PRAISE FOl

We Are Going to Be Lucky

"At the heart of this fascinating and educational tale about a soldier and his wife during wartime is a wonderful love story. Lenny and Diana become relatable almost immediately. Their excitement at their experiences—the eagerness with which they anticipate their few reunions, the battles he is in, the pregnancy and birth of their daughter—draws readers in and allows them to live through the era as ordinary people experienced it day in and day out."
— Richard Aquila, author of *Home Front Soldier: The Story of a GI and His Italian American Family During World War II*

"This is a truly remarkable story, contextualized just enough by the editor to provide the reader with a sufficient understanding of the history of the times without taking away the daily realities of a young couple making their way through letters and the occasional souvenir, till their final reunion. It pulls you in in such a way that you will not want to put the book down until the finish."
— Melissa Suzanne Fisher, author of *Wall Street Women*

"The correspondence of Lenny and Diana is a compelling account of the war though the eyes of an American soldier in Europe and his wife who stayed in the United States. The drama centers on the birth of their first child in America and Lenny's increasingly dangerous war. Lenny was to go on to become an eminent scholar of John Milton, and these letters show the young scholar at work, struggling to obtain research materials while recovering from serious injuries sustained at the Battle of the Bulge."
— Gordon Campbell, University of Leicester

"Is there any genre of writing more immediate and soul-bearing than the love letter? In *We Are Going to Be Lucky*, Elizabeth L. Fox allows us inside the lives of one New York couple as they endure the challenges of living apart through World War II—Lenny from the battlefront and Diana at home in Brooklyn. From arduous training to the difficulties of factory work, from the hopefulness of pregnancy to a near-fatal injury and painful convalescence, this carefully edited collection of correspondence reveals the pain, sacrifice, and everyday struggles—and magnanimity—of the Greatest Generation, and the universal beauty of human connection."

— Julie Scelfo, author of *The Women Who Made New York*

"This remarkable collection of letters gives us a unique glimpse into the experiences of a World War II soldier and his wife on the home front. The correspondences between Lenny and Diana are both relatable and fascinating—full of funny anecdotes, powerful impressions of combat, profound insights into human nature, and a shared hope for a better world. Elizabeth L. Fox, the daughter of the letter writers, has edited this collection beautifully, vividly bringing to life a deeply personal love story within the dramatic context of a world war. From page one, we find ourselves rooting for this couple—for their commitment to fighting for justice, for their daily triumphs and struggles as soldiers and parents, and, ultimately, for them to be 'lucky' enough to hold each other again in a time of peace."

— Andrew Carroll, editor of *War Letters: Extraordinary Correspondence from American Wars*

We Are Going to Be Lucky

WE ARE GOING TO BE LUCKY

A World War II Love Story in Letters

EDITED AND ANNOTATED BY

Elizabeth L. Fox

excelsior editions

Published by
State University of New York Press, Albany

EXCELSIOR EDITIONS
is an imprint of
STATE UNIVERSITY OF NEW YORK PRESS

For information, contact
State University of New York Press, Albany, NY
www.sunypress.edu

Library of Congress Cataloging-in-Publication Data

Names: Miller, Leo, 1915–1990, author. | Miller, Diana F., author. | Fox,
Elizabeth L., 1944– editor.
Title: We are going to be lucky : a World War II love story in letters / edited by Elizabeth L. Fox.
Description: Albany : State University of New York Press, 2018. | Series:
Excelsior editions | Includes bibliographical references and index.
Identifiers: LCCN 2017040336| ISBN 9781438470580 (paperback : alk. paper) |
ISBN 9781438470597 (e-book)
Subjects: LCSH: Miller, Leo, 1915–1990—Correspondence. | World War,
1939–1945—Personal narratives, American. | World War,
1939–1945—Campaigns—Western Front. | Soldiers—United
States—Correspondence. | Married people—United States—Correspondence. |
Love-letters—United States. | Miller, Diana F.—Correspondence.
Classification: LCC D811 .M517 2018 | DDC 940.54/1273092—dc23
LC record available at https://lccn.loc.gov/2017040336

This book is dedicated to my parents,

Lenny and Diana Miller,

who possessed the insight to write meaningfully,

the devotion to communicate frequently, and the

wisdom to preserve their correspondence. May

their legacy live on, through their grandchildren

and future generations, and may it resonate with

those who seek justice for all people.

Contents

Acknowledgments

I am most indebted to my parents, Leo (Lenny) and Diana Miller, who preserved their wartime letters and who taught me how to live by one's ideals and principles to make the world a better place.

This book wouldn't have been possible without the support and love of my husband and best friend, Sid, who believed in this project and supported me, allowing me to spend many hours reading and rereading the letters and sitting at the computer over the past five years. His understanding and knowledge of the history of World War II contributed greatly.

My daughter, Amy, an accomplished playwright and screenwriter, was my sounding board and supported me during all the trying times. Her professional knowledge taught me how to strengthen the manuscript. My son David sorted all the letters by date and inspired me to start reading them. With his passion for history and research, my son Jon motivated me to keep going.

My brother, Fred, took the time to type my dad's war memoir "Rifleman's Road" into the computer for easier access to reference that material. He also provided valuable insights while reading the manuscript.

My uncle Eddie (Lenny's younger brother), often referred to in the letters and also a veteran of World War II, has written many short stories and novellas recording family stories. He also shared his memories of the war and personal family history with me through several conversations.

My friend Alice Levine, a professional editor, guided me from the conception of my book to its completion, always sharing her knowledge of the publishing process and editing expertise. Matt Young, a published author and editor, who read the manuscript, encouraged me and gave meaningful suggestions. Matt also provided technical support early in the process. Shirley Gang's editorial suggestions were of great assistance.

Connie Rosenblum, retired *New York Times* City Section editor, believed in the project and encouraged me to continue. Her careful, thoughtful editing skill helped me focus on the main themes of the story and prepare the manuscript to be sent to publishers.

Jim Williams II, dean of Libraries at the University of Colorado, who knew my dad from his visits to the university library provided guidance and support. Darren Pratt, director of the University of Colorado Press, deserves special mention for his suggestion that I submit the manuscript to SUNY Press.

Finally, I acknowledge and thank my team at SUNY Press, starting with Amanda Lanne-Camilli, my acquisitions editor, who recognized the importance and uniqueness of my book and whose advice and assistance was invaluable. Chelsea Miller, Amanda's assistant, also offered her skill when needed. Laurie Searl, my production editor, worked with sensitivity and devotion to support me through the production and book design phase. Her attention to detail was only surpassed by her artistic eye, her vision for the book, and her commitment to the project. Kate Seburyamo and Michael Campochiaro, my marketing managers, brought their knowledge and expertise of the marketing process to promote the book and to help me develop my marketing plan.

Preface

From Letters to a Book

For as long as I can remember, a large cardboard box was hidden away on a top shelf of the linen closet in the New York City Stuyvesant Town apartment where I grew up. My mother never took down the carton or looked at the letters it contained, which for her were a painful reminder of a difficult time. My father did look at the letters and also amended them by adding locations and other details that had not been permitted by the censors at the time they were written.

After my mother's death in 1994, I took the box to my home in Colorado. Inside, I discovered several thousand letters written over three years and tied together in packets with ribbons or rubber bands. Time had taken its toll and the rubber bands had disintegrated, but the paper remained intact.

As I read the letters, I remembered my father proudly showing me the Bronze and Silver Star medals awarded to him for valor in combat, each in its original box with a corresponding strip of ribbon. I recalled seeing the huge captured Nazi flag that he had been given by the Belgian Resistance and sent home as a war trophy to be used to raise money for the war effort at political meetings.

Reading these letters was a profoundly moving experience, and I needed to find a way to preserve and share their story.

Initially, the huge jumble of letters felt overwhelming. The letters in the carton were not in any chronological order, until my son David took on the task of sorting them.

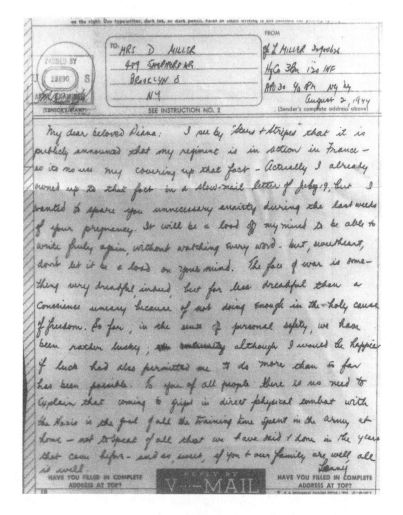

V-mail

The letters were written both on stationery and V-mail. V-mail was a secure process used during World War II in which letters were censored, copied onto film, and printed on paper at their destination. They were reduced in size to 3 by 4 inch paper and then photographed. Over time, they had faded. I often needed daylight and a magnifying glass to read the V-mail. I also had to become familiar with my parents' handwriting; my dad's presented much more of a challenge than my mom's.

I began by reading my dad's letters from overseas, thinking they would be the most interesting and wanting to learn more about his experiences in action. I quickly learned that his letters contained much more of interest than just limited descriptions of warfare. While reading his letters, I became curious as to what my mom was doing at the same time.

Knowing that I was born while my dad was fighting in France, I realized my mom's letters contained valuable information about the daily lives and struggles on the home front. It was only then that I understood the letters told a story, the conversation of two people talking to each other, with questions often separated from their responses by weeks because of mail delays.

Next, I read the earlier letters from his basic training and her time at home, working and preparing for the birth of their child. Finally, I looked at the later letters sent after he was wounded. I found a wealth of information from two educated and politically active people, recording the social history of the home front as well as military life and combat experiences.

The letters became the core of my book. The biggest challenge was deciding what to include and what to leave out. I began by excerpting the most meaningful sections of the letters and complementing them with several selections from a collection of poetry or "lyrics" my dad wrote during the war. I also read the six small notebooks and the summary letters, in which he recorded his experiences and events in more detail, in down time and during recovery. These notebooks became the source documents for his "novelistic" memoir "Rifleman's Road," with sociological and historical perspectives, written during his long recovery. These added additional background to the story I set out to tell.

In 2014, my husband and I decided to travel to Belgium to visit sites that are referred to in the letters. Fort Eben-Emael, which was closed in 1978, when my parents visited Belgium, was now open to the public, on a very limited basis. I arranged to coordinate my visit with an Army group from Weisbaden, Germany. During the initial orientation to the visit, the guide asked me to share with the group why I was visiting. It was very moving for me, and for them, as I told my dad's story. We walked through the great hall where my dad had found the Nazi flags he sent home. We toured a room in the fort featuring photos and historical information about my dad's 30th Infantry Division. We also visited the town of Bastogne to see the museum and the huge memorial dedicated to all the Americans who fought in the Battle of the Bulge.

Personally, most moving for me was the time spent walking the streets in Malmédy and finding the bridge and paper mill, all referred to in this book. We tracked down an elderly woman who knew the family my dad stayed with in 1944, only to learn that the daughters my parents had reconnected with in 1978 had recently died. We saw the fields and hillsides that my dad and so many other soldiers trekked through. We stayed overnight in Spa, visited Stavelot, and other nearby towns, following my dad's footsteps.

We also visited the International Museum of World War II in Natick, Massachusetts. It was founded by Kenneth W. Rendell, who has devoted his life to building the most comprehensive of private collections of World War II memorabilia. The many letters from famous World War II figures, photographs, posters, manuscripts, and the wide variety of artifacts added to my knowledge of this period.

My research included reading other published collections of letters, and interviewing my dad's brother, Eddie, who shared his firsthand memories.

The next step was to provide the connective thread for today's readers by adding historical background information for context and understanding. During the process, there were several technical questions to answer. At first, I used ellipses to indicate where I had excerpted from the letters. However, because of the number and length of the letters, there were so many ellipses that they detracted from the readability, and I chose to eliminate them. I also tried to correct spelling and grammar errors to reflect their level of education because many of the letters were written hastily and under very difficult conditions. Finally, colloquial expressions common at that time were left in for authenticity. For example, the word *swell* appears repeatedly.

I read and excerpted from the letters for more than three years. The result is a story told from letters seen through the lens of my eyes.

Introduction

In May of 1943, when World War II was raging thousands of miles away, my parents, Lenny and Diana Miller, a young couple from Brooklyn, embarked on a remarkable daily correspondence that would last until 1946. Lenny, age 28, was an infantryman with a passion for historical research; Diana, age 26, worked in the milling department of a machine shop in the Brooklyn Navy Yard, making periscopes for the war effort.

They began writing to each other, as Lenny entered his year of basic training for the infantry, in Mississippi. They continued through his shipment to Europe in June of 1944, and his service in England, France, Belgium, Holland, and Germany. Lenny fought with the 30th Infantry Division, in some of the most critical battles of the war: at Saint-Lô, in the recapture of Fort Eben-Emael, in Aachen, the first major action on German soil, and finally, in the Battle of the Bulge around Malmédy, Belgium.

Because of Lenny's knowledge of foreign languages (he knew Yiddish, some German and French, and later taught himself some Flemish and Dutch), he became a scout in the infantry. He wrote of making contact with local underground forces and interrogating German prisoners of war as they were captured. He recorded the life-threatening injuries he suffered during the Battle of the Bulge, and his long and arduous convalescence in England, and later, America.

There are many collections of letters from soldiers, but it is rare to have access to both sides of the correspondence. Under the most difficult circumstances, my father saved my mother's letters, sometimes in his gas mask, in small packets, and from time to time sent them home to preserve along with his. My parents wrote to each other sometimes more than once a day for three years. There were nearly 2,500 letters, many up to ten handwritten pages long, covering a wide variety of subjects.

The letters track the couple's decision to have a child, Diana's pregnancy, the birth of their daughter, and the joys and anxieties of raising a baby in the cramped two-bedroom walk-up in East New York, Brooklyn, where Diana lived with her parents after Lenny enlisted.

The letters include nuts-and-bolts details of Lenny's lengthy training, the skills and teamwork needed to survive in combat, and the experiences of a woman engaged in community war work. They contain reflections on the political and social conditions of the time, particularly with regard to economic and racial injustice. They deal with such timely matters as rationing and financial problems, along with the mundane details of life—Sabbath dinners, health concerns, difficult bosses, and cramped living quarters. Many were love letters.

In these tens of thousands of pages, Lenny and Diana poured out their deepest feelings, and in the process left a remarkable portrait of two people full of hope for the future in a world engulfed in fear and turmoil.

Lenny and Diana were first-generation Americans. Their parents came to America to escape persecution and poverty. Lenny's family came from a Galician shtetl, Dobromil, in the Austro-Hungarian Empire. Lenny's father, Saul, was apprenticed to a tailor in Galicia and spent several years in Berlin, where he perfected the needle trade. He made his way to New York, where he reconnected with Lenny's mother, Ida, whose family had also emigrated. They were married in New York. Saul was a garment worker all his life. He was a union organizer and leader in the International Ladies Garment Workers Union. For a time, the family tried their luck in business, opening a dry cleaning/alterations store in Rockville Center, Long Island.

Most of Lenny's years growing up were in East New York, Brooklyn, surrounded by his extended family of aunts, uncles, and cousins. He was the eldest of four children, followed by Rose, three years later, Harriet, three years later, and Eddie, four years later. He grew up in an Orthodox Jewish home where his mother kept kosher. Lenny never ate anything non-kosher until the army. A favorite family story was that Lenny tasted corn on the cob for the first time in basic training, and all the "farm boys" from the Midwest in his outfit made fun of him for eating "cow" grub.

In 1935, Lenny was the first in his family to graduate from college, taking advantage of free tuition at the City College of New York. His strong interest in history and political science led him to a PhD program at Columbia University. He never completed his dissertation after his mentor passed away unexpectedly, but this passion stayed with him. His brother, Eddie, also graduated from City College after the war, and became an art teacher in Queens, in a junior high school.

Diana's family came from Sokolievka/Justingrad, a shtetl in the Ukraine. Her parents knew each other growing up. Her father, David, was eight years older, and came to New York as a young man. He returned home to marry his childhood sweetheart Adele, and together they immigrated to America. They also found work in garment sweatshops. Their children, Diana and Lucy, five years younger, grew up in Brooklyn, in a culturally, but not religious, Jewish home. Eventually, others in their family came to America.

Diana graduated from Hunter College, and Lucy from Brooklyn College. In many families at that time it was unusual for girls to attend college, but their parents believed in education for girls, and it was possible with free tuition. Diana went on to earn a master's degree as a dietician at Columbia University, and Lucy earned a master's degree in social work at Washington University in St. Louis.

After graduating, both Lenny and Diana struggled to find employment in the aftermath of the Great Depression. Both were idealistic and politically active, as was common in their generation. Having grown up in poor immigrant families, they were deeply committed to racial equality and improving economic conditions for all people. Lenny found employment as a caseworker for the New York City Welfare Department, and rose through the ranks as a union leader. Diana worked as a dietician in hospitals. It was a family joke that Diana's recipes could serve hundreds of people and weren't easily adapted for a family of four. Lenny also participated in the CCC (Civilian Conservation Corps), a public works relief program, over two summers. Here, he first experienced organized discipline and physically demanding outdoor work.

In 1938, Lenny and Diana met at a party. Lenny often shared the story that he told a close friend that night that he had found the woman he would marry. They lived only a few blocks apart, and during their courtship, Lenny's brother, Eddie, often carried notes back and forth, since neither had a telephone at home. They were married in April 1940 and moved into a tiny one-bedroom apartment in Brooklyn.

During this time, Lenny was encouraged to continue his union leadership rather than enlist in the armed forces, but by 1943, although older than the typical soldier, he knew he had to do his part to stop Hitler. Both the threat of Hitler's advancement and increasing concern for their many family members still in Europe and Ukraine, convinced him. With Lenny away, Diana, now working for the war effort, became more active as a union organizer, and volunteered as a community organizer and teacher of night classes. Diana and her sister, Lucy, moved back in with their parents because they could no longer afford their own apartments.

Diana and Lucy's situation was common, as it seemed "everyone" went to war. All of the young adult males, unless they had a medical exemption, did. In Lenny and Diana's immediate family, Lucy's husband, Babe, served in the Navy on a destroyer, his brother, Paul, served in the Navy on a submarine, Lenny's brother, Eddie, served in the Marines and was at Iwo Jima, and Lenny's brother-in-law Mike served in the Army until he received a medical discharge. The support and love from their extended families at home, who all lived locally then, was key to keeping up morale and courage, whether through frequent visits to those at home, or ongoing care packages sent to those away.

Writing letters was the only way for a soldier and his loved ones to communicate. Time was set aside each day to write. Waiting for letters, often delayed weeks at a time, added tension to their already strained daily lives.

There are fewer and fewer survivors of my parents' generation, and it is increasingly important to tell their stories. I hope this collection will inspire others, as it has inspired my own family. In today's world of email and social media, it is hard to imagine a father waiting every day for several weeks to receive the letter announcing that his child has been born.

It is my hope that readers will see not only a glimpse of their parents or grandparents, but a piece of themselves in this record of the triumphs and sacrifices of ordinary people in an extraordinary time.

It is the story of two people who were deeply in love. who survived one of the most harrowing eras in American history, and who were passionately committed to making the world a better place.

We Are Going to Be Lucky: A World War II Love Story in Letters is a story of wartime. It is my parents' story.

Part I

Training

1

Induction

May 7, Aboard Train

Dearest,

Have finally got going — had lunch at Penn. Station — We are on a train that must have been used at Lincoln's inaugural but Max & I have good seats.

Lenny

May 7, 9:30 P.M.

Dear Diana,

There's every likelihood that our group will be shipped out at once — destination, of course, unknown. We have been told that it's "48 or 72" hours, & no visitors or receipt of letters. So far, so good —

Lenny

May 8, 1943, Camp Upton[1]

Dearest darling wife,

I got the "Hook" this afternoon — my double dose of anti-typhoid & anti-tetanus injections & my right arm & shoulder are rather sore.

Darling — are you well? Honestly, are you in good spirits? If it relieves your feelings go right ahead & cry once in a while — don't go on

---

1. Camp Upton was an induction and military training facility built in 1917 for World War I. It reopened in 1940, again as an induction and training ground. In 1944, it was used as a military hospital, and in May 1945 it became a prisoner of war camp when five hundred Germans were housed there. In 1947, the facility was taken over by Brookhaven National Laboratory, which operates it today. Lenny was inducted and began his military training here.

3

accumulating it in yourself 'til something like a tooth shoots your nerves to pieces.

My barracks are two story-cream-painted wooden structures. I've a cot with a mattress. But no sheets or pillowcases — they're a little short, a few men had no cots, so I was satisfied with what I had. The one nuisance is the time (hours) wasted between doing things — the things themselves aren't bad. Yesterday we were received in a big hall — fed & given 3 exams. Today we used up the morning being "classified." I think I'm headed for my infantry!!! I am classified "semiskilled"! Later we got 2,500 lbs of uniform, fatigue clothing, equipment, etc. The distribution of some 75–100 articles, in all sizes, to about 1,000 guys in one day is really well organized — very praiseworthy.

The Negro troops were segregated from us as soon as we got off the train, a miserable scene, & they've been kept apart, even to separate benches at the theater where we saw the films.

Lenny

May 9, Upton

Hello, dearest,

Right now your husband is sitting in a cool breeze in the checkered shade of a pine grove, midst fragrant pine needles and fluttering white butterflies, under a clear blue sky. The segregated Negro troops are playing baseball off on the far left. Down the company street a few squads are being drilled. Most of the fellows must be parading hundreds of miles to nowhere. I'm reclining at ease, having just showered & I am writing (my greatest pleasure) to my dove.

Well, personally, I think we should have Sunday afternoon off. This post seems to act on the "Satan finds mischief for idle hands" theory & keeps us going even if there is nothing to do. Fourteen of us including me were marched to camp prison, where we were given picks and shovels, with the army's usual lack of reason, & led out to the woods. We were then initiated into the mystery of road building, to wit. You swing a pick to break up hard ground (nary an earthworm or an ant did we turn up) barren, hard-packed sand, then shovel it level to 4 inches deep, and square the edges. Tomorrow the hole will be filled with flat stones & cement.

The guys all cooperated in fine spirit. It was necessary, tho, to combat the "WPA" theory of doing it leisurely & to get them to hustle. When they got the idea that in this job & all our work we are digging "a road to Berlin," as one said, all went well.

What's privacy anyhow? We are called "privates" but we sleep 50–72 in a room, our bags and clothes are all unsealed, our baths & toilets are public — no privacy anywhere. Our phones are not private either, and only English may be spoken.

Beloved, I wear your name all the time. My brass identification disk — 2 of 'em I wear bears my name & ASN[2], & your name & address, & the letter H for Hebrew.[3]

Lenny

May 9

Dearest Lenny,

I'm so happy to have received the Special Delivery from you yesterday and the phone call today. You can understand I was disappointed not to have been able to speak to you myself darling but I was glad to hear you are OK. Love, I am writing this letter but I cannot mail it until I have an address. I hope that will be soon.

Your,
Diana

May 9

Sweetheart,

I'm stuck with KP for the night shift (6–12). This afternoon's task I'd rather forget. See Sinclair's "Jungle" for Jurgis Rudkis's experiences in the fertilizer plant. As one of our detail said, after 3 hours shoulder deep in the sewage settling bed, "I don't want to look at a piece of s—t again." I don't mind if it's really necessary but I know this wasn't.

Lenny

May 10

Sweetheart,

Since you say you cannot receive any mail, I am keeping the letter until I get an address from you. Lenny, darling, my spirits are good. As a matter of fact I am surprised at myself. I am reacting much better than I thought I would. As you have said many times — we can never really be apart even though there is distance between us. Only tonight when I received all those letters from you did I cry a little.

---

2. Army Serial Number.

3. Although American dog tags cite religion to ensure that a soldier's religious needs will be met, some were reissued without religious affiliation listed because identification of religion, such as H for Hebrew, could increase a soldier's danger if he fell into enemy hands. Presumably, when in combat, Lenny wore a tag without his religious identity.

Beloved, I keep a date with you morning, evening, and all during the day. I look at your beautiful, smiling picture and know how lucky I am to have you as my own.

Diana

May 11

Dearest,

It was "bitchy," after a hard afternoon, to go on evening duty. Our group of 20 made some 3,000 sandwiches for today's shipment & packed them. Then we had a late arrival, at 11:25 of a new group of rookies to feed & wash dishes, tables, floors, etc.

Four guys from our barrack were "shipped out" today to the general envy; well, here's hoping.

Today I did absolutely nothing to earn my $1.66-a-day pay, and I'm very annoyed at it. That's the major reason why I'd like to be shipped — they just fritter away the time here. At the telephone center where several score were waiting to put through phone calls it is easy to sit a couple of hours with no questions asked.

Are you settled, dearest, as regards to bed & bureau?[4]

Beloved, today, with your letter, I have a close two-way conversation with you. I'm glad you are in good spirits — while I hope you won't cry too much or cry at all. I still repeat I don't want you repressing your emotions to the breaking point. Honestly, dearest beloved, I am (in spite of my irritation at wasting time) very content at being here.

I would only be more content if I were tonight put behind my favorite — the machine gun & told to cross over to Dunkirk & Calais. Darling beloved, you know my two passions are the struggle for freedom and historical research, and my love for my mate is the catalyst which makes both possible to me. With a soldier's wife like you at home, & the army job now mine, there's no guy in Upton as happy or with a life so full.

Lenny

May 11

Dearest Lenny,

It's hard when today is Tuesday to read a letter written on Sunday because I feel that by now there must be much more news. Maybe you

---

4. Diana and her sister, Lucy, are back sharing their parent's two-bedroom apartment in East New York, Brooklyn. This required several purchases to accommodate everyone's needs.

have even left Upton, well, I'll have to learn to be patient and I am learning.

Diana

May 12, 8:30 A.M.

Dina,

5 days have passed — the longest "separation," so-called, since before our marriage. Except for the "detail" work, this place is like a dude ranch. There's no real war effort. What opportunities for training & morale building are going to waste — can't wait to be shipped.

Lenny

May 12

Dearest Beloved, Lenny

I am sitting down to do the thing I look forward to all day — write to my beloved. The best part of every day, my sweetheart, is when I read your letter and write to you. I wrote and mailed a short letter earlier — this again I shall keep 'till I have an address.

My days are very much routine — I work during the day and spend my evenings fruitfully as always.

Lenny, I know I do not have to write you a "pep-up" letter but it seems that a number of very unpleasant tasks have come your way. Darling, whenever I feel so tired on my job that I want to sit down and rest or whenever I find it very hard to get up at 6 A.M. every morning, I think of how much I hate Hitler and Fascism and how hard I want to work to destroy it so that I can live with my husband again and together we can raise a family in a free America. So darling, every time you have an unpleasant job even if it is an unnecessary one — it is a means to an end — it is part of your fight to destroy the horror and misery of Fascism so that our children can live in a free America. The work I am doing is mostly for the Navy. The best part of me — my husband — is in the army, I think that we are making our small contribution to the winning of the war.

Lenny, I returned your ration books and I received a letter acknowledging them today.[5]

---

5. Rationing or restrictions on certain foods and goods was introduced because voluntary conservation on the home front wasn't adequate. Civilians received ration books. Typewriters, gasoline, bicycles, shoes, nylons, meat, cheese, butter, canned foods, firewood, coal, jam, and canned milk were among the items rationed.

I love you so much. I know I have said it before but just for the record, darling.

Your,

Diana

May 13

Dearest Lenny,

I'm really so happy you received my letter of Monday. I'm also happy you are now satisfied with what you are doing. I know how much you wanted to be in the army and I shall try to be a good soldier's wife here at home where my job is so that together we shall help destroy Fascism and build a good life for ourselves and the future. Do you know anything of what branch of the army you will be in?

The bed & bureau situation will be settled Saturday. We bought the furniture and it will be delivered then. So far Lucy has been sleeping with my mother so I have been very comfortable.

Darling — I know that you are very happy to be in the army but I am glad you wrote it to me because it makes me happy with and for you. Also I am so proud to be the wife of a soldier who I know will be an example of a good and patriotic American. I am so proud to wear the service pin which says to everyone "My husband is in the army."

Good news internationally — war in Africa has been successfully concluded and there are reports of riots in Holland.

All my love,

Diana

May 14

Hello,

Fellows' general morale is A1. There are guys here who are all-out, like our friends. There are guys here who say — I tried to keep out, appealed 4 times, but they've got me, so I'll make the best of it.

Lenny

May 14

Darling,

Lenny, I am writing this letter in your old room which is now Harriet's and Mike's.[6] As I sit here, I remember many beautiful times we had together in this room with the lovely view out the window. I

---

6. Lenny's sister and brother-in-law moved back in with Lenny's parents.

remember especially the night you proposed to me. I know just what you mean when you say in your letter, "I don't miss you because we are together." I feel the same way but I also miss you.

Diana

May 15

Sweetheart Love,

Your usually patient husband is becoming annoyed. We were told we'd be shipped to camp in 48 to 72 hours; here it is 9 days & nary a sign of shipment.

Lenny

May 15

Dearest Love,

I wrote you before that we are only working 'til noon on Sat. now. Sweetheart, for the last two days I have been doing a very interesting job in the shop. It is very important.

Love, this is the second weekend, you are a soldier and in camp. I cannot say I am getting used to spending Saturday night without you because I shall never be used to it.

Your,
Diana

May 16

Hello,

I am writing to you in the middle of a small riot that is raging all around. Some dozen guys from my barrack are on the shipping list. They took a lot of M's but skipped me & my particular friends here. The guys on the list are elated. Although staying here appeals to many, once they know they're due to go they want no more delay. Of course, they don't know where to they're going; all the troop movements are military secrets. After lunch, still determined to work, even on these miserable details, I was marched out with the company, and left with about 100 waiting an hour on the drill field. Finally we were taken into the woods to pick up "things that don't grow" — a mass time killing. From these observations & others I have passed to you, you can well understand why I am so eager to go somewhere, where we have real training, where we have regular foot-lockers, closets, laundry service, regular mess, where evenings & Sundays are different from weekdays etc. Eleven days gone: what a painful waste for me, especially when there's so much I want to do.

Darling, don't get the idea from all this that I am down in the mouth or blue or disheartened. On the contrary, I am as serene, confident, unruffled as always: my gripes are merely my hungering after full living, my appetite for action, and learning, my eagerness and impatience to be further along the way.

Lenny

May 16

Lenny darling —

your phone call this morning still has me smiling every few minutes. How I love to hear your voice. Dearest, I hope that you are feeling OK and getting enough to eat. Please take good care of yourself. How do you look in your uniform? You must look so handsome.

Darling, now that I am all settled in my mother's house — I have gotten a lot of new things, bed, chest and closet but the house looks a little like a storage place. My parents are very good-natured about it though and are trying to cooperate to make me very comfortable.

Sleep well tonight and my arms will be around you and my love will be with you.

Diana

May 17

Dear Diana,

Adding to the "sociological" notes I've sent you on the Negro troop: everyone notices that they inject a markedly original kind of rhythm into their marching, conveying some of their culture-psychology. Whereas we all say, shouting in unison, "One-two-three-four" they use two variants — they usually say, in a swing-it fashion, "a-one, a-two, a-three, a-four." Since we are very segregated I have not been able to discuss this with any Negro soldiers, & so can only record it as an observation.

Since I'm on KP tonight, I won't ship tomorrow, so now I pass into a class of fellows who having been here 12 days and find their eagerness to ship out balanced by the expectancy of a pass in 9 more days. Of course most of us will be shipped by then, some of us on the 20th day, just before we are eligible for the pass home. However, I still prefer to be shipped out, hoping I go to an infantry camp like Meade. Of course, there's the chance I'll go to Mississippi or Seattle or Algeria or Ireland — but wherever I go, beloved, your presence goes with me & my presence stays with you.

Lenny

May 18

My Lady Love,

Here's hoping this is the last letter I write to you in Upton 'til I pass through here again on my way to honorable discharge. It was swell to be able to get you on the phone this morning. At first your firm wouldn't call you on the phone & was asked your foreman's name which I finally remembered. It cost me about $1.50, mostly for overtime, but I was very glad to be able to speak to you before I go. You understand we do not know where we are going. I think we are going to a basic infantry camp and as you asked on the phone, I am happy.

Sweetheart, I hope I didn't get you so excited that it interfered with your work since you were summoned suddenly from your milling machines & surface grinders before you could collect yourself.

Lenny

On His Way

May 18

Sweetheart,

Today's phone call from you was a complete surprise. Dearest, thank you so much for letting me know that you were being shipped. I know that since you have left Upton and I don't know yet how far you are going, it may be a few days before I hear from you.

All my love,
Diana

May 19, Leaving Indianapolis

Hello Diana,

Since we continue to travel fully ignorant to where, I'll write now & have this ready to mail wherever we are in the morning. I finished the letter just before Pittsburgh. Pittsburgh looks like Detroit with a lot of smokestacks, there are bridges over the rivers here & we saw some relics of the past, rear paddle Ohio-Mississippi riverboats. We passed Weirton, W. Va. & Steubenville, Ohio — and from there on it looked as if we wouldn't see a town again ever — All thru there has been hot debate as to where we are headed.

While geographic distance between us increases every second, I feel your presence with me as vividly & alertly as ever. Oh, Diana, Dina, "Divina," how I do love you!

Lenny

May 19

Darling,

While I was waiting for the thunder and lightning to end, I thought to myself — where is Lenny? Is he traveling to the beautiful sunshine of California or Florida, is he going to the desert of Arizona or New Mexico? Is he going to the high mountains or the lowland, or is just going over to New Jersey or even back to Brooklyn? Darling, I am hoping that the next time I take a trip it will be to see you.

Diana

May 20, Fulton, Ky.

Beloved,

We're south of the Mason Dixon line now & still don't know where to — but now it's southward. Got my first sight of cotton bales —

Well, darling, I have now loved you in 10 states in 48 hours, and in some for the first time — Illinois, West Virginia, Kentucky, Tennessee & Mississippi. Well it's Mississippi for sure & most likely Shelby. I expect to get my address in the morning.

Lenny

May 20, postcard, en route to Memphis

My dearest,

Just got my first sight of the Mississippi, where the Wolf River enters at Memphis. THIS IS A RIVER. Have been traveling since Tues. evening, now second day — These states are large!

Lenny

May 20

Dearest Love,

I called home when I left work and Lucy told me that there are 2 postcards and a letter for me. She said one card is from Upton, one is from Pittsburgh and the letter is from Ohio. I am assuming since there was no return address on the envelope you are still traveling. I am so eager to know where you will finally be, but I am learning to be patient.

As soon as you are settled write me what I should send you — any of your presents, or books, or radio, watch, knife — anything at all.

Diana

2

Basic Training: The First Six Months

Camp Shelby is a military post near Hattiesburg, Mississippi, founded in 1917. It served as a training site for reserve units of the Army and active units of the Army, Navy, Marine Corps, and Air Force. It was the nation's largest, at 134,820 acres, state-owned and-operated field training center. The 69th Infantry Division trained at Shelby in preparation for World War II combat. Lenny was stationed at Camp Shelby from May 21, 1943, until June 6, 1944, when he was sent to England.

The first six months focused on the basics. Time was spent on building extreme fitness through calisthenics and long marches with full gear. The soldiers were introduced to basic weaponry through films and actual practice with rifles, bayonets, grenades, and gas masks. There was map reading and lots of book learning followed by tests to assess competence. Infantry tactics, including concealment, observation, scouting, and patrolling, were taught. There were repeated patrol maneuvers in the heat of Mississippi.

A New Kind of Army

May 21

Dear Diana,

We finally pulled in here about midnight, about 52 hours of train time. We were loaded into trucks on the double & brought out here, for a day, to the 272 Anti-Tank Co. of the 69th Infantry. We have been transported from late spring into mid-July weather. Our barracks are one-story frame

Mississippi

buildings with a screen section running all around. Estimates are that
70,000 to 120,000 men are here. Max & Henry are in the other barracks.
There are small flies like at home, but also large flies, 1½ inches long &
buzzing like a bomber plane. There are several oak species & a kind of
pine with very long needles 8 inches or more, growing like a broom.
We have been chatting with some boys from No'th Ca'lin', Fla'da, and
Miss'sippi' — kids, boys of 18 and looking younger.

Something tells me there's a brainy officer somewhere around here. I
have seen such a sequence of intelligent things happening that I am quite
amazed and pleased. We are treated as human beings, American citizens, rea-
soning creatures & as gentlemen. We were all given a personal interview by
the first sergeant & by the captain himself. Both asked a lot of questions, by
way of getting to know the men well, but in a friendly manner.

By the way, in this Mississippi climate, you sit absolutely motionless in the shade and perspire like the devil. Our schedule calls for basic training to Sept. 4; 14 weeks beginning officially 6/1/43 but actually tomorrow. No furloughs possible 'til then except in extreme emergencies.

I'm in a "headquarters company," why, I don't know. A Hq. Co. administers the affairs of a battalion, which has 4 line companies. Our 272nd Inf. regiment has several battalions; my battalion is antitank, handling rifle & 37 mm. gun (a light cannon used against tanks). We are part of the 69th Inf. one of the most famous regiments in World War I and the tradition is exploited to the full. A Hq. Co. has a lot of duties; they learn the same battle drill as a line company but, in theory, are back of the line of combat. There's no way of knowing if it's good or bad — all I can do is try my best & hope it comes out OK.

I went to Friday night services in one of the chapels here. The rabbi-chaplain made the customary excuse for giving up "kashruth" [dietary laws] & the "shabbos" [Sabbath] as sacrifices of living in a free land.

I salute my beloved darling & finish this letter so I can turn in full of thoughts of her whose love follows me no matter how far I roam, nor how long I may be away.

Lenny

May 21

Dearest,

Just came home from your parents. They are both going up to Segar's[1] next week.

I just finished a budget session. This month my budget is sort of confused because I have a lot of bills to pay — gas & electric, $8.73, insurance (about $8.00), debt to father ($10 used for Mother's Day presents). I received a raise today to .56 per hour. That makes it $32.48 for 52 hours work. It is certainly enough considering my main expenses are room & board ($6.00 per week), furniture storage ($7.00 per month), clothes and personal.

Lenny, write me all about this new camp you are at. What kind of people there are, the location, the towns if any are near — all the details like about Upton. Talked to Dora on the phone — she hasn't heard from Joe since he left this country but she heard from the War Dept. that he arrived safely — where she doesn't know.

Diana

---

1. A summer vacation guest house in the Catskill Mountains.

May 22

Dear Beloved,

This morning we were addressed by our division commander, the Maj. General; a good military talk, one that set the tone. This is a new division. It will set up its own history & tradition & it will be the best in the army. We had a lecture on "morality": an officer who stressed that you're human, so be sensible & use prophylaxis. Then a doctor did a fine job on the ravages of venereal disease.

Louis, the colonel gave a good explanation of our purpose which is to train well, to kill as many Japanese & German soldiers with as few losses as possible. As for discussion of the war aims, of that there is nothing. The theory is all wars are the same & the soldier's duty is to fight them.

Last night Max & I "went out" after supper. We walked over to the PX, shopped around, and then over to look at the theater, a handsome place, seating perhaps 700. Then we went to the Service Club. It's a two-story structure with a cafeteria, a lounge with ping pong & pool tables, dance floor & entertainment room, a library, a music room, and soft chairs & tables with free stationery.

Lenny

May 22

My love,

Although I am so eager to know where you will be, love, I feel the way you say in the letter — since you are quite far from home already and frequent visits will not be possible, it doesn't matter too much which state you will be. Though I cannot mail my letters just yet, my darling, you know that I sent you my love and kisses.

Your,
Diana

May 23

Dearest,

Hattiesburg, our nearest town, 15 miles away, is very swollen by war wives & soldier visitors. Even though, there is little to attract one, it's the only place to go & many do, for liquor (which has to be bootlegged into camp; only 3.2 beer is sold here), for a "dose of clap" or for simple curiosity.

I signed the payroll today, but no pay in sight.

Lenny

May 23

Lenny, Dearest,

Helen and I went to the movies where we saw "Desert Victory," an English documentary about the fighting of the 8th Army in Africa. It shows actual scenes of the battle and I know you would be especially interested because the infantry and the machine guns are featured. The other picture was a musical.

Today I went to see your Aunt Minnie and your cousin Bea and the baby. I had a nice time except for a few unpleasantnesses. Ruth spent 2 hours complaining about how hard it is for her with her husband Leo in the army. Of course, he is only in Jersey — she sees him twice a week and speaks to him daily — but I guess she did not realize she was talking to a girl doesn't even know where her husband is.

Diana

May 24

Well, My Love,

Mississippi's flats, white — glaring dry sands, hot molten sunshine pouring, beating down on your helmet, pith helmet burning hot, the air stifling hot pressed like forced steam on your brow, red flashes dancing in your eyes, marching up and down 'til your brain is swimming and you think you have passed the limits of human endurance, and still you go on breathing the scorching air-fumes, men noncoms & officers alike falling into a slow half-step instead of the full stride. And then, at last, 10 minutes time out.

After four days here, you don't bother with a raincoat — you let it pour when it rains as it finally did today, & you're happy to be wet because you know it will be hot all over again when the shower ends.

Lenny

May 24

Dear Lenny,

I have just come home and found your special delivery with the address. I'm so glad you got the *infantry*.

I know you will think I am silly but is there any possibility of a furlough in the near future? I expect to get a week's vacation in July and I want to come and visit you. Do you think we could work it out? This is the first time there has been so much of the country between us, but darling as you say, it just means that we have loved each other in that many more states.

Diana

May 25

Good morning, sweetheart: We'll fall out any minute now but here's a good morning kiss for you.

This afternoon I went over to the Station Hospital for the orthopedic consultation. It seems that with whole infantry divisions here there's plenty of foot trouble; there were 400 or so on line, & they took my appointment papers & said they'd call me when they get around to me — maybe months, some of the guys in line said.

Mused a deal today on the Milton manuscript[2] & what I could do on it from long distance. I was wondering if you could follow some directions by mail to sort out certain material from my notes, & send it to me to work on.

Lenny

May 25

Hello Dear,

It is hard to think of not having a furlough for at least 3½ months. Even if not, I feel now as though I can hold my head up high and know that I am making a contribution to the war both in my job and through my beloved. We will have earned our happiness after the war is won,

I'm sorry you have come into such heat but from your letter you seem to be more pleased with Shelby, better food and more intelligent officers. What is Mississippi like? I can only see it as a yellow spot on the map.

Diana

May 26

Dear Dina,

I went to the Service Club to read Sunday's Herald Tribune. (NY papers are 2 days late here.) Then I got hold of an atlas & finally located myself on the map. Shelby is about 15 miles southeast of Hattiesburg, which is southeast of Jackson, Miss. It's been a fine day. It was really cool, New York cool, at dawn & while blistering hot now, our drill was interspersed with (open air) classes, in the shade, so I'm not at all tired. I wait for photos — of you, of our families, of our former home.

Congratulations on the raise!!! From your reckoning, you should save $15 a week easily. About my uniform & stuff — I did get a full winter

---

2. Lenny would work on this manuscript, begun in graduate school, whenever he had free time.

outfit, coat & gloves at Upton & now I have no place to store it away from the moths. I wear in the main two uniforms; from dawn 'til 4 I wear fatigues, heavy duty olive green herringbone twill shirt & trousers, wool socks, service shoes, and helmet (plastic model, good for work in hot sun), no tie. Also leggings, into which trousers are stuffed like knickers — For retreat & evening I wear suntan shirt, trousers, tie, overseas cap; khaki socks & low shoes. Cameras are taboo so it'll be some time before I can send a photo.

One of the things that has to change before we can have victory is civilian morale. That's why I emphasized, in my farewell address to the 81 union staff that we will never have a decent, free world until we are ready & willing to lay down our lives for it; & if we aren't willing, we'll discover that any other kind of life just isn't worth living.

Lenny

May 26

Darling —

I'm so glad you seem to be more satisfied with Shelby. The modified Ruml plan seems to be about to pass in Congress — 75% of last year's taxes forgiven.[3] I received your income tax statement for what you owe. I will let them know you are in the army.

Lenny, my darling — I love you so — I spend all my day talking to you and send you love messages through the skies.

Yours,

Diana

May 27

Good Morning Dear,

Naturally, good as our outfit is, there are some blokes among noncoms & second lieutenants, and instead of making progress sometimes we retrogress — as today — when we were over-drilled on old stuff to the point where a good group became a sloppy, careless, indifferent shuffling outfit. I did relatively well on the sighting exercise in fact quite well. The sights on the M-1 are easier for my eyes than the Springfield, & I was able to place on the bull's eye quickly, without strain.

This morning we had a very good training film illustrating all the basic weapons of infantry, and how to recognize them when under fire by lis-

---

3. Ruml, director of the New York Federal Reserve Bank, developed a plan for withholding tax from a paycheck.

tening; it is interesting that the person shot at hears first the bullet or shell in motion, overhead or approaching, then the explosion as it lands & last the explosion from firing, because the bullet goes twice as fast as sound waves.

Lenny

May 27

Dearest Lenny Mine,

It's so good at the end of the day to sit down and write to you and read your letter. By now, since you have been a soldier for 20 days, I have become a little adjusted to my new way of living. Living back with my folks even though they have been swell is not easy. I feel as though this is just a stay-over place for me. I cannot think of it as home. It is also hard because Mississippi is not a real place to me, just a spot on the map.

I can understand what you say about wives following their soldier husband. There is an article in the paper by our favorite woman columnist. She condemned it quite harshly. I agree women have a role to play at home, but I also know it would be heaven if we could be together.

Diana

May 28

My Dearest,

'Tis Friday night, hot, hot, hot; & we're tired. You're probably at my mother's, having a good supper, and reading from my letters.

Darling, I'm proud of your spirit & wouldn't trade you for anyone else. My concern is to do a job as good as my wife & sweetheart is doing.

Lenny

May 28

My Love,

I didn't go to your mother's tonight because she and your father are in the country. This weekend I shall see Miriam and discuss with her visiting plans. I am definitely planning to see you in July.

Yours,
Diana

May 29

Hello Dearest,

Moving day — We have been assigned to our functions during basic training which begins in deadly earnest on Monday. On the barrack roster I see "Int." after my name, which the fellows say is "intelligence & reconnaissance." That doesn't mean any compliment; it means I am (theoretically) a scout, going ahead to draw fire and make the enemy reveal his position so that the next body can come up close to them.

Have begun to reread with great pleasure, Milton's "Of Reformation" — I am as infatuated as ever with his rolling organ tones in his prose.

Got my steel helmet; it's lighter than my fireman's helmet; & a beautiful new gas mask. By the way all my equipment is beautifully brand new. It's a long time since I've had a lot of new clothes!

Here in Shelby, you are a much bigger part of me than at home: not that I loved you less at home, but there I had to devote time to my job and to my civic duty as a fireman. Here I have only one task, to be a soldier, & a good one, & that leaves me many, many hours to spend with you.

Lenny

May 29

My Lady Love,

Here, in a quiet room at the service club, surrounded by books and more books I stop a moment to relax and send my warm love to my beloved. 'Tis Saturday night — We've always had Saturday nights, walking together, dancing, visiting friends, reading, chess playing, seeing a good film — even the tired Saturday nights when you were working so hard at the mechanic's school.

Lenny

May 29

Darling,

Lenny, please realize that mail takes about 3–4 days to reach me and then 3–4 days 'til my answer reaches you although I write immediately.[4] When I look at Lucy (she hasn't heard from Babe in 2½ weeks) I realize how strong one must be today.

Diana

May 30, Memorial Day

Dearest,

'Tis Sunday and I practically had the day off — only one formation. Lee and I were going up to the service club, when a call comes for me to

---

4. Diana responds to Lenny's disappointment at not receiving mail yet at Shelby.

go to the orderly room. When I got there, there were 11 others; and we were all handed a 2 inch square of red cloth and told to pin it over the left shirt pocket, as a sign that we are acting squad leaders, and if we make good, we will maybe become regular squad leaders, that is, corporals. It means I'm on my way!

As you say, if you could visit me here, it would be a dream — nothing else can quite describe it.

Lenny

May 30

Dearest Lenny,

This afternoon I spent with Myra, Leah, Bea and Winnie and the two children. It was very pleasant — out of doors and relaxing. Everyone is so interested to make sure I am not lonely. Darling, as you can see from my letters, I am trying to keep myself busy over the weekends so that my morale will be good and I will be a truly exemplary soldier's wife.

Diana

May 31

Dear,

Today was fairly easy. The heat was made a little more tolerable by a steady wind from the Gulf. We were not drilled on the parched drill area, but out in the woods, under field conditions, with field rations. So most of the day we sat on green slopes under oaks & pines hearing lectures on gases, military discipline, & sanitation — except for double timing the only hot work was calisthenics, which I enjoy, & preliminary bayonet drill.

Lenny

May 31

Lenny,

Thank you so much for the division insignia. My first present from you in the army — How glad I am that you did well in the sighting exercises.

I have discussed visiting you with Miriam and it looks as though we will be able to come together.

Since today was a holiday, I was with so many friends. All of us army & navy wives tonight had a jam session about our wonderful men. Pretty soon there won't be a girl left from all our friends who is not an army or navy wife. Ken & Wally are leaving next week. Sam is being inducted in June.

Diana

June 1

Hello Dear,

Today will be another day in the field wearing pack & gas masks. What a day! Luckily there was a steady gulf wind all day. I must have lost 4 quarts in perspiration. For the first time, I carried a rifle & bayonet together, plus mask & pack.

Today we had more on gas drill & I whiffed a bit too much, but it's past now; and grenade throwing; & bayonet practice. It sounds short as I write it, but from 7:00 to 5:00 we are on the go in this hellish heat. We got 3 to 5 minute breaks an hour & a few minutes extra at lunch. There was a gag — "Boy did I gain weight in the army; before I was inducted I weighed 125 pounds in street clothes, now I weigh 225 pounds with my pack & rifle."

In general, as I've written we see no Negroes: the soldiers are segregated, & the few civilian employees are all in menial tasks & stay at a distance.

Lenny

June 1

Lenny darling —

I know what miserable weather you must be having and how much more difficult that must make your infantry training, but my darling, we must learn to work under severe hardships so we can become steeled fighters and the best trained soldiers.

You ask what I am making at work — same job for three weeks — ever since you left — it requires cutting teeth in a rack. Of course they must be perfectly even and accurate.

Yours,
Diana

June 2

Hello,

Another day out in the field — a bitch — Calisthenics was OK; then practice tent pitching, then gas mask drill. We had to run 400 yards with gas masks on & that was fierce, because it cuts your air supply even while it purifies it.

Lenny

June 2

Dearest Lenny,

I'm glad you are better satisfied with your permanent quarters. Write me more about being a scout. From what you write, it would seem to be quite a dangerous job although of course under battle conditions everyone is in danger.

You know dear when we were home together — with our busy schedules we did not see each other any more during the week than we do right now. What I mean is that with reading your letters and answering them I probably spend as much or maybe more time with you now as we did then. Of course weekends are different.

Diana

June 3

Dear Diana,

I got my first pay installment of $15 tonight, so I have $36 in bills & $1 in loose change. That's plenty. Also I may go to Hattiesburg to examine its historical aspects, & I will have to buy a packet of condoms without which I cannot get a pass to town — laugh, darling; that packet will undoubtedly last me for the duration, so I'll get it in a metal container!

Lenny

June 3

Darling,

You make me so proud of you all the time especially when something happens like being made "acting squad leader." I know there are a lot of maybe's 'til being a corporal, but as you say you are on your way.

Diana

June 4

Good Morning,

A very interesting morning in infantry tactics — concealment, observation, scouting & patrolling — The army has learned a good deal from the Pacific Island fighting. They also read us the latest bulletins — A. V. Alexander's[5] statement on the Nazi subs sunk & the smashing of the Nazi Air Raid at Kursk.

A bitch of a day, one of the hardest & hottest, & in a second the whistle will blow to fall out for a night march.

Lenny

---

5. First Lord of the English Admiralty.

June 4

Lenny Dearest,

I was finally able to hear the record you sent tonight.[6] It was simply tremendous — so wonderful to hear your voice. It sounded exactly like you — very clear and beautiful. When I got to your parents tonight for supper — I brought it with me. Everyone was so thrilled.

I got another raise today, only 2 weeks after the other one. I think the reason is I acted very disappointed with the first one which was only 6 cents, and my foreman also felt it wasn't enough. This one was 8 cents per hr which brings it up to 64 cents per hr or about $37.50 per wk. with overtime.

Now the most wonderful news — I found out I am definitely getting a vacation from July 10–19. So Mississippi, here I come. Since I have only 10 days I shall probably spend 6 with you and 4 traveling. Shall I spend the extra money to take a Pullman? It is quite a bit, but this will be my vacation and I don't want to be too tired.

> *Your,*
> *Diana*

June 5

My Dearest,

To really understand my letters & how they are written, you should sit in the sun, turn on all the gas jets on full flame 'til the temperature is about 105 degrees, sweat & perspire thoroughly — there, that's just right. We eat salt pills bigger than aspirin at every meal to make up for the drain of salt in sweat. I am in a hutment with 18 — 20 others. A hutment is a rude sort of shack, elongated, with 2 side doors, one floor only, all wooden with an open screen running all around the four sides. Inside are only our cots, two stoves, and a shelf running along the walls. Under the shelf is a rod for clothes on hangers.

Last night when I fell in with my company, and the regiment, with several others, marched out at twilight. We walked in silence because we were practicing a forced march approaching enemy lines — think if you can, of long column on column of young men in green uniforms, green helmets, browned faces & brown rifles alongside of the green blending into the forest we were entering. We've got to go six miles in an hour & a quarter. The guys suffered from heat & sweat, from dust & thirst, from

---

6. Soldiers could record a short message on a 78 rpm record to send home.

fatigue & nausea, from every kind of ache & pain. But they felt "now we are becoming soldiers" — this is the real test, not those "right faces" & "left faces." They felt they must come thru now, even if they had failed before. For all the lack of discussion of war aims, everyone knows the score even if it isn't expressed; we are in for a battle. For myself — my morale is something over & above that. Fighting morale is so much a part of my life these past 8 years that the incidentals of being away from wife & home have no effect on it, so long as I am in the fight.

Lenny

June 5

Beloved,

I have just come back from a very tiring day but such a pleasant one. This morning I worked until noon. I met Miriam and we bought the watches — one for you and one for Max. They cost $40 apiece wholesale. The watch for you is a present from my parents. We went to Penn. Station to inquire about our visit to you. We got wonderful news. There is a train called the "Southerner" which goes direct from N.Y. to New Orleans and makes a stop at Hattiesburg. It takes 26 hours. Arrives in Hattiesburg, Sat. night at 6:30 —

Diana

June 6

Dearly Beloved,

Even one's day off is very busy. I double shined my shoes. I washed & aired some more clothes. I stood in line 2½ hours for a haircut. While in line, read through the June issue of the Infantry Journal which had a lot of practical battle experiences and articles.

Food was swell today. Over 40% of our company was in town on pass, so we had doubles on all, & being Sunday, plenty of leisure. So at breakfast I had a whole grapefruit, whereas to get a ½ here is miraculous; at lunch we had the most delicious apple pie. Max, Henry, and I went into the guest house to inquire. We can arrange for a room for you, or two of you, at 75 cents a night. The rub is that we can't spend any time in the guest house with you.

Time is a different thing here from home. There are no "weeks." You don't remember whether you are here a day or a month! This morning and last Wednesday are all the same. There are no calendars, no daily newspapers, and you make no "dates" or appointments. Everything is predetermined by the training plan. One result is to minimize our separation.

All the days between our last parting & our next meeting will be, to me,
like as when one goes to sleep & arises again; there's no sense of anything
in between.

Lenny

June 6

Dearest,

Well, darling, we finally hung the service flags today. I had mine
for about 10 days but Lucy had trouble getting a Navy one, so I waited.
We hung them both over the couch — we want more people to see
them.

You ask about the Giraud De Gaulle unity?[7] It is a great victory because it includes all anti-Hitler and anti-Vichy French forces. It is also a
victory because it was extended on the basis of cleaning out the Vichy —
men and fascists in the colonial administrations.

Lou called and said he had such a nice visit with you. He said you are
looking well and he had the highest praise for your attitude. He said you
should be hard as nails by the time I see you.

Diana

June 7

My Darling Love,

Today in fierce blazing sun we marched 3 stretches, totally about 12
miles. We double timed, wearing gas masks, which is enough to kill anyone, about 200 yards — I wouldn't do that to anyone except if I felt like
torturing a Nazi.

Lenny

June 7

Dearest,

Congratulations on your first anniversary as a soldier (1 month). This
is now the longest time I have been separated from you. The way you
describe the marching and drilling with full pack, I almost feel as though I
am by your side — helping you through the grueling tests and giving you
fresh courage to go on.

Diana

---

7. This refers to an agreement between the French generals, Henri Giraud and Charles
De Gaulle, to coordinate the campaign to liberate France from Nazi Germany during
World War II.

June 8

Hello,

I must be toughening up. Except for an extra dose of tear gas in the gas chamber this A.M. (really a closed tent), and about 500 yards double timing with bayonet fixed on rifle (you're not fit for much after that!), I am quite rested & un-tired at this time.

As regards your coming here nobody in the army knows anything now of what will be July 10 & if they know it doesn't matter because it will probably be changed. It is always possible for something unexpected to make it impossible to see each other — especially if Europe is invaded by then all bets are off. But, dearest, it's worth the trying. ·

Lenny

June 8

Dear Lenny Darling,

I arrived home early tonight intending to write you such a nice long letter but we had a blackout from 9:30 'til 11:15. There has been a good deal of excitement about a speech by Churchill in which he says we are now ready for an invasion.

Diana

June 9

My Dearest,

At 5 to 10 I got a call to go to Battalion Headquarters & up there to find Lt. Hamilton meeting with our intelligence section. I think I made a good impression. He is Battalion Officer in charge of intelligence work & I'll probably have more to do with him.

Today has been an easy day: mostly we were belly-crawling in under-brush concealment downhill. The idea is to keep out of sight — & it is amazing — 100 yards of open woods with underbrush completely hid 175 men so you could only see 4 or 5 of them & when they moved, only an expert rifleman could catch any at all. That's only practice but it helps give everyone confidence that we will not simply be mowed down but will have a good chance to go on fighting under fire.

There have been 5 AWOL cases in our regiment, although for less than 24 hours. The malefactors were all assessed $15 fine & 15 days hard labor — which means pick & shovel 5:30 A.M. to 10 P.M. Dearest, if it is true that the Southerner will make it in 26 hours, & will bring you here for Saturday night, then take it. The main consideration is that we have Saturday and Sunday.

Lenny

June 9

Sweetheart,

I shall leave Friday and arrive in camp Saturday. Lenny — in your description of the night march with gas attacks drill, you seem to write as though you are trying to tell me how difficult it is, how every muscle & nerve is strained — and yet you seem to feel as though I don't understand. Perhaps I have not been expressing it in my letters but I understand the tough training you have. Of course, I know there is no comparison, but my job in N.Y. takes almost all my strength out of me. Lenny, I wrote of the terrific hot spell we had. I know I cannot write descriptions like you can, but as I worked — the sweat pouring from my body — I was so wet and hot that before long I noticed my arms and face and neck becoming a distinct green. I was frightened, but some of the men told me that always happens in the summer. The brass we work on reacts with the acids in the skin and leaves a distinct green covering. I now stand all day long because I am on a new machine, which is so high that it is impossible to sit. In spite of this, I go on day after day because my fighting spirit and my determination make me do my job.

A number of people in my shop and outside have asked me why I don't go and stay with you in Mississippi. It is hard for me to explain it to them. They think I am heartless. People say, "I wish I could be like you," but say it with a nasty undertone and they really mean, "There must be something wrong with you."[8]

Diana

June 10

My Darling Wife,

This morning, after physical training, we had bayonet drill. This always starts with about 400 yards double time with the bayonet in front. For variety, they lay the rifles & bayonets midway between two lines of soldiers — each line races out to grab it — the one who gets it tries

---

8. Diana is referring to those wives who chose to follow their husbands to military bases. It was a controversial issue. Although many did travel to and stay with their husbands, Diana and others remained home. Crowded trains, inadequate housing for married couples, high prices near bases, and frequent moves were among the concerns cited.

to keep, the other to take away — wrestling: Well, I got it first, & in a second my opponent was on me trying to get it. We wrestled fiercely, & he had me down & rolling, but didn't get the rifle & I didn't shake him off so it was a draw. In real combat with a Nazi I would no doubt have bitten a big hunk out of his leg, & I hate to think what he'd have done to me.

Lenny

June 10

Dearest,

Today was a pretty nice day in the shop. I am on quite an interesting job now and the foreman is just beginning to let me set up certain things myself. Of course, he doesn't let me do this half enough, but still it is better than when I first came here. Little by little, and oh, so slowly, he is beginning to have a little more faith in women's ability, but he is still convinced that "woman's place is in the home as a decoration."

Although I have been with other people a great deal, the time of the day I look forward to is the hour I spend with you writing & reading your letters and talking to you. People say to me, "You must be so lonely especially since you were married over 3 years before your husband left." I always answer, "I am not lonely as long as we have each other, no matter what the distance between us is."

I saw a very cute cartoon. A woman with a baby in her arms says to another woman pointing to the baby. "We call him Furlough." Well, when I come to see you I will bring my equipment, so that we won't have a "Furlough" unless we decide to.

Yours,
Diana

June 11

Dear Love,

I learned about our schedule, delaying your visit. Thanks a million for the watch. It is a wonderful thing to have here when time is so rare a commodity. I can get a great many things done which hitherto I couldn't because now I can judge precisely how much time to leave myself. I want to lie down & relax for five minutes before I dress into my hike uniform for tonight, so I'll sign off with a special shower of kisses for no special reason at all.

Lenny

June 11, Friday

Dearest,

I have just returned from your mother's house and a delicious supper as always. They teased me because I would not read them your entire letter, but only parts which I felt they should hear. I try to make my Friday night visits very gay because of course they all miss you.

I expect to arrive in Hattiesburg on July 10 on Sat. and leave July 18 on Sun. We are planning to make train reservations this week. As soon as we write we have the train reservations, you can reserve a room. Maybe if you can get a pass, we can visit New Orleans — only 3 hours away. It is such a historic city I feel it must be worth seeing.

Is there any chance of your meeting us at the station in Hattiesburg? Do we take only summer clothes? Do we need bathing suits?

Diana

June 12

My Dearest Darling,

We both know, for we learned it together, that our love can have its fullest expression and development only in the struggle to free our country and all countries from the hateful cancerous dragon that now befouls our fair earth. To root it out from all sources, to let free nature run its own beautiful course: to love and to struggle — the sum of happiness.

Your passionate soldier,
Lenny

June 12

Dearest Husband Mine,

I called my mother after work to know if there was a letter from you and when she told me there was a letter and also an air mail special delivery, I went home immediately. Of course dearest, I was very disappointed at not being able to come when we planned. I knew there was a possibility of having to change our plans. I'm glad you found out, before we made more arrangements. As you suggest, I shall come the last week in July or 7/23–7/31. I shall speak to my foreman to find out if I can change my vacation.

Diana

June 13

Hello Dearest,

You say something about understanding the toughness of my training; & my letter suggests that I feel you don't understand. We don't understand each other, do we? I have proudly told everyone that my wife is a production soldier whose daily work hours are two hours longer than our basic training hours, and who goes on to do vital civilian war work every evening. And dearest, when I write of our labors here, no matter how detailed I may speak of our sufferings, & at times that is the only word to use, you know that I am not complaining. I write plainly, to give you a strictly factual account day by day. My only expression of the day's fatigue goes into these letters, & if they're heavy sometimes with the day's fatigue, you understand I am thereby working off the burden & relaxing. I never for a moment forget that the most severe test I have had or will have here in camp will not compare to the first day or any day, I go into battle.

Mike and I hiked to 66 St. (We're at 51 St.) to get a seat on the bus; and off to Hattiesburg. The town is a serviceman's city — no civilians in sight except for store personnel — only soldiers & soldiers' wives. If Mike didn't stop at every candy store, and lunch bar & soda fountain to "nosh," maybe we'd seen something: as it was, 2/3 of the time was spent in waiting for a steak. We "bee lined" to the Forest Hotel, best in town — they have rooms for $3.50 to $5.50. Reservations can be made now at 3 weeks in advance.

Before we got our passes, our first sergeant informed us that the M.P.[9] arrest & jail any white soldier who enters a street in the Negro section of town, so this aspect of Southern life is not easy to look into. We observed that the bus terminal has a "White Waiting Room" & "Colored Waiting Room," toilets say "White Men" & "Colored Men" on the door; theaters have a separate door labeled "Colored Entrance," and the restaurant where we ate had no Negro patrons. Negroes walk the streets alongside of whites, however; & in some places, like Woolworths, appear to work together but behind the food counter only. The Negroes I have seen on the street are a quiet (is it sullen?) lot.

The New Orleans papers mainly ignore the Negro community in the news. Their want ads do not specify religion like New York papers do but they do have three kinds of "color" specifications: "white only,"

---

9. Military Police.

"white," and "colored" which refers to mixed race. The Hattiesburg paper shows much more overt prejudice: Negro is always with a small N; "Negress" is used too.[10]

Lenny

SEARCHING FOR NEWT KNIGHT IN JONES COUNTY

While in Hattiesburg, on June 13, Lenny stumbles on the story of Captain Newt Knight, the grandson of John Knight, who was awarded land grants for service in the War of 1812. He left the Confederate Army and led a rebellion of poor whites and blacks, seceding from the Confederacy and forming The Free State of Jones, over three years, in the very same part of Mississippi. While Lenny crawled through the same swamps as Newt's band, in his spare time he plodded methodically through Newt's story in the county libraries, and visited with Newt's son Tom, who wrote a book about his father's story. Seventy years later, interest in this story resurfaced, with several new books that led to the 2016 film, *The Free State of Jones*, which drew Matthew McConaughey into this largely unknown Civil War story.

June 13 8:40 P.M.

My Lady,

Dearest, I'm very excited over a "find" — my nose is on a hot trail. Here's the story, I have turned up, in a guide to Mississippi by the WPA.[11] A Federal Writers' Project published by Viking in 1938 tells the story of

---

10. Enclosed with this letter is a clipping from a *Guide to the Deep South* to be given to soldiers to teach them how to act in accordance with local customs in the name of national unity. The article describes an episode near Jackson, "Two white lieutenants, it was reported, took a colored soldier into the café and ordered three beers. The waitress served the officers and asked the negro to drink his beer outside. The officers angrily left. If the negro had been from this section, he would have told the officers that he preferred to drink his beer in one of his own cafés, with his own people."

11. Works Projects Administration was the largest and most ambitious New Deal agency, employing millions of unemployed people to carry out public works projects, including the construction of public buildings and roads. It also employed artists in projects in the field.

the Civil War & how Mississippi seceded. The citizens of Jones Country sent an anti-secessionist delegate to the Secessionist Convention. Assembling in Ellisville, they declared Ellisville to be the capital of the "Free State of Jones," and led by Newt Knight, captain, they maintained a guerrilla band that declared & waged war on the Confederacy. They hid out in the Leaf River swamps, where we have our practice marches.

Lenny

June 13, Sunday

Darling Lenny,

This is going to be a very hard letter for me to write. Since I am not very adept at leading up to things gently I shall just tell you. Your Aunt Minnie died Friday night. The funeral was today. The entire family behaved quite well under the circumstances because they were prepared for it. I attended the funeral and went back to the house with them. They were all quite calm when they came home and your mother was OK. She was making a real effort to behave well, because she had to help Aunt Minnie's daughters. Your mother, Aunt Mary & Uncle Benny are sitting "shivah" at the house with the girls and Leo, who is home. I shall see them in a day or two.[12]

Diana

June 14, Sent special delivery, air mail

Dearest Diana,

As I telegraphed you earlier tonight, we expect you on June 24. We have arranged lodging for you at guest house #3, which is nearest to us (about 10 minute walk). Tomorrow night, I'm going to Hattiesburg to try to get rooms with a private family for you, where we may have some privacy — at guest houses we can't come in beyond the lobby. When you come to Hattiesburg on Thursday, we'll probably not be able to meet you. You'll get the bus to Camp Shelby for a 20 cent fare. When you get to the camp gate, tell the M.P. you have reservations, they'll phone in & then issue a pass to you.

Lenny

---

12. Shivah is a week-long mourning period in Judaism observed by the immediate family after burial. Family members gather in a family member's home and receive visitors. In the evening, a prayer service is held to recite the kaddish prayer for the deceased.

June 14, Monday

Sweetheart,

Lenny, I hope so much you say for me to come.

Your,

Diana

June 15, 6 A.M.

Dearest Lenny,

Received telegram 1 A.M. telling me to come June 24. Hurrah — Must stop now — have to go to work.

Diana

June 15 Western Union telegram

OK PLACE RESERVED — COME JUNE 24 TRY TO BE HERE UNTIL JULY 4. LETTER FOLLOWS — LENNY

June 15

Dear Dina,

The eye doctor said my last lenses were OK for 20/20 — He said I ought to be limited service & I said I'd rather not & he said 20/300 calls for it — so I repeated I didn't want limited service; so he went to the major, who agreed with me. Well, the upshot is they are giving me 2 pairs of G.I. glasses, built for service rather than looks. In addition, I can have the Rx filled in Hattiesburg, at 40 % off, by ordering thru the PX account. I got the order for a new lens & a new extra pair. Then I will have 4 good pairs of glasses, which should last me at least through the duration!!

Lenny

June 15, 7:50 P.M.

My Love,

This is still the army, no pass, no can go. I'll try tomorrow to find a place to stay in town. Bring along a little alarm clock in case I stay over so I can get to camp for "reveille."

Lenny

June 15, 11:30, A.M.

Lenny Dearest,

I sent you another night letter tonight telling you all is arranged and we are coming next week. The Southerner is all booked until July 15 so that is out. The Pullman fare is $93.00 and hard to get a reservation. We had to take the regular coach — $53.00 round trip. I hope nothing comes up to interfere.

My dearest, how beautifully you describe our love and how wonderful it makes me feel to read it.

Diana

June 16

My Dearest,

Your coming in on Saturday morning presents some problems. I'm going to try to get you a room (two rooms, one for each couple, in town), and you'll have to go there from the station; I'll try to get a weekend pass as soon after 5:00 as I can.

Lenny

June 16

Lenny, as I said in the telegram, we are planning to leave Thurs. June 24 at 6:30 P.M. to arrive Sat. June 26 at 5 A.M. Beloved, beloved — just a few more days to wait.

Diana

June 17

My Dearest Darling,

"Gosh" — as you say — I am looking forward to your visit. Doing one's duty is well, & the army is OK by me, but even at home there comes a time when duties were relaxed & I turned to embrace my wife, to talk, to love.

In 8 minutes we leave for night operations; a fierce east wind is blowing up a fine storm, & I am dog tired after a day that was twice as hard as yesterday.

Lenny

June 17

Dearest Lenny,

Just came home from visiting your mother and the rest of the family. They are beginning to accept your aunt's death and think about other things again.

By the end of next week we shall see each other and that is all that matters.

Your,
Diana

June 18

Dear,

Today we learned how to stand barehanded when an enemy comes at you with bayonet & to disarm him & finish him — 4 different tactics for different situations; one of those things that gives you great confidence & assurance another little thing — we were taught to test for land mines. We have also been shown, on night march what a rifle shot looks & sounds like at distances up to 1,000 yards & other noises at like distances. I am working very hard in rifle marksmanship — we have 4 hours a day in it & I hope to really do a good job in spite of my miserable right eye.

Lenny

June 18

Darling,

What you write about Hattiesburg is interesting. Of course the business about segregation of Negro and White is very shameful — one of the evils which the winning of this war should begin to overcome.

Lenny, my darling, each day that passes now seems so long to me because I am getting so impatient. I reread your letters every chance I get, on the train, while I eat, while I sit down to rest — all the time — I always have 5 or 6 with me.

Diana

June 19

My Dearest Diana,

The moon in Mississippi is its one redeeming feature. Whether it is the southerly latitude, or the fact that we are out in open country, at any rate the full moon here is much bigger than at Shepherd Avenue.[13] Well beloved — next Saturday night in this time 'twill be no letter to you — but lips to lips.

Lenny

June 19

Lenny, sweetheart, tonight I spent Sat night with you by writing to you but next Sat night Whee! This afternoon I took care of all my last-minute shopping for the visit and had such fun thinking, "Will my darling like this?" and "What will he say?" Tomorrow I shall get all my things ready

---

13. This is the street where Diana lived with her parents during the war.

Diana visiting Lenny in Hattiesburg, Mississippi, June 27, 1943

and pack. I spoke to Miriam and we decided to leave on Tues as you want us to. I hope you were able to get the pass and arrange everything in town, but I'm not worried. Darling, I shall practically arrive at the same time as this letter.

Diana

June 20

Dear My Love,

Well, darling, those 2 patches of prickly heat turned out to be a nasty dose of poison oak on my left arm & throat, & I do hope it's mostly gone when you get here.

Lenny

Diana and Lenny in Hattiesburg, Mississippi

June 20

Lenny Dearest,

I am practically all set now — I shall pack tomorrow night when I come home from work. My father is going to help me take my things to Penn. Station because he works right near there, so I won't have any problem with heavy valises. Just a few more days — I know I keep repeating this but it's just how I feel. I still have to work two more days so I must remain calm. Tuesday, from work, I shall go to Penn. Station, meet Miriam and then we're on our way.

Diana

June 21

Hello Dear,

Well, that skin business is poison ivy, according to the doctor. My first sergeant saw me & suggested he could use me in company area "today" so it wouldn't get worse by sweating & scraping a rifle sling over it.

Lenny

June 21

Darling,

I have just finished packing. I will be in touch with you on Thursday when I get to Hattiesburg which will be before this letter gets to you. However, I cannot go to bed without writing to you, so just a short note.

Yours,
Diana

June 22

My Dearest Darling,

If our plans work out right, you will be on your way to Hattiesburg when this arrives. It is hot; I am sitting still in my hutment. This is the second working day that the poison ivy had kept me from duty. The shocking news of the Detroit massacre came over the radio this morning.[14] At once the southerners in the group proclaimed that the north coddles the "n—rs," the "n—rs" [*sic*] must be taught to keep their place, that stringing them onto a fast car, or lynching a few every so often was the best way.

Lenny

DIANA HEADS TO MISSISSIPPI

[Break in letters during Diana's visit to Mississippi]

---

14. Race riots in Detroit from 6/20–6/22 resulted in deaths.

GOING HOME

July 2

Dear My Love,

Darling — this past week of your visit has been pretty much of a dream, from the first misty moment when you were swimming down the guesthouse stairs into my arms, as happily surprised to find me there, right through to our sweet parting sorrow.

Lenny

July 2

Dearest Husband,

The train has just pulled out of Hattiesburg and I'm on my way home. This morning I walked down to your company area and was told the headquarters platoon went on the range about 4 A.M. this morning. Good luck, beloved, I know you will do well — all my love and hopes go with you so that you do a good job. The train, I am on is not air conditioned, but I have a seat and that is most important. I'll have to change at Chattanooga and then at Washington. Some of the girls I know who went to visit their husbands in the army told me that you feel much worse when you go home. I don't agree with them at all. It's true that I didn't want to say goodbye, but I feel wonderful for having had this week together. Now that I saw you and can think of you always in your daily routine, eating, working, marching, in your hutment, in the service club, etc. it makes it much nicer and brings us so much closer because we have been in camp together.

Diana

July 2

Dearest Lenny,

On this trip back I am seeing plenty of poverty. We are passing dozens of small towns in Mississippi and now in Alabama, and all along the tracks are old, broken-down one-room shacks with holes in the walls for windows and no doors even. We have passed hundreds of them — some where Negroes live and some where White people live.

I've never seen such poverty. We must be passing through a pretty poverty-stricken section now — cows grazing alongside the railroad tracks and so thin and sick looking — the people we can see from the train window also so thin and anemic looking. More and more we grow to understand why we must fight this war.

Diana

July 5

Dearly Beloved,

By now you are back at home. The hike out here was a strenuous one — about 13 miles in 4 hours, leaving when it was still dark night. We are living in or more truly, out of field pup tents. My bed is Mississippi clay soil which I have strewn liberally with pine needles & covered with a blanket and mosquito netting. Our tents are pitched in a clearing in the woods. All day long the air is full of cracking rifles and echoes of other weapons.

Lenny

July 5, 6:30 P.M.

Hello Diana,

I was all settled when an order came for me & two others to strike our tents & return to camp by truck. So here I am on guard duty, 24 hour shift, 2 hours on guard with 4 off. Theoretically, we have a 2 hour rest after guard but I expect a snafu again, to be called out to the range when my sleep time arrives. It's the army all over.

Lenny

July 5

Dearest, you may think I am stressing the business of army wives staying with their husbands, but after being with you in camp and seeing what goes on there — you can't help thinking about it, and discussing it. Sleep well, although you are probably not too comfortable sleeping on the ground.

Diana

July 6

Dear My Love,

Well, I'm completing my first experience with guard duty and the first & last shifts were the hardest. Walking guard is a dull bore — you change rifle from right to left shoulder, & back every half hour, salute an officer once or twice a day, & just pace slowly round and round a 6-block area.

Lenny

July 6

Dearest,

Since you probably do not see any newspapers now on the range I'll tell you some of the news. The Germans launched an offensive this week around Orel[15] and lost 586 tanks the first day. The Red Army is repulsing the enemy. Also General Sikorski[16] was killed in a plane crash.

Yours,
Diana

July 7

Dear Diana,

It's unbelievable but I've practically a day off!!! No duty has been given me 'til my next 24-hour guard shift. Over to the Service club for a real holiday — on the porch, reading — I chose Freud's "Basic Writings" — I wanted something not too difficult, yet something to learn, something non-military.

Lenny

July 7

Sweetheart,

The letter I received today is postmarked Sunday, July 4. In reading I relived my entire stay with you. Darling, I want you to know — I wasn't blue or sad on my way home — but as we said to each other and as you write in the letter — it was harder for us to part now because we know what we would have to face better than on May 7. I am so glad you wrote it down in a letter, because now we have it written out and such a beautiful time together we should have it written out. Not of course that either of us would forget, but I wanted a letter with this in it, so that we could refer back to it again and again.

I did go back to work and it was good to get back. Today is 2 months that you are a soldier and I am a very proud soldier's wife.

Your,
Diana

July 8

Sweet Dina,

My last tour of the 24-hour shift is over, & I'm just resting here 'til

---

15. On the southern front in Russia.

16. Prime Minister of the Polish Government in Exile.

we are dismissed. We walked the post together, my gun & I. Somehow I began to sing our well-known Yiddish Hebrew songs but even the jolliest have such a melancholy note that very soon I was in a deep vein of homesickness; but it was pleasant to be homesick for once, out there alone, to have a lump in my throat, and think of everything that home means to me.

Lenny

July 8

Goodnight beloved,

In 5 hours (now it is midnight) you will be starting your day because you are 1 hour ahead of us. Shoot well, Lenny. I love you.

Diana

July 9

Dearest,

Hooray for the allotment! Can it all go into the B fund?[17]

Lenny

July 9, Friday

Dearest Lenny,

I have to work the whole day tomorrow, because I am on an important rush job. I couldn't refuse especially since I just came back from vacation.

Diana

July 10

Hello,

So far the 5 of us who are holding the company area have no orders about the range, but I expect to be called any minute.

Tonight will bring your first letter from home — I'm eager for it. Tonight I'll be a-thinking of you & my folks together having supper. With Mike gone, & Eddie soon to go please read from my letters, give my folks cheer; & I'll always be with all of you in spirit when you get together on Friday night, until the grand reunion when victory is ours.

Lenny

---

17. An allotment refers to when the military automatically takes money from the paycheck and sends it to a dependent spouse. B fund refers to Lenny and Diana's special savings account for their future child.

DIANA AT THE BROOKLYN NAVY YARD

Diana and many other women found a significant role in the war effort for themselves. Employment opportunities for women opened up as more and more men left the workforce. It was very important to Diana to contribute to the war effort. Like Lenny, she was strongly committed to stopping Hitler and making the world a better place.

Diana took classes to train as a machinist. She worked at the Brooklyn Navy Yard, the largest shipbuilding facility in the country, along with seventy thousand other men and women. Her job was to build periscopes for Kollmorgen, a well-known company and a leading provider of motion systems and components for original equipment manufactured around the globe. The work was exacting and often required standing on her feet for hours. Working with the older male, long-time employees and supervisors, was often challenging, as was learning to work with other women from very different backgrounds.

During Diana's time at Kollmorgen, she became involved in organizing the union local, jeopardizing her position. Once she knew she was pregnant, she left the factory work, but spent a lot of time trying to find work that was less physically demanding. She was unable to find something suitable, although she kept searching for several months. She needed to feel like she was contributing, as well as needing money to supplement her husband's army pay, and to not burden her parents. Finally, she was resigned to stay home and wait for the birth of the baby.

July 10, continued on July 11

Dearest Love,

I came home from work at 4:30 p.m. As I write, there is a special broadcast from North Africa on the invasion of Sicily. I guess you know about this already. Isn't that swell?

One of the great inconveniences of living with my parents is that I have so little privacy. Our apartment is very poorly constructed for 4 adults. The rooms are not separated enough and you cannot really go off by yourself.

In my shop,[18] we are very busy now and the men are even working today. We have gotten some new orders that are a rush and we have to fill them as soon as possible. My community war work has also intensified and needs more of my attention. We feel at the present time to help the war effort more we must become a much more inclusive and larger group and we are working in that direction.

You write that Mississippi has been transformed for you since I was there with you. I feel the same way, but about you. Now I think of you walking to the service club with me, in front of the guest house, meeting you on 51 St. and 2nd, in mess, in town, at the USO, and all the other places we were together.

Darling, I forgot to write this but I broached the question of another raise with my foreman and he told me that before I could become a really higher paid worker, I would have to buy some tools. Well, I couldn't right now until I pay back $65 to my father that I borrowed. Lucy's father-in-law offered to loan me tools for the duration. That will help me a great deal because with our plans for Sept. I may not be in the job long enough to pay for me to buy tools.[19]

Yours,
Diana

July 11

Dearest,

I think of our plans for September a great deal, mostly because I am not fully decided yet and I want to give it a great deal of thought before I see you and we come to a decision. There is no doubt in my mind that I want to have a child. The only doubts are am I capable physically and otherwise of taking the responsibility upon myself until you can come home to share it with me, and is it right to take the time now from other work. When you can, write me about how you feel on some of these questions.

Diana

---

18. Kollmorgen Factory in the Brooklyn Navy Yard.

19. This was the first reference to plans to become pregnant.

SIDELINED: JULY 12–AUGUST 3

July 12

Dear My Love,

Well I'm determined to get these pesky "boils" cleaned up[20] so I'm up to the Station Hospital, as I'll never get better while on guard duty or doing creeping & crawling in underbrush. There's no reason for you to start worrying: you must know that the army reckons "either full duty or the hospital" & leaves no range between.

Lenny

July 12

Hello my Darling,

A group got together this evening and I learned the good news that another group of our friends have been sent to England. The allotment came and went into the bank. Of course for the B fund. What else?

Diana

July 13

Dear Diana,

I do hope you are not troubled over my being in the hospital. It's a quiet ward with finger, arm & foot infections, none very "serious" although painful & interfering with duty. The nurse says it will be OK only after several weeks. Unhappily, dearest that means that this term of basic is pretty near killed, my chances of an early rating ditto, & at the very least I'll have to do basic all over.

Lenny

July 13

Darling Love,

I tend to agree with you on the names for a girl — Elizabeth is very nice and fits so well with our last name. Perhaps Elizabeth Clara would work. We shall finally decide when we see each other. I am also very partial to Nellie but I guess you are right — she might not like it and we wouldn't want that. A boy would be Freddie without any question.

Your,
Diana

---

20. Infected poison ivy sores.

July 14

Dearest,

Another long day here in the hospital, I was reading Anatole France. As I've written before, I am far better off here than in the company, my pain is gone — only unhappiness is to lose time from the war: that I shall try to make up by redoubled effort when I am recovered.

Lenny

July 14

Dearest, there was no letter from you today. I don't quite understand the reason unless you were sent out on the range again.

Diana

July 15

Dearest,

This morning I whiled away with Franklin's autobiography. Sweetheart darling, I am sorry it will be sometime before I can write you really jolly news — we must be patient 'til I can be fully recovered & resume my training & duties.

Lenny

July 15

Dearest Lenny Darling,

How are you feeling? How are the infections from the poison ivy? How is your finger, which you write is the worst? Do you still have to take codeine? Your Monday letter made me very concerned about you. My first reaction was to run and grab the train so I could get to you and take care of you myself. I hope you will get proper care and that it will heal up quickly.

My foreman resigned this week. He felt he was being mistreated by the company and his health was being affected because of the strenuous work. Since he resigned there has been havoc in the department. The set-up man expected to be made foreman but he wasn't. A foreman from another department who knows nothing about the milling machine was made foreman. Now the set-up man refused to do set-up. It's a very bad situation because those of us who cannot do our own set-up are in a pickle because there is no one to help us.

Diana

July 16

My Dearest,

Last night I read Aristophanes's, "Lysistrata," the most 20th century of his plays. This morning I read his "Plutus." These days I could do tremendously with the Milton manuscript I have racked my brains but can't figure any way I can work on it here; let alone the lack of library facilities. Just another thing to hate the Nazis for!

Lenny

July 16, 10 A.M.

Dearest,

I am writing this note while I sit here watching my machine. You know that one thing I shall learn as a result of your being a soldier is patience and discipline — There have been days when it has been so hard for me to work. It's so hard for me now not to run to you, but I must learn this because even though I could go to you now — it would be wrong to leave my job and evening work. Also Lenny, there will come a time when I won't be able to run to you because you won't be in America. I must prepare myself for this.

Diana

July 17

My Lady Love,

Tolstoy's "War and Peace" so far doesn't hold my interest; maybe it's the translator. Tonight I left your letter to write — Saturday evening, so we could be together the while.

Lenny

July 17, Sat.

Lenny Dearest,

It is needless for me to say how I felt to read that you expect to be sick for 2–4 weeks. Dearest, please do not be too unhappy about this unfortunate situation. Don't feel as though all your chances in the army have been cut short. You really don't know yet just what missing this part of training will mean.

I am trying to help you get better even though I cannot be by you right now — I do soothe you and caress you and try to help the pain go away. I also want you to be a good soldier. I want to be a good soldier's wife — a war worker and a civilian defense worker.

Diana

July 18

Dear My Love,

After a week here I find reading quite tasteless. I find writing more pleasurable a way to pass the time. My infections continue to retreat. But I shall be here surely another week. The edition of Tolstoy's "War and Peace" proved hopeless — exchanged it for a Shakespeare.

Lenny

July 18, Sun

Dearest Lenny

I was all ready to go to the country for the day with friends when my father called me. He had just gotten an attack on his kidneys — the other one from the one he had trouble with last year. As you remember, he was screaming and writhing with pain. I called the doctor who gave him an injection, which is all he can do during an attack. About an hour later the pain became easier and he has been resting comfortably.

I am writing you all this because I don't like to keep anything from you as I promised you, and because I feel better to talk to you about it.

Yours,
Diana

July 19

Hello Dear,

Sat this morning out on the lawn in the pine tree shade & read "Othello." And having nothing else — turned to "Winter's Tale." The bombing of Rome caused a flurry in the ward. A number of the fellows felt we're too needlessly squeamish about cathedrals & such, & should give the enemy what they gave London. I, too, lover of antiquity that I am, am ready to say "let all that perish, but let men be free," if need be. But if we can spare Michelangelo's frescoes & the Vatican library, we should by all means.

Lenny

July 19

Beloved,

My father has been fairly comfortable today. Dr. Shaw thinks the stone is very small and it may come out by itself. Even worse than the kidneys is my father's mental state. He is very downhearted and extremely unhappy.

Darling, regarding our plans for September, I realize why you say I will have to make the decision but I still want it to be a joint decision because it affects both our lives and our future. What you say about my giving up my war job and other activities, I cannot disagree with in normal peace times, but I am not sure that the same applies in war. We are people who realize what is at stake in this war, and we realize we have to give up personal pleasures now till we have won the right to have them. Otherwise dearest, I would be with you right now.

Diana

July 20

Dear Diana,

I have been promoted to "mess hall patient," which means I march half a mile to meals & back instead of having a tray brought to me. It means that I'm soon getting out of here.

You, in the midst of your war job, turning out battle periscopes & spending every other minute rallying people for more sacrifice & war effort, must indeed be shaking your head sadly at your fainéant husband who eats & sleeps & reads Greek dramas as if there was nothing in the world but beauty & sunshine.

Lenny

July 21 8:45 A.M.

Dear My Love,

As my last thoughts at bedtime are of you, so are my first on waking of my sweetheart, wife, coworker & co-fighter. I am comfortable; & only eat my heart out at the thought of wasted time, at the thought of God knows what they have done to my personal & G.I. stuff back in the hutment, & worst of all, there is a growing & persistent rumor that the 69th is being shipped to Ft. Meade, Maryland & if I'm still here then I'll miss out on the royal chance to be only 4 hours from you & 1½ hours from the Library of Congress. Read Sophocles, "Antigone" this morning and it was really good. Hurray for the taking of Enna. But in all my life I do not understand this nibbling strategy that pecks away at the periphery (just Sicily) dawdling away the time — unless of course, as ever, politics is holding back the strategy.

Lenny

July 21

Darling,

Your letter made me feel good because you seem to be back to your usual self — I guess the relief of having yourself properly taken care of and the fact you are improving account for this.

Diana

July 22

My Dear Girl,

It's been a hot night & hot day, with very little encouragement to do anything. The classics pull on one, too. Thanks, sweetheart, for the second letter today — like all of your letters, it's reread 'til the print is fairly worn out.

This afternoon I positively disciplined myself into finishing "Henry IV" — Shakespeare's Falstaff. After your letter I turned with much more life back to Aristophanes, "The Frogs." Brave lass, thanks again for your words of encouragement & comfort — you're a real mate, and I'm proud of you. You've done a darn sight more these 3 months gone, at your job & other duties towards winning the war than I have; though I'm in training, & as a soldier get all the glory.

Lenny

July 22

Dearest Lenny,

A nice thing happened at work. I have a new foreman. He called me over and asked me how much I was earning and when I had my last raise. In a couple of weeks he would ask for another raise for me.

Diana

July 23

Dearest,

It was a terrific shock to hear of your father's sudden illness. I do hope it's only an alarm, and will not return. Hurrah for Palermo & Bolkhov. The Straits of Messina were identified by some ancients with Scylla & Charybdis — may it prove both to Hitler & Mussolini.

Lenny

July 23

Dear Beloved,

Happy anniversary darling — 39 months![21] I am glad you can get to the library to get things to read. I know it is hard for you to be inactive all day, especially since the pain is gone. I'm so sorry my mail is not brought to you regularly, but it does catch up with you every few days, doesn't it?

---

21. They counted the months they were married.

Continued Sat. July 24

Yesterday I had such an upsetting day at the shop — I cursed and fumed all day long because my new foreman is not too competent. I told him on Thurs I would be finished with the job I was on by Friday noon. I expected he would prepare a new one for me. Well, I finished at 10 A.M. and didn't get a new job for the rest of the day. I spoke to the foreman who said, "As long as I know you could not help it, don't worry about it." I couldn't convince him it was war production that I was interested in.

Diana

July 24

Dearest Diana,

From the "Times Picayune": it seems as if one or two hefty cracks at Italy & Mussolini's Imperium will crack. There seems to be a real to-do over the Balkans likewise.

Finished reading "Faust" The library is exhausted — there are hundreds of volumes there, but none worth reading.

Well, I've just been told by the "ward boy" that I am now a sweeper — which means one other and I sweep the ward, office & private rooms attached every morning but I'll be glad of the chance to feel useful again. 'Tis also a mark of my "improvement" and progress toward getting out of here.

Today is a month since the glorious 24th of June when you drifted mistily into my eager arms at the foot of the guest-house stairs. Magic day, when I fell in love with you again for the nth time —

Lenny

July 24, Sat

Dearest,

Lenny, do you know that today is exactly one month that I came out to Shelby for our dream visit? We need some time together every few months (of course only as long as it will be possible).

Today I attended synagogue services, quite a new experience for me. All day long — especially this morning and evening while I am in my room I have heard the services from the "shul" in our back yard.[22] I practically feel as though I have been there.

Lenny, let's go for a little walk together now because I haven't been out all day. We shall walk down Pitkin Ave. for a few blocks and perhaps

---

22. Diana and her family celebrated Jewish traditions and holidays and were immersed in "Yiddishkeit." They didn't participate in synagogue life.

stop at the ice cream parlor for a soda. Remember the peach in pineapple sodas? That's another thing to look forward to when victory comes and they make all the flavors again.

Your,
Diana

July 25

Hello Diana,

As usual, one day no mail, next day four letters. I'm so happy to have these 3 additional snapshots of you. Dave just came over & spent an hour with me. He confirmed what I guessed — 14 guys got Pfc.'s — & now they are taking exams for corporal, and my platoon has been at intelligence school for a week, & are going to combat range for a week. Shucks: now I'll really be a yard bird.[23]

Lenny

July 25, Sun.

Sweetheart,

The news came over the radio today that Mussolini's resigned. It is hard to tell just how much this will mean but it may be very important. Also there was a conference held in the Soviet Union of German prisoners who formed a "Free Germany" committee. They issued an appeal to the German people to revolt against the Nazis. How are you? How is your finger?

Diana

July 26

My Dearest Darling,

The hot news of Mussolini's "resignation" was buzzing thru the mess hall & of course today's newspapers were scarcer than hen's teeth. The crisis must be fierce inside Italy and the effect in the Balkans, in France, in Spain & in Germany itself must be terrific. Now that the mighty has fallen, his name will be kicked around like a dog's name it is, everywhere. Capt. Stevens, my company commander, came this afternoon to see how I was. He told me the interesting things the company is doing but in reply to my questions felt I should be able to catch up.

Lenny

---

23. A cooked chicken — he is referring to having fallen far behind in training.

July 26

Dear Lenny,

Today I was doing a job in the shop which was very mechanical and required hardly any concentration and therefore the whole day I was thinking of you and talking to you.

Diana

July 27

Hello Dearest,

V letter came today from John. He says he has "not been altogether aloof from the fighting" & has done interpreting with Nazi prisoners; but is not doing yet what he was trained for.

So I open up my stationery carton and there you are smiling up at me spreading sunshine all over the ward. Never can I understand why I was so lucky as to have you choose to give your love to me. A bear hug tonight — I'm well enough in the finger for that.

Lenny

July 28

Good Morning Dear,

The Mussolini disappearance hullabaloo has already sunk here. All morning spent in cramming the manuals sent by Capt. Stevens; but they are so dully written & tiresome. A tremendous part of it is just memorizing hundreds of symbols used to designate terrain features in maps, military dispositions in relation to the same, interpreting aerial photos (which vary according to time of day, seasons, angle of camera, etc.). Many of the guys in the ward are asking the nurse if a portable radio can be brought in so we can hear FDR's speech tonight — it's really a demand. (P.S. Who do you think got them started?)

Lenny

July 28

Hello Dearest,

You must know by now of the collapse of Mussolini and that he was kicked out. This is a tremendous victory for the Allies and is the first country in which Fascism is smashed. Of course, we must wait for further developments — how this new Italian gov't acts — the Allies are demanding unconditional surrender. Five different political parties in Italy today asked for the destruction of all the Fascists.

Diana

July 28

Dearest Love,

Tonight I had my class. We've had 4 sessions — we plan to have 12. I think the students really like it because there is a steady attendance of 16–17 and because they have all told me so. Next week we are going to a movie together as part of our study of our allies. Tonight I ended very early because Pres. Roosevelt was on the air at 9:30. He made a good speech. He spoke on our attitude towards Italy — isn't much point in my repeating his speech. You will probably have read it or heard it.

Diana

July 29

My Dearest,

I have spent the day so far with the manuals that take hours of concentration.

You ask repeatedly about my finger. Well, there is still a surface cavity with the flesh healing from underneath. The doc said today I may get out before 4 weeks (today's 19 days). Outside the finger I am in perfect condition, except getting soft from doing nothing.

Darling, you can tell your folks again that their gift is marvelous: a soldier with a watch is king. Always I used to have to borrow watches, ask the time — now they come to me.

To better master the material I am outlining & taking notes on the manuals now. 'Tis slower but helps fix the attention on much, which as I have noted is very dry-as-dust in content.

I feasted in our ward kitchen on the pumpernickel that Hersh brought me, and the sardines in alleged olive oil (boneless fillet, American) faintly recalled the rich flavored Portuguese kind we knew before the war. Gastronomically, war is doubly hell.

You must be tired from your week's work. Everyone in the ward knows you work harder than we do, except when we're on maneuvers or bivouac.

Lenny

July 29

Beloved Husband,

Things on an international scale are beginning to move rapidly. As you know Churchill spoke and said we will not make any deals. Unconditional surrender is our only term. Roosevelt reiterated this. Yesterday's paper reported 50,000 people demonstrated in Milan. The Free Germany movement broadcast daily to Germans thru the underground asking the Germans to overthrow Hitler. Roosevelt made it very clear that we will apply the four freedoms to others and that we will not reduce them to slaves. He promised this to the Italian people if they surrender.

Now Roosevelt warned that we must not become too optimistic. There is great danger of this over optimism. I see it all around me in my shop. There it takes the form of, "Now that the war is practically over, I guess we better start looking for other jobs." Also a number of large war plants have begun to convert little by little back to civilian goods. Some war plants are going from 3 eight-hour shifts to 2 ten-hour shifts.

Lenny, continue to write me all the things you are reading. That way I absorb a little culture too.

Your,
Diana

July 30

Dearest Lenny,

Today I really had a pretty miserable day at work. It seems that every Friday something happens — You know I have told you of all the practical jokes that the men play. Well, this afternoon took the prize. When I returned from lunch and started to work, in about 10 minutes there was a terrific odor all around my machine. I couldn't discover where it was but I knew it was limburger cheese. It made me quite sick and I had to go upstairs and lie down. When I came down again, I learned that it had been spread on my electric light which is attached to each machine. When the light became hot, the cheese just smelled absolutely vile. They did it to me and another girl. She became so sick she had to go home. It may sound funny but it wasn't. I'm all right now — completely over it.

Diana

July 31

Sweetheart Love,

Following the usual morning routine, which consumes all the time from 6:30 to 9:30, I went over to chapel for services. Chaplain Fine gave a very sensible sermon, discussing the future of Jews in Poland, Palestine & Russia — From there I went to the Red Cross Auditorium, which was jammed, for the distinguished guest, Walter Pidgeon, the actor.

All afternoon spent in disciplined grind — Advanced Map. Already, I can read a 6-mile photo of Sicilian coast, printed in the latest "Life" & pick out details like plowed fields, fences, streams, which the untrained eye would completely overlook.

The healing finger comes steadily closer to the surface & I begin to be able to bend the first knuckle. These daily bulletins sound silly to me — the affliction is so slight in scope, there's been no pain in two weeks, the bandage is a pitifully small thing.

The last glow of the setting sun has unfurled a long crimson banner on the horizon. I sit in a screen sun-porch, facing away from that fading glow, towards northeast, towards my sweetheart. What are you doing this night, I will not know for 3 or 4 more days — but that you are thinking to me as I am thinking to you, that we both know.

Lenny

Aug 1

My Dearest,

A warm day, hours and hours of intense concentration & note taking on advanced aerial photography; & tactics of the rifle squad. A month has slipped by since I kissed you and hurried away, leaving you at the guest house — another month of loving you so far away, and yet to be farther, before we can be together again for good.

Lenny

Aug 1, Sunday

Dear Lenny,

Dearest, please have a little patience with me because I really have had a number of bad days lately when I haven't felt well and when I write such a little bit to you.

Diana

Aug 2

Hello Beloved,

Hooray, Hooray, Hooray!!!! I'm getting out tomorrow!!! Doc just said so!!! I'll have to go to the dispensary to have the dressing changed every day or so but it's no reason to remain confined here any longer. Whoopee!!

Lenny

Resumes Basic Training

Aug 3, 10 P.M.

Dearest Lenny Darling,

I interrupted this letter to go visit to your family. There have been reports on the radio and in the evening press of riots in Harlem — 6 killed — hundreds injured and arrested. Mayor La Guardia spoke on the radio and said everything is being done to stop it — 10:00 curfew has been declared in Harlem, more police stationed there etc.

My darling Lenny — now it is August already — remember last August — the month of the weddings — your cousin Leo's and Ruth's and also Harriet's and Mike's. Remember how pretty Harriet looked and what a beautiful usher you were. And soon dear — 2 months from today Oct 2 will be Lucy's and Babe's anniversary. Lucy has gotten so thin lately. Although she has a lot of courage and her spirits as always are good, she does worry a great deal. It is now six months that she hasn't seen Babe and with mail so irregular, you can understand the strain she is undergoing. You know, dearest, I hate Nazism and Hitler and Fascism with every fiber in my body for all the misery and suffering that it is causing all over the world. Especially when it is happening to someone close to you whom you love very much —

Diana

Aug 3

Dear Sweetheart,

I'm back in my suntan uniform once more. I still have to wear a clean bandage on the finger for a week or more, but I can go back to duty.

Today is Tisha B'av[24] — the day the Jews were expelled from Spain under Torquemada's order, the day Columbus set sail for America.

Lenny

Aug 3

Darling,

How are you my dearest? You write so little about your finger. Is it almost healed now? You are in the hospital almost 3 weeks already.

Darling — on Italy — there is much more clarity now. The Badoglio

---

24. The traditional date of the destruction of the First and Second Temples in Jerusalem.

Government has not surrendered to the Allies and therefore we must say, "The war continues."

About the riots in Harlem — They were started by rumors that were spread about the killing of a Negro soldier (one was actually wounded). We can see that this is not a repetition of Detroit. It was not rioting between Negro and white people.

Every time I start to say goodnight to you, I write some more. It is like when we used to go to bed and say goodnight a dozen times before we finally fell asleep.

Your,
Diana

Aug 4

My Darling Love,

Today I serve my country as latrine orderly, executing some 20 miscellaneous orders: sweep & wash the floor & showers; wash the toilet bowls, urinals & sinks, make a fire in the hot water stove & shovel coal on it as needed, stick around all day keeping the place clean.

The August heat surpasses anything in June or the 11 days I saw in July before going into the hospital. Fierce is no word for it — it's not the heat that bothers me, but the clothes soaked in sweat.

Lenny

Aug 4

Dearest,

Tonight I went to see "Black Sea Fighters" with my class[25] and it was enjoyable. It is a documentary film about the siege of Sevastopol in the Ukraine. It shows the wonderful defense of the city and how they were able to delay the taking of the city for over 200 days, and destroy many Nazis. Especially interesting were the actual scenes of the fighting. It showed much of the work of the scouts and just what their job is which was particularly interesting to me.

Diana

Aug 5

Ducilima,

Today I am sort of attached to the A&P (Ammunition & Pioneer)

---

25. This refers to classes about current events that Diana taught with others at a local community center.

Platoon, & I am looking forward to it eagerly. I want to learn all angles of the business.

A busy day! I helped build a real Abe Lincoln log cabin, splittin' rails with wedge & sledge hammer for the roof, which we put up today. I lifted logs that I never dreamed I could hoist — the cabin interior is about the size of my old room at my mother's.

Lenny

Aug 5

Dearest Lenny,

Congratulations — dearest on you getting out of the hospital on Tuesday. Your next letter will probably tell me what is going to happen to you with your basic training. My darling — in the time since we were last together about 5 weeks ago it has been harder for me — our separation — than before. I have had a lot of worries — you in the hospital — and I haven't had hardly any relaxation at all. Also the heat of July made my job that much harder.

Diana

Aug 6

Dear Diana,

An easy day, rather easier than I like — I want some real muscle-tone exercise after those idle weeks in the hospital — Again into the "jungle" with the A&P platoon — finished the cabin.

Well, I also had an experience today, one of those heart-in-mouth affairs & bit my under lip plenty. In some places it is out of the question to build a road, so they fell a tree so that it lies across the gully. There are three we crossed repeatedly. Well of course the log wobbles as you teeter along and the other log is pulled along by a wire — just when you want support it gives way: your mouth & stomach merge. The idea of this bridge is that when soldiers are crossing they will have a sniper fire at them (blanks, of course) & you must not lose your balance.

Lenny

Aug 6

Hello,

The news on the war fronts is great. Orel and Belgorod retaken and the Red Army push is on. Also British Army successes in Sicily —

Lenny, do you hear me whispering sweet love calls to you? Do you see me smiling to you? I am right now and I want you to know it.

Diana

Aug 7

My Lady Love,

This morning was fair: an hour of policing up the motor pool area —
an hour of calisthenics, one on a manual of arms & an hour of walking on
a series of compass courses. I volunteered to lead one of the groups — we
ended up rather a distance from where we should have, but the alibi was
the compass was badly affected by electric lines overhead.

After lunch I saw Lt. Hamilton who heads the intelligence section
which returned today from a week's field practice & arranged with him to
make up what I missed.

For no reason at all I felt I wanted to go to town — probably because
5 weeks in camp is enough! In town — went to the Hattiesburg Public
Library. It's pretty hopeless for research, though good for general stuff.

Now beloved, don't get too excited or hopeful but the talk of furloughs for us sometime between Sept. 5 and Dec. 1 is daily more persistent. Also only 3 or 4 more weeks to basic; but the training after will be
even more strenuous, as we will go on protracted maneuvers repeatedly.
As things set up now, I can possibly hope to earn Pfc. In the remaining 3
weeks; corporal that was in my lap before the hospital, looks impossible.

Lenny

Aug 7, Saturday

Dearest Lenny,

Today has been a very long day but a nice one. This morning I worked
and after I met Lucy and we went shopping for a coat for her. I did buy
some things for a package for you.

Gosh darling, what is a yard bird? What does latrine duty consist of?

You have missed so much study and opportunity but dearest, there is
so little one can say. There is no point saying "don't feel badly" because we
do both feel very sorry about this. It was a very unlucky break.

Diana

Aug 8

Dear Dina,

One of the nicer fellows in the intelligence platoon lent me his notes
on the past 3 weeks. I spent from 9 to 4 copying his notes & trying to
master them. It will be impossible to make up the days & days of field
practice in setting up observation posts & listening posts and day & night
patrolling but at least I will get this book stuff down as fast as possible.

Lenny

Aug 8

Lenny Dear,

Do you know how much money we have at present with the last allotment check?

Post Office	$500
Bank	$130
Bonds	$225
Pension	$169
Total	$1,024

Isn't it swell?

Yours, Diana

Aug 9

My Dearest,

There's a heavy rainstorm pouring down & we'll likely not to have retreat. It is the heaviest rain we've yet had: the walk past the mess hall is under the flooded waters. It has been a very easy day — my first in intelligence school: all class work, sitting down in the shade. This morning a one-hour examination, in which I knew 47 out of 50 answers. This evening I shall spend again in the manuals covering what I missed. The intelligence school ends next week, so I only have a few days to catch up.

Don't worry about when you see me next. My attitude is that we'll meet again when victory is won & any chance to get together before is pure luck & we are going to be lucky.

Lenny

Aug 9

Dear Darling,

I had a busy day today. The entire milling machine dept. is on vacation except myself and one other fellow. The night shift is working days this week. I have to work with the night foreman but he is OK.

Diana

Aug 9

Dearest,

The main reason I am writing this letter is to tell you how much I love you. I came home tonight — really ready to fall into bed, but after reading your letter I feel so much better.

The news that Churchill is in Canada and will meet with Roosevelt has hit the papers. I hope it will mean more action and fireworks in Europe.

Your, Diana

Aug 10

My Beloved,

In about 2 weeks or less there will be big exams on the six week's school & in those 2 weeks I must catch up the 4 weeks I missed while doing these 2. When I spoke to Lt. Hamilton about making up certain technical work, he expressed confidence that I'll be fully caught up.

Today we spent some hours on code & decoding. Then we studied air photos under stereoscope lenses, they made flat pictures transform instantly into a miniature 3 D model.

Lenny

Aug 11

My Lady Love,

To send you my love tonight Mississippi sunshine & raindrops wove a rainbow across the blue-white skies, reaching from south to northeast, a pale, distant rainbow, but a huge one, reaching over towards you.

Today was another long day of classroom work — about 100 in a lecture hall; much dull repetition but also some fascinating exercises in which a huge map-sketch of a battle front is shown us & a series of live problems are set out for us to solve.

The enclosed cartoon about rationing from "Esquire" is one of the best war cartoons, I've seen yet.[26]

Lenny

Aug 11

Dearest,

Roosevelt and Churchill are conferring again — we shall probably know soon what they have discussed. I'm very glad you saw Lt. Hamilton and that there is a good chance you will get back with your old squad.

Diana

Aug 12

My Dear Girl,

Furlough talk is the main conversation these days.

A hot day in the field today, practicing motor patrolling — an art. We repeated a 6-mile hike including that killer hill I have written about. If I

---

26. A woman is in a butcher shop and says to the owner, "I knew when the army started to feed my Sammy they'd have to ration the rest of us!"

ever have to hold a defensive line, I'd want it at the top of a hill like that. Only men with hearts of steel & lungs of iron could climb that hill & still be able to fight at the top.

Lenny

Aug 12

Darling,

When you read this letter you will be as surprised and delighted as I am writing it. Babe came home last night. We were sleeping peacefully when suddenly we heard my father get off the bed to answer the door. We were a little started because it was 1 A.M., but he opened the door and there was Babe. There was so much excitement and we didn't go back to bed until 3 A.M. He looks wonderful — gained 8 lbs, sunburned and looks very well. He was away over 6 months. He will be here until Sunday night and as you know Sunday is Lucy's birthday. He is stationed in Boston. She is going back with him until he leaves, probably in a few days.

Diana

Aug 13

Dearest,

An easy morning & a fierce afternoon — I am tired! After lunch we were divided into 5 man patrols, & given a problem: to leave from a certain point & proceed reconnoitering for enemy installations up to the Leaf River, with a detour up a certain creek; & to be at a certain area within 2 hours — well, they were a strenuous 2 hours. I volunteered to be patrol leader. Well, our course took us up & down the steepest hills I have ever yet climbed. You climb up at an angle of 50, 60 or even 85 degrees, & you slide down vertically on the other side. We meandered into a big swamp, & when the 1½ foot deep mud gave way to green slime & undetermined water, we took the risk of getting off our route, skirting the swamp, & fighting thru the jungle underbrush to locate our course again.

Lenny

Aug 13, Friday

Dearest Lenny,

My mother is better and my father continues OK. I've my fingers crossed on the furlough. I know dearest that we shall meet again when victory is ours — but I do like to see you every chance we can.

Diana

Aug 14

Dear Diana,

I must be getting re-acclimated to the heat — it is fierce today, but I only sweated moderately & moved about without the awful sense of imminent collapse that Mississippi heat induces. This morning we went on a little 6-mile hike. After lunch I finally nailed down the Regimental S-2 (intelligence officer) & got the remaining schedules I need. Now I'll be able to finish the makeup work.

Over to the service club and the librarian trundled out two huge packages, my requested material from the State Archives. I'll write as soon as my research yields further "dirt." The few hours on Newt Knight has been my only relaxation this weekend.

Dearest beloved, even if on tomorrow's CQ.[27] I am lucky & can squeeze in 4 or 5 more hours of study, it will take every night & spare minute to cover the arrears work.

Lights go out in a minute—but I'll lie awake looking up at the moon and thinking of you.

Lenny

Aug 14

Hello,

I'm very glad to receive short letters from you if the reason is intensive work and study. Please darling, just write to say you are OK. Use all your time to study and catch up. I know what a job you have to do in the next two weeks and I'm rooting for you.

As I sit here alone talking to you, with a beautiful full moon shining in through the window, I think how lucky I am to have you to come home to every night. Now, of course, with your daily letter, I feel as though we are together when I read and answer it.

Diana

Aug 15

Dearly Beloved,

CQ duty is letter writing day for most guys, & there are many overdue letters; but I'm giving precedence to the manuals. Diana, dearest, I am preparing a little surprise for you, which will be explained in the

---

27. Charge of Quarters.

enclosed envelope. Please do not open it until Sunday, Aug 22. It should make you happy but only if it is not opened prematurely.[28]

Lenny

Aug 16

Dear Love,

Tonight we were all asked to submit requests for furlough dates from Sept 5 to Nov 30.

A sedentary day of boiling in the sun, in open air classes! According to a number of guys, I hit a "possible" on the first part of the exam last week — in military organization that means 100 %. On the second part, I doubt I did nearly as well. During the afternoon, Lt. Hamilton cited a remarkable example of a certain soldier who, though losing 4 weeks in the hospital, had managed to get manuals & schedules & keep up with the class.

Only 48 hours — if they grant the furloughs — well: seven weeks in which to dream of you, and one crowning week to be with you: aren't you happy?

Lenny

Aug 16

Dear Lenny,

I had a very busy day and evening. We had a discussion of all the teachers tonight about our classes that proved fruitful. We are planning new methods of teaching. It is a problem since so many young people of various opinions attend the classes.

I finally mailed you the package today with the three books and some good things to eat.
The way you allot money makes me laugh —
it is so like you. Don't stint yourself on anything that you want. I'll be able to send you any money you need to come home on furlough.

Love, on the furlough — all I can say is Whee! — I don't want to get too excited until you are actually here.

Diana

---

28. This is the first reference to Lenny enclosing a letter for Sunday, so Diana would "receive" a letter even on the day mail wasn't delivered.

Aug 17

Dear Dina,

There are some days in Mississippi when the heat becomes so fierce that it replaces consciousness — you don't think, you don't breathe, you just suffer that all pervading heat.

This morning we were divided into patrols and sent out, 6 patrols, to gather, to work out our own strategy & take a certain fortified hill; later we held it on the defensive. We all make plenty of mistakes, mistakes which are cheap now as the dirt we wallow in all day — but we learned an awful lot! I led one patrol — this was my first combat patrol — we blundered but learned.

The marks of the second half of the test came out today; I made 88, the highest (with 2 others) in the battalion.

Lenny

Aug 17, in pencil from work

Darling,

I'm writing to you now because with a house full of company tonight, I'll have little time. The job I'm on now takes about 20 seconds a cut and I get bored just watching it.

Dearest, I have been discussing production problems in my shop in a number of my letters. It doesn't seem to be a problem in my shop alone but rather widespread. In yesterday's paper the leading editorial was devoted to this question. For the last 3 months our entire production has been behind schedule. This is vital for a successful invasion of Europe. I have to stop now because I must be careful that no one sees me. I am not holding up production because my machine is running as I write. As you once told me a good soldier has to know when to goldbrick.

Diana

Aug 18

Dearest Lenny Darling,

Every time you write about the furlough week, I get goose pimples.

Your,
Diana

Aug 19

Dear Darling,

Tonight this letter takes precedence over a miscellany of duties, & a little sleep — my hunger for you, my desire to speak to you compels it. It's been a long day — both class & practical work and 4 exams in the afternoon. The sweat ate through the watch band, so I got a new one, a cheap one (50 cents) at the PX 'til I get a better one in town.

Lenny

Aug 19

Dearest,

Lenny — how could you do that to me? You know how curious I am and you ask me not to open the envelope until Sunday. Of course I won't, but three whole days. To have the letter in my hand and not be able to open it, really requires self control.

It begins to look like the furlough may really happen. Make every effort to reserve the Southerner home and back. We can spend the dough — don't worry about that. I'll be happy to know you will travel in an air-conditioned train with a reserved seat and no changes. I've heard of people who have to stand all the way.

Diana

Aug 20

Dear Sweetheart,

Patrolling is good — I'm getting used to the "jungle" — I can head off thru dense thicket & forest, drop down steep hillsides, cross mud banks & streams, trip over vines without falling, & rush thru brambles & brush without a scratch, & all without losing direction.

Lenny

Aug 20

Lenny Dearest,

The news is very good. Several islands off Italy surrendered today — We're on the march to Kharkov.

Dearest, I'm not sure from your letters when your exams are. I shall be rooting for you.

Diana

Aug 21

Dear Ducilima,

Happily this mild New York like August heat continues.

A snafu this morning — tangled order & conflicts, rather uncomfortable; but it straightened out finally and we were sent out at a fast clip to join part of the company at the grenade range. The six-mile round trip (in full pack) was as little remarked by the men as if it were 6 blocks. We were shown exploding grenades — fragments fell close to my squad — but we wore our steel helmets & our packs on our backs, to eliminate the danger.

One learns fast in such practice: I found that even if one has to lie face flat in the open group facing a grenade or other explosive attack, one can with practically no movement dig a few inches under the face so as to have a space & yet have the helmet cover you down to the ground.

Over to the service club where I finished the manuscripts on Jones County — The plot thickens & becomes more complex. Knight was conscripted to the Confederate Army, & was a sergeant but went home on a furlough & "forgot" to return — instead organized his band. I have a lot of fresh details as to the battles his company fought. There are still no clues, as to his relations to Negroes, the most crucial question.

Lenny

Aug 21, Saturday

Darling,

I was home all morning — cleaning but we were done at 11:00 A.M. There was no letter from you again and I am a little concerned. In today's paper there was much about the Quebec Conference of Churchill & Roosevelt. Though no official statements yet, a number of officials have made speeches which discuss the difficulties of a European invasion. Also a few papers have headlines today that a big Japanese attack was planned by the conference. The news from the front continues encouraging.

Diana

Aug 22

Hello Diana,

Last night I left the service club early intending to get a long night's sleep — & found a rollicking party on in my hut; so I joined in, threw in a can of your, again, much-liked candy & told tall stories with the best of them. After supper I went to see "So Proudly We Hail" with Veronica Lake & Claudette Colbert, a very stirring film. Only mail was from Pop today, who is very faithful & sends me a long Yiddish letter once or twice a week. It's peculiar because we never corresponded in Yiddish before; I answer in Yiddish because my mother reads it more confidently than English & because the language exercise is pleasant intellectual amusement.

Lenny

Aug 22

My Beloved,

Cudgeling my brains for weeks to determine a way of getting you a letter on Sunday has yielded no solution. At last I have determined to write you an 8th & extra letter, and enclosed it sealed, for you to open next Sunday — as an experiment.

Now maybe this is counting chickens before they are hatched, but right now the most pleasant thing I can think of is my prospective furlough.

Lenny

Aug 22 not to be read until Sun., Aug 29

Dearest,

Again I greet you on Sunday morning. Such a summer's day is a perfect day to dream of love.

Lenny

Aug 23

Dear My Love,

Mississippi heat is back. Very routine training today, class & field — I am glad you were teased by the sealed surprise envelope: you will admit that half the value lay in the surprise.

Well — in two weeks basic is over. Then starts maneuvers, in many ways much tougher — weeks & weeks on bivouac, in Louisiana swamps. The taking of Keska is amusing & puzzling: because the job of intelligence is never to lose contact with the enemy, & here they pulled away without our knowing it. Hooray for Kharkov![29]

As a souvenir of hitting the earth fast under Saturday's grenade fire I have a sprinkling of poison ivy blisters on my wrists, hands & shin — but I've got them under control with iodine. No more lost time for me 'til we see Berlin!

Lenny

8/23

Dear Lenny,

Happy anniversary! Lenny a very happy 40th anniversary to my beloved soldier!

---

29. Keska, in the Aleutian Islands, Alaska, was invaded by the Allies to rout the Japanese invaders. Kharkov was a huge battle in Russia.

I had such an unpleasant day today. On Friday I mentioned to my foreman I would be late today and arrive at 9:15 A.M. He didn't make any negative comment, so I assumed it was all right. However, when I arrived this morning, the supervisor made a terrific row and wouldn't let me work today at all. It was very, very bad — first of all it made a bad impression on the other workers, secondly I lost a day's production and pay and thirdly it was just a messy situation.

Dearest, congratulations on doing so well on that exam. Your description of your K.P. duties was very enlightening to me because it is the first time that I know that you have been on K.P. in Mississippi.

Lenny, do I have to remind you that I have a first-class husband. Dearest, don't be so impatient. I am so pleased that you are being given the opportunity to continue with the other men. The stripes will come.

> *Your,*
> *Diana*

Aug 23, Sunday

Dearest,

I was so happy and thrilled to receive a letter from you on Sunday and such a wonderful one about our furlough week together. I just can't find words to tell you how I felt. How did you ever think of it?

Darling, if at all possible I would like to meet you at the station when you come home. It will mean an extra hour together and then we can have the first greeting to ourselves before the rest of the family sees you. Also dearest, I agree with you that we should inconvenience Lucy as little as possible. First of all because I want to sleep with you and also it would be so nice for your mother, for us to spend a few nights there and have breakfast with her.

> *Diana*

Aug 24

Dearly Beloved,

More exams this morning — It hurts me to get 18 questions of 20 perfect & lose 10 points on material covered in my absence & not listed on the schedule. There is indifference to making up work — many men are in my fix & never bother picking up missed work, since they don't give up their evenings. What they expect of these guys in combat, I don't know. The October list was read at retreat & I am scheduled for Oct 5. It's a 15-day furlough!

> *Lenny*

Aug 24

Sweetheart,

When I came into work this morning not a word was said, so I just started to work and continued all day. Lenny darling, when you write about jungle tactics that you are learning and how you are learning to get along in the jungle, I get a little concerned because those are things which I know nothing about. Perhaps I should start getting used to climbing trees and hills and crossing creeks, because as you know I am not good at those things, and you might want to continue this even when victory is ours and you come home. My Tarzan husband may require a jungle mate.

Whenever you have some sort of night duty, you write me such glorious love letters.

Diana

Aug 25

Dearest Dina,

Snafu — As usual — First, furlough dates are shifted: mine to Oct 8th. Second, I am ordered without appeal to "apply" for the ASTP,[30] though I'd much rather stay in the infantry. The course lasts from 3 to 9 months. While a number of stripes have been passed out this week, although none to yours truly — Intelligence calls for 1 Sgt. (filled) & no corporals — so unless he or we are transferred, Pfc. is our limit here. (But I'll be content just with one stripe right now!)

Lenny

Aug 26

My Beloved Husband,

In spite of hard work, I did not have a satisfying day. At work, we had another one of those "mistakes" — I'm beginning to think they happen too regularly. I finished a job at 10 A.M. The setup man set up a new job which should not have been put on my machine. There is a machine which can do this particular job quickly and efficiently but he put it on my machine where I have to do it by hand, which is slow, inefficient and very painful. When I questioned the foreman, he said he would not have my work ready until tomorrow. I worked on it till 10 A.M. By that time, I had made 20 pieces and both my hands were so cut up with little cuts that

---

30. Army Specialized Training Program, at select universities, to develop technical skills in officers and enlisted men.

I couldn't go on. I went to him and raised the roof. He finally agreed to put it on the other machine and 1,000 pieces were made from 10 A.M. to 5 P.M. He found another job for me to do until my work is ready tomorrow. Think of it, dearest, in terms of production — 50 times as fast and no cuts or bruises.

Diana

Aug 27

My Lady Love,

The forced march this morning was a strenuous test; & 'twas a good thing we stopped at the point we did! The rest of the day I was in a sub-command post with 3 others, sitting on a rotting moss-covered log & waiting for action that never came.

Lenny

Aug 27, Friday

Dearest Lenny,

I had a much better day at work today. I finally got a decent job and I was able to make up for some of the time wasted yesterday.

Darling, you write about 10 or 11 days at home — gosh — I'm speechless.

Be very careful about the poison ivy. I get so scared about it.

Diana

Aug 28

Dearest,

Your husband is in a very aggrieved and melancholy frame of mind. After our usual Sat. half day of training we are normally dismissed to scrub & clean our hutments & then are free 'til Monday — but first I got dragged into a detail to draw a map on a stencil, which cost me 3 hours this afternoon; & then was all set to get a pass to town, I was handed Sunday KP — Naturally I couldn't go to town anymore. Two Sundays in 4 to have detail is a pain in the neck.

I'm afraid it can't be the Southerner, we must save the money. At best furlough will cost, all in all, over $100.

Lenny

Aug 28, to be opened Sept 5

Dearly Beloved,

Labor Day weekend: the first we spend apart since we know each other.

Lenny

Aug 28

Lenny Dearest,

Today has been a long day but a fairly nice one and tomorrow is a day of rest and I can sleep late.

Your Tuesday letter came and it seems you are coming home Oct 5 — a little over 5 weeks more and for 15 days. It troubles me that you miss some of the exam questions through no fault of your own. My love, I'm very proud of you — that you can get such good grades after having been out 4 weeks but I am also concerned. Right now if you miss one or two questions in an exam — it's not decisive, but later on, in combat — I can only hope you and the other boys that have missed work will be able to learn it before you go into actual battle.

Diana

Aug 29

Dear My Love,

Furlough talk, tickets, traveling gear & painting the town red has supplanted all else. Tell me dearest, are not the first leaves falling from the trees on Shepherd Avenue, the ones which are earliest with cat skins in the springtime?

Despite every precaution, I am again a good walking sample of poison ivy, with a handsome swelling on my left forearm & streaks on my right arm, forehead & other spots. It's still, happily, nothing like the last big attack.

Lenny

Aug 29

Dear Lenny,

Sometimes, dearest, I feel that our dreams are too much of the past — I know it is easiest to dream of the past because we have such wonderful six years to remember, but, my darling, together we have an even greater future. Darling, when we will be at peace again and people will be able to live happily and securely, what a place for young lovers like us, Lucy and Babe, Harriet and Mike and so many scores of others. What fun it will be to have a home again — now we are both boarding even though I am with my folks and sweetheart our new home will have a family of 3 or 5 or maybe more.

Lenny, now for the news I promised you I would discuss. The Ohio AFL had a convention a week ago. They called for an immediate land invasion of Europe. Roosevelt and Churchill gave "limited recognition" to the French Committee of National Liberation. Since this committee represents all anti-Fascist and patriotic Frenchmen, they deserve full recognition. Sumner Welles, Undersecretary of State and advisor to FDR, resigned under pressure this week.

Your,
Diana

Aug 30

Dearest Beloved,

Here is one soldier who will be glad when this week's corps exams are over. Today they inspected huts & buildings, so latrines were locked up to guarantee they'd pass.

Lenny

Aug 30

Darling husband,

You write about your furlough being shifted to Oct 8 — well, that isn't too bad.

I agree that you have certainly earned a stripe — but darling — the army has its own methods. It's so hard to have patience. I'm so eager to know what's going to happen with you and with the furlough, but I guess I will know as soon as you do.

Your,
Diana

Aug 31

Dearest,

I really ought — or ought I? — to be using every second to study tonight for tomorrow's big corps exam, but my impulse is to write to you before all else. This was a less wearisome day. There was plenty of lobbing around, but two good periods helped. One was identification of German & Japanese uniforms — mainly we had had only dry lectures before & you can imagine how confused one can get to have every kind of uniform in the Nazi army rattled off at you. Today they brought out mannequins of Nazi officers & men, & pinned all the various insignia on, so at last, one day before the exam, we really got an idea.

Your Friday letter at hand: I do hope you can go up to Kauneonga[31] for the weekend, & I wish I could be there with you: read Spinoza and swim in that beautiful Silver bath.

---

31. Kauneonga Lake is in New York State.

This is the 4th anniversary of the war: let's hope it is the last. Distant as the end seems to the men who direct our strategy, there may yet be bigger surprises than any that have yet come in our war of surprises.

Only 39 more days — see how fast they go — 'til I see you again. 'Tis sweet to fall asleep a-dreaming of being with you again, & I shall do my best to make you happy because you make me so happy.

Lenny

Aug 31

Darling,

There is talk of a joint Anglo-American-Soviet meeting in the near future. The Soviet offensive is moving leaps and bounds. Reports also came from Sofia that mass demonstrations are being held against Hitler Germany, and against a gov't that sold out to the Axis. The time is ripe for a European invasion.

Diana

Sept 1

Dear Dinika,

This is my first "evening" off in many, many weeks, & I need it! The corps exams took place today. The morning was farcical — we were hiked out a piece; the examiner read off a question & our instructors called on a soldier to answer. Naturally, they called on their reliable good answerers. There was a little written & practical work. The afternoon was more real — we set up command & observation posts — dug foxholes & camouflaged them, ran messages, etc. — 4 hours of strenuous labor, in a steaming jungle with rain pouring down constantly. Tomorrow we have an exam in physical training and then exams & basic are just about over. A new 7-week intelligence school will be conducted immediately after.

Saw a headline about Churchill saying a second front will be opened at the right time, as we marched out this morning: what's it about?

Lenny

Sept 1

Dearest Lenny,

I am enclosing a union flyer for Local 1225 of the CIO: "Initiations in U.E. — Local 1225 costs $2.00 plus 25 cents for the book. Dues are $1.50 per month — but Kollmorgen employees aren't expected to pay dues until the management signs a contract with the U.E. (Don't worry — they will!) Almost all our members are voluntarily buying war stamps every pay day. They buy more than $10,000 per week and have bought over $150,000 in the Third War Loan Drive. Most of our members also contribute voluntarily, through our Union, to American and Allied War Relief, U.S.O., Greater New York Fund, Army and Navy Relief, etc. We are also very proud of the fact that our members contribute hundreds of pints of blood regularly to the Red Cross. We have no personal quarrels with the bosses — but in this war emergency we know that organized workers produce for the war effort better than unorganized workers. A.U.E. shop is a "Victory Shop." It is your patriotic duty to make Kollmorgen a member of the U.E. family of Victory Shops! Join the UE CIO — ORGANIZE FOR VICTORY! It's the American Way!

Your,
Diana

Sept 2

Diana,

Today we had an hour on first aid for the nth time; & then another hour of calisthenics — only I went to the gas chamber. The chamber is a large airtight room where you go first into tear gas, with your mask on, to test the mask, then without the mask on, you go in after it has been filled with chlorine gas, & put the mask on — this giving the simulation of actual mask drill in the face of real danger. We were double-timed around the room several times after we got our masks on. While the mask is wonderful against lung irritant gasses, it doesn't give you much air, especially when you're panting from heavy exertion.

They've passed out some more ratings, including corporals. I continue to be the only Pvt. (aside from one other) in the intelligence section, everyone else is a Pfc. & it is very humiliating.[32]

Lenny

Sept 2

Sweetheart,

I'm really quite concerned. The poison ivy you mentioned seems to be getting worse. Lenny, I know it isn't your fault, because you are trying, but can't anything be done to check it or perhaps to immunize some of you boys who are so susceptible to it? Wasn't 4 weeks in the hospital due in large part to their neglect enough?

---

32. It is possible that antisemitism was the reason for not being promoted.

Nothing special happened in my place today. Two other fellows left for the army. In my shop they are not getting any more occupational deferments for young men unless they have children. As a result 27 or 28 young fellows are expected to leave in September with a similar situation in Oct. and Nov. This has meant the hiring of more girls and 2 new girls came into my department last week. It may also mean there will be more opportunities for girls. They are so hesitant about giving a girl a break, it just makes your blood boil but sooner or later they will have to.[33] Darling you received a letter from the Dept. of Welfare with an official notification that your job is waiting for you when you are honorably discharged from the army.

Diana

BEYOND BASIC: BIVOUACS AND MORE

Sept 3

Dearest,

We seem to be scheduled for a night march & bivouac. I find myself sort of groping & feeling empty: no goal ahead. It seems that a Pfc. is even hopeless. So it's taking a little mental readjustment to figure out how to be a good private & like it. I have never, even as a squad leader, put on any airs or lorded it over the men; & discipline is second nature to me, so if I can restrain my first nature (initiative — too much for this army!), I'll just continue blending in obscurely with the other men & do what's expected of me.

Probably more important, I feel somewhat lost in the world scene, events have moved with great rapidity since the outline I drafted in the hospital & I need to chart the course again.

Lenny

Sept 3

Hello darling,

I guess by now most of your exams are over and I hope this weekend you will have some time off to relax.

I got another raise today — 6 cents per hour, which brings me up to 70 cents per hour now. This brings my weekly pay to $40.60 for 52 hours of work.

The news came over the radio today that Italy has been invaded by the British 8th army and by Canadian troops. This is their first operation

---

33. An example of employment discrimination against women.

on the Continent; let us hope it is really what we have been waiting for. Some of the best commentators said this week that a military decision over Hitlerism is within our grasp this year depending on a major invasion of Europe. A concentrated effort is being made by the reactionary forces to put all the responsibility for wavering and retreats on Roosevelt, but he is fighting much better than most of his liberal critics who yell he is betraying them.

Lenny, the War Manpower Commission has issued an urgent call for 1,000,000 women to take jobs within the next six months. They are the only reserve available for the growing labor shortage. This will mean that the majority will have to come from housewives with children and the W.M.C. finally realizes that special provisions will have to be made to enable these women to work. There are at present 17,000,000 women working — an all time high!

Diana

Sept 4

My Dearest,

Last night was an experience! First we had a speed march (both ways) going 1½ hours each time sans a halt (normally halt after 1st 45 minutes, & after 50 minutes thereafter); as soon as we hit the bivouac area we scattered out as in pre-battle conditions & dug slit trenches (one-man affairs 2 feet deep, big enough to hold you) — and lady, I take a big size trench.

Then I went on duty as a messenger to go in a hurry a mile or more through dense woods from one command post to another, & get back to your post — well, it's miraculous I found my way back each time, only once straying a little, only once falling into a trench.

Supper was not given out 'til 10 & then under complete blackout. We slung gas masks at all times; also slung rifles; & since I was moving all the time, not knowing when we'd pull out, I wore my full pack a good deal of the time so as not to have to run back 400 yards to my "shelter." It was raining while we were out there, which kept things a little cooler. My fatigues have been wet thru & thru since Wed. now.

This morning we had "off," which in army life means clean your mess gear, brush the mud off, wash socks, etc. We are now "on the alert": i.e., subject to call at a whistle's notice, ready to move anywhere.

Lenny

Sept 4/5 for Sept 12

Hello Diana,

Tell me something of the approach of the fall season at home. I can recall that mid & end September is one of New York's most beautiful seasons. Your food loving husband had a sudden memory of home at supper tonight. It recalled our happy kitchen with its maple furniture & blue trimmings, and your mother's kitchen with fragrant (prewar) steaks. Of course to me "home" cooking includes not only my mother's fried chicken on Friday night but your mother's blintzes.

Lenny

Sept 4

Dearest husband,

I worked until noon and then I went to Helen's.[34] I had a nice time since I hadn't seen her all summer. She has a very acute social problem. She is 26, unmarried and there are very few available, worthwhile men left in NY. Were she 16, 17 or 18, she would have a lot of time, but she isn't getting any younger and she is very aware of it. Being a psychologist, she doesn't put this problem in the back of her mind, but she tries to help herself by putting herself in a situation where she can meet other men. It made me realize how exceptionally fortunate I am to have you and be your wife. Difficult as the present situation is for us, it is so much harder for a girl who is alone.

Diana

Sept 5

My Lady Love,

'Tis hot & muggy & nerves are on edge as we prepare for the signal to move out. I'm all packed & set. Well, it will be the Southerner after all, you win. Before I forget — this Southerner ticket is cleaning me out — I'll be left with about $2. Send me a $20 postal money order tout-de-suite. Geez — 3 month's pay just for furlough fare.

About 2:30 came the alert signal. I was assigned as intelligence man & camouflage checker — finally we pulled out — by truck! No walking! On arriving there the intelligence men were recalled & sent back to camp by truck thus escaping a week's bivouac; no fun in that.

Lenny

---

34. Mom's lifelong friend from high school.

Sept 5

Dear Lenny,

I recall our Labor Day weekends together. Lenny, remember how in 1939 when we sat at breakfast listening to the opening tumult of this war and I had a sad expression on my face Irving said to me, "Don't worry Diana, Leo isn't going yet." He said it in jest, but we knew that this would reach every person and every home before victory will be ours. Darling, of that whole circle of people, that is our Flatbush friends — you are the first to be a soldier. I hope you managed to have some time off this weekend. I know how much I need a day off after 6 days of work and you working 14.

Diana

Sept 6, Labor Day

Dear Diana,

'Tis verily like a holiday evening tonight here, though we did have duty (school) today because the first furlough group has been pulling out. School began again today & woe we are going to repeat the past school; despite our excellent showing in the corps exams & the manifest waste. They promise a ride to the Hattiesburg Air Base to really see some airplanes instead of photos.

You may well imagine that a mere review is not going to keep your husband's restless cerebellum occupied, & I've already jotted down a schedule for the coming 4 weeks. To begin with, I am going to review my French. Further I intend to put in a concentrated effort on some subjects the class dabbles in but never tackles: chemical warfare; air & tank vehicle recognition etc.

Thanks for the news item: 17 million working women — that is grand!!!

Lenny

Sept 6, Labor Day

Darling,

I'm really very worried because this week my class is on the Jewish question and Zionism and I know very little about this.

Diana

Sept 7

Lenny Dearest,

My brain has been taxed to the limit. Remember I wrote you I was worried about my class because I know so little on the Jewish Question.

I had to do something about it. I came home from work, ate supper and got busy. For the past 3 hours I have been in the midst of books, booklets, newspapers, anything I could get on the subject and I think I have a fair curriculum. I shall only really know after the session tomorrow.

Yours,
Diana

FURLOUGH FEVER

Time together was extremely important to the soldiers and their loved ones, especially for those who were physically separated, often for long periods of time. The anticipation of being together, even for a short time period, was tremendous. Visits of a wife or a girl-friend to Camp Shelby were often brief, limited by the soldier's schedule, and did not allow for contact with their extended family. Diana only visited Lenny at Camp Shelby once.

Furloughs allowed the soldier to go home to both wife and family. The anticipation was often dampened when frequent sched-uling delays occurred, often several times before the actual furlough came through. The letters reflect Lenny and Diana's hopes and dis-appointments as the delays mount up.

Sept 8

Dearest Love,

A strenuous day: two speed marches, one at the start & one at the end, carrying us way over 5 miles; scouting & patrolling, & map orientation in the field, all laborious work.

The news of Italy's surrender has started a wave of war-is-over feeling here. The "unconditional" part of the surrender is the significant thing IF IT IS REALLY SO. Of course, it is good news; what "ally" of Hitler will stay now in the face of threatened invasion?

It's days like these without mail & no idea of when your mail may come that makes separation real. A month hence at this hour I'll have been 10 hours on the train speeding up towards you as fast as I can push the locomotive. We've all got that furlough spirit!

Lenny

Sept 8

Dearest,

Well, I needn't have worried about my class. When I got to the office,[35] I found a discussion being held on the international situation. I got permission for my class to attend because I felt we would learn more from this. It was swell and it gives me another week to do some studying on the Jewish Question before I teach it.[36]

The tremendous news today — The unconditional surrender of Italy — this is a great victory and it is indicative of growing military and political crisis in the ranks of the Axis.

Diana

Sept 9

Hello dearest,

This has been a beautiful day — must have been about 50 degrees at dawn. It's about 75 now, really choice for hutments.

Myself, as you know, I'm plagued by the writing hunger. I'm conditioned towards it from my earliest childhood when my father bred in me a reverence by reading me only the "sublimest" of Shakespeare, Isaiah, Schiller, and Heine and taught me that the pen must be used interchangeably with the sword in the continuing liberation war of humanity.

Lenny

Sept 9

Dearest Husband,

Today was a good day. In the shop I finished a job which I have been on for the last 10 days. It was beginning to get very monotonous and I was very glad to finish. Usually when I finish a job I wait a few hours before I start on a new one; today no time was wasted. For a change, the set-up man who was busy told me to go ahead and set up the new job myself. As you know this is unusual because they don't want the girls to learn too much, but I took full advantage of the opportunity. I set up the new job and made the first piece. He checked it and told me to go ahead because it was OK. He also told me he didn't think I would be able to do it because it was a complicated job, he thought I would fool around with it until he had time to come over and do it for me.

---

35. Her volunteer office was located in a local community center.

36. Lenny sent Diana an analysis of the current political situation related to Jews to help her prepare.

After work three of us went down to the union. Since among the three of us we felt we could bring about 20 to a meeting, we agreed to have one next Fri. and begin to lay plans for organization. Let us hope and work for a union shop as soon as possible.

Diana

Sept 10

Good morning dear,

Here I am on Cq at Bn Hq, & have already put in 1½ hours study in chemical warfare on my own. I am shivering with cold. Yes, shivering here in Camp Shelby. Read, dutifully, a couple of hours of French.

Lenny

Sept 10, Friday 12:15, A.M.

Dearest,

This evening, I spent with your folks. It was very nice to spend a Fri. evening there after the whole summer and as was to be expected we had a delicious meal.

Re the budget — I do want to discuss it with you, but here is a little about it. I only get $33 cash out of the $40.60 ($4.20 goes to income tax, $3.00 to bonds and .41 for Social Security).

Monthly Budget Expenses
Board $24
Personal $ 24
Kenwood $ 7 (storage of furnishings)
Phone $ 2.50
Allotment to bank $ 50

I have returned $65 to my father, given $20 for charity, paid $9 dues, $4 to doctor, $6 birthday present Lucy, $3.59 visit to Babe, $4 package to you and $5 for other extras such as pictures, stationery, stamps etc. Write me what you think of the budget.

Your,
Diana

Sept 11

Dear Love,

Sometimes your husband does the stupidest things, like reaching for a fly ball with one hand when it's just out of reach, with the result that my right hand "pinky" took a terrific wallop and hurts like the very devil. The game was good nevertheless — softball. We won 18–6.

Lenny

Sept 11

Darling,

Love, your mother has told me not to write this to you, but I don't
agree with her on keeping secrets from you while you are away, just as I
don't do it when we are together. Your cousin Frances had an accident on
her way up to the country to spend her vacation in the Catskills. When
she arrived, she called and got directions. She took a taxi. The driver didn't
follow her directions and she became frightened. Although it was daylight,
country roads are quite devoid of cars now. She asked him to go a certain way and he didn't. Finally she asked him to stop so she could get out
and walk. He started to go faster. She became so frightened she opened
the door and jumped out of the speeding car. She broke her ankle, and
bruised herself all over. Fortunately, after she jumped, the first car that happened along was a doctor, so she had immediate attention. She said that
they picked the driver up later, but she was afraid to press charges.

Love — 4 weeks from today we shall have a date. A Saturday night
together —

Diana

Sept 13

My Dearest,

A moment ago the full moon rose into view — a sight to behold: the
full moon in Mississippi is ever so much larger & golden than in the north
— so I smiled a huge smile to you, & turned to write to you. Tomorrow I
am to appear before the A.S.T.P. board. I still don't know whether it is to
be desired or shunned.

Lenny

Lenny dear,

You ask about Italy. Unconditional surrender in time — There has
been and continues fighting between the Allies and the Nazis who are in
Naples, the Brenner Pass between Italy and Austria and in other parts of
Italy. 1) Fighting to cease between United Nations and Italy. 2) Prison-
ers of War to be released and not sent to Germany. 3) Italy not to help
Germany.

There was a great deal of festivity in New York at the Italian surrender.
Terrific doings on Mulberry St. in Little Italy — demonstrations, street
corner rallies. In the afternoon when the news came through, the Garment Center was like Times Square on New Year's Eve from what I heard.

On Thursday night there was a victory rally at Madison Square Garden. There was a lot of hubbub in the city but it died down quickly — I think people realized after the first excitement that the war is still not won.

Diana

Sept 14

Dearest,

A gala & holiday air prevailed today. We had class to 10 A.M. & then rolled out in trucks 'til we reached Hattiesburg. Finally we're off for the big parade — light packs, suntans, rifles with bayonets fixed slung over the shoulder, & plenty of sweat, steel helmets — lines of 9 abreast, thru the residential & business streets. Trucking back, we rode thru a corner of the Negro community (which is barred to us on our own time) — the ramshackle unpainted huts, one-room affairs, with ragged folk about, little unkempt vegetable patches.

Lenny

Sept 14

Lenny Dearest,

What a swell surprise and wonderful help that an air mail special delivery came tonight with your outline. I had been going crazy all week — I did have an outline prepared but I felt it was very weak on Zionism.

Diana

Sept 15

Hello,

Up before dawn and we were hiked out where we dug foxholes. Tomorrow will be exciting — the infiltration course — crawling under fire.

Lenny

Sept 15

Dearly Beloved,

Today was hectic — I've just sat down after 18 hours on the go. I quit work at 4:30, went to the office and taught my class. You were really a life saver. I could never have done it without your outline. Next week is my last session — on the working class — and I should not have any difficulty preparing that. Please take care — how's the pinky now?

Your,
Diana

Sick Call Again

Sept 16

Dearest Diana,

After breakfast, I went on sick call account of the joint between my last 2 fingers on the right hand (hurt in Saturday's ball game) which still hurts & is swollen. I held out 5 days but with a big night problem on tomorrow night, decided to risk sick call again. I had to hike to the hospital, where I got immediate service & a negative report after 3 pictures being taken — no fracture indicated. So back to "soak it in hot water" — the universal remedy and now I soak both hands.

Well, on returning, I find to my dismay that the intelligence school, which was to go to the infiltration course at 1 P.M., had been switched to the morning & I'm left out. So I located a company going out in the P.M. & got permission to go with them. I voluntarily took along my rifle & bayonet, knowing it would mean long hours of cleaning after from dragging it thru the ground. But as a scout I'll need to carry the rifle on just such occasions, & it's precisely in such an exercise that most closely approximates battle conditions. It was the best experience I had in my whole training so far — the nearest thing to combat — & I know I'll never be afraid to do the same in the real day.

Lenny

Sept 16

Dear Lenny,

How are you, dearest? 22 more days to go — I am trying so very hard to have a lot of things finished and to be free when you are home.

Diana

Sept 17

Dearest,

Must finish preparing — blacken my face with soot & prepare for night patrol.

Lenny

Sept 17, Friday

Lenny,

We had the union meeting tonight. Twelve of us met with the union organizer to begin to lay plans for organization. I think that this was a pretty good showing — these are not people who are merely willing to join the union. They are like myself — they want to work to unionize the entire shop. We aim to sign up 100 workers in the union by next Friday. We aim to get 75% signed up by next month. Then we plan to have a big educational leaflet campaign outside the shop. If necessary we may have to hold an election and we must be sure of a majority. We intend to convince people to join for the following reasons — wage increases through equalizing pay for the same type of work between men and women, for upgrading many of the workers, and for those at their top salary the incentive pay system.

Secondly — seniority — many of the workers are worried about their jobs after the war and especially the older workers who are earning more and are afraid that the lower paid ones will be kept. Then there is the whole question of grievances and an apparatus to settle them. The oldest, highest skilled workers are friends of the boss — they belong to the same club and they will be tough. Among the younger men, the firm has gotten them deferments and they are afraid to lose this. Darling, you can imagine how good it is to be doing this type of activity. With all the problems that exist, we shall be moving forward and working to organize more workers and to win better conditions for us all. Isn't that swell?

I'm anxious to know about the A.S.T.P. business. I'm also not sure if it is desirable because I don't know what it will mean and what you will be doing.

If you cannot get shoes — then you will have to use one of our tickets and buy a pair here.[37] Your mother asked me when you expect to arrive. She said everyone wants to meet you at the station also. I couldn't say anything but I would so love to have the first hour with you alone until we get home.

Your,
Diana

Sept 18

Sweetheart,

To resume where I stopped last night, dipping into the hutment stoves for soot, we blackened hands, faces & necks 'til not a spot of natural skin color showed, not even on the eyelids — the effect was outstanding: first our faces wholly disappeared in the dark, which is essential; secondly we did not even recognize our closest associates until a second look.

---

37. There was a shortage of shoes and Diana is offering Lenny one of the family's shoe ration coupons.

We were marched at nearly double time to a location I've never been at before — the patrol leaders were handed a map & told to scout for enemy listening posts. In darkness when lights are forbidden, in dense woods a map is as useful as a bass drum. So by the light of a cigarette lighter, I drew a pencil course on the map, and estimated distances. We were off into the woods: night had fallen long ago, & a steady rain made the obscurity palpable.

Then the forest became jungle, tangled vines & thicket tearing at our uniforms. Suddenly the ground began to slope downward more & more steeply. The blackness was so dense before us that we moved along now holding one hand on the shoulder ahead of us. And suddenly the four men before me disappeared even from arm reach, & we heard the splash of water, and not a second later I was flying, "kerplunk" into the morass. It seems we reached a cliff and the slippery mud gravity had greatly accelerated our progress.

Lenny

Sept 19

My Dearest,

And it rains, rains, rains — The rain dominates all: we are going out to bivouac for one or two weeks — we leave at midnight, and we know we are going to be soaked.

Worked last night on "Samson Agonistes," of all Milton's works it requires the least research, & so is easy to work on here.

A bustling evening, packing duffle bags, planning supplies, rolling pack, an extra cleaning & oiling to the rifle — Now to catch 40 winks — maybe I can sleep an hour before we march out.

I'm including a clipping with the title, "Posse Kills Negro after Farm Slaying."[38]

Lenny

Sept 19 for Sept 26 [Sunday special letter again]

Dearest Diana,

The rabbis of old were wont to ask: Why did not Moses lead the Children of Israel from Egypt to the Promised Land along the easy shore route,

---

38. "A posse near Shaw, in Bolivar county, early today shot and killed Whitey Hall, 35 years old, Negro, who defied officers to capture him after he shot and killed W. D. Brown, 42, a Shaw plantation manager." Lenny's comment is "This is legal — but still a lynching."

hardly a three-day caravan journey, but led them 40 years through the hardships of the desert and wilderness, past mounts Sinai and Hozeb and roundabout Jordan? And they answered, the folk who went forth from slavery were tainted with the servile yoke, they would have too easily succumbed to a temptation to return to slavery in Egypt unless they were steeled in forty years of struggle to be a folk worthy of freedom, capable of exercising their liberty. The human race is now passing through its forty years — and the seeds of the future free men and free woman are planted in us.

Lenny

Sept 19, Sunday

Dear Lenny,

Last night I was a bad girl and stayed out till 3 A.M. with Myra. I had a very nice time. She looks well. We had so much to discuss. It was really so good to talk to someone who feels like I do about basic questions. We discussed wife camp following, our work, our plans, having a baby. She plans to live with her mother and they have taken 6 rooms.

Hull[39] made a speech emphasizing that there is a basic field of agreement among the Allies in their common need to defeat the Axis and to prevent future aggression in the post-war. He stressed that the need for cooperation far outweighs any differences that may exist. In regard to the Soviet Union, he said, "It is our desire and our settled policy that collaboration and cooperation between our two countries shall increase steadily during and following the war." However, only by indirection did he touch upon the key question of shortening the war by a second front — when he referred to the mutual assistance derived by the Red Army and the Anglo-American armies from the offensive in the Eastern Front and the invasion of Italy.

Red Army captured Bryansk. Surging ahead — The papers have been going to town on the difficulties in Italy. It was so bad that Gen. Clark issued a statement denying that the position of our troops was even desperate. Of course, they met resistance. At present our 5th Army and the British 8th have joined and it seems they are pushing ahead into German held lines.

Yugoslavian People's Army has captured Split — Yugoslavia's biggest port on the Adriatic and has occupied a sector of the Dalmatian Coast.

Diana

---

39. Cordell Hull was secretary of state, 1933 to 1944.

Sept 20

Dear Diana,

I write from a damp & cramped pup tent in a pine tree grove — a heavy thunderstorm is raging and everything is rather wet. Well, my prone shelter dug for air raid protection is not perfect for a bathtub: it is full and overflowing with water. Bivouac in cold & rain is one of those hardships that you never get used to.

With the golden glow of furlough days ahead, especially the warm smile of my darling — really you have no cause to worry.

Lenny

Sept 20

Dearest,

We had a blackout tonight. In your description of the infiltration course — darling I felt as though I were with you. How I wish I could fight side by side with you, but then it might be distracting. Seriously though — I am glad you are having this experience now. I can tell from your description that you are gaining confidence and I know this training is invaluable for you. Was it live ammunition?

Your, Diana

Sept 21

Dearest Diana,

'Tis quiet mostly — Last night I headed for the nearest campfire to dry my fatigues & shoes & promptly fell knee deep into one of the foxholes (one for every man here) which, with the rain, were brimful of water. (I'm going to dig my foxholes with a drain on the bottom hereafter).

Delighted at the union meeting — only: how come you don't mention boosting war production which your plant needs?

Beloved, darling, sweetheart, if all goes well — soon we'll count only the minutes 'til we meet — as it approaches. I tremble when I think of it with the apprehension that something may snafu it. I want to give you the grandest fortnight you've ever had.

Lenny

Sept 21 for Oct 2

My Love,

When you read these lines, three full months will have passed since I kissed you and bade you goodbye at the guesthouse terrace. We couldn't know then that the days would bring Sicily and Salerno, Smolensk and the Dnieper, & Split — what may not the next days bring? As I have said often, when the guys here need the prodding, we want the war to end with victory soon, but we'd hate not to get our lick at bat. To get an early chance "up at bat" — & help in the final push — that would be swell.

Dininka, my beloved, every time I go through a particularly bad piece of training, full of hardship & misery, the one thing that carried me through is the flash that comes to mind — "You are learning to do this right so you can come back to your Diana & make her happy."

Lenny

Sept 21

Lenny Dearest,

What a full and wonderful day this has been. After work I came home and prepared for tomorrow's class. It will be the last session. At 9:15 I went to meet Myra to hear a grand old lady. I was quite tired but when I think of her 60 odd years of service and I compare them to myself and I think of how at 11 P.M. she was still arousing her audience to win the war activity, can I feel tired? When she spoke of the need to use all our energy in the struggle today — well, Lenny, I felt as though I could hold my head up high for both of us.

P.S. Some 30 people have signed union cards in these 2 days.

Diana

Sept 22

Dinika,

You were nearly cheated of a letter, tonight by Mississippi climate — all the envelopes stuck tight & useless — but I was able to get from a guy who just came from furlough today.

This morning was OK — patrolling & again I learned a lot. Ordered to break camp, roll full field pack & be ready for a speed march at once. 176, 1 yard paces, a minute, when 140, 1 yard paces just about taxes me to the full — the idea was 5 miles in 50 minutes, as much uphill as down. Well, here's the sad & humiliating story — at 4 ¼ miles I was thru. It's the first time I've fallen out on a march, & there's no greater unhappy soldier in Shelby.

Lenny

Sept 22

Dearest,

All day long I have wanted to write. I have had a very difficult time in my shop in the last few days. First I have had a great deal of aggravation on the question of production — I waited from yesterday 1 P.M. till today 3 P.M. to get a job set up so I could work. I have written you this many times but each time it happens I have much heartache until I am working again. I wrote we agreed to sign up 100 people this week. Well, although in some departments it is coming along, I have not been able to sign a single person as yet. It is almost impossible for me to approach the men — they just won't discuss anything serious with a girl. I have approached some 12 girls already. In only one case I did get a promise to sign a card and she changed her mind because of fear. She is only on the job 3 weeks and has 2 children to support. The girls are a clique mostly Italian and Spanish Catholic. I have never been able to break into it, partly because I am Jewish and partly because our interests are so different. They are un-married and go out to meet fellows.

Diana

Sept 23

My Lady Love,

I learned a lot today — for a change I volunteered to be enemy detail — so I practiced infiltrating behind enemy lines to locate their cover and post. Another scout & I were able to capture the enemy command post. We were able to come around the rear under cover of the brook timber (trees grow along brooks) & bayonet all the out guards & "hand grenade" the C.P.

I'm trying to rest my weary legs just now before we go out on a night problem — this has been a tiring week, & the toughest is yet ahead. In spite of all precautions my right forearm is girdled by a broadband of poison ivy — heaven only knows how it got under my sleeve. When I go on a night problem, when you simply cannot look for it before dropping to the ground, I am resigned to getting some more.

Lenny

Sept 24

Dear,

It was an a-1 patrol I led last night — perfect discipline — no one spoke a word in 3 hours. We came in at midnight, after going some 2 plus miles thru wholly unknown pasture & woods, changing direction 3 times, & dried our wet feet & shoes & trousers by the fire. Must strike tents, roll pack, pack barracks bag, fill the slit trench & the drainage ditch — then be ready for the return march, likely to be 15–18 miles.

2 A.M. — Got in a little while ago after marching steadily since 7:30 P.M. — couldn't straighten my shoulders out for half an hour, from

the weight of pack, etc.; on my back — but the hot shower was something like a long forgotten dream.

Lenny

Sept 24, Friday

Dearest,

After work we had the union meeting. I would estimate that close to 50 cards came in this week. We discussed continuing the campaign and we elected a committee to appear at the union each week and we would hold a meeting when necessary. There are many problems but by and large, it seems to me we are progressing.

Diana

Sept 25, Saturday

Dear Diana,

Right now the last strains of Shubert's "Unfinished" are fading out as I sit in a cozy little room at the USO cottage on Hemphill Street. I'm relaxing. Lit out for town as soon as I could get a pass, have bought a pair of shoes at last, also some wool socks & other needs.

The bond drive decorates the town with pretty girls at bridge tables everywhere; displays of military equipment with price tags — $330 for this light machine gun, etc. The shoe salesman in the J.C. Penney store said he sold $2,000 worth today — the press carried huge appeals last week, criticizing the poor showing of Forest County & calling on the little man to come across.

The bivouac week was good once the rain passed. Thursday we had the first experience with "C-Rations" — canned "hard tac"; we'd been warned in advance, but it turned out to be OK. If we feed 4 million soldiers overseas that way it explains some of our shortages! We got 6 cans for the day: 3 bread units, 3 meat & vegetable units. We quickly learned how to make coffee & cook the food over an open fire in our own mess gear.

Over to the service club to find the State Archives have sent James Suet's "Look Away," which has a garbled fictionalized chapter on Newt Knight but not the book by Knight Jr. that I want so much.

Lenny

Sept 25

Lenny,

Finally my Saturday night pleasure — the time I spend with my love. You ask about the union program and why boosting war production is not included. I have raised this question a number of times but the organizers feel we must raise this mainly in terms of incentive pay. A number of people have told me they won't join the union because they will lose their freedom — You can't stay out when you want to, you can't ask for a raise whenever you wish, you can't go to the bathroom, etc., etc.

Diana

Sept 26

Dear Darling,

You can't imagine how happy I am to hear that there's a real union being organized in your place at last. We who are here in camp training for the big battles ahead know that unions, strong unions, mean better production, so we can get the weapons and jeeps & telescopes & field glasses that we need fast. Then when we know there's a union in your place, will I feel like a friend of mine is looking after you — that you can't be fired for no good reason, that your security is watched over, that there's no petty chiseling on your pay or Social Security.

I can imagine some of the older men in the place may feel they have got along so long without one that they don't need one now. But who is going to look after their seniority rights to the job when the war is over and industry switches over to a peacetime basis? Nobody — unless they all get together in the union & protect themselves. Have your whole department sign up by next week. They can do that much "for a soldier's morale," yes?

Lenny

Sept 26, 3:45

Dear Diana,

As to your shop problems: long distance advice is limited. As to getting at the girls socially — how about inviting two or three over for a quiet evening? They go seeking fellows but I warrant, with the war on, plenty sit home week after week and will welcome an invitation. Maybe if they are very Italian conscious, is there any good channel for funds to help Italian patriots (anti-Axis fighters)?

As far as the men, they will readily discuss things seriously & will respond to a woman's agitation. I've seen it in laundry, garment, civil service & now that women are cracking into machines the men here too will accept, even if judgingly, the leadership of a girl. Are they making ends meet under present prices? Are they going to have jobs after the war? Have any men signed up at all? Involve them as much as possible.

6:45

A large unit from the 69th is being sent overseas currently — men are being recalled from furloughs. So far no intelligence men are included, & no married men. Besides this big group, last week a call came for German & Italian translators to leave at once for overseas.

Lenny

Sept 26, Sunday

Dearest Beloved Lenny,

I promised you a news summary:

1. Irmalinsk retaken — fighting on the outskirts of Kiev.

2. A number·of trade unions have come out for a Second Front.

3. Decision against Bob Wood has been reversed by Oklahoma Court of Appeals. He is free.[40]

4. Registration for election starts tomorrow. The most important contests are for Lt. Gov and City Council.

5. Churchill spoke on his return to England. It was a disappointment to many — The real cross Channel second front, it is clear from his speech is not to be opened immediately. The decision to hold a 3-power conference is being organized and planned now.

6. There is much discussion on the Manpower problem. This week Bernard Baruch[41] put his finger on the key — housing, transportation, bad living conditions — There is still debate on drafting of fathers — pro and con.

7. Anthony Eden[42] finally revealed publicly the true mission of Rudolf Hess[43] — he offered negotiated peace — apparently in an effort to get Britain out of the war before he attacked the Soviet Union.

8. Shostakovich just finished the 8th Symphony. He says it is an attempt to look to the future – the postwar world.

---

40. Robert Wood was convicted of criminal syndicalism. He appealed and the decision was reversed. Syndicalism is a revolutionary doctrine in which workers seize control of the economy and the government by a general strike.

41. Bermard Baruch was an American financier, philanthropist, and statesman.

42. Anthony Eden, British foreign secretary from 1935 to 1955 and Prime Minister from 1955 to 1957.

43. Rudolf Hess, deputy fuehrer to Adolf Hitler from 1933 to 1941, was sent on a secret mission to Britain in May 1941.

Lenny, 13 more days — dearest, it will soon be time for us to decide when we should stop writing as soon as you know definitely when you will arrive. It's cold in N.Y. now. I think you should wear your uniform and perhaps bring your field jacket.

Your,
Diana

P.S. Your Sunday letters are terrific. You write such beautiful thoughts you almost make me feel like crying.

Sept 27

Darling,

I am glad you wrote the Wed. letter as you did — the one where you fell out on a march. I know that it eased you to tell me about it. Sweetheart, I would so like to write words that would make you feel that it was not a serious thing, but you are too intelligent and we both realize that we must learn to endure all tests and meet them. I do feel you put a little too much stock in it. We know that your training will teach you your weaknesses as well as your strengths. If you knew all that you are learning now, and if you were in the best shape physically — then your training would be unnecessary and you could go right into battle.

Diana

Darling,

You know among the people I know, just a handful have war jobs during the day and participate in community affairs at night. It's really hard, because I know that I try to the best of my ability to carry on both, but I find that I must have a rest every few months.

Diana

Sept 28

Diana,

A dull day in the field, a waste of time, since we all know how to dig & camouflage.

Lenny

Sept 29, Rosh Hashanah

Happy New Year, my beloved husband — It was a good description of a good patrol that you led.

I'm glad you are being innoculated for poison ivy. I hope it helps you.

Your folks again asked me about when you arrive. I told them I thought Sat. Oct 19 at 1 or 2 P.M. Of course, since it is Yom Kippur your mom won't go and she doesn't want your father to go — but if you arrive at night she expects to be there.

Diana

Sept 30

Dearest Diana,

Tomorrow's another speed march like the "other" & I'm ill at ease about it but your letter helps.

Well, with the injections to prevent poison ivy, I am currently having my worst poison ivy affliction with the exception only of June.

Last night I went to Rosh Hashona services. The chapel was quite full — over 100%. By the .way, there are about 25 permanent Jewish families in Hattiesburg.

Up to the service club to return the "Samson Agonistes" I find by the Herald Tribune someone has been blaming the delay in invading France on Churchill.

If this letter sounds a bit blue in B-minor, blame it on the poison ivy & furlough uncertainty. Believe me, when I find myself on the train flying to you a week from tonight, the whole train will be aglow with the happiness of your Lenny.

Lenny

Sept 30

Dearest Love,

There was a good deal of excitement in my shop today. We organized a blood bank through the Red Cross. They brought a unit to the shop and took donations there. We had been working on it for about a week and we had over 250 people signed up. It worked out well. The blood was donated on company time with their cooperation.

The company has definitely discovered that people are joining the union and I think they also know who started it. Their main strategy has been to try to frighten a few of us and also to scare the others away from us. They have not come out in a frontal attack yet but last Tues. my assistant foreman called me over and said in a very angry voice, "I hear you are going to join the union." Since I didn't want to commit myself either way to him, I just said, "I'm thinking about it." Then he went into a 15–20 minute attack against unions. When he finished, I wanted him to know he hadn't frightened me so I said, "I'm still thinking about it." And I walked away.

Lenny darling, by next Thurs. — you will be taking the train at midnight I hope.

Your, Diana

Oct 1, Friday

Lenny Dearest,

It is very good to be able to write Oct. now, just a week from tomorrow and we'll be in each others arms. I've just come home from your folks and everyone is fine.

I was surprised that you know that some of the men are going overseas. Isn't that usually secret? Dearest, if you should be one of the men chosen to go, I will be disappointed but we understand you are being trained for a job as soon as the army calls you to perform it. I know if possible you will try to see me before. I have decided to write to you every day until you are here.

Diana

Furlough Hopes Dashed

Oct 2

Hello Dear,

This morning the official word came that I am one of the 7 unlucky ones whose Oct 8 furloughs are cancelled and we won't know of any new furlough dates indefinitely. This is the army, you get what you get & obey without murmur.

My basic is over, I am a soldier. No more rookie; from here on in, 'til the war is over and won, at any moment I may head out to combat without any chance to kiss you or speak to you.

Lenny

Oct 2, Postal Telegraph

SNAFU — SO MY FURLOUGH IS POSTPONED HOPE FOR END OF OCTOBER OR NOVEMBER LENNY

Oct 2 for Sun. Oct 9

Dear Love,

Well — there will be longer separations, when I cross the seas, and letters won't come every day, nor any enclosures for Sundays, and will endure that too, and go on loving and fighting, 'til the day we can lay my uniform aside in the mothballs.

Lenny

Oct 2

Dearest Lenny,

How are you? — Just another 6 days now — next Sat we have a date.[44] Today I went to town. I was shopping all afternoon to prepare for my beloved's furlough homecoming. I bought shoes, a bag, stockings, gloves, a cigarette case and stationery. I haven't spent any money on clothes all summer but I spent about $22 today. I hope you will like the things I bought. Tomorrow, my mother has promised to sew for me at least one new dress.

The war from the front news is swell. Naples is ours — 460 White Russian towns retaken. The situation on the home front continues critical. Most of the press now discussed the "political necessity" of the second front as a counterweight to Soviet advances. The second front is a military and political necessity in order to defeat Hitler. Without a second front, we cannot be assured of a victory which will guarantee for us and the world a more stable and peaceful postwar. We cannot wait to see how things develop — we must go in there fighting and help determine how quickly and thoroughly Hitler will be defeated.

Diana

Oct 3

My Dearest,

By this time you have received my telegram, and know the unhappy news of the delay in our furlough. Poor darling — it's a cruel disappointment for us both. I wish I could say cheerfully I'll get the furlough, even if it's late. However, to be honest, I don't believe it will work out: as the alerting of more men for overseas goes on.

Let me tell you about one of the more interesting days I have spent in Mississippi. Planned to go to Laurel in Jones County to see what could be learned about Newt Knight on the spot. I got a pass to Hattiesburg and decided to take a bus. Of course, there was the perennial unpleasantness of the "colored" section in the rear. Since Negroes are a majority of the population, but only 6 or 8 seats are reserved for them, they must often wait hour after hour for a seat, while "white" sections may be half empty. Noted with mild dismay none of the persons I wanted to see were listed for Laurel or Ellisville — neither Tom Knight (Newt's son) nor B. R. Sumrall nor Mrs. E. M. Devall names on the WPA typescript.

---

44. She doesn't know the furlough has been canceled yet.

Picking out of the list, one with initials "W. W." — (Coinciding with those of Knight's lieutenant) I hiked over to the house — Mrs. was in — Mr. would know about it & wouldn't return until 6. I strolled out along the business section. The Loren Rogers Memorial Institute, where there's a reference library. Librarian pulls out T. J. Knight's little book I put down $1.00 deposit & borrow the book at 2 cents a day. This is Mississippi's only museum.

Returned to Mr. W. W. Sumrall, who received me — He seemed eager for a favorable account to be written up — the Tom Knight book is crude.
Lenny

Oct 3, Sunday

Beloved,

It is a little difficult for me to write now because your telegram has just arrived saying your furlough has been postponed. I am so eager for mail which will be more explicit than the telegram. I am still hoping you will have yours even though it may be postponed.

Lenny, we are new soldiers, you and I, we must learn to take the way of a soldier's life — at least I must and these things help teach me. It may be a little premature to raise this, but what are the possibilities of my coming to see you again for a few days. Of course, with all the time you spend on bivouac and hikes, it may not be practical, but what do you think?

Your Sunday letter gave me such great joy. No, darling, we shall never regret "the price we have to pay." I am happy, darling, although a few tears are trickling down my cheeks, because we are doing our share in the great struggle of the people, and because we are in love.
Diana

Oct 4

Dearest,

I was up this A.M. at 2, to breakfast & hiking off in dim darkness for hours & hours — to 11:30 A.M. We dig in and pitch tents. This is the best bivouac area so far. Fires begin to dot the landscape — they keep the snakes away — we killed one about 4 feet long today while gathering firewood.
Lenny

Oct 4

My Dearest,

All day I was hoping for a special delivery from you to tell me more news regarding your furlough, but I shall have to wait for your regular Sat.

letter. I had two letters today — both before the telegram. It was a little difficult to read them because they are so full of your furlough and because you are concerned lest something happen to change it. I do hope to see you before you are included in the group leaving for "overseas" duty.

Darling, don't be sorry you have to write me news that might not be the happiest regarding your furlough or "overseas" duty or anything else. I'm so glad you always write me just what the situation is. I do the same regarding news from home. I am not a child. I realize full well why you are in the army — what your job is and what is expected of you as a soldier in the infantry. I have never fooled myself in regard to your going into battle.

It would be unreal if I were to write that I am not concerned about you. I am very much concerned darling. I read somewhere that a man who wants to live and has something to live for has a better chance to live. Well, I think you and I have both — we want to live and we have much to live for — we have hope and faith in the future of America — we have each other — we have our children (as yet unborn) — all these things make it worthwhile and possible for us to fight and do our part in this great struggle for freedom.

Lucy came home from Boston today. She was at the commissioning of Babe's new boat.[45] She doesn't expect to see him again before he puts out to sea. The indications are that his boat will be in the Pacific fleet.

Your,
Diana

Oct 5

Dearest Lenny,

Well, I guess I shall have to accept it. Until now I just couldn't convince myself you would not be home this Sat even though I had your telegram. I guess we had planned and talked about it so many weeks — even after your telegram I hoped for another change and you would still come. But tonight, your Fri. and Sat. letters say your furlough has definitely been cancelled and no new dates set yet. I don't want you to try to get special privileges, but I have seen plenty of boys around N.Y. with the 69th insignia. So darling, try to get a later date. I'm much relieved about what you write about the second speed march. You did much better than the first as I knew you would. Lenny, it's funny for you to write that my

---

45. The USS *Remey*, the flagship of Destroyer Squadron 54, sailed from Boston through the Panama Canal and was deployed in the Pacific as an escort to submarines.

"sane" letter helped you. You know dearest, that you are usually the "sane" one and I am the opposite.

Diana

Oct 6

Dearest,

Yesterday's rain cut my shaving & washing time down, so today I reveled in a thorough job, having been able to get a whole helmet full of water, over a gallon; & so I was able to wash sox & underwear too!

Let it not surprise you that we know of a huge overseas group moving out of here. My current plans are nil; we don't know if we go in Friday night or stay on bivouac next week, or next 5 weeks.

What's happening? Is Kiev retaken, are we near Rome, what of Yugoslavia? The only news trickling thru is that the Yanks & Cards have tied in the first 2 games of the series.

Lenny

Oct 6

Darling,

Today was a very difficult day for me. When I arrived at work, I wasn't feeling well. I guess it was a combination of physical and emotional strain. I have tried very hard not to be emotionally overwrought and although I have been able to control it on the surface, you know what happens to me inside. In addition, I have had a cold for about a week and I'm quite tired. To top it all off I didn't get a job from 10 A.M. on. Darling, by noon I was in a pretty bad state. I left at noon, but I didn't want to go home and lie there alone. So I went to Fort Tryon Park. There I spent several hours relaxing in the beautiful atmosphere. I feel ashamed of myself because this is a sign of weakness on my part — but on the other hand, I do feel much better now.

Diana

FIVE MONTHS IN THE ARMY

Oct 7

Darling Lenny,

I came into work feeling much better than yesterday. I had the opportunity to work on a big machine (the kind that the men work). One of the men quit yesterday — I don't know how long I will be on it — the job is very hard physically. I had to mill a "clearance," a space the size into which another piece fits. Of course, it has to be very accurate. The difficulty was due to the shape of the piece and the type of cutter. It was necessary for me to have the machine very high — too high for me to reach and I had to stand on a box all day. Also because the piece was a casting — it was not smooth finished — I had to set each piece separately depending on its particular size. Then because of the type of cut, I had to feed it by hand which means that I had to turn the handles all day long. Although I was quite tired at the end of the day — it was a good day's work.

Diana

P.S. Lucy says that even when Babe comes home after the war has been won, she will be writing him letters from habit — it's close to 2 years for her now. I'm beginning to feel the same way.

Oct 8

Dearest,

Camp is broken, awaiting the call to move out. We wait for sundown & march in dark. Last night was even more beautiful than the one before — how I longed to have you by my side.

Lenny

Oct 8, Friday

Hello My Darling,

I've just come home from a very tiring day and I'm really glad I don't have to work tomorrow because of the holiday. After work, I went to the union and I'm enclosing a leaflet given out in front of the shop for the first time.[46] We did not have any reaction at all today — but it did stop the union baiters at least for today.

Diana

Oct 9

Dear Dinika,

Yesterday, as we marched in from bivouac, it hurt me, as it always does, to see the squalid unpainted rotting shacks the poor farmers dwell in, the

---

46. Flyer addressed to all Kollmorgen employees: Join the U.E.- C.I.O. (U.E.-United Electrical, Radio & Machine Workers). "It is the U.E. who seeks to stabilize wages—to eliminate unfair and disruptive wage inequalities to promote wage incentive plans so that every increase in production can be registered in a corresponding increase in worker's pay envelopes. The U.E. also protects its workers' job seniority. A U.E-C.I.O-shop is a victory shop—organize for victory: If Sperry can do it so can Kollmorgen!!!!"

wretched patches of corn and sugar cane, the furrowed faces of the local folk. How rare is a fat Mississippian! And these are white folk.

The march back was a rough one — we made about 19 miles in 4 hours, only 3 halts, a real stretcher; but I did it well.

Lenny

Oct 9, Yom Kippur

Dearest,

I knew today would be a difficult day for me. All day long, I couldn't help thinking — but today my Lenny would have been home. Well, I feel rested today. I slept almost 12 hours last night.

I shall include the news survey from the United Automobile Workers' Convention: 1) they came out in support of Roosevelt for a 4th term, 2) for a struggle against the defeatist spreaders of suspicion and poison who divide the U.S. from the Soviet Union and Britain and are pressing towards a negotiated peace with Hitler, 3) for continuation of no strike pledge irrespective of the impatient attitude of some employees. They had 1979 delegates from 533 locals.

The proposed three-power conference of U.S., S.U., and G.B will be very important and perhaps even decisive. The decisive conference on the second front was at Quebec where it was decided not to have a second front this year. News from the war front — great—— Dneiper River crossed — fighting progressing in Italy. The London Daily Herald has finally recognized that the guerrilla campaign in Yugoslavia is the people's liberation movement led by a man named Tito. His forces are organized as a regular army. At the head of this movement is the Yugoslav anti fascist council embracing more than 60 members representing all classes, all social and religious groups. It is extremely significant.

Diana

Oct 10

Dear Diana,

Camp is quiet — 1/6 out on furlough, perhaps 1/3 shipped out last week.

Lenny

Oct 10, Sunday

Dear Lenny,

I hope you agree I should get a coat. I haven't bought one since we have been married. My black one is usable for daily wear, but I need one which will be new and dressy. Of course with prices sky high, I shall have to spend quite a bit on it, so I will get a plain clothe coat with no fur trimming. The coat will still cost about $70–75 but I really do need it.

Diana

Oct 11

Hello,

Your ever extravagant wife just came home from spending more money. I went to the tailor tonight and picked a nice fitted coat. It will take about 4 weeks to be ready.

I wrote you a long news summary Sat. but to answer your questions — Kiev is not yet retaken. Today's news is that the Soviet forces have smashed the Germans back beyond artillery range of the Dneiper bridge-heads south of Kiev, and to the north are closing in rapidly on Inomel and Vitebsk.

The Yugoslavian people's army is fighting the Germans around the Italian city of Trieste at the head of the Adriatic and today's communiqué said the Germans have fallen back in several places. Other people's army forces are fighting in Croatia to capture Zagreb.

I can imagine what a good time you had on Thursday being in charge of your men. I can just see you directing a campaign. Lenny, dearest — as soon as you get back to camp from bivouac will you try to find out anything you can about the furlough or your status. I guess it's silly for me to write this because you will without my telling you, but I am so eager to know.

Diana

Oct 12

Darling,

Right now our whole company is lined up at the dispensary for physical checkup & no one has to tell us it is a pre-overseas checkup. There's a powerful rumor there will be no more furloughs. Of course, it is army policy to grant a furlough from port of embarkation to those who have not had any: but there is no promise & no money back guarantee.

It was a very tired & sleepy Lenny who went out on guard duty last night. Up at the same time for a strenuous day of creeping & crawling and scouting & patrolling —

Lenny

Oct 12

Dear Lenny,

Well, today is Columbus Day — passed hardly noticed by anyone —
Only the school kids were off. I celebrated by going on a book-buying
spree although not for us. I had intended to buy good things to eat for our
friends overseas, but changed my mind since the overseas package is so
limited in size. For John and Paul, "The Basic Writings of Tom Paine" and
for my cousin Jack two novels "Mother" by Sholem Asch and "The Sea
Wolf" by Jack London. I spent about $2 for each.

You write you may not be able to let me know in advance if you get
a furlough suddenly. Just come straight home. Regarding my job it will be
OK. Other girls, their husbands have come home suddenly and they've
had no trouble getting time off.

Your,
Diana

Oct 13

Diana,

I was homesick today. I'm beginning to get that pent-up feeling so
many of our guys complain of: I'm not beginning to make a fraction of
the contribution I could here; 9/10 of the time is frittered away with
non-essentials, & no opportunity to apply any of the abilities I have. The
whole set-up is so utterly confining and I get stuck on miserable petty
things which I despise & therefore don't bother doing well, & that means
not getting bigger responsibilities.

I'd love to say "Come at once" but we're going out to bivouac, likely
for 2 weeks in Oct. and in Nov. we go for a 5 week bivouac. If I am
alerted for overseas, I shall definitely wire, "Come at once," I do want so
much to see you again at least once — then I'm ready to go to the ends of
the earth for the duration, and probably will.

Lenny

Is There a New Furlough Date?

Oct 14

My Dear Girl,

A new furlough date has been set for Oct 26.

We went to our class and waited. Well, a snafu was on, instructors
hadn't come. Then Lt. Johnson said, "Miller, get up and give a talk on

current events." I upped to the blackboard & started the discussion, & carried it on 1½ hours.

In the afternoon, 2 U.S. soldiers showed up in German uniform, with Nazi equipment, who explained German military organization in detail. They threw in a speed march. I did it in 56 minutes this time, 5 miles, but still a minute behind the column.

Lenny

Oct 14

Dearest Lenny,

Today was a little better than yesterday. Another leaflet was handed out in front of my shop.

Diana

Oct 15, Friday

Darling,

I've just come home from one of the most thrilling gatherings. It was so crowded we had to get an extra hall — over 6,000 people. The program was tops — people from many different groups — from trade unions and other youth organizations.

You write your company will send one Army Specialized Training Program candidate a month and you are one of four on the list. Does that mean you have been accepted? What will happen if you are "shipped" or alerted to be "shipped"? Do you know what you will study if you are sent to school?

Do you think we are doing right in waiting for a "furlough?" Don't you think I should come to see you right now while we have a chance? I'm so afraid that if we continue to wait, you will be "shipped" before I see you once more.

Yours,
Diana

Oct 16, Saturday

Dearest Diana,

"Brrr" — cold December winds blow — In this weather I walked guard last night. So we're changing to our winter olive drabs this weekend. I had hoped to leave after lunch but have just been notified of another detail. Worse yet — they put me down for battalion CQ for tomorrow Sunday. It would have been my 3rd weekend CQ in a row. The other detail — 10 of us privates had to wash & wax the floor of the officers' club for their dance tonight. One good thing today: we were shown a film, "Baptism of

Fire," a realistic portrayal of 3 soldiers in their first battle. The film showed some of the more horrible kinds of death & mangling in battle, not as in Hollywood films but pretty close to life. I'm sure a number will pay much closer attention to their rifles hereafter!

Lenny

Oct 16

Lenny,

As you know you have a birthday coming this Friday. I have been to all the stores and I couldn't figure out a present. There is no article I could think that you need. That boiled down to two items — books and things to eat. You asked me not to send books because of lack of space. I was left with the second. I want to explain some of the things because you may question them. First I am taking a chance with two bars of chocolate. Then I am sending the mayonnaise, marmalade, salmon & crackers. Write me if they were enjoyable and if it is wise to send things like that. I also mailed you a present from my folks today. It is a home-made strudel. My mother worked very hard to prepare it.

Lucy went to Boston. This will definitely be the last time she'll see Babe before he ships out. Babe's brother Paul is coming home again. He and three buddies have the longest submarine service record of the present war so they have been taken off active duty and will be assigned to a base at home for the time being.[47]

Darling, I have been thinking a great deal about the question you ask regarding having a baby. I still feel in the main the way I did before. I want to have a baby very, very much — but I think the reasons for not having it begin to take precedence although I have not fully decided yet. The main reason is I'm afraid to take on the responsibility alone. If I felt confident I could manage physically, I wouldn't hesitate a minute. Also, dearest, if we should have to be apart for a number of years I don't feel I could care for a child and work also — and financially I would have to after the first year or so. But darling in spite of all I have written, I do so want to have a baby. I hope, you understand, what I mean — write me what you think.

Diana

---

47. Paul served on the USS *Seawolf,* assigned to the Pacific Fleet for several years. On October 4, Paul was on shore leave when the *Seawolf* was sunk (most likely by friendly fire), and his shipmates were lost at sea.

Oct 17, Sunday

Dearest,

I met several of our old friends today who send you regards. How much more content are we than people who are uncommitted or those who do not see where they can go. You can say to me, "Thanks for not taking the news of my furlough so strongly." I can be strong about anything that is demanded of me, and I hope I shall be able to meet the test as the tasks become more difficult, as they undoubtedly will before they become simpler.

Lenny — my heart is so full of mixed emotions now — I guess you don't know whether you will get a furlough or not. This indecisiveness is a trial for both of us. If you arrive on the train that gets in at noon, you will have to contact me at work. You can call me there and insist you must speak to me. If they ask, I work in the milling machine dept. and my foreman is Mr. Perkins. You can also come directly to the shop at 2 Franklin Ave. and tell the guard at the door to call me out.

Diana

Oct 18

Hello,

Last night we marched out at 11 P.M., with 10 minute halts once an hour, 'til 7:30 this morning, a map distance of 27 miles, in full field pack & rifle. So I have skipped a night's sleep & done our longest march so far.

Lenny

Oct 18, for next Sunday, Oct 24

Sweetheart,

Happy to report an innovation by me — Hitherto bivouac has meant everyone forgets the war, account of no newspapers. Well, I arranged for papers to be sent me, and had a big war map & board brought out on which I have chalked up the fronts & latest bulletins.

Dearest beloved — tho' I fear almost to write it, lest snafu bring grief, when you get this, I'll be almost ready to take off on furlough — I can't wait!

Lenny

Oct 18, for your birthday, Oct 22

Happy birthday to you sweetheart –

Lenny, this is our first "celebration" day that we cannot spend together and it is hard to take. Let us hope and struggle to make this, your 29th year, one to be long remembered as the year of the crushing of the Fascist tyranny and of reestablishing a world where people can again celebrate their birthdays with the ones they love.

Your Thurs. letter received and the news of the new furlough date. Even though I know of all the possible snafus, I can't help being excited. It was so good to read your Thurs. letter. It's the first happy letter I have received in several weeks and it made me happy too.

Your,

Diana

P.S. I guess you'll bring home all your letters that you want to save so I'll keep them here for you.

8:10 P.M.

Dearly Beloved,

Surprise! I am back on my hutment cot! A note addressed to me in Lt. Hamilton's hand addresses me as "Pfc." Thinking it was an error I decided to ask why the delay in my promotion. Lt. Hamilton said, "He's going to be "Pfc." — but no official word yet.

Lenny

Oct 20

Dearest Lenny,

By the time this reaches you, you will be almost on your way — I hope, oh, I hope. You don't say when I can expect you, although you did write you are scheduled for Oct. 26, next Tues.

Things are becoming increasingly difficult in my shop, in terms of getting organized because the company is trying to scare many people. I may have difficulty getting time off to be with you because of what has happened to other people in the last week.

Diana

FIRST BATTLE PRACTICE

Oct 21

Dearest Diana,

Your double letter of birthday greetings & your two overwhelming packages came tonight, just in time for my birthday. There are 7 birthday cards adorning the shelf above my cot. Well, this birthday business has driven out the really important news of the day — today we stormed the German village of Traurigdorf and took it in the assault; it was my first battle experience & also the first time I led a squad, 12 men including rifles and a BAR[48] team into action, and brought them through safely to victory, with commendation from the observing officers.

Traurigdorf is a little town, with a main street where several German squads remained entrenched, while our main forces had bypassed it. Our platoon of 3 squads attacked thus: first mortars opened up, then machine guns, & under cover of both we attacked, moving up. So at the sound of the mortars — I led my squad out through the woods 'til we reached rifle distance (I got commendation for controlling & maneuvering the men thru dense woods.) Traurigdorf is an actual model city and a sorry wreck is a village that has been the scene of a battle!

I learned an awful lot — the need to know every man, as a team, relying each on the other's performance; the need to advance without a second's hesitation in the face of fire, because you'll lose more lives by the hesitation; the tendency of men to bunch up to stand up instead of crawling. The squad leader must concentrate on directing his men, firing only when necessary.

Lenny

Oct 21

Darling,

As the time grows nearer, I'm getting a little jittery — every time the bell rings I get scared it might be a telegram of a negative character.

Diana

Oct 22 (Dad's 28th birthday)

Dear My Love,

After yesterday's birthday eve powwow came a dull day, one of those unsatisfying time wasters on communications all day. Supper was a mess — rations are worse: one slice of bread, boiled onions, ½ frankfurter (boiled, tasteless), squash, & Jello. So Hersh & I added a can of salmon, mayonnaise & olives, & strudel, & made a meal out of the mess. What works best — "Olives, mayonnaise, marmalade: all grand, but impossible to keep — send only the smallest sizes, for one or two days, & don't send them all at once."

The nervous strain you feel at my furlough is fully shared by yours truly. It is practically in the bag now, in 72 hours I'll be on my way!

Lenny

---

48. Browning Automatic Rifle spits bullets like a machine gun.

First Furlough in Brooklyn, New York

Oct 22, Friday

Dearest,

Happy Birthday darling — I certainly hope you had a nice day.

Diana

Oct 23

Dearest Diana,

At last I had my crack at the rifle range, & am fully "qualified" as a rifleman. My score was 152, qualifying required 140. I am by no means satisfied by the score & intend to do at least "sharpshooter" (165) next chance I get.

Lenny

Oct 24, Sunday

Darling,

How are you my darling? I shall not write you a long current events account — we'll talk about it when we are together — I hope.

Diana

Furlough in Brooklyn, New York

HEADING HOME—FIRST FURLOUGH

Oct 25, 2:50 A.M.

Dearest,

Waiting in the Chattanooga depot — Walked out a few blocks but all is deserted & closed, so back to the stuffy station. The views from my train window, until early night blotted all from sight, woodlands, only slightly marred by the wretched cabins & poverty stricken hamlets of Mississippi and Alabama; it was dark when we rode through Birmingham.

I had 3 seat-mates: first a 69th soldier, a refugee from Spain in '37, Cuba '37–'39. Second, a young Oklahoma girl: her husband stationed at Tuscaloosa, after a tour of overseas combat service, so she'd been to see him. Next came a Coast Guardsman, being discharged — had seen much anti-sub duty.

Beloved darling, it's hard to sit here waiting oh so long for the train that is to take me to you — to our grand reunion.

Lenny

Oct 25, 1:00 A.M., USO Postcard

Diana,

At the USO lounge in the Chattanooga Station — had a good cup of coffee & egg salad on whole wheat for 25 cents and a better cup of coffee with doughnuts for nothing in the lounge.

Lenny

[Two-week break in letters while Lenny is home]

Back in Training

Nov 9, En route back to Mississippi

Dearest,

This train, practically a 69th special, is somewhere in Tennessee. So far a very quiet & uneventful trip: I have a comfortable window seat. I got the seat at Washington. It has been dreary & rainy and little to look at. The sandwiches you prepared have been swell & my mother's cookies grand.

Lenny

Nov 9, En route

Darling Diana,

Tomorrow I'm back at work. I want to clear my deck for action: it is not good to carry a mind full of fresh furlough memories into camp — I don't want to forget them, "no" I don't but one needs to distill them, digest them, extract the fighting morale essence, & store the rest safely for future times.

To the Chinese Restaurant to talk our hearts to each other, and decide our biggest decision since July 1, 1939! Sweet Diana, I've known all along how much I love you — but never have I felt it so much or realized it so much as those 4–5 last minutes in Union Terminal: and I promise you again to do all I can to come back & enjoy with you, the fruits of our victory.

Lenny

Is She Pregnant?

For those in the service and their wives, a major decision was whether to try to have a child. Lenny and Diana share whether it is a good idea for them, given all the uncertainty involved. They made their decision, in spite of significant concerns Diana expressed, which included how she would manage alone.

As Lenny's first furlough home became increasingly delayed, it must have become apparent to them that the opportunity might pass, as so many of his fellow soldiers in training began to receive orders to ship out overseas. They were lucky, and Diana became pregnant on his first furlough.

In many of Diana's letters there is much talk about being pregnant, how it feels, what type of work is suitable during pregnancy, and choosing the obstetrician and the hospital arrangements for the birth. She expresses their parents' fears should Lenny not return, and Lenny's mom's superstitions regarding pregnancy. Diana also writes of her loneliness and her fears for the future.

Nov 9

Dear Lenny,

It's a little hard to write to you because — well for two weeks we talked all our letters.

Lenny, I feel fine — just a little impatient until it's definite, but more and more eager every minute.

How is the trip? Are you sitting? I was anxious to walk through the gate last night and see if I could see you on the train, but Irving wouldn't let me — I guess he was right because we had said "so long" enough times. Dearest, I told Irving and Edna I think I am pregnant — I just had to tell someone.

Diana

Nov 10, Back in camp

Dearest Wife,

In spite of all my philosophy and my understanding, I have a hefty dose of the "back from furlough blues." I have spent the whole morning setting my stuff to rights. But don't worry about me, dear: by the time you read this I'll probably be thoroughly readjusted again. It appears we go on a 4-week bivouac from next week on; and there's a report that maneuvers — the real thing starts after that.

I'm so impatient to hear how you are.

Lenny

Nov 10, Postcard

Dearest,

I've just come home and I want to mail this card so you'll know I'm OK. I had a good trip home and a seat.

Diana

Nov 10

Dear Lenny,

I spent last night with Irving and Edna. They coaxed me to stay but I took the 1 P.M. train out of Washington. I had a full seat to myself all the way. The trip was uneventful, but I was able to do a lot of thinking on my way home. Dearest, I thought of the past two weeks and all that happened. I'm really so glad we had this opportunity to be together, and that we took advantage of it to make a most important decision. I feel fine — in fact too well because I have been taking it easy — I wish the next week will pass quickly so I can go to the doctor and really know.

I shall have to keep it all to myself before I tell anyone else. I've had a little difficulty explaining that I'm not going back to my job — they don't quite understand. My folks think I have gone out of my mind because they can't believe I'm quitting because the work is too hard for me. They know me too well for that. Well, in a little while, I guess they will understand better.

Your, Diana

Nov 11

Dinika,

Rose this "morning" in midnight darkness and was it cold!!! I wore my wool undershirt & sweater as well as fatigues & field jacket. In the afternoon we were set to cutting photos of enemy vehicles and aircraft from "Life" and other such publications. Love, there's a rumor that the next shipment is November 23 for Army Specialized Training Program and that I'll be on the list.

Lenny

Nov 11

Dear,

I'm fine, darling — and getting more and more, sure every day. Tomorrow, I intend to go to my shop and to pay a visit to the union. I hope I won't have any difficulty. It will be a little difficult to explain to my union colleagues without telling them the complete reason for my not wanting to return to work.[49] Each day that passes, I become more certain of my present status. I'll be so glad when this transitioning stage is over.

Diana

Nov 12

Dear Diana,

Well, I have 4 hours free this afternoon — we might have a night problem, firing in the dark, so I'll have to borrow a rifle & clean it. (They have this miserable, discipline breaking system of issuing your rifle to someone else when you go on furlough or hospital.) So far, this morning a total waste, for the hundredth time, we dug foxholes & camouflaged them.

Darling sweetheart, how are you developing? Anything show yet?

Lenny

Nov 12

Sweetheart,

Lenny, please don't be concerned about me — I have been feeling fine — I am becoming more and more, sure of my condition each day. I intend to go to the doctor during the later part of next week. Dearest, I shall find out at once about my unemployment insurance rights and then I may not look for work at all. In any case, I shall not look for a new job until the doctor tells me it will be OK for me to work. I would rather be careful than take any chances.

Considering all the qualms I had before you came home, you were just what I needed. Talking to you helped me to understand some of the doubts and questions that I had. Also, now that it begins to look like a reality, well, I'm so happy and proud that I feel I can conquer any problems that arise. Darling, I know as soon as I tell our folks I'll feel much more comfortable, but I'd like to wait. I shall probably tell my mother as soon as an opportune moment arises. I spoke to her last night again about the question generally and her attitude was still the same, but I hope she'll react more favorably when she'll know that I'm the one.

Your parents, especially your father thinks I have taken leave of my senses. They keep asking me how come I gave up my job. I told them I need a rest but they didn't understand. Love — I was at my shop this afternoon and I quit. I didn't have any trouble at all. I was really sorry to leave because I was proud of that job. I was so happy to be able to say I

---

49. Strenuous factory work wasn't considered suitable for a pregnant woman.

was a war worker, but I hope my new job will be even better and certainly as important. I also went to the union and explained why I left. I used "ill health" as the excuse. Gosh this letter is all about me. Write me what's happening in camp?

Diana

Nov 13

Dearest,

Last night's problem was very interesting & well worth both the late hours out in the keen cold and the tedious hours of rifle cleaning. To wit: we were guerrillas! So we learned a lot about ambushing, and teamwork too.

Lenny

Nov 13, Saturday

Lenny, darling,

I feel fine. It's difficult because no one knows, and my folks are worried I've left my job because I'm not well. This evening I told Lucy and she was very happy. Lucy agreed I should not tell Mom until I've seen the doctor. Lucy was funny — she said she suspected it.

Yours,
Diana

Nov 14, for Sun. Nov 21

Darling,

Sitting in the USO at Laurel waiting for the bus — And I am flabbergasted, for once, on what to write to you! What does one write to a pregnant wife? I know I should have studied your Hunter College prenatal care course! It's still so new: and you being back at home, so that I miss the show, put an awful strain on the imagination. You have all my love and best wishes for an easy time of it — gee, I do so hope & pray so!

Lenny

Nov 14, Sunday

Dear Lenny,

I'm feeling very well. I'm really beginning to have hopes that all is as we want it to be. You know I still can't get used to the idea of not working for a while. It seems so strange. As soon as I finish this letter, I intend to go for a long walk. It is a very beautiful day today — cold and wintry but sunny and dry.

Diana

Nov 15

Dear Dina,

I had 4 hours of making overlay maps for the maneuvers. Love, in this maneuver, we may be 9 days with no chance to write or send mail — we may be without rest for 48 or 72 hours — so please don't worry if there's a 10-day delay in mail; I'll try my best.

Lenny

Nov 15

Dearest Husband,

These days I feel as if I need to depend on you more. It's a strange feeling but I think you understand. It must be the most glorious thing in the world for people who are in love to spend a pregnancy together — but my darling, I promise you I will share it all with you through the mail.

By the end of the week, I shall be ready to start on my study program in earnest.[50] I'm sorry to write this to you, but your wife is fundamentally a very lazy person I am discovering. I relish the idea of staying in bed until 8 A.M. and not getting up in utter darkness, in a cold apartment. I think I shall take advantage of this for the next months, because after that, from all I have heard, little ones require attention at all hours of the night.

I understand that it will be at least another month before the doctor will be willing to say anything definite. However, I shall visit him at the end of the week.

Diana

Nov 16, Postcard

Dearest,

On the bivouac — no stationery, only postcards available — It's cold but I am in those laughable but very warm sweater and "long Johns," knitted by Bea that are so long they reach from my torso to my feet.

Lenny

Nov 17

My Darling,

If I'm busy for a few hours — I forget about my new condition and then I remember and I'm so happy. The only thing that bothers me is

---

50. The study program consisted of topics to study and books to read, put together by Lenny to fill the time productively while Diana wasn't working.

I'm not doing as much now. I'm very sorry I had to give up my war job because I feel this is no time to be taking it easy.

Diana

Nov 18

Dear Lenny,

It makes me unhappy to read you haven't heard from me in three days. My darling, I have been writing daily. Please dearest, don't be concerned about me — I really am fine and taking good care of myself. The only thing that bothers me is that I am not doing enough and that I haven't told my folks yet. It's funny, Lenny, but I think this moving back with my parents has made me feel that I am a child again. When I was out of the house, they got used to the idea I was on my own and capable of making my own decisions. Now they seem to feel again I should consult them. Well, I'm not really too concerned because Lucy seems to be quite willing to take an apartment with me. We figured out financially and I'm pretty sure we will be able to manage it. We'll see what my mother's reaction will be and we'll decide then. Besides, dearest, just as my folks never were the most important factor in any decision that I made — they couldn't be in this either no matter what their reaction will be.

Diana

Nov 19, Postcard

Dear,

Waiting for the chow truck to reach us in the forward positions & hungry! The days are brisk & autumnal, but the nights are long & icy, sleeping on the ground with frost piling up white like a snowstorm. But we sleep & dream of home!

Lenny

Nov 19, Friday

Darling,

I get tired much more quickly now than I did before. I'm not sure whether it is due to my new condition or to accumulated fatigue. I feel so changeable these days. Sometimes I feel very confident and thrilled about the new addition, but once in a while, I get a little scared and I think of all the problems.

Diana

Nov 20, Postcard

Dearest Sweetheart,

Last night for the first time out here we were permitted a fire at our post so we were "comfortable." We are so used to the hard ground by now that a mattress will seem off.

Lenny

Nov 20

To My Dearest Husband,

Here we are spending Sat. night together again. Your march must be taking you many new places. I hope you will write all about it.

You know darling — I'm not used to the idea yet — every once in a while I forget it. Now that it is almost 2 weeks since you left, I guess we can be fairly certain. This week I shall go to the doctor. From what I understand, you have to skip at least 2 periods before they can give you the test to determine pregnancy, but in another 2½–3 weeks I should be pretty definite. I am a mixture of feelings, both very thrilled and happy and concerned and a little scared.

Your,
Diana

3

Basic Training: The Second Six Months

CAMP SHELBY, MISSISSIPPI
NOVEMBER 21, 1943–JUNE 4, 1944

The second six months focused on longer bivouacs away from camp in conditions more similar to what would be encountered overseas. It included activities in swamp conditions as well as winter conditions, preparing the soldiers for deployment either in Europe or the Far East. This second phase of training was critical to a soldier's survival, not just because it simulated real combat, but also because it aided in the development of teamwork and leadership skills among the trainees.

Nov 21

Dear Diana,

I spent the afternoon on a quiet knoll with Hersh. It's an Indian summer day. I am sending you an article from the "Welfare Reporter" of 11/13/43 which was sent to me. It references my speech at the union saying, "The conference was climaxed by a stirring address by Private Leo Miller, former member of Local 1's executive board, who spoke proudly of the wonderfully efficient U.S. Army, which he felt was fully prepared to accomplish any tasks it was called upon to perform."

Lenny

Nov 21, Sunday, somewhere in South Mississippi

Diana,

We are "off" today so I can at last write. We have been, & are, out on a 9 day "problem": an enemy force has landed at Gulfport, and we are fighting it — naturally, hours are fantastic: some nights we are on the go without stopping, some days we lie in a foxhole & sleep for hours. Some nights, intelligence has been on guard all thru the freezing darkness, & one night, we captured our enemy prisoners in a brisk fight. We are constantly on the go. All our supplies on our backs — besides heavy pack we carry overcoat, rifle, field glasses, heavy wire cutters, several tons of ammunition (so it feels), always wear pitch helmet, never take rifle off.

Dove: although I've left it for last, your present condition is with me always — and it is so unspeakably wonderful to know that you are happy in it. I pray you will have an easy & comfortable time.

Lenny

Nov 21

My Dear Diana,

Tomorrow or Tuesday we leave on a 9-day march & maneuver which will take us almost to the Gulf of Mexico and so mail may be a little snafu'd. Today, I rose before dawn, I dressed & caught a bus, using a blank pass Lt. Hamilton had given me some weeks ago, that I saved for emergencies, I got the 7:50 A.M. bus to Laurel and walked to the house of Tom Knight — and met him, spending 4 hours there. He is 83. When I told him what I was interested in, he told me details no end; & answered a hundred questions. It seems that he really knows less than he claims & had to consult others to write the book. Apparently old Newt wanted his life story written by his Negro daughter Ann — she's a teacher in Alabama. In spite of everyone's warnings he himself brought up mention of this aspect of his father's life & spoke frankly. (He didn't tell me what I learned later in the day, that his twin brother Matt also married a Negro girl, & to meet the law that a white man must have Negro blood to marry a Negro girl, he drew blood from his intended by a pin & swallowed it.) I rather fancy that Newt was more advanced on the Negro question than Tom, who shares the chauvinism of the southern poor whites. Regrettably there are no copies left to sell.

Off to Betty Myrick, a grandmother who seems to have some material to round out the story — missed the bus and went into the library. Then rush off to grab the bus & ride out in the country, & her cabin is even more ramshackle than T. Knight's; and worst — she wasn't home. So I returned to camp.

Lenny

11/21 for Sun 11/28 (This is map overlay paper.) — No peeking

Dear Diana,

One curious thing about this open-air bivouac — I, who rarely dream find I dream, oh, so happily — of home! Every night for 6 nights I've dreamed I was home with you. Last night I was home on furlough. You were there with a cheery glow & swelling belly.

Lenny

Nov 21, Sunday

Dearest,

Your Sunday letter greeted me and it left me all in smiles — You say you don't know what to write to a pregnant wife — sweetheart, you must keep writing as you always have. I am no different now than I was four weeks ago when you came home. I look exactly the same and feel pretty much the same except that I am rested.

I guess we are really going to be parents, huh? And I promise you when you come home to your family after the war, we will have another baby if at all possible, so that you can see first hand just what is involved.

I have been looking through the newspaper this week and find there isn't much to say so I'll write a summary. The most important developments are on the political front. The meeting of Churchill, Roosevelt and Stalin seems to be pretty definite for the near future. This meeting will set the big offensive, soon so that the war in Europe will be ended before the summer of 1944, and that the war with Japan can be finished by the end of next year.

Diana

Nov 22, in a Foxhole, Hill D, Somewhere in South Mississippi

Dearest,

Well, today has been a training day, really the first since we're out. It was real training to spot trucks, jeeps, soldiers, anti-tank guns etc. at ¾ mile off, locate their command post & motor pool, determine the direction, & phone it into HQ. Then about 1:00 the enemy attacked with tanks and riflemen, although our men fired back, all was in blanks, so naturally the enemy came on & the tanks broke through our main line of resistance. The action was good training, although it lost a lot of reality, in that there were no casualties.

I hope your letter will come with tonight's chow truck & tell me more of my developing parenthood! And, of you, my darling?

Lenny

Nov 22

Lenny,

Today is an anniversary that I think we should celebrate — it is exactly 6 years that we met in the community center on Elton St. I remember so well when Pete brought me over and introduced us, but I didn't realize, until I had seen you several times, you were the one for me.

Diana

Nov 23, Hill?

Dear Darling,

On another nameless hill: we are not given any large-scale maps, & our route has been thru wide reaches of country: we have seen only one farmhouse in 9 days. Friday we go out to the wilderness again. Tonight there will be no fires after 5:30 P.M., — so we'll be blue. Of course, our severest hardships are not equal to anything in combat.

Lenny

Nov 23

Dear Husband Mine,

Tomorrow I'm going to spend the day just relaxing and getting some sunshine. I think I am going to have to provide for more rest because I tire easily. I shall go to the doctor on Friday. The longer I wait, the more he'll be able to tell me, but I'm getting too impatient.

Diana

Nov 24, HQ Co, Dayroom

Dear Diana,

Back in Shelby & we are glad! Nine days (the soldier says "nine f—g days") without a bath, without bed, chair or shelter from the frost and wind, without rest; and as we were, started to realize, also without sight of women as our truck jogged into McLaurin, Mississippi. Except that we have endured so much that increments of hardships and weariness hardly registered, this last day was the hardest. None too rested from previous toils, we moved into our final bivouac area, and prepared for the night attack. I was detailed as guide for the forward assembly with 5 in all. I'd never been in that area before at anytime and in ½ hour of darkness had to memorize in detail the layout of a ¼ mile area of woods and meadow accurately.

We were a little behind the main line of the attack, we could dimly see the firing & hear the shouting about 5/8 mile away, & once a "rocket's red glare" caught us in its glow. Mostly our group froze & shivered & ran forward in half-mile stretches as the front line advanced. The objective gained by 12:30, we dug in at the command post: a dreary 6 hours of darkness (no moon 'til 5 A.M., & only a sliver), of icy wind, of gloom & weariness, I dug and dozed in the foxhole, & camouflaged it in the darkness about 3 times — finally gave up any attempt to rest at 4, and just stood around in the cold with a few others 'til dawn — the longest night we ever spent in the army, one guy said.

At daylight the long march back — more wearisome miles than we cared to count, 'til finally we reached the trucking point & cut the remainder to an hour's ride.

Your mixed feelings is what is to be expected now, beloved: I also am very happy when I think of you soon to be a mama; but also I worry about your health; and I also worry about you having enough money for all your needs. So I am delighted when you write you are well; as to $ — I still hope to raise my army pay in the next 9 months.

"Dinika," I'd prefer you not to go to any work & not to take any chances — no amount you might earn is worth it. Don't join me in "worrying" — that is my responsibility as papa; you know the mama bird sits on the eggs in the nest and the papa bird brings her nice fat juicy worms he digs up from the dirt — so I'm thinking how to get juicier worms for you!

Lenny

11/25

Dear Diana and "?"

A little after midday, a careful observer might have noted a distinct grin appearing quietly over the horizon and slowly spreading as it settled comfortably on the countenances of several thousand soldiers in the 69th Division. Since preparations for an historic Thanksgiving dinner were under-way was no secret, that to supplement the regular rations, all the reserve profits from the PX were tossed in; a late bulletin yesterday heralded the arrival of four turkeys, 120 lbs. in all. As we entered the mess hall at 2, dazzling tablecloths covered the bare boards out of sight; napkins at every place — and such a display of eats! And music too! Last night, my first bed sleep in 10 days, was mighty sweet too. Also did a $2.50 job cleaning my rifle from end to end. Issued to me when we left on the 9 day problem, full of dirt & rust, & repeated cleanings in the field, where dirt comes easier than it goes, didn't set it as I like my rifle to be — now it's a beauty again.

Well, they passed out the Sgt.'s stripes today and made 7 new Pfc's, but you notice my address-rank is the same. I'm so used to being passed over I didn't even wince; but of course I am fast losing any desire to stay in a company where promotion looks hopeless after 7 months of hard work. I'm sorry, because you could use the dough.

Lenny

Nov 26

Dear,

Today is "light duty" — wait for orders for the big division problem and meanwhile get shoved from pillar to post as only a lowly private can be — picking up matches on 2nd Ave., mopping HQ's floor. That's when I feel most keenly my yard bird status.

I explained to Lt. Stevens my Newt Knight research & the problems I face in continuing it. He agreed to ask the division special service officer on my behalf for 1) time off when I'd be on detail, not field work 2) transportation especially in going to Jackson and the places that cost money. He felt time off might work but transportation less likely; it is an unusual request. I'm just wondering how far one could travel to see some records or documents!!

I keep wondering about your unemployment insurance benefits — don't delay: if it's enough you may not have to look for any job at all.

Lenny

Nov 27, Somewhere south of Mc Lauren

Dear Diana,

This would be a lovely picnic area; I'm prone on a natural bed of pine needles six inches deep; this pine forest is open and the sun comes thru brightly. We are supposed to be in a big attack, starting 8:00 A.M. tomorrow.

At lunch we were raided by a single fighter plane which disrupted chow & delayed us — of course you're not going to stand in a chow line when a P40 is ripping up the area with imaginary machine gun fire — the plane practically sheared the treetops off; it was so low.

For all you know "?" is a month en route now & only 8 months to go. Dearest beloved, I so hope you keep on in the best of health, I am so happy we went ahead without further delay. I hope you are as happy. How I'd love to have you beside me lying here on this warm bed of pine needles, run my fingers thru your hair, kiss your eyes and caress you all over.

Lenny

PROBABLY PREGNANT

Nov 27, Saturday

Sweetheart,

This afternoon I went to Dr. Shaw and he made me feel very confident. He said he cannot be sure yet but that he is pretty sure. He said when I

have missed my second period, I can be sure. That means by the middle of
Dec., we can be sure of it. He said I was right to give up my hard job, but I
could take an easy job of the type we thought if I desire it. He felt it would
be better for me to keep myself busy. Therefore, in a few days, I shall look
around for a job and see if I can get one that I feel will be OK.

He told me to come back to him at the end of Dec. and if I am pregnant then he will put me on pre-natal care and explain to me what I have
to do and how to take care of myself. He spoke to me about having a baby
at the present time and was quite sympathetic. His own daughter, whose
husband is in the army, is due to have a baby in Feb. Well, now I shall tell
my folks at the first opportunity. Then in about 2 weeks when I am sure, I
will tell your folks. Lenny dearest — I'm really quite thrilled. He said I can
expect the baby in the middle of July.

Diana

Nov 28, Sunday

Dina,

Today was as hard as Saturday was easy. At 4 A.M. we moved out
reaching the battle line at 8 A.M., & went at once into attack, which
lasted without interruption 'til 4 P.M. It was a magnificent exercise: the
entire division attacked 3 regiments of infantry in line on a 2 mile wide
front, supported by the 4 artillery battalions, rifles, 37 mm guns, 105 and
155 howitzers & mortars & machine guns all going throughout. It was
valuable to see and hear the mortars fire. Towards the end of the "battle"
I had to go out across the battle area some 2–3 miles to a certain forward position, and trekked out across the shot-up area: seen close up, it
was a scene of horrible desolation; the barren brown grassy hillocks are
dreary enough in the drizzle, but with trees battered to burnt stumps by
gunfire, blackened meadows from the incessant barrages, roads turned to
quagmires by rain and traffic, bridges wrecked — everything a wreck &
shambles.

Lenny

Nov 29

Dearest,

I have a pass to town & will take off after lunch. I am going to the
Miss. Southern College. During the last few days I have had a hard
struggle with my morale. I find I no longer have the resilient morale I had
in April — May — June and during the first weeks out of the hospital in
August. The miserable hospital stay, the continued humiliation of being a
yard bird sans promotion, and 50 other factors pull me down.

There is a general low level of morale. Snafus are depressing and you know how many snafus we face in our intelligence squad's functioning & misuse, time wasting drives me to irritation. There's the miserable feeling of physical exhaustion without value or purpose — like yesterday when my back crumbled under a full pack which I'd never carry in combat, but had to carry all day because they make no provision for a transport vehicle for intelligence. There's the lack of any companionship. There's no perspective either that the 69th will be a unit in combat.

Lenny

11/29 for Sunday, Dec 5

Dear Diana,

It is not surprising that you find dissatisfaction in your present jobless career. It seems to me you are failing in one respect: you are not planning your time, & it will fritter away. Give thought to forms of activity which are practical to you. Examples: 1) There are hundreds of issues on which letters need to be written, to Roosevelt, to Congress, the state officials, to various newspapers. 2) Have you thought about helping with a girl's page? Cooking, beauty, culture, war jobs and conditions, all the sort of stuff such a page would need — a little thought and care in writing and you could help fill a real need, without physical exertion.

Lenny

Nov 29

Dear Lenny,

You write about Gen. McNair's praise of your outfit. In today's newspaper he said that this war will be won by the land army. He said the Infantry is the decisive factor and that victory over Germany and Japan will depend on the price the Infantry pays. I thought I wrote about the unemployment insurance. I was there about two weeks ago and was told that I couldn't get any because I left my job voluntarily. Last week, I spoke to Bob about it. He called a friend who is an expert and he said if I left the job because of it being too hard for me, I may be entitled to it, but I would have to go out on a job if they sent me to one. I shall go again this week and see what I can do.

Diana

Nov 30

Darling,

Just came from seeing "Battle of Russia," no 5 in the training film series on "Why we fight?" And it's terrific! It's compulsory for everyone.

I was glad I was in a very OK frame of mind. The letter I wrote to you yesterday was getting things off my chest. Yesterday went to town and rode out to Miss. Southern College. The Library's rather a hope than a fact; mostly bare shelves & empty corridors. At 5 they closed the library, so I hung around the soldiers at the Army Administration School & "infiltrated" into their chow line, & had a fine supper.

I reflected on these "soldiers" who sleep in a steam-heated brick building & book study all day and decided I'd rather be at Shelby & bivouac in the frost any day — And it brought me back that precious sense I've been groping for, the sense I felt when I came into the army; that no matter how wretched one may be in the army, it would be mean, vile, & miserable a hundred times more to be a civilian at present.

Lenny

SHARING THEIR NEWS

Nov 30

Dearest,

Lenny, dearest, I told my mother this evening about our baby. Finally, after dinner, my father went to a meeting of his society[1] and we were alone. She reacted just as I expected her to, perhaps even a little better. She was not surprised, because she said she suspected it since I stopped working and she knew I had been thinking about it. She said she wasn't angry because she understood my feeling about wanting to have a baby and that perhaps were she in my position, she would feel the same way. She said for me to try to understand that she is worried about me and with you not at home, she is even more worried. I think she will get used to the idea soon and begin to be a little happy about it.

Of course, she assured me of as much help as could possibly give me. She wouldn't even hear of my moving for the time being. She told me she would tell my father in a day or so. If you wish, you can write to my folks about it now. I'm still going to delay before I tell your folks until I have skipped my second period. By the way, my mother said she wasn't subject to nausea during pregnancy. Well, so far I haven't felt any morning sickness either — I hope it continues.

Diana

---

1. Organization of people who emigrated from Sokolievka/Justingrad, in Ukraine.

Nov 30, 2nd letter

Dear,

It is good to hear about Dr. Shaw's diagnosis and attitudes. However your husband is not as easy to convince about taking a job: I agree only if: 1) you actually get a light, sedentary job with little traveling and limited hours; 2) you quit at the slightest indication of fatigue beyond normal limits. The only reason why I consent at all, besides your own desire for useful activity, is that since I am unfortunately unable to give you more than the bare necessities, your "own earnings" will get you some additional comforts and maintain your emergency reserves.

Lenny

Dec 1

Dear Diana,

In typical GI fashion, we were roused at 4:30, breakfasted at 5:00, turned in bed rolls at 5:30 & were ready to march at 6:00 & now 8:25 & we are still waiting. So I have put in a couple of hours good reading in the December "Infantry Journal," as fine an issue as ever.

Lenny

Dec 2, Somewhere in Mississippi, near Wiggins

Dear Diana and?

Well, we finally left yesterday, we marched from about 9:15 A.M. to 6 P.M., and it was the most rugged march we ever made. We have gone longer distances, but the terrain was fierce: one whole hour we went uphill, & it was the longest hour I can remember.

When we finally arrived my feet were sore as blazes, I couldn't straighten my back, my shoulders pained & sore from the terrific pack. The hike brought a July sweat out of us in December, the chill leaving us soaked & cold while we sweated on. But your rugged husband stays well.

Please let my folks know my letters in more detail, since writing is very hard under these bivouac conditions. If we go into an attack for 36 hours, it will be all I can do to send you a card. As in the previous bivouacs, when I crawl into my sleeping bag; & pull my coat on me, I dream of home. Last night I dreamt I was home on furlough again, looking after your swelling belly; and also enjoyed a fine plate of chicken & "lokshin."[2] Tell my mother, "It was a Friday night dream, of course." Best thing is these dreams always leave me feeling good.

---

2. Yiddish word for noodles.

Night's drawing on & no fires tonight — we've been on the move since 2 P.M. after waiting in the rain from 11 to 2 for the truck to move — & riding in open truck in the rain some 25 miles, 2 hours by Miss. dirt roads. Now digging in & am 4½ feet down & a couple more to go —

Lenny

Dec 2

Dearest,

This morning I went to the Unemployment Insurance place again. Well, after being sent from Manhattan (where I registered) back to Brooklyn, I finally filled out an application. Tomorrow I have to go to Schermerhorn St. to register for employment, but that doesn't mean you have to take the job they send you on. After tomorrow, it will be simple, I hope, I'll have to report every Friday to the Pitkin Ave. office to sign that I'm not working. Although it may only come to $10–$12 per week, but of course even that for a period of 18 weeks would add up to about $200 which would be swell.

Diana

Dec 3, Friday

Dear Lenny,

I really had a pretty crummy day. This morning I went to register for a war job with the Manpower Commission in order to satisfy the unemployment insurance. I thought it was a formality but I found out differently. Their attitude is you can't get unemployment insurance unless they cannot place you in a job. Since they have plenty of jobs to send you out on at present, very few people get insurance, especially if they have a skill like I have. They immediately wanted to send me on 4 jobs — all milling machine jobs. I know that if I had gone out, I would have been hired so I tried to stall them. I said I couldn't go out on a job like that because of poor health. Well, I was bombarded with questions and I really felt terrible. I got a long lecture on not letting a skill like mine go to waste.

Finally I was able to get them to agree if I brought a doctor's note — they might release me from war work and let me register in the clerical section. On Monday — I shall bring them a note which I hope will make it possible to take a non-essential job. Since I want to be very choosy and careful before I take a job — I think I shall stop bothering with them and try to get a job on my own. I'm OK — I'm really so happy when I think that in 8 months the war could be won, what joy to have you home with me so we could share every little thing together.

Diana

12/4

Dearly Beloved,

Yesterday was rainy all day, a heavy drizzling rain. We were down to about 5 feet in the hard white soapstone-like clay, chipping slowing because digging was very hard, & we were starved; and no hope of chow 'til 10:30 when word came "non-tactical;" could light a fire, stop digging in & seek some comforts.

Finally chow came about 9, so all was right with the world again — especially since it also brought our first mail in 4 days.

Well, today began pleasantly by rain clearing & Sgt. Jameson saying I'd lead a class on maps; the class being about 60 members of the company. They are puzzled by the discussion & class participation method. It's tactical again now, & we are being ordered to dig in our foxholes again; the same ones we were ordered to fill up one hour ago. Do you notice how I write so much in detail? It shows how starved I am for conversation here.

Lenny

Dec 5, Sunday

Dear Lenny,

Your Sunday letter upset me quite a bit this morning. After thinking about it, I feel I must explain my present situation to you more adequately. Dearest — I am not goldbricking and I have tried to plan my time. You have no idea how much time it took me to settle some things as my insurance, the pictures, my tailor, the unemployment insurance, etc.

Dearest, some of the suggestions you make are good and I'll give them thought. I'd like to continue my evening community work.[3] I write many of the things we put out — letters to organizations, to clubs, to individuals. We are planning a rally for Dec. 7 — to launch us in Brooklyn. I promise to do all I can to keep you proud of me, only give me a little time to see where I am going.

I'm glad you were able to get to the library. The time you spent in the library seemed to do a great deal to help you straighten yourself out after the letter you wrote last Mon.

I know that the army pays the doctor and told me he has an authorization for one of his patients already but since the doctor doesn't get paid until after the baby is born, there is no rush. Next time I see Dr. Shaw

---

3. In addition to working full-time, Diana volunteered at a local community center raising money for the war effort, and teaching classes on current political events.

I shall discuss the question of money with him — my father will see to it that he doesn't charge me too much. I hope that what the army gives will cover most — if not all of it. I'm not exactly certain as to what Dr. to have. I know Dr. Shaw has a great deal of experience with obstetrics and he has taught at Long Island College Medical School, but he isn't an obstetrician. My mother suggested he be the pre-natal doctor and that for the delivery we have another doctor present with Dr. Shaw.

Diana

FINAL DIVISION TRAINING: PREPARING FOR COMBAT

12/6 for Sunday, Dec 12

Darling Wife,

This is the 3rd time I have begun this letter and both previous times I couldn't write; it seemed there was something I wanted to say very much — but I knew it would make you sad & so I didn't want to say it — but nothing else would come from my pen that was worth writing. And I still don't want to write that letter — it would be about a subject a soldier in a combat outfit doesn't like to think of, & usually keeps pushed back away out of consciousness. But every once in a while it comes up when I read detailed accounts of the Tarawa fighting, why I don't suppose a single American soldier at that island came back unhurt, and 2 of 5 will stay there forever.

Dina, my beloved, my wife, my mate, my mother-to-be, there are hard jobs to do and hard things to say. But one thing I've got to say right now — it's one of those things that you can't explain, but like I had to love you when I did, Dina, as a soldier I can't guarantee to keep one promise to you: much as I'd like to, much as I'd want to — I have a feeling I've promised you I'm coming back when it's all over. I've got to feel I've no such obligation — that my only obligation is to strangle the Nazi serpent, before all else.

Dearest, we know we'll have a better, more beautiful world, a world we've built with our own suffering as its cement & mortar, and I'm glad you will have our child with you and I hope oh so much to return to you in our joyous day of victory because the reconstruction of the world, on new foundations will need me too, & "me" means all our fighting generation, and precisely in order to come back safe I must feel free to devote all to the battle without any hesitations, without any reservations or looking backwards. Do you understand, Diana! I do hope I haven't made you terribly unhappy. Rest assured I'm training myself far beyond the army's demands to be a good soldier capable of surviving any number of battles — smile at me bravely as you did when we parted at Washington, and tell me you understand.

Lenny

Dec 6

Dear,

This morning I went to the War Manpower Commission with the note from Dr. Shaw. The note was inadequate. The decision was I would have to try an easier job at a milling machine. I saw that it was useless. She wouldn't let me register for clerical work. I shall try to go and get a job without the release.[4] I hope to have a job by the end of the week — I'll work as long as I feel OK.

Diana

PEARL HARBOR PLUS TWO YEARS

Dec 7

Dear Lenny,

Today is the second anniversary of Pearl Harbor. I have just come home from an excellent rally dedicated to the memory of Meyer Levin[5] by a young veteran of this war who made the dedication. He was wounded in action and he received the Purple Heart. Three hundred young people in Brooklyn gathered to decide how they could best help win the war.

Diana

Dec 8

Darling Husband,

Today is exactly a month since you left me standing and took the train back to Mississippi. I've spoken to a number of army wives and most of them feel that after the first few weeks they get used to the separation. I don't feel that way at all dearest, do you? Each passing day, makes it more

---

4. Release form was needed to allow Diana to be referred for clerical work.

5. Meyer Levin, a war hero and a bombardier pilot, was the first to successfully destroy a Japanese battleship. This mission occurred three days after Pearl Harbor. A year later, he died, sacrificing his own life to save members of his crew.

difficult and I feel it more keenly. When I think that yesterday was seven months you are a soldier, I get such an empty feeling inside of me. Today I went out to look for work. I went to two dep't stores and two other places but they weren't satisfactory for me.

> *Your,*
> *Diana*

Dec 9

Dearest Diana,

This morning I had 2 hours of classes on air photo maps & on traveling by map & compass, and while you know I enjoyed that, it was tough — a class of 60, in open air, with no blackboard, only 5 maps to work with, the greatest variation in development & ability & lots of other things going on as distractions. Still I held their attention.

I made up some good problems as we went along & I used the photomap as a puzzle, to have them figure out what certain objects were. A photomap is an air photo of an area about 10 miles square on which a house looks like this "::" and trees are 2 sets of 4 dots one on top of the other.

> *Lenny*

Dec 9, Part II

Dear,

So the A.M. was nice. Lt. Kellogg said he heard I'd taught a map class today & would I go right over and teach one to the drivers at the motor pool. So with 5 minutes to prepare a wholly different approach & considerably different content, there I was thinking very fast in front of some very critical truck drivers.

My father writes about a Times clipping you advised not enclosing. If it's the Times, & camouflaged with 2 or 3 sports and indifferent articles, by all means let it be sent. When we get only 12 to 36 hours between bivouacs, newspapers are often available only for one day and 4 or 5 day gaps are inevitable — back papers are not kept around here.

> *Lenny*

Dec 9

Dear Lenny,

I've been looking for a job all day with no success. It isn't going to be as easy as I thought to get a satisfactory job. Most of the jobs advertised in the newspapers either required real skill in bookkeeping or stenography which I don't have, or they are 5½ or 6 days at $18 a week.

Darling, I just can't understand your letters these last few weeks. You — were always the calmest — most even keeled person, and who kept me on an even keel — I don't know what has happened to you. Every one of your letters just doesn't sound like you at all — in some you sound like my cheerful and satisfied Lenny — eager to do the most important job facing anyone today — to be a soldier in the war for freedom — and in some you sound so dissatisfied, and as though you don't quite understand why you are in the army. I've been worried about you.

Don't misunderstand me, it's not that I don't want you to write truthfully how you are, rather, I want to understand why this change has taken place and see what we can do about it. You have given several reasons but I don't feel they are the key to the problem. The fact that you have no stripes — I don't think that is enough to make my Lenny blue. The fact that you don't know exactly what will happen to you — you are getting a great deal of training even though you may feel a lot of time is wasted — and you still feel you will be going across in 3 months which was the original projection.

The fact that I knew, you were happy in the infantry and in training to fight — that all your letters were full of understanding and pride, helped me to feel that way too. And now when I need your letters most, to help me through this period — you seem so uncertain and are letting snafus and other wrongs dull the horizon and dim your perspective.

Lee — I'd like very much for you to write a letter to my folks. It may not have been too difficult to tell my mother, but neither my mother nor father, are happy about the baby. That bothers me a great deal.

Diana

Dec 10

Dearest,

'Twas a rugged day: our regiment attacked northward near Deep Creek High School and ran into the enemy early. Col. Lewis was thrown in on the left flank to find another way to reach our destination. I, holding a wide front on each side of the road, pinned down by enemy fire & holding its own by virtue of 2 machine guns and a mortar section. Second battalion came into the front & quickly overran enemy lines, taking a number of prisoners. Since we were practically in Alabama by now, the return by truck was a pleasant ride.

Lenny

Dec 10, Friday

Dear Lenny,

    I couldn't go out to look for work this morning. I couldn't do much of anything since for the first time, I wasn't feeling well. I did feel nauseous most of the day. I just came home from your folks. I purposely went to your mother's house early to tell her the wonderful news. I can't help telling you I was a little disappointed — more than a little. You led me to expect she would be very happy. Well, she wasn't at all — she was quite indifferent. She asked me very little — just what month I was in. I tried hard to get her to talk about it — but she kept changing the subject. She asked me not to tell anyone for the present — I'm very sorry she feels that way. I didn't tell your father or anyone else.[6]

    Gosh, Lenny, you and I must continue to be happy and thrilled about the baby even if none of the other relatives seem to be. I just don't understand them — most families welcome a baby.

    Your mother told me they had mail from Jerusalem this week. Your grandmother is not well. It seems she is losing her eyesight and she needs extra care. I'm very sorry about this, but I guess at her age, it is to be expected. It seems that she will need more money than she has been receiving up to now. Your cousin Edith suggested that all the grandchildren give a certain amount monthly, a dollar or two. I agreed without any question.[7]

Diana

Dec 11

Dearest Diana,

    Free — and it feels so peculiar! I have a pass, but nothing to coax me into town tonight. Think I'll spend the evening in reading & physical exercise. We had another physical check up to see if everyone of us is fit for overseas duty.

    It seems you are procrastinating lately, or maybe it looks that way from a distance, to a soldier who's trained in instant reaction to a situation. As to

---

6. Diana later learns that Lenny's mom is superstitious and doesn't believe in talking about pregnancy until after the third month, to keep the evil eye away.

7. Lenny's grandmother, a widow, eloped with the local milk delivery man and moved to Palestine with her second husband. They were Orthodox Jews who believed that in Jerusalem they would be the first to greet the Messiah.

no rush in registering, don't be so sure: there is such a thing as first come, first served — Most babies currently born are servicemen's children & there are limited beds.

Dina, spare me the extra anxiety and do everything earlier, not later. I'm in a position where I may be overseas any week, & I do want to be sure everything is provided for.

Lenny

12/11

Diana,

Here is a sample of one phase of my work: the rough draft & a carbon copy of the sketch overlay of our battalion bivouac area. This is made to be laid on top of a photomap. The sketch shows the location of our 2nd battalion. We have become quite skilled in this phase of our work & it's a common joke that, "We can't be going out yet on bivouac etc., the intelligence hasn't made the overlays yet."

Lenny

Dec 11

Dearest Lenny,

Today has been a typical Saturday. I feel much better — practically back to my usual self. This afternoon I went to the tailor to get my coat. I think it looks very nice. I had to pay $45 on it and my father lent it to me.

The most important news of the Teheran Conference — the declaration guaranteeing the "independence, sovereignty and territorial integrity" of Iran and welcoming her participation in post-war collective security, symbolizes the actual regard of the Big Three for the smaller nations.

Diana

12/12, Sunday

Dearly Beloved,

I wish I could spend an hour or so with you this afternoon. It's cold here but bright and sunny — and I miss you.

I spent a couple of hours last night & again this morning on "Samson Agonistes," which was pleasant. Well, that leaves only "Paradise Regained" unfinished; and the rough draft of the last parts of the Theology.

The rumor mill has it 1) P.O.E. (port of embarkation) by Dec. 27. 2) Maneuvers begin in February, when we go to Tennessee, 3) A new furlough series begins now. But no one knows what we shall be doing tomorrow!

By the way does your father know about your pregnancy & what does he say? It will be good when everyone knows already.

Lenny

Dec 12, Sunday

Dearest Lenny,

Since I just read your Sunday letter, I am very anxious to answer you immediately. Lenny, darling, you write you do not want to make me sad — sad is really too shallow a word to us. I have thought of this often, painful as it is, because, knowing the type of outfit you are in, I can't help worrying because I understand so well that in our lives the battle comes first, then I must write to you now that I know you may not be able to keep your promise. I always felt you meant that you would learn to be a good soldier that you would master our weapons and because of this you would be able to fight well, do a good job and then be able to come back after victory was won. I always allowed for an accident because I recognized that what may happen at the battlefront is not always predictable or controllable.

My husband, I certainly wouldn't want any promise you made to me to ever be a drag or an obligation to you — that is not what our marriage is based on. But I do think the promise as I interpreted it above is something you can agree to, and still go forward into battle feeling that your first and main job is to crush the Nazi Fascists.

My darling — if it will not be possible for you to come back to us, very frankly, right now as I write it, I can't conceive of how I will live. But I do know that if this is demanded of me, I shall do my best to live. And most of all I shall try to bring up our baby as you would do, and as you would want it to be brought up. But I do hope so much that you will come back to us — we need you so very much, my darling, and I know that you want to also. However, as you say, for you to come back safely, you will have to devote all of yourself to the battle and that is as it should be. I am smiling at you as when we parted. Not a happy or a carefree smile, but a smile of understanding, love and admiration.

I hope this answer is what you wanted. If you are satisfied, then let us again put this subject away and hope that we'll never have to live through it.

Diana

12/13

Dear Diana,

I am sending you my watch. I hate to burden you but it's very impractical with our bivouacking to try to get it repaired here. With that over, I can tackle your two blue letters of Wed. & Thurs. It's a bad deal — I get you blue & that makes me blue — must get to break that up at once. First off, well, dearest, with the "Sunday Special" about combat duty, which I hope didn't upset you too much. I finished the process of overcoming the mass of depressing circumstances that were bothering me. All my letters since should have eased your mind. I am "calm" & "on even keel" — as ever.

Stripes — it's not a simple thing. That petty & insignificant Pfc. stripe is so slight — but lacking that one stripe is all that prevents me from making an application for Officer Candidate's School. Everything goes by rank in the army.

Diana, you must stop counting the months of my absence. I have forgotten the count, & don't want to remember. Just keep your eye on victory as the time of our reunion & forget any dates except the months 'til the coming of our baby. How wearing your job hunting is. I pray that it is settled by now.

Lenny

12/13 for Sunday, 12/19

Dearest,

'Tis new and strange, to be so fixed upon the calendar, as we have never been before, ticking off the moons; when the moon has been full eight times more we stop counting the months, and start counting the baby's birthdays. It's a great temptation to talk of our baby dear, but let that wait. And when this cruel war is over, and the bright sun of freedom shines again over the peoples who now give all to win it, we'll build ourselves a happy home again with baby's room, and the Persian styled rug & torchiere lamp — and hundreds of books and music.

Lenny

Dec 13

My Husband,

This morning I looked for work — still no luck — I'm getting a little discouraged, but I shall continue to look. I had a meeting to discuss my new community work. I'm also going to do union membership work

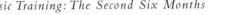

which will be a key job until Feb. 28 when the enrollment drive will end. You know we are aiming for 5,000 in Brooklyn.

Diana

12/14

Dearest Diana,

'Tis 8:02 I'm told (It's woeful to be without the watch) — We are waiting in our hut for orders — I presume the rain has put a crimp in the schedule.

Well, I've had my half day in the rain, & I guess it's enough for 3 or 4 months or so! We went by truck — to the close combat range; but got wet enough & cold enough, standing around in the rain for our turn, going thru the course & waiting for the return.

The range was interesting: the course consists of 6 concealed targets that are sprung on you from trees, shrubs, & the ground all of a sudden, while you are wading knee deep in swamp in fairly dense forest & thicket — just as a patrol might run suddenly into enemy while out on reconnaissance & have to shoot pronto the target in sight for 1 to 4 seconds — so you must be really fast on the draw & on the trigger.

I don't know what has gotten into our parents. Do they think it was an unplanned accident & we need sympathy, or are they going prudish on us?

Lenny

Dec 14

Darling,

This morning there was such a terrible storm. All day long, I worked and got my records in order. This union membership work is quite complicated. It involves a lot of record keeping and money, so I have to be careful and up to date. I've already gotten another person to help me.

Diana

Dec 14

Lenny Dear,

After looking for work unsuccessfully all morning, I spent the afternoon shopping (for stockings and things to put in a package to you) and I went to your mother's to get cookies she baked for you. In spite of the fact I have been busy and I'm doing many useful things, I'm bothered because I'm not working and I could use the money, but most important is that I feel it is wrong for me not to be working when there is such a labor shortage.

Love — I had three letters from you today. For the first time in so long — they were fairly cheerful. I guess when they give you a real job to do such as teaching map reading, then you feel you have accomplished a little.

Yours,

Diana

Dec 15, 11 P.M.

Dear Lenny,

I am sitting here shivering with cold. Today was another one of those extremely cold days. The steam stopped about an hour ago. It may seem funny to you after sleeping out of doors on the ground for so many nights to hear me say that it is cold indoors, but was so bad this morning I didn't go out to look for work. About 2:30 P.M. I went to the office and worked.[8]

Sweetheart, darling, I actually have no doubts now. I shall apply for maternity care as soon as I have seen Dr. Shaw and he tells me it's definite. I understand you want to have everything settled before you go into combat, but we just can't rush things. You can trust me.

Diana

Dec 16

Dear Dinika,

A weary, drooping sad sack of a husband is writing you. The past 24 hours workout took more out of us than some 3 or 4 days of previous bivouacs. Not the work itself — strenuous as it was — it was a repetition & refinement of the division attack with live ammunition of two weeks ago, but only 2nd Battalion took part, & only used blanks because there was an enemy detail.

We moved into bivouac & that wind kept blowing and it began to get colder & colder. We got to work on the bivouac overlay & determined our location & assembled the company overlays & discovered we couldn't draw in that wind which numbed fingers & froze nose & toes. Dark fell, that cruel wind kept cutting & cutting. Supper came finally at 8, a little warmth poured into us — and fumbling around in total blackout, we locate our individual blanket rolls. Well, we were to sleep to 2 A.M., but there was mighty little sleeping. That needling, knifing wind didn't stop for a second. So I gave up at 12:30 & got up & walked up & down to keep some life in my toes. At 2 A.M. we breakfasted, still in blackout. To last us 'til our next meal 18 hours later — Right after breakfast, we hiked out

---

8. At the neighborhood community center where Diana volunteers for the war effort.

because hiking makes us warm again — hiked from 4 to 7, when we went into the attack, which lasted 'til afternoon.

The duty assigned to me was simple, though rugged, going with the forward lines. The battalion commander sent us through woods in a shallow valley. I knew we'd find water there: my scout experience told me that; well, the 8-foot stretches we crossed on the trembling vines & slippery fallen tree trunks. I waded through to save time. To my surprise the ice filled waters were warmer, and instead of my feet getting colder, they were warmer where they got soaked (up to the knee). I realized the air temperature must be much below 32 degrees, which was the presumable water temperature — and so the water was warm to the touch!

About 11 A.M. I got another surprise. As a disciplined soldier I have learned to conserve water. So my canteen, filled before I left yesterday, remained untouched all thru the hikes & last night. When I ate my dry cheese sandwich, I turned to take my first sips of water & found my canteen was frozen solid. Well, the official report said it was 14 degrees this morning & probably colder in the night.

Will I appreciate a knitted helmet? Boy, I'd have paid well for one last night! Send it on!!!!

Lenny

Dec 16

Dearest,

I went to see the placement director of Local 16 regarding a job. I had the letter of introduction and I told her the truth that I had had a war job and that I was pregnant. She went to a lot of trouble and finally placed me in a temporary job for 1 week doing general office work and typing. I start tomorrow — hours are 9–5 and I'll get about $28. I felt it was worth taking it because I want to see if I can work.

Dearest, I had your Sun. letter today. I'm glad you could do some work on Samson Agonistes — I'd love to see it.

I feel well and "Junior" is OK. Do you realize at the end of the month, I will be entering the 3rd month? Gosh.

Diana

Dec 17

Darling,

Waiting for mail call. Right now everything in the world is overshadowed by the wretched fact that tomorrow our one day off, since Sunday, we return to bivouac.

With regard to Mrs. Zimmerman's knitting circle, I don't like to ask too much — but if it is within their scope there are a couple of other deserving soldiers here who are also freezing on bivouac — who are good guys too — so if 3 more helmets and 2 sweaters could be made it would be nice.

'Tis Friday night — one's recollection and feeling for such evenings becomes dulled in the army & it's good that it does, because one would get homesick & unfit for duty if one dwelled on it. I guess you're at my folks for a pleasant evening there.

Lenny

THE FLU SCARE

Dec 17, Friday

Dear Lenny,

Well, I'm a working girl again. The new job was pretty good today. I did some mimeographing, collating, typing etc.

On my parents' attitude — I try hard not to let it bother me, but living with them I feel it so keenly. Lucy has the flu. There is a mild flu epidemic in NY and throughout the country — nothing too serious. Well, my mother goes around as though the world has come to an end. My mother can be so unnecessarily dramatic.

As far as your mother is concerned — in the two weeks I have seen her since telling her and she warned me not to tell anyone else — she only asked me how I felt — nothing else. I had hoped she would tell the rest of the family, but she hasn't because no one commented tonight. I don't understand her attitude at all, and why it has to be a secret.

Diana

Dec 18

Darling Wife,

For your answer to my "Sunday" letter, a million thanks — the thanks you feel in a squeeze of the hand, the glance of an eye. With your love and understanding, I am always safe from harm.

A rugged day — On that so called "trash detail." I was one of a crew of 5 that hoisted 20 tons of soft coal ashes onto a 2½ ton truck & unloaded it at the dump — lifting not the garbage or ash cans you see in New York but huge gasoline drums, so heavy that all 5 of us were needed to heave them up. We were all sore at losing our one free day, & at getting our uniforms not merely filthy but seriously damaged.

News: I am ordered to take a week's course in first aid. The theory is I will be an instructor in first aid for the battalion thereafter. While I am chosen no doubt because of my map classes, it cuts me off from intelligence section for a week.

By the way, Frank (as a native born of Germany) has done some translating for Nazi prisoners at the hospital — & reports they are as anti Semitic and as vicious as anything you have heard and assert Germany will win the war.

Lenny

Dec 19, Sunday

Hello,

I had your Sun. letter this morning and it was swell — the nicest one I've had in a long time. Sun. morning is our time together and when you are home again with me, it will even be more so, because with you working all week, this will be the morning that you will spend with me and the baby — eat breakfast together and then we'll take the baby out to the park and walk, and hold hands, and be together.

Diana

Dec 20

Dearest Diana,

Today we scorched the earth of some more square miles of Mississippi, as we attacked & stormed Everett Ridge: green & brown autumn fields turned charred black & gray ash, and rivulets of flames broadened to roaring pools where rifle, machine gun & artillery barrages set the dry pine needles & old stumps on fire. And of course, I am tired, very tired; and forgetful — already I observe in myself & others the forgetfulness of combat, one reason you know, for veteran's silence on combat experience.

I can remember a halt sometime yesterday afternoon in which I dug a prone shelter, & had to fill it up even as I was putting the finishing touches on it, for we were moving again. Then, as night fell, we were setting up a defensive position digging observation post fox holes. They just forgot about us at support, & we blundered our way back just in time to get some soupy stew. Then back again — to take turns at watching & handling the phone, in shivering cold.

We watch the far off bonfires of a non-tactical bivouac of some other outfit, miles away — no bonfires for us! The defense phase over, we move into attack, repeating the division firing exercise. Then the long & tiresome road home & I'm almost too tired to eat supper.

Lenny

Sun. Dec 20 for Sun. Dec 27

Dearest Darling,

Midst the dice gaming and the profanity, & short tempers of tired men, the Christmas spirit is rising. Carols are hummed, sung & butchered; cards are sent & received; the mail clerk bends double under the weight of packages and gifts, & candies & cakes are tendered on every hand. Central in the Christmas atmosphere of '43, to me, is the image of the mother and child. Yes, my dove, furloughs are coming again, 7 day furloughs. Perhaps as early as February, perhaps as late as April — But let's not plan too much for it — snafus are even more likely at this stage.

Lenny

12/21

Dear,

The attitude of our mothers had me stymied a bit & racking my brains as to what to do.

Today was a halfway interesting day on explosives. The first hour was the best — demonstration of explosions of dynamite, nitro-starch Bangalore torpedoes, various types of fuses & how to handle all of these for demolition purposed. Later sessions on mines, booby traps, gapping a way thru a mine field & sketching the area were mildly interesting. We seem to be moving along real training lines this week & that is swell.

Lenny

Dec 21

Dearest,

I'm not feeling very well. I have a cold that has given me a lot of trouble today and I'm very anxious to get into bed now.

I'll try to get the knitted helmet sent as soon as I can. Also the gloves, but the helmet comes first because as you say, you'll get new gloves from the army. I'll see what I can do about some extras for the others, but I can't make any promises.

Diana

REAL LIVE GRENADES

Dec 22

Dear Diana,

This morning we threw real grenades, 20 ounces of concentrated death — pull the pin & 5 seconds later its deadly shrapnel & exploding

TNT, & you better have ducked! And this afternoon we stormed a pillbox — the flamethrowers were really something; & I found it quite to my taste to go running through a cut blasted in the barbed wire, right through burning grass (3-foot-high flames), diving into shell holes to get a crack in with my M-1.

That all sounds like a swell day — Actually it should have been. Yet, it left me very disgusted. What was wrong was officer stupidity. Well, we are ordered to march & we marched — and marched. We ended by marching 10 miles, still ignorant of why & wherefore; and since we weren't expecting a hike, we were all sweating in our woolen underwear & none had brought our canteens.

Finally, we arrived at the grenade court but still didn't dream we'd get the real grenades. Then when they were passed out we got only one a piece — & then 1/3 didn't get any at all!!

Frankly, I felt a nervous sensation in my stomach as I un-wrapped the container & took the cast-iron grenade out, & pulled the safety pin — 5 seconds is a mighty slim safety margin, if it should slip or fall & was mightily relieved when it flew from my hand to a safe distance and exploded. But once you've thrown it, you're an old hand at it.

I deliberately ran thru the fire, tho' I could have avoided it; but I wanted to see if I could go thru it under real battle conditions; & found I could run 25 yards with no harm at all — of course I didn't stand in the fire but ran through it & didn't even feel it.

Lenny

P.S. Enclosed is the safety ring & pin from the grenade I threw today. Aside from the curiosity value it might be used as a novelty buckle on a belt: not very pretty but very meaningful.

12/23

Dear,

The afternoon spent 4 hours on the bazooka [a rocket-propelled antitank weapon that can be carried by a single person]. They had a movie showing how it works & how it's used & then we went out in the rain to see it fired. It's amazing — a stove pipe fitted with an electric flashlight is all it is — but it sets off a rocket loaded with explosives & a steel cone which bores thru heavy tank armor plate & smashes concrete blocks.

Lenny

12/24

Dear Diana,

Today I added another weapon to my repertory — the U.S. caliber 30 M. As a gun it isn't worth s—t, as the soldiers would say: too damn erratic.

Let me tell you not to make you blue, but to show you again that I am overriding all the depressing influences: 1) It was a nasty, wet, rainy, cold day; we fired in our clumsy raincoats, full of mud after the prone position. 2) Because of the weather officers and men alike had only one idea, to scram & so it was all rushed thru perfunctorily, with only "let's get this god damn nuisance over with spirit."

Lenny

CHRISTMAS 1943

Christmas night, 12/25

Darling Diana,

It is the sight of other women, alone or with their men that makes me feel ever so much the warmth of your love. This is especially true on a day like today, when a lot of men had their wives visiting.

Well, today we Jewish guys did KP (5 of us, me included), and also CQ. 7 latrines & officers mess. Finished about 7, & left with a month's supply of hard candy. I could have taken more only your package came & also a cookie package from Edith. Then I went to the Field House, in a driving rain, very eager to hear the Kryl Symphony Orchestra. You know how music starved we are without even radios available to us. But what is a day at Shelby without a snafu? There was no concert — no explanation.

Gee think — next Xmas we will be a family!

Lenny

12/26

Dear Dina,

I got away from camp to the Jewish Welfare Board Hanukah program. Today was my first day at the First Aid School & snafu reigned supreme as usual. Called for 11 it began at 2; the instructor, a last-minute substitute, drove all night to get here; etc. etc. No provision is made for food for us, while the companies are out on bivouac.

Roosevelt spoke on the 24th — here it's the 26th & not yet have I been able to get a copy of his speech!

My love, you should be rounding out your second month now & getting ready for definite word by your standards. I am eager to hear what you do about a job now: I hope so much you don't have the pain of protracted job hunting. Dove, I have already saved up $30.00, so that I have enough to pay my furlough ticket home, & with Jan. & Feb. pay I'll have enough for a pleasant vacation for us too when I get my furlough papers!

Lenny

Dec 27

Darling,

The first aid textbook assignment is 108 pp., for one night, which is rather a pace to my taste; and so I must turn to the book while there are yet a few minutes before the instructor opens. This afternoon was varied by a little practical work in bandaging and pressure point control of bleeding. Finished at 5, by the time I got over to the mess hall having shaved, showered & changed, the meager rations were much reduced — so grateful for the two packages from Edith & you!

Class is assembling as the first glimmer of dawn tints the heavens a dreamy blue in place of the dull beclouded black of all last night. Happily for our bivouacs, it did not rain, it was only cold.

I finally got hold of Roosevelt's Xmas speech. You'd think with all that it says of the effort to broadcast it to our overseas men, the officers at Shelby might have let us listen in — but oh no. Probably 98% do not even know there was such a speech, let alone the principles of United Nations unity etc. it developed.

Please write me about the new Soviet anthem — the text if it is available and, also a full account of the railroad and steel situations, please. On the job — well, if you can knock out $40 a week on a light job I can't object!!! No, dear, you don't have to send me any money. As a matter of fact, if you hadn't gotten this job I'd have sent you some because I know you aren't able to manage on $50.00 a month.

Latest rumor which seems well founded — a 3 week's continuous bivouac beginning Jan 28 — that looks like the wind up of our 9 month training schedule. After that who knows???

Lenny

P.S. I've written a letter to your parents, in Yiddish. Frankly, it has me worried lest they misunderstand & be offended. I'm enclosing a translation, so you can know what it says, just in case it produces the wrong result.

Dear Parents;

For the New Year I can wish you only one thing that both your wandering sons-in-law should be able to move your "boarders" out!

Diana has written me that the news of her pregnancy has caused you some concern. This is understandable and we did expect such feelings, a little, but we also expected some satisfaction and pleasure. Believe us, we did not take this step or make this decision in a light moment without responsibility, but after we had thought it over and talked it over for a long time. And therefore I want to give you the reasons for which I think that you should be greeting Dina with joy and happiness — emotions which she is in need of, to have the spirit and courage to carry through the coming months. We have well understood what sort of burdens will fall on Dina, particularly at a time when her husband is far away & will be farther. We have well understood the financial burden.

Despite that, we felt that we who for so many years have been engaged in the struggle to rescue the world from Hitler barbarism, we who have sacrificed so much for this struggle, have also a right to the natural good things & joys which every person has a right to. When we came to this decision, we understood that the full responsibility was our own, and we never had any thought that there should fall on you either the financial burden or the responsibility of a home for our "family." From you, beloved parents, I expect this one thing that same love which you have always shown to our Dina and me. (And, no doubt, Dina may come sometimes for a mother's advice!) I want to hope that the New Year 1944 will therefore be crowned for you not only with Hitler's downfall but also with the bright smile of your first grandchild.

Lenny

Dec 29

Dearest,

It's funny writing that you hope I have a easy time job hunting. Matter of fact, I got a job today by telephone through a friend without even leaving the house. Of course the salary is nominal, 50 cents per hour, but I think it might be interesting for a few days. I'm taking the place of a sick secretary.

Diana

Dec 31

Dearest,

They're calling the roll of the written exam marks in Red Cross School. Your husband batted 100 in written, but there are several practical

& oral tests to follow. If all goes well, then your Lenny will feel justified in having gone & played hooky a little last night. Your see, the Red Cross business is a lot of learning by rote, "what the book says." I detest learning by rote, the textbook is elementary; it's far too dogmatic. It doesn't make a lot of things clear — It's really ambiguous in spots; so try as I might I couldn't get myself to study last night, neither the text, nor the instructor's guide, nor my notes. I did read carefully an article in the January "Air Force" magazine on artificial respiration under combat conditions.

Later — White chauvinism shows itself in devious ways. The instructor & book stress "red–white–blue" kinds of unconsciousness, wholly ignoring the fact that these symptoms apply only to "white" complexions & reflecting the"my-back-is-turned-where-my-colored-brother-is-involved" situation. When someone in the class asked what to do in case of a Negro, where complexion wouldn't help to determine the cause of unconsciousness, it was as a chauvinist gag.

3:45

School's finished. I've now passed as a qualified instructor. Some 10 were flunked. They'll be given some make up chance.

Dearest, as 1943 faces away into past history, one beautiful memory is imprinted upon it, one I shall never forget, and as I say "au revoir" to you now for the last time this year I kiss the smiling face that bade me "au revoir" last November.

Lenny

Dec 31

My Darling,

And so it is New Year's. Everyone is expecting so much from this year of 1944. We have been promised victory in Europe. Certainly we can say that 1944 will be a year of great decisions. And my darling, for you and me, 1944 will be an important year — the year that we become a family.

Diana

1944 BEGINS

Jan 1, 1944

To my Darling Wife,

A Happy, fighting, victorious New Year! I read the new manual on handling prisoners of war (part of our intelligence work), much enriched by our 1942–3 experiences, & also the Infantry School (Ft. Benning) booklet on fighting at Salerno & Guadalcanal; the former was particularly good & critical. Midnight brought the explosion of many firecrackers apparently saved from combat problems & occasionally some firearms too.

And how are you, my lady? What's progress? Will there be a very different "Dininka" when I see you next (I hope soon!)?

Lenny

Jan 1

Dearest Lenny,

You know, beloved, gosh are we lucky. Myra also tried to become pregnant while in Memphis and after all that time, she isn't. She has gone to the Dr. and he said everything is OK with her. She still wants to be pregnant, and the only way it can happen is, if she goes to Florida where Burt is, and stays with him until she does.

Diana

Sunday for Jan 2, 1944

Dearest:

A Happy New Year! As 1944 dawns with the promise of victory in Europe & progress towards victory in Asia, I send you my wish that it be an easy year for you, with easy fruition when the time comes. Probably it is too much to hope for that next New Years all will be settled & I can be home with you — at least let it be the last New Year of separation for us and for millions of young couples. Still there's a grand prospect ahead — you'll be a blooming mama, with a "?" on your knee — and in Europe 'twill be curtains for the Nazis: everything we've been fighting for all these years together coming true.

Lenny

Jan 2, in an envelope marked for Sun., 1/9

Darling,

The average married guy like me has his wife's picture prominent on the shelf, writes home daily, and is half the time ready to go over the hill to see her. Do I miss you? Hell, yes!!! It's only that the beauty of our love is that it isn't a contingent love, it doesn't depend on this, that, or the other, but is full in itself; and so knowing why we must do our respective duties miles & miles apart, we can go on loving across the states, talking to each other, sharing our thought and keeping so close that "missing one another" isn't the one cloud that crowds all the sunshine out of the sky.

Although all the time I'm wishing so much that I could be beside you in your present pre-motherhood stress — and although we know that no river rushes more surely nor more eagerly down to the sea than you and I will rush to each other the first moment that duty grants leave. Sweetheart, I love you —

Lenny

Jan 2

Dearest,

It's strange but these days I find I can have a very nice time by taking it easy for a whole day, whereas previously, I didn't like to stay at home ever. It must be my new condition and perhaps old age is creeping up on me too.

On the steel and RR situation,[9] by now both these crises are settled for the time being because of Roosevelt's swift action which must be highly applauded.

There is a very serious outbreak of anti-Semitism throughout New York — especially in Washington Heights. And a New York Supreme Court Justice and court reformer David Peck outraged every anti Nazi American by upholding the legality of Hitler's anti Jewish laws. Two German refugees, whose insurance policies were confiscated by the German Nazi gov't because they were Jewish, brought the suit.

The story of the heroic resistance of the Jews in the Warsaw Ghetto on Passover, April 19, 1943, is a very wonderful one. It is a truly heroic story of resistance, and although they were finally subdued, they managed to resist for 42 days and there was a much heavier death rate of Nazis than there were Jews. There was also a report from London that a Jewish guerilla army of 3,000 fighting under the blue and white Jewish flag and the Polish flag have been harassing Nazi forces in the Lublin sector of Poland for months. There have been two wonderful victories on the Soviet front. Zhitomir has been recaptured and in the last 6 days, 22 Nazi divisions have been routed and over 1,000 towns retaken.

Your,
Diana

1/3

Dearest Diana,

I am sending you a photo souvenir booklet of Shelby. You will recognize it is life as seen by the public relations office, not as seen by the

---

9. Labor union strikes.

suffering soldiers. It may — no doubt — interest your folks & my folks. Last night I picked up an easy dollar. Since it was raining & I didn't care to go anywhere but only to write you & do some reading, it was a bit of a problem because the hut was full of men — confined men & visitors playing pinochle, dice etc — noisy. So when the Sgt, a pleasant chap, came in & offered a buck for someone to sit in the orderly room for him & sleep there in his stead so he could pack for furlough, I accepted — it's quiet and was a favor.

Dina — I don't like this "tired" business at all. Let me know what Dr. Shaw says. Maybe you shouldn't try to work at all?? No chances are worth taking. Nothing you could earn would be worth it.

Lenny

Jan 3

Dearest,

I went to see Dr. Shaw today. My father saw him on Sat. and although he didn't arrange any specific amount with him, my father said he won't charge too much. I'd rather know the specific amount. I know it will be very reasonable.

More important though is what Dr. Shaw told me today. He said everything was fine. I told him about how tired I feel and he said it was nothing to be concerned about because many women have that reaction for the first few months. He said I could continue to work for a while yet. Oh, yes, he gave a note to the War Manpower Commission that I'm in the 3rd month of gestation.

Diana

1/4

Dear Diana,

Last night did some reading in the history of the rifle. Saw the headlines about Soviet advance on the Polish frontier. Good deal! When the hell do we get moving?

There's been so much talk among the men of "no jobs after the war" — so I tried to figure out some general principles by way of showing a practical solution within the framework of present economic & social facts, sort of thinking thru the economic post war transition; nothing too deep & nothing original; seeking a simple picture which GI's could appreciate.

Tomorrow's bivouac — strange how it's dreaded by everyone! That infectious dread even touches me; after 10 days in a sheltered hut it isn't easy to face the frosts & rains again. A few nights ago someone repeated the common line, "Oh the 69th is all f—d up, it will never go over as a division, we're not fit for combat etc. so I "flared" up tactfully & controlled and let loose on the subject of how much training do we need to be a good soldier — and is the bivouacking training or not — and what division is better than ours after so much time — and isn't it all really a rationalization by guys who are a little afraid to face combat, who are letting themselves forget what peril America & their families are in — and wouldn't the attitude towards hard duties change the minute they face the cold steel or hot lead? Well, the effect was instantaneous & electric — a complete reversal of sentiment in that small group & we all felt lots better.

Lenny

1/5

Dearest,

Today we go out again. Meanwhile — just sitting around waiting for orders. There was a beautiful dawn — Mississippi's glowing salmon gold in waves over the clouds — and then the lingerie blue breaking through — and then the clouds came back & all is overcast again.

Again no mail — I miss mail so much when 2–3 days go by without it — I will dread weeks sans mail. Love — be well, won't you please???

Lenny

1/6

Dear,

Second day out on this problem & so far nothing has happened. We rode out some 45 miles from camp yesterday by a roundabout route. We were amazed, first, to have supper at twilight instead of waiting for 9 or 10 P.M., when total darkness takes all the joy out of eating, enjoined by tactical conditions (everyone 10 yards apart, so the 3 washing cans stretch out 100 yards in blackout). Although we couldn't be sure since no orders came at all 'til it was all over, we were allowed to sleep all night.

This morning after breakfast we were given the customary two so-called sandwiches (dry white bread, a thin shaving of bologna on one, a dab of apple butter on the other) & loaded on trucks, & rode another score or so of miles, & we don't know where we are now or what the situation is.

Lenny

Jan 6

Dearest Husband,

Yesterday was not such a good day for me. It was one of my nauseous mornings. I felt pretty rotten until about noon but then it cleared up and I was O.K again. It's nothing to worry about except it is so annoying and incapacitates me. I awoke this morning feeling much better then yesterday and quite rested.

My darling, now, more than ever before I want you by my side. I don't mean that I would want you not to be in the army, but I mean that I need you near me. And so if we do have a few days together before you leave America to go and do a real job — I just would like to be with you and lie in your arms and talk to you about many things.

Diana

1/7

Dear Diana,

We were interested to see how we've learned to take cover, to advance under fire, to attack without fear of the enemy — even though we knew the enemy's fire was blanks like our own, it was a very real battle to us.

Glad you quit your job & for heaven's sake, don't take any but a sedentary one! And for my part, don't take any job at all. Nothing you might earn could make up for any injury to yourself, your health or the prospective kid.

Lenny

Jan 7, Friday

Dear Lenny,

The letter that you wrote Rose about a wonderful secret — well, she and Eddie have been driving your mother crazy all week with questions. She hasn't told them yet so when I came in, they started to bombard me.

Your father walked me home tonight and he told me that the reason your mother hasn't told them is that there is an old Jewish superstition not to say anything until it is noticeable. Well, now I know your father knows definitely.

I looked in a book — a physiology book — that has a picture of an 8 week old fetus — it is very tiny but it has definite shape — a head and a body, etc. I guess our baby really looks like something now.

I have some news for you. I have stopped smoking. It's about a month now. I don't even miss it. First I save money and then it's also good for my health.

Diana

Jan 8,

Dearest,

This is one of those non com making days and they always have a very depressing effect on me. I know that both Sgt. Johnson & Lt. Hamilton (who passed thru last week) have renewed their nomination of a Pfc. for me. About 10 days ago, there's been no action. Honestly, if I didn't have the self discipline & understanding of a consistent Democrat, it would be enough to drive me "over the hill" & I'm not exaggerating. Even if I ever do get the one stripe now it will be a miserable anticlimax.

We were given to understand that from Jan 28 to Feb 20, or so, we shall be on bivouac, & thereafter we'll probably move. You know of course that we are about to launch major offensives in Europe & Asia, & there'll be millions of troops moved all over the map.

Lenny

Jan 8

Darling,

The outline you sent me of post-war economics really set me thinking. We always said that the military policy will be a correct one, and then we can hope for a correct post-war policy. I think that Teheran makes all this possible. My one criticism, and you may have avoided it intentionally in the group you were talking to, is no mention of the Negro problem — both as a source of labor and as a source of buying power. We can only hope to achieve real national unity when the Negroes will be included as real equals.

Diana

1/9, written on U.S.O. paper

Dear Diana,

The waste of time here is appalling. So far today I've been on duty since 5 A.M., or 9 hours, & have done exactly nothing.

This is Sunday & everybody is off duty except intelligence & some communications. As a "Sunday privilege" they let us have a fire; & the sun has come out again & the blessed blue sky, so it's not unpleasant.

Enclosed is a message, the official kind used in maneuvers & combat if available. They're triplicate — one for the message center & one for the writer & come-in-handy books with carbon all set up. It says, "From a pine grove near blue Goose Creek beneath blue skies in a quiet nook, where the sunlight streams in, like sunlight seen below a lake surface. I send you my love and my presence close to you." Rose, bless her, has sent me another cigar box of cookies, just as I was finishing Mom's, so that plus the chocolate & candy you sent me, plus some hard candy left from Xmas so I'll be set pretty fair for the next 3 days.

Lenny

Jan 9

Dear Lenny,

The news of the past week:

    1. The film critics awarded "Watch on the Rhine" as the best movie of 1943. It is interesting that they chose this type of a movie.

    2. More Anti-Semitic outbursts throughout the city and La Guardia ordered an investigation.

    3. The Polish gov't in exile is making a big fuss about the Red Army's so-called advance into Poland.

    4. The anonymous statement regarding the effect of strikes attributed to Gen. Marshall has been seized by all the anti-labor elements to be used as a weapon against the Pres. From all reports of the press interview, Gen Marshall did not attack labor but pointed to the results of the strike threats. What he said is true — that it does delay victory.

Diana

1/10, USO paper

Dear Diana,

Leaving for bivouac in a few minutes — so there's only time to say I love you & pray you and "Junior" are well.

It's cold — frost on the ground & my toes are icy even before leaving camp!

Lenny

1/10, USO paper, Somewhere in South Mississippi

Darling,

We've ridden some 20 miles or more this morning on the open antitank truck, & are well frozen; although the sun's bright overhead. We've stopped at this point a few thousand yards back from where we are going to make a defensive stand against an enemy regiment; being tactical, no fires are allowed, so, as is usual when the temperature drops below 32 (below 20 is more accurate today), the infantryman loses his usual aversion to digging & instead of skimping, digs him a deeper & more elaborate prone shelter (slit trench) — digging warms one up fast. A very fine afternoon,

amazing! Sgt. Johnson, Ben & I went out on route reconnaissance by jeep.
It was a very fine exercise in photomap reading, really good, & we forgot about the cold, as we plotted positions, filled in ridges & valleys (not
shown in a photomap, which like all photos doesn't show relief) and other
tactical details.

Lenny

Jan 10

Dearest,

I'm so very sorry that my mail to you is so irregular — I know how you
feel because last week I didn't have any mail from Thurs. to Mon. Please
know that I am well and writing. Beloved, I think of you everyday all day
long — my love should reach you even when mail is a little delayed.

Lenny

1/11, written on U.S.O. paper

Dear Diana,

The battalion convoy lining up on 52nd — riflemen loading on trucks,
rifles poised, light combat packs on overcoats, steel helmets strapped on;
jeeps for communication men, ton and a half with their antitank guns
trailing, antiaircraft 50 cal. Guns mounted on various vehicles; bustle.
On the road — long convoy, vehicles 80 yards apart, serpentine, stretching from horizon to horizon — F company marching back at dawn, G
Company having moved up to the front lines to relieve them: we envy G
Co, they have C rations (canned), better than our fresh meals; F Co up all
night in the outposts shifting wearily back.

I received a Yiddish letter from your father in reply to me. It is rather
gingerly written, and seeks to assure me they will do everything to make
you comfortable, & that any conception that you may have to the contrary
is unfounded.

On your smoking: again for heaven's sake, don't try to save money
that way. I have no objection to your not smoking, just as I never had any
objection to your cigarettes, & wouldn't hear of your stopping on account
of my non smoking. Don't abstain from smoking if you really crave a cigarette, unless you really know it's injurious to you or the baby.

Dove, sometimes I think back at the cold nights when we left our cozy
warm home & went out to a meeting or activity — how hard that was.
Dina, "taint nothing compared to how hard 'tis for a soldier to crawl out
of his blanket roll out in the swamps to go our on night patrol" — and
we are all but indifferent to that now. As we are to all discomforts: but

love-words do not come easily under these circumstances. Yet, I do love you, my sweetheart!!! Ever so much!!!

Lenny

Jan 11

Dearest,

Last night was really something very special — I'm so sorry that we couldn't have been there together. It was a typical political rally of its type — crowded, enthusiastic, and wonderful. Teheran has made possible a new type of post-war world.

Every time you write me a long account of a bivouac or other training — I am filled with admiration for you, dearest. All the difficulties you endure — I feel that especially now because every little thing makes me feel so tired. I find I cannot look for work and it interferes with so much that I want to do.

Diana

Jan 12

Lenny,

Your mother was really funny tonight. She sort of apologized for having shown very little excitement about the baby — saying that was the tradition.

Diana

1/14

Dearest,

Tonight I am on guard, all "oisgeputzt"[10] — in my new leggings, shiny shoes & best uniform, all of which will be covered by mud & soaked by rain, but such is the army. Guard is, as I've often said, soldier's work & I don't kick at it, even if I'd rather not have rain when post walking.

Last night I tore off 2 pages from the letter I wrote you because it was too blue sounding — but really I am at my wit's end as regards a personal perspective in the army. It's clear that if I stay here I'll never accomplish anything. As I have said before, only my deep self-discipline & understanding, the fact that I am here voluntarily & not because of the draft, only that keeps me from going AWOL. The promise of combat experience remains as a personal perspective, a slight hope that this wasted time will yet be redeemed.

Lenny

---

10. Yiddish transliteration for "all dressed up."

1/15 69th Infantry Division Camp Shelby, Mississippi paper

Dear Diana,

Lt. Kellogg notified, he said, that he was officially now S-2 Sergeant not just acting and he wanted to talk over some of the deficiencies. Gradually the complaints came forth — the abuse of our personnel, using us as errand boys & floor moppers instead of trained men, depriving us of our compasses & field glasses which are given as decorations to officers & noncoms who don't even know their use, giving us a double burden of detail, battalion plus company, etc. I brought up my oft denied promotion as a grievance of the whole group, & Sgt. Johnson seconded it with bitter emphasis, asking where else is a private used to teach classes & still remains a private.

My delayed promotion is a scandal in the company so Sgt. Johnson went to ask about my stripe & he reported to me that he was told that it was assured but that it was not yet formally typed up.

Lenny

Jan 15

Dearest,

I think to myself what is Lenny doing this Saturday afternoon? Perhaps he is out on bivouac working hard on a problem or is he perhaps relaxing after a hard week's work. I hope the second is true and that you have some time off. There was no mail from you today — Lee — it will be so hard to take weeks without mail. I feel so empty when it skips just one or two days.

Diana

PRIVATE FIRST CLASS AT LAST

1/16 Sun

Dear Diana,

It was almost perfect weather to start sewing on the chevrons in the sun glow.[11] — A pleasant chore, whose tedium was compensated by the release of tension & humiliation that has dogged my steps for over 5 months. Now I am still far behind my ex-red patch colleagues who sport 3 stripes & soon will have an arc below, but at least have some prospect of advancing & approaching them.[12]

---

11. Chevron usually refers to an emblem, but in this case it is his first stripe.

12. Lenny finally gets his Pfc. stripe.

I went to the library & worked a couple of hours on Milton — the character of Satan, a subsection to Paradise Lost. It's beginning to take shape but will take some more labor.

Lenny

1/16 for 1/23 Anniversary Day

My Darling,

In the warm April sunshine today my heart warmed also to the memory of May 28, 1938, when we rode home together thrilled in the springtime of our love by our discovery of each other. We were partners in action that day, in grim yet youthful action, hoping to save our Spanish boyfriends & girlfriends & check the advance of the monster which, we knew, if unchecked, would separate many of our American boy & girl sweethearts.[13]

And now that I have at last broken the ice and come through with my first stripe (little as it is!) I am oh so happy because I know you will be happy; and I am happy to be your baby's father sharing with you in partnership your creative work, your woman's work, as I advance towards greater achievement in my man's work of protecting my woman and my woman's babe.

Far away as I am from you I never raise my rifle but that I feel as if I am putting one sheltering arm around you while I beat off the enemy terrors with the other.

Lenny

1/16, Mon

Dearest,

Sweet, thanks & thanks — but hold up on further refreshments as I'm a little overstocked right now! As usual the good things come in floods & even the voracious denizens of hut 2 have their limit!

On furlough, I won't hear of your traveling out here, lugging baggage in the crowded trains, all strained. And besides I'm almost never in camp, almost always out in the woods 30 to 40 miles away. If there's no delay, my turn should come soon. I should get my chance in March. It's not at all far off. You made me smile in today's letter — do you inspect your belly every night to see "if it shows"?

Sweet, confidential — not even to be breathed to my folks or to your folks I decided today to ask for an application to Officers Candidate

---

13. Lenny refers to the Spanish Civil War.

School (OCS), & will speak to Lt. Kellogg about it first chance, likely tomorrow. I doubt very much that I will get it because I compete against 3 stripe men and better, but it's a chance not to be passed up.

Lenny

Jan 16

Lenny,

Remember I wrote you the 5 points that Roosevelt has proposed in his speech to Congress this past week. Well, the one on a labor draft has gotten the most comment pro and con. Labor should approach the President's proposal with the understanding that the President's objective here is to smash the defeatist conspiracy against the national war effort and to promote the unity of labor, farmers, middle classes, patriots, capitalists and our men and women in the armed forces — a unity essential to victory and a peaceful, progressive post war America. The labor movement fully accepts the principles embodied in the President's proposal that every able bodied man and woman shall serve the war effort where most needed — on the home front or in the armed forces.

Diana

1/18

Dearest,

It was another lovely spring day — I was able to walk outside in fatigues without field jacket. The New Orleans press gave front page prominence to the Pravda item citing Greek & Yugoslav sources for a rumored secret British meeting with Ribbentrop.[14] It aroused a big wave of anti-Soviet feeling today.

Edgar, by the way, forgot to limp this afternoon — he's cultivating a limp as the time for our unit to go overseas approaches & it aroused some amused talk.

Lenny

Jan 18

Dearest Lenny,

In the first letter you write of your own "perspective" in the army. I don't feel, however, you are wasting time. If you are given a chance to use your skill against the enemy all these months of training, hardships, separation and snafus will be useful.

---

14. Nazi foreign minister.

I don't understand why you are not being given any recognition while you are being given important tasks it means they do recognize your ability. Is it because of another reason do you think?[15]

In regard to stripes — I agree — it would be a great help — financially, etc. But even more I want them because I know how much they would mean to you. Lenny, I'm always a little surprised when you talk of AWOL. I don't take it seriously because I think its just soldier talk — but being a civilian myself — the thought of deserting one's post is very far away from my thinking and it always jars me when you write it.

> *Yours,*
> *Diana*

1/19

Dearest,

Tonight I hope to speak to Lt. Miller about O.C.S. & I wish he knew me better! Not having been a squad leader during the time Lt. Miller has been C.O., naturally I had no opportunity of coming in contact with him or showing what I can do. So an awful lot depends on this one interview.

Mail from Irving & Edna — he's betting it's a boy & wants to know the name. Funny neither of us has given a thought to whether it is a boy or a girl. I guess we'll be satisfied with whatever our love produces! And as to the name, they'll wait 'til we're ready to announce it in due course.

> *Lenny*

Jan 19

Dear Private First Class,

I'm so happy for you. The baby also sends his best wishes to his Daddy. I don't know why I always think of the baby as a he — it's really not certain yet although I think the sex is determined already.

> *Diana*

How I Learned to Drive

1/20

Dina,

Today was another "tiddly-piddly" day: morning, talk by Sgt. Miller on patrols, O.K but old stuff, in the P.M. — we had the interesting experience of setting off dynamite sticks, blowing craters & knocking trees down —

---

15. Diana may be suggesting antisemitism.

learning how to set fuse & primer & handle the explosive sticks of nitro. But it was balmy, spring-like, & the instruction not too good & so we dozed. Lt. Miller stepped in the hut. He's a swell guy.

I used the chance to snag myself an enrollment in driver school beginning tomorrow. If I learn to drive, it will be a worthwhile week. I won't be a regular driver but to be able to take off in a jeep when necessary is invaluable. I hope they will let me attend, since I must begin from scratch, & they don't like that.

Lenny

1/20

Dear Diana,

I reported to the motor pool at 7:30 & worked till 5:00 — not all of the time, but I did get to drive a jeep, & I am on my way to a driver's license. There were many hurdles today. First of all, the driver's school is designed to teach an experienced civilian driver how to drive an army vehicle; it makes no provision for beginners. So when we discovered that non-experienced persons were sent back — well, I immediately became an "experienced" driver, only I haven't driven for about 10 years.

Lunch hour I grabbed hold of Cpl. Di Matteo, our motor noncom, & explained the situation so he borrowed a jeep & took Hersh & me out on a side area, & showed us the ropes, & let us get the feel of it. So we each drove around a circle 125 yards in diameter about 15 minutes & arrived at school just in time to load on for the afternoon's practice driving. We had too much fun to mind anything, even if Hersh once stepped hard on the accelerator instead of the brake & ran us into a ditch, & even if the guys in the jeep behind (we drove in "convoy," or a column of jeeps, 100 yards apart) said I steered like (wavy line). Could I help it if the road was a winding one?

Now beloved how are you & the precious cargo you carry? It's about time for another examination, isn't it?[16]

Lenny

Jan 20

Dearest,

You know darling, I've been thinking — when you come home from the army, our life will be quite different. You and I — we are accustomed

---

16. Enclosed is a newspaper clipping of "Post-Natal Exercises Designed to Make Figures Slim and Firm Again."

to such freedom — it will take some time to adjust to a baby who will make such demands on us.

I cannot work — I feel very tired — my appetite is very poor — all my thoughts and all my plans are in terms of the baby first. Sometimes this worries me a little — but then I think of the baby — ours — yours and mine — I feel so thrilled.

Diana

1/23

Darling Diana,

I got that guy Doug to go down to the motor pool with me & did about an hour practicing on the jeep — backing, turning, and shifting gears. It was a warm May spring-like day & everything was pleasant except for the post-firemen who couldn't understand why I should back the jeep into their white lawn fence and demolish it as effectively as if a tank came through. But even they were pleasant & amazed when I came back later with Doug & sawed & hammered them a new fence.

On AWOL talk, it may sound peculiar but when a soldier here goes AWOL no one considers it as "deserting one's post" unless he intends to stay "deserted." It is considered the one & only relief a soldier can turn to under extreme pressure. Now don't think I'm going over the hill or building up a case — I'm just recording fact. Many officers speak of AWOL as showing a soldier has gumption & courage, in fact.

Lenny

Jan 23

Lenny,

I sometimes wonder at how I can be so lucky to have you in love with me. You write so beautifully to me — I sometimes wish that I could write as well. I hope that my letters mean even a little to you of what your letters mean to me.

I shall write the news of the week:

    1. The CIO[17] has accepted the invitation of the British Trade Union Congress to attend the World Labor Congress in London on June 5th. The AFL[18] has not accepted.

---

17. Congress of Industrial Organizations.

18. American Federation of Labor.

2. The report in Pravda that 2 British officials met with Von Ribbentrop[19] to ascertain conditions for a separate peace sure did raise a fury. The note was intended as a warning that there are pro fascist forces in Britain who might be interested in a separate peace. The British gov't denied knowledge of the meeting, which is good. That there are forces in Britain working against the best interest of the gov't there is no doubt — so let us take heed.

3. The railroads are back in private hands. The happy ending speaks more than anything how eloquently the President handled this situation. The workers were awarded wage raises higher than the Brotherhood leaders were prepared to accept.

4. The Soviet offensive around Leningrad is terrific — Yugoslavian Partisans have retaken Jaice, their capital — Yanks and British are advancing on Rome.

Diana

1/23, for Sun, 1/30

Dearest,

"Carissima mea," while we are dreaming — you wrote you feel it's a him but I can't say anything like that — perhaps it's because I'm so much in love with its mama that I wouldn't be at all surprised if it came out a pretty little black-eyed girl with a blue dress on! Actually I'm quite neutral; be it a Freddy or be it a Betty baby, as long as you are well & the baby is well, I'll be happy with my family.

Lenny

1/24

Dear Diana,

Busy all day. Right after supper we go out driving again for 4 hours blackout driving — which leaves no time for letters tonight.

Just returned from a 60 mile drive by night, during which I drove 20 miles, half in complete blackout & half with lights & was very much surprised at how easy it could be. Then — as we checked in at the end, the miserable officer in charge rules Hersh & I out completely, account of no previous driving experience — Oh well: I have proved to myself that I can drive, & I have learned enough to handle a jeep in an emergency.

Lenny

---

19. Foreign minister of Nazi Germany from 1938 to 1945.

1/25

Dear Diana,

The day was rugged but very valuable training — it'll give you goose pimples & stand your hair on end, but 'tis-a-nothing: motorized patrolling. Speed is vital, because the area has the no-man's-land, 5 or 10 miles in front of our lines, & only speed can protect you if you find the enemy you are seeking, — so you dismount from the jeep while it is still running & jump on ditto — while you scout on foot, the jeep turns aside & hides in the woods.

As to loss of "freedom" & the demands a baby makes on you — well, "dulcissima," just think how much your "freedom" was curtailed when you married me, & what "demands" I have made on you — how could you endure them! Love, I'm not worried about our married life & house life after the war: in truth I am very impatient for its "problems"!

Lenny

Jan 25

Dear Lenny,

Love, I'm glad you will learn to drive a jeep. I'm anxious for you to know how to drive in case of an emergency — so I'm really hoping you'll get a chance to learn.

Dearest, today I am taking it easy. It may seem to you that I spend a lot of time taking it easy, but I haven't been entirely without any effects. First I have very little appetite. Then I feel very tired. I feel ashamed to write you that I feel tired after you are the one who is working so hard and really doing so much to help win the war. You have to drive yourself beyond the point of exhaustion, whereas I can take it easy whenever I wish. But I guess pregnancy is a strain on your body.

Diana

1/26

Dearest Sweetheart,

I am very tired & will have a severe day of KP tomorrow (up at 5:30 & we have to do the pre-moving cleaning up) — oh those god damn army officers who pull a dummy fire alarm tonight, a special floor washing session & hold retreat a half hour longer & figure out 20 other ways of wasting our time when we are most busy.

Lenny

Jan 26

Dearest,

I am due at the Doc's next week and I'll ask him to recommend exercises that I can do at home, when the time comes. As far as the present is concerned — I am not allowed to exercise according to Dr. Shaw. I am only supposed to walk — and that I do. Because I've written you so often about feeling tired, please don't let it worry you dearest. I understand it's not an unusual symptom.

Diana

Jan 27

Dearest,

Sometimes I think I'm losing my mind — I awoke this morning so elated — so full of spirit — it took me a few minutes to realize where I was. Then I understood — I had been dreaming that I had a letter from you that you were accepted for OCS. I guess it was wishful thinking on my part.

Well, dearest — this will be a short letter — even though my love for you is tremendous. I love you so — but I'm going to lie down and rest.

Diana

Jan 28

Dear Diana,

Somewhere, miles away, where — Who knows? Had a rugged day and am all wet thru & thru with sweat & the skies are still rain clouded.

Time begins to move faster for you, doesn't it? Honest, I envy you: you have a set definite task, with a normal time limit, and can therefore do a good job: but any amount of effort on my part means nothing, from what I can see. Luck plays so great a role in the army.

Lenny

Jan 28

Dear Lenny,

Looking at my mom and pop today — I kept thinking — it's a wonderful thing to be celebrating your 32nd anniversary together with your husband. Thirty-two years seems like a long time to me, but my mother says it passes very quickly. She found it a little hard to celebrate today with her two "sons" away, but I know your letter helped a lot.

Lee, I'm very sorry about the driver's school. It's just that sometimes I wonder how the army decides to do things. I'm very glad you did have some practice in the jeep though, because it many come in handy some day. Today is the day that you will go out on the long 3 week bivouac. I hope you will have good weather and you will learn a lot.

Diana

Jan 29

Dear,

Shortly after I finished the preceding letter — the officer in charge of the road guide detail suddenly took off in the truck, leaving word that we should rejoin our companies — an outrageous act: we were stranded with 90 pound packs, not counting gas masks, rifles & other equipment, like my field glasses, & we had been dumped blind, with no idea of where we were, & only a wave of the hand — "over there" — to show us where the division was.

Well, by dint of scouting, we finally hit the right turns in the roads & trails, and after 1½ hours trudging with that load (which is supposed to be vehicle-transported, not carried), we at last found an out guard of our battalion.

The fact that we unanimously said we wanted to sleep & to hell with chow (unheard of) was taken as the ultimate indication of what we'd been through. In truth, it was rugged, while I am glad it showed me we could lug a load like that cross country for 3 hours, besides time on the road, it was not at all a desirable experience, and we slept like logs in our bedrolls 'til 6 A.M. — despite a steady drizzle that fell all night.

Lenny

Jan 29

Dear Lenny,

Regarding money, I really am managing very well so far. I don't think you need to send me any of the $57 at present. Keep that for your furlough expenses.

You ask about changes — well, I think that for most people that know me very well, my waistline has gotten bigger. Love, do you realize that I'm going into the 4th month in a few days!

Diana

1/30

Dearest,

We hiked across rugged country & valleys in utter darkness; the unpleasant angle was, that as usual, we were left to shift for ourselves — &

while we arrived safely it was no fun — arriving at 3 A.M. on foot while the rest had come by truck at 10 P.M.

Lenny

Jan 30

Dear Lenny

Today's letter which I have read over and over — was so thrilling to me. As far as our budget after the war — I'm not worried. I'm truly too impatient to face these "problems" — I know that I'm not so terribly spoiled yet because I've been able to adjust myself to a budget of $50 per month after one of $200 which it was when I was working.

Diana

1/30

Dearest,

It was like a late day in May, warm, sunny & bright. It was so lovely that one is almost tempted to daydream, to see myself charioting up to our doorstep in a jeep & hoisting you and the kid in & perambulating off into the blue horizon — you with your telephone & me with my jeep, how will we ever be able to resume our staid budgetary household economy after the war?

Lenny

1/31

Dear Diana,

First of all, I am very concerned about your continued loss of weight — it is sort of lasting too long to suit your husband; — that some discomforts & even pains will be part of your pregnancy we expect, that's regrettably the woman's end of the deal, but we want you to be well.

It takes very little to make a soldier's life wretched & very little to make him happy. Dismal & wretched were the feelings of the four of us at the KP last night, although I swallowed mine & tried to cheer & inspire the guys — wary from Friday nights cross country, full field traipse, from the rain soaked ground we slept on that night, from Saturday's running around & a night withdrawal, during which we hiked some more 'til 8:30 — & got only 2 hours sleep before we took off to set up the observation post weary from a long day of duty there — & comes the order not that we are relieved by fresh men but that we are to stay up as listening posts all night, taking turns sleeping — with our bedrolls.

I soon learned that you "gotta" go way out to the enemy lines to hear anything because the sounds from our own lines, our own guard challenging, our own patrols coming in & out, blanket all enemy sounds. Meanwhile the enemy kept up a steady fire on the left flank, but was silent on the right, where we were — my guess is they weren't there. Well, it was a long and rugged trip, in which we mainly had to hide from our own patrols because they were "trigger" happy & inclined to fire on us as enemy — and 'tho they only fire blanks, the flashes would show our lines to the enemy. I was inadequately dressed for the cold night, & no way of getting the stuff. From now on I'll keep my long johns & knitted helmet in pack, which I usually have with me.

About dawn it became evident that the enemy had withdrawn during the night, clearly under cover of the firing on the left.

Lenny

Jan 31

Dear Lenny,

The matches, band aids and one napkin are in a separate envelope — I'll send you a napkin in each letter while you are on bivouac. No one can convince me that in a two week period Sara couldn't find one hour at home to make a scrap book for a soldier in a hospital or she couldn't knit a sweater in a month. I am upset — I know there is a group in Brownsville of ten women who took their baby carriages one sunny afternoon and with signs on them like "My Daddy is a Soldier" — collected some 1,500 signatures on the soldier vote petitions in about 1½ hours.

Diana

Feb 1

Dearest,

Takes very little to make a soldier wretched — as we were wearily preparing our "beds" last night, Sgt. Major Langley announced the Intelligence Section would take 1 hr shifts on C.Q. through the night. We, who'd been sans bedrolls & "sans" real sleep for 2 nights, were up in arms but Sgt. Johnson was mad too, & he stomped over to the Major & demanded that we be off since there were plenty of men who'd slept all night & all day too. So we were let off & slept.

Lenny

Feb 2

Dearest,

I paid a visit to Dr. Shaw this afternoon. He was very satisfied with my condition. He examined my abdomen and said he could feel the baby

from the outside and it felt like a 3 month old fetus. I tried to feel it too
— he showed me where and it does feel like a hard mass.

Diana and?

Feb 3

Dear Diana,

As usual on the day of departure there's only time for a hurried note
— rushing, packing, rolling the roll that's always too full, etc.

Lenny

Feb 3

Dear Lenny

As I walked home from Linwood St. station, I looked up into the sky
and saw the moon. Tonight as you sleep under the stars somewhere in
Mississippi, Lenny, did you talk to the moon too? And if the moon could
tell you what is in my heart. Lenny, since Dr. Shaw told me he could feel
the baby, I've felt differently about it. It has almost become something real
to me.

Before, as I had written you, it's been hard for me to imagine it as
something real, but now I'm beginning to feel differently. And my baby's
father — well — the moon knows how I feel about him and promised to
convey my message of love and kisses to him.

Your,
Diana

Feb 4

Dear Diana,

Yesterday after the rain soaking morning, we were told to expect chow
at 4 & to go into action soon after. But in very war-time like fashion, &
of this I shall not complain, the counterattack was launched at 2 — which
meant waiting until dark to eat & a forced march of great severity & strain.
Arriving at the scene of action, we scouts went forward to various duties.

This all lasted from 4:30 P.M. to 4:30 A.M. — no sleep at all this night,
& the 4th night without "normal" army sleep (by me 5 hours is "normal"
army sleep). At 4:30 our battalion withdrew, having completed its mission,
& withdrew making another forced march many miles, from 4:30 to 8:30
A.M. without a halt.

Well — if I can go 4 nights without any real sleep, topping it off with
a 36 hour stretch of no sleep & high exertion, I can do it in real battle. By
the way, I love you —

Lenny

Feb 4

Hello darling,

How is my dearest who has been bivouacking for over a week now? I've not had any mail since you've been out on bivouac.

I bought the vitamin pills. They are a special kind — $6.00 per 100 which is quite expensive but since I only have to take 1 pill a day they should last over 3 months. Anyhow nothing is too good for our baby — if the Dr. feels I should take them. We want to make all the guarantees that we can that the baby will be healthy and happy.

Diana

Feb 5

Dear Diana,

It's a matter of deepest regret that the father of your coming baby has to keep writing & asking after your health, as if you were a distant friend or relative — instead of my own beloved whom I can stand by close to hand all the time.

Received your letter with what I asked for: thanks. Matches are a rare & precious thing here, because there is no form of supply, they're forever getting wet in rain or swamp, & wind forces you to use several at a time. Besides the occasional fires we are permitted for warmth & light & odd cooking, we have other uses — I have to burn mail envelopes so they don't fall into enemy hands as identifications of our unit.

Lenny

Feb 5

Dear Lenny,

Hurray — I had two long letters from you today. By the way, our mail-man only rings the bell when there is mail from you or Babe. The letters show all the difficulties you have had on bivouac, and how many unnecessary hardships you have to face. I'm truly sorry but I'm glad I did hear from you because this has been a lonely week.

Dearest, don't be concerned about me now, as I've written you I have been feeling better the last few days. As for my appetite, it's improving.

I'm so glad you write me long descriptions of the things that you do. But I wonder, do these snafus take place in battle also? I hope that the officers learn by these mistakes.

Diana

Feb 6

Dear Diana,

Some Sunday! Hiking from dawn to 2 P.M. at least 25 miles — and then lugged by truck like baggage 'til 5:30, maybe 75 miles more over dirt track roads — so we are all a bit sore in a number of localities. It's again "somewhere in Mississippi."

Lenny

Feb 7

Dearest,

Maybe the army does it deliberately or maybe it's snafu — But look: at twilight we arrive at a place after a nearly 100 mile trip, dig in (no easy job) & eat supper at 9. We go to sleep. At 11 we are awakened to eat breakfast!!! — Told to be ready to move at 12:20. At 12:20 we load on trucks — and sit 'til 3 A.M., when we move out, arriving at 5 A.M. at a point 8 miles away — unload, & dig in & start maneuvers.

We were summoned & moved out in the direction of the firing which was active all morning. Forty eight hours of waiting made us eager — I decided to do some shooting too, as I have a deal of "arms" & my rifle needs cleaning anyhow.

Lenny

Feb 7

Dear Lenny,

Edith and I played a few games of ping pong in a place on 14th St. I played two games — I'm sure it was OK. After that we went to eat in the Chinese Restaurant that you and I ate in the first night you came home on furlough. You remember when it was raining so hard and where we made such an important decision.

When I read one of your letters about how hard you are working and I think of how I am taking it easy and just growing a baby which is plea-surable even if sometimes painful — I sometimes wish we could change places. But then I see how silly that is — you couldn't possibly be doing my job at present and I'm sure that I would not make a good infantry soldier. I doubt very much if the life that you describe would be physically possible for a woman.

Diana

Four Months Pregnant

Feb 8

Dearest,

Today is the official day that I enter my fourth month of pregnancy. Isn't that something? And I am feeling better — just like the book says — the first 3 months are the hardest and the chances for a miscarriage are the greatest — so I'm glad they are over.

Diana

Feb 9

Dear Diana,

When the rain came last night, Max & I turned into our tents; it was close & warm, after weeks of free, open air all around. The winds increased steadily but we dozed off. About 11:30 P.M. I awoke to hear the storm really reach fierce proportions — the wind howled & blew like 60 — our little pup tent filled with wind like a sail, & billowed out like it would take off — the ballooning sides heaved and strained at the pegs & at the ropes— but the battered, old tent held — & we stayed dry. And then as we were congratulating ourselves at our luck, a sudden gust came along & whipped at my raincoat, draped over the open end, & whoosh — it was gone. I leaped forward & strained my eyes thru the grey rain & midnight gloom — but no sight of my raincoat.

Figuring how many weeks pay would go into another raincoat went out to find it. As I reached outside of the tent, back around to the side, gingerly (if you touch the canvas it starts a leak) & there was my raincoat safe & sound, held fast by one button, a little precaution I had made when setting up.

The rain clouds are overhead again & it's cold — And 10 more days of this to go. Fading twilight: wonder if in combat I'll also stop to write a word in the middle of digging me a foxhole. Since the previous paragraph, I have made about a 25 miler on foot to a new combat area, have been on 2 rugged scouting missions, finding a lost battalion & now (am tired!) digging in while awaiting further orders.

Lenny

Feb 10

Dearest,

Your Feb 4th letter shows you are feeling better & that is swell. Your husband is rather groggy right now, tired, & dirty. I have had no sleep (of my own volition) since Monday night, & washing is out in the middle of attack, especially when my half canteen of water must last me at least 'til tonight, & possibly 24 hours after that. As to sleeping, we have had no night patrolling in ages, & a good night patrol is worth more than sleep — I can sleep after the war, but only good patrolling will bring me back to my bed!

We penetrated nearly 4 miles, which is damn good going on foot, at night, without being detected; I led the way, as point, & Sgt. Johnson followed thru the woods.

Now this should please you — In that darkness, with my eyesight, my scout craft was still so A-1 that I detected 5 patrols coming our way; in each case, we discovered the telltale motion of the shadow thru the night, or heard the muffled footfall, or whisper; long enough to conceal ourselves to either ambush or halt or pass the patrol.

We agreed, afterward, that in combat we'd have had a 50-50 chance of doing each patrol successfully & returning. Before we set out, we were both certain that we'd be captured; you just can't expect not to be discovered when you are moving into strange territory & the enemy is camouflaged & waiting for you. Well, we attacked at dawn, & have been on sundry lesser missions all day. This battle will go on at least another 24 hours — so will my work. But so long as it's real scouting & soldiering, it's well worth the exertion.

Lenny

Feb 13 While digging a foxhole

Dear Diana,

Max & I huddled close together, all night, in a dug out on the side of a hill, all night, the icy winds cut through our uniforms & blankets & we woke with skin chapped, frozen & lame all over, to greet a day of grey skies & colder winds yet, so cold our canteen water freezes.

Rumor is we return to camp 2/18. While the hardships of maneuvers are so much our life already that they could last a year now, just the same, I'll be happy to get chow again & into clean clothes, & read, & catch up on back mail — Of course, we'll be out on another long bivouac again after a few days.

The food situation is very bad now. We simply are not getting enough food to do a days' work. The only real meal is supper, & it has been adequate only 2 times since we are out. So as a result, a black market in candy has arisen & those who can afford it eat huge amounts. To counteract this, the major has authorized the chaplain to bring in daily a certain amount of chocolate. My reserve rations are about gone; except for my last reserve which I keep in case of being separated from the unit for a long time, is all gone. We are just not getting the calories a day to do a job in our company.

By the way, your knitted helmet has been a lifesaver these cold nights of sleeping on the ground; where formerly I had to use my overcoat to keep my head & shoulders warm. I can use my overcoat as a 3rd blanket; & whenever I have to go somewhere where I can't lug the overcoat & may get stuck overnight without it, the helmet is in my pack with me all the time.

Well, we moved out, so I filled that hole & we came to a new place (hiking) & I dug a new foxhole and now we have moved from there to another place yet (hiked) & now I am in my 3rd dug foxhole. What a way to spend a Sunday!

Lenny

Feb 14

My Love,

Tonight I'm toasting my feet by a little fire in a pine grove. It has been a rugged & a fast moving 24 hours! Last night it was fiercely windy & bitterly cold and dark as a subterranean labyrinth in the scrub oaks. We shivered painfully in the night 'til chow was finally brought up & our blanket rolls with it (Those go on the kitchen truck while we are in "combat.") Sgt. Miller came up & directed me to post guard. We are used to such sleep wreckers, & I for one am never reluctant to do guard duty. Along comes Lt. Kellogg & very apologetically tells me Regiment has ordered a 7 man patrol to report, period. After I rounded up the guys from their scattered places & quieted their "bitchen" & decided on specific equipment, we were off thru the night.

For Feb 14, To Diana, on not sending you the Red Cross's card

O Harlequin Kissed Columbine,
Or was it Pantaloon?
Who serenaded Adeline
Beneath a tipsy moon?
What miners stomped with Clementine
When size 9 were her shoes?
Let's skip the twisted eglantine—
That went out with the swoon,
Dispense with lace and crinoline!
I'd rather pet than spoon,

And need no cards to do my wooin'
With you my Valentine—
                                                        Lenny

Feb 15

Dear Diana,

As usual G.I. snafu makes the difference between tolerable & intolerable conditions. Today was a warmish, sunny day; & it was "non-tactical" — so we all planned to bathe in a creek & wash (Oh would I love to wash my fatigues & underwear; even in my helmet if I could arrange to dry them. I'd even sacrifice all my drinking water for a day to that.) But instead — we were dragged out to fill in old foxholes dug one & two years ago & left unfilled by some earlier division.

On bonds: buy a 10-cent stamp a month.[20] That's our share, 'til we can do better. Just participate —

I can't wait to see you, be the changes slight or big, — tonight I was told that I am tentatively on the list for April furlough — but whether I'll be where I can come home is another story.
                                                        Lenny

2/16

Dear,

I miss you this morning, Diana, as we wait for the signal to move again after filling in foxholes.

My Diana, the sweet playmate I met & loved 6 years ago, she's now bearing a child: it's hard for it to seem not like a stranger's affair, because it's so far away. This too is part of the heavy price we pay for building a world in which our child can live proud & free.
                                                        Lenny

Feb 16

Lee,

There are so many questions in my mind about the training you are getting. All the letters you have written since you've been on this bivouac seem to indicate that your training is so disorganized. No one knows quite

---

20. War savings stamps were issued by the U.S. Treasury Department to help fund participation in World War I and World War II. They were aimed at common citizens. The lowest denomination was 10 cents and collections of them could be redeemed for Treasury Certificates or War Bonds.

what to do — guys try to hide out of work, nobody caring if they get the training or miss it, as long as they can get away with it — mistakes galore — and your work in the intelligence section seems to be so makeshift — just as long as they keep you busy.

Is it just the incompetence of the officers or is that confusion part of the training? I get so worried when I read your letters and think that your outfit will probably soon be going into the real thing and you seem so unprepared.

Diana

2/17

Dearest,

A weary Lenny writes a day later, after a day of pain & suffering which can only be exceeded by combat. Yesterday we hiked in rain at a killing pace, soaked in sweat beneath and rain above, from 2 to 10 P.M. (at least 25 miles) with no break after 6, in mud knee deep that sucked you in & threw you down — 'til muscles cried out for pain and the brain reeled; and when in blackness of rain & forest we ended, there was no chow — no food for 25 hours & we just lay down in the wet grass & mud & dozed as the rain fell on us. I could go on for pages on our misery — but that's war, so it goes. I love you.

Lenny

BACK IN TRAINING CAMP

Feb 18

Dearest,

Back in camp — The painful memory of that hike in mud & rain & lying all night in mud & rain — well, it's a foretaste of combat horrors & has to be considered an asset; but I'll take my fighting in dry, mild, Indian-summer weather, thank you.

Unpacking my barracks bag & suitcase I had curious feelings. A foretaste of how we will feel on unpacking our stored beloved home furnishings — feelings of pain, at the thought of happy days missed, feelings of happy memories, & joy at having them again — pain at seeing them creased & shapeless, but knowing they'd soon be OK. again; and wondering as one is surprised at things forgotten.

They handed out a flock of 3-day passes tonight & I got one on the basis of my work. I could go to New Orleans but I plan to go up to Jackson & have a look in at the archives on Newt Knight.

Lenny

Feb 18

Dear Lenny,

Eddie is very busy seeing everyone before he leaves on Wed. He still doesn't know whether he is in the Navy, in the Coast Guard, or in the Marines.

Diana

Feb 19

Dearest,

I want to write you briefly so I can send you the money order right away: It's $50 as you see, as follows: $30 for your own budgetary needs, as you see fit, representing $6 saved from each month's pay and $20 furlough money for you to hold or bank — anyway, that is to cover our expenses for if & when I get that week at home.

Lenny

EXCURSION TO JACKSON, MISSISSIPPI

Feb 20

Dearly Beloved,

It's warm & humid here at the Tri-State Bus Terminal at Hattiesburg, where I am waiting (an hour to go) for the bus to Jackson.

Lenny

Feb 20, 10 P.M. Written on Jackson Defense Recreation Association, Service Men's stationary

Dear,

Rode up on the bus with Mr. Douglass who repairs & installs refrigerators, en route from Shelby to Jackson — He served 11 mos. at Camp White last war, thinks we have it tougher; the war's biggest effect on Mississippi is higher prices, higher cost of living. He is father of 4, oldest, 18. There were 6,000 Republican votes last election & will be more this year. Of course the poll tax keeps a lot from voting — it takes $2 for 2 years, & many don't bother paying.

Lenny

Feb 20, from Jackson YMCA, for Sun. Feb 27

Dear Diana,

In this altogether new locale, I send you once again a Sunday special — with all my love.

Coming up here on the bus, some fleeting images came thru & brought a smile to my face — my Dina, my gal — and her daily self-inspection, checking on the production schedule. Well, you were a fine machinist, & this construction should come a lot more instinctively. Our baby can grow up feeling that it was not procreated by some selfish and self-seeking wish of mama to keep papa out of the draft, but that it was born in joy to be a joy to itself, created by proud, brave fighters who were building a new world for the youngster.

Lenny

Feb 20

Lee,

I shall write you the news:

1. The Fraternal Council of Negro Churches prepared a report of very serious Jim Crow practices in Southern Camps. The things that were emphasized were cruel treatment by nearby civilians, policemen are cruel, and German war prisoners receive more courtesy than Negroes. Shelby was one of the camps visited and listed.

2. There have been several articles in the paper recently about the good progressive work of the Dept. of Welfare in getting people placed in jobs and actually helping them.

3. For the first time German war prisoners in this country will be permitted to receive an anti fascist newspaper, like the German American.

Diana

2/21

Dear Diana,

The Y redeemed itself with genuine hot water for a shower last night — one doesn't realize that there's never hot water at Shelby. Had breakfast in a little place opposite the Old Capitol, & started my day there. In one wing is preserved the rostrum of the old house where Henry Clay & Andrew Jackson once spoke, where later the Secession Ordinance was adopted, & where Jeff Davis made his last public appearance. There, also, was adopted the 1890 convention with its prime design of keeping the Negroes out & down. Next to it is the pretentious "modernistic" War Memorial. It houses the State Archives where I worked from 10–3. In the main, I only picked up details but I did get to a number of original sources on the Knight business. By the way, the War Memorial also houses a Mississippi Hall of Fame and in a big case, the original Secession Ordinance on display. It also has a painting of 2 KKK'ers in genuine costume, blood red with white trimmings, & white hoods with red eyes, nose & mouth.

At the Greenwood Cemetery asked the Sexton if he could show me the grave of John R. Lynch. Yes, he said, & led the way.

> SEXTON: "I never knew his first name. It's not on the stone. Nigrah wasn't he?" (Note the compromising form)
>
> ME: "He was Secretary of State, wasn't he?"
>
> HE: "Yes, or Treasurer, or something."

I stood at attention for a minute in silent salute to this man who, in death as in life, carries on the fight for equality for Negro and white, because there are mighty few cemeteries in the U.S., north as well as south, where Negroes are lying beside white. Lynch was a Reconstruction leader.

Lenny

Feb 21

Dear Lenny,

Sweetheart love — one of the letters I had today was a love letter — like my Sunday letter before you went on this long bivouac. It made me so happy, but with tears in my eyes.

Diana

Feb 22

Dearest,

Somehow I feel sort of good tonight — don't know why exactly — but very much — a loving towards you.

How is my growing family tonight? I have developed a tremendous sensitiveness to baby & children's pictures & the first infants I saw over the weekend sort of set me unsteadily gyrating.

Today — one of those filler days — Jackson being a capital city is metropolitan in air: it's small, a mere 40,000. Its "antebellum" monuments & buildings are few — it was burned in the Civil War & nicknamed, "Chimneyville" as only chimneys survived the fire. Of course under the army's restrictive policy it was impossible for me to visit the Negro community; but it was noticeable that Negroes appeared to move more easily than in Hattiesburg; (40% of Jackson is Negro) their homes came closer, schools nearer, Negro schoolchildren walking on "White" streets — never so in Hattiesburg.

The phone book showed a few AFL locals. Musicians, Construction, Teamsters, but no CIO —

We are receiving replacements from overseas units: so they are sent into Infantry, a guy, Marv, not in our hut, a nice guy, with 2 years combat experience, Guadalcanal, etc., in the COAST ARTILLERY — he doesn't know beans about Infantry. And then Staff Sgt. McClarren, a wounded veteran, a malaria victim, they send him here & offer him a civilian disability discharge cold, which he properly rejected & then tell him he's cut to private because his leg wound prevents him doing Staff Sgt. duties. Most overseas guys who are here are very cynical, very bitter. Don't know what's coming next. We expect a 15-day march (March emphasized, not maneuvers); & beyond — well, all kinds of rumors are afloat, & "shipment" predominates over "maneuvers."

Lenny

Feb 22

Dear Lenny,

I've just kissed Eddie goodbye — he leaves tomorrow morning. I spent the evening with your folks. Your mother was swell — as when you left — brave and trying to be cheerful — The rest of the group was likewise. It hardly felt like farewell until they all said goodbye. Eddie is a kid or so he seems to me — after all when I met Eddie, he was 12, but he has good spirit and is the type of clean, healthy guy that our country needs today. I'm sure he'll get along OK.

Your,
Diana

Feb 23

Dearest,

So Eddie's left today. Here's wishing him an easier time than I have had. Today was one of those wretched days of wasted time. Sgt. Johnson decided to call in all maps & replace damaged & lost ones & return 'em to the companies. So all day we sorted & unfolded maps (each company has about 200 air photo maps) & nothing else.

Next bivouac is Mar 2 to 15th or 20th. Better send two smaller packages a week apart than one; smaller than the ones you have been, even. This is a march with weight on my back & space at a big premium.

Lenny

Feb 23

Lee,

I just came home from your mother's house. When I came there, she had been lying down and she looked as though she had been crying. I talked to her, made her eat lunch, and I'm sure she felt better when I left. Eddie called while I was there. He is in the Marines — he was chosen for it. He's disappointed about not having gotten the Navy but he's a good sport. The marines are such a tough "outfit" I hope he'll be OK. He's going to Paris Island — I think it's off South Carolina.

Diana

2/24

Dearest,

A rugged day — very tired. At 5:30 I was awakened & told I was on K.P. It's Thursday & since I'd expected Sunday K.P. it was almost with relief that I reported on duty.

To add to the tension, 3-day passes are still being issued, if one can be lucky & tie a 3 day pass, one can get to N.Y. & back & still have a day or two at home. You can imagine how a day before Friday, one feels to be on K.P., unable to get out to apply for the passes About those passes — so if I'm not already home when you read this, well I have to wait 'til April for furlough.

Lenny

Feb 24

Dear Lenny,

This morning I went for my maternity girdle. I wish you could see it — with laces on both sides for expansion purposes.

Diana

Feb 24

Dearest,

Here it's November — December — January — February since I've seen you. Well, if I was overseas, & in action, I'd say "well, here I am for the duration." But when one is still in the United States — gee whiz — And furloughs are so problematic — here 1,000 guys are going "out" — overseas, most likely — & many sans furlough; and our 9-month program at Shelby ends Feb 29 — while there's word of a 15 or 18 day maneuver in March, all is up in the air. So — now I'm waiting for the pass on pins & needles.

Lenny

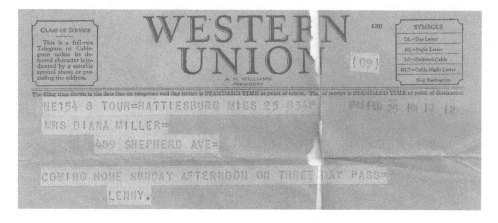

Western Union telegram, February 25
"Coming home Sunday afternoon on three-day pass — Lenny."

FOUR-DAY FURLOUGH PASS
AT THE END OF NINE MONTHS OF TRAINING

2/29, 6:25 P.M.

Dear Diana,

As you see it isn't 10 minutes since we smiled goodbye — I'm in the coach, seated, & writing. Swell sweetheart darling, always ready to give me a brave sendoff. That's the girl I love. Well, now that I'm a-leaving of you, the first hush discordant note of reality has crept in. Otherwise, from the time I got the pass and meeting you, the family & being with you, & seeing the changes — sweet changes — by developing maternity, are all a rare & precious dream. What was so wonderful about these 48 or so hours together? It wasn't like our furlough — not anything so remarkable about what we did — no great decisions made & enacted. It was just being together, for a little while, & so unexpectedly, too, that made it so happy, so like a dream. My love — be well. Soon again, perhaps, meanwhile, the battle —

Lenny

3/1 Postcard en route

Darling,

Still dreaming — won't wake up 'til Mississippi! Have a good seat, slept some last night.

Mar 1

Darling Husband,

The activity of the afternoon and the fact that it was a strain to say goodbye to you — made me tired. I awoke this morning and just as we thought would happen I felt as though it was all a glorious, wonderful dream. Lenny, was it really true? Were we in each others arms yesterday? I feel so tremendously happy at having seen you — so glowing and smiling all over me. I'm sad at your having left — now more than ever it is difficult for me to let you go.

I feel so relieved at having seen you — I was quite concerned after your letters describing the 21-day bivouac. But you look well and healthy and you feel so tough and hard.

Love from both of us,
yours, Diana and?

BACK TO MISSISSIPPI

3/2

Dearest,

We're supposed to be packing for the 15-day problem but the order's unclear as to when or what. Talk about snafus. Believe it or not, this morning I was handed a GI driver's license — yes! Now I hope they don't call on me to drive before I can get some practice!

Dearly beloved, it was worth millions to be with you these few days. It's got to be my inspiration to do everything to finish the war & be able to come home, when all is done, & be with you (baby too) always —

Lenny

Mar 3

Dear Lenny,

It no longer seems funny to me to feel that flutter in my belly. I've felt it several times since Sun. and I'm pretty sure it is our baby making itself felt. I'll ask Dr. Shaw on Mon.

Diana

Mar 4

Dearest,

The statement from the Dep't of Welfare came with your earnings for 1943. You earned $744.33 until Mar 5th.

Lee, I'm really beginning to blossom out. I think it is even more noticeable than when we were together last weekend. Probably in another
week or so, it will be unmistakable and if you are able to come home in a
month — my goodness!

Diana

Mar 5

Dear Sweetheart,

So far, since breakfast at 5:30, I have done nothing. A few months
ago that would have made me very unhappy, but today I am quite indifferent. It's an old story now. You see we do have a one-day "problem,"
eyewash mainly, because Gen. McArthur is somewhere around on a visit.
Meanwhile G Co. passed by, & a guy told me that Hersh was a simulated
casualty — so I went over to where he was lying — with an imaginary
"fractured skull," "unconscious," bandaged by the first aid medic, & waiting for the ambulance which came 2 hours late — so we conversed the
time away, since we haven't really talked since before his furlough.

Did I say I was indifferent? Perhaps it would be more correct to say
I have been depressed to the point of unconsciousness. But I have some
terribly blue moments & evenings & days, from this endless waste of
time; times when I welcome the release of an hour's dozing to release
the mind.

Lenny

Mar 5

Lenny,

How are you, beloved Lenny? Last Sunday with all the excitement of
waiting and seeing you — meeting on the steps and lying in your arms
at night — all of that seems so close to me now — but as the days pass, it
again begins to feel like a dream and such a glorious dream.

Diana

Mar 6

Dearest,

This morning was a wretched waste — in the rain marching on a
compass course, stuff we did in basic. We have new "experiences" — wood
ticks, just now, also rattlesnakes. I had to go to the medics to have an ob-
streperous wood tick yanked out of my belly — didn't hurt but a nuisance.

Lenny

Mar 6

Dearest,

This afternoon I went to the Dr. All is well. He said that since I am OK so far, there is very little danger of complications because the first few months are the hardest. He said I still have time before I have to register and reserve a place in a hospital so I'll wait until I go back to see him in a month.

Diana

Mar 8

Dear Diana.

This is a "care of equipment" hour — so my wife is to be "cared" for too. It's cold; I'm cross-legged by a fire. Hersh, Frank, Joe, & Max are asleep because of weariness which I share — but someone has to stay "alert," & I don't want to sleep by day. Last night we marched, after a full days work, from 7:30 to 2 A.M. and the wretched officer in charge did not give us the regulation 10 minute breaks every hour, but 2 minutes, & less which is not enough to relieve acute local fatigue — so all our joints are in pain, especially knees and ankles.

Well, we are only a dozen miles from the Gulf. All in all, with yesterday's scouting we hiked 45 miles in about 32 hours, besides other incidental walking. We ended shivering with chills, & too broken & lame to even build a fire.

Lenny

Mar 9

Dear Diana,

To begin in sequence — At 5:30 A.M. yesterday the cursing 69th was wakened & took off again on the final stretch to drive the "enemy" into the sea at Biloxi. It must be that they fled before our approach, and we halted in the Magnolia State Forest & pitched tents, & busied ourselves in miscellaneous chores.

Then — as conquerors — we were given the freedom of the coast — no passes needed!!!! — Unheard of liberty!! So I hopped a GI truck. Thalassa![21] The Bay of Biloxi — and then Biloxi itself, a neat city — I saw the Gulf of Mexico for the first time! So I strolled out along Beach Ave, filling my eyes with the sea, amazing how it made me homesick, I

---

21. Greek expression of joy upon first seeing "the sea."

never thought it meant so much to me — but 'tis true that I've not seen the sea since 1942, & my sea memories — our sea memories — are all beautiful ones.

Lenny

Mar 9

Dear Lenny,

I'm very glad that I am still well enough to get around. It would be hard for me to stay at home all the time now. The way I have scheduled my time now so that I am at the community office about two afternoons and two evenings a week — I find this work very satisfying.

Dearest, it hurts me so much that your last few letters have been depressed, that you feel as though you are wasting so much time, but I understand how you feel. You say you look for my letters — I don't know what to write to make you feel better.

Diana

Mar 10

Dear Lenny,

I went to 14th St. to meet my mother and we went shopping. I bought a coat — a loose coat for the spring — blue — very appropriate for my present condition. I was so glad to be able to get one for $25 because it saved my mother the job of sewing one for me.

Diana

Mar 11

Dear Diana,

It rained last night; & in the rain, we broke camp & marched out — "we," 5 men of the S–2, all the rest rode sheltered, we & the Rifle Companies walked in the downpour thru mud & on hard concrete, many foot weary miles, 'til we are now 25 miles from the sea. Slowly, by fireside, I am drying out.

Your gift package came — pity it couldn't have included hamantash-en.[22] Everything came in good condition; but Hellmann mayonnaise jars always break in transit. The pears a delight — we never see pears. Of course all the S–2's joined in enjoying the cookies. My dearest, as I read of your "blossoming" I get such a tremendous feeling of happiness, of being

---

22. Traditional three-sided Purim cookie.

in love with you, of being your man, of being united with you in this child to be — it's all so beautiful!

Lenny

Mar 12,

Dear Diana

At 8:00 I was told to be prepared to do the whole demonstration & class by my self, as Lt. B was due elsewhere; but presently all training was cancelled, & we've had a free day. So I relaxed my still aching feet & read "Time" & "Newsweek" to catch up with the news. Rumors are rife: we all know the Shelby days are numbered.

Lenny

Mar 12

Dearest,

By the way, on the income taxes — I have finished the entire family and they are ready to be mailed. Ours is very satisfying — we shall get $10.00 back and we'll be all paid up for 1942 — that is for the money you owed.

Diana

Mar 14

Dear Diana,

A "June" morning, fragrant, fresh: white blossoming trees (Dogwood? Magnolia?) We're taking our ease after a "short" hike, only 3 hours — only one county, while yesterday we traversed Jackson, Harrison, & Stone.

Word is tomorrow we have a record distance hike, a rugged affair; & my feet — all our S-2's feet — are pretty battered already. I've just soaked my "bleeding stumps" in my helmet full of water & am going to relax 'em from now on tonight. Wasn't Uman[23] just retaken? It'll be long before you hear anything of your family there.

Dear, don't place any expectations on that furlough date. The fact that we leave on maneuvers during that period may delay the dates, as well as add to the distance & cost.

While I am fiercely eager to get over into action — oh, I'd be so happy to be in the first wave of the western invasion — I wish that I could make a flying visit back for a weekend to see Jr. whenever he/she comes!

---

23. City in central Ukraine.

But I expect to be far away by then! "Gotta" get this war over "so's" I can sit down & soak my feet for about 6 months!!!

> *Lenny*

Mar 14

Dear,

This morning I went to Army Emergency Relief to apply for maternity care. I was amazed at how simple the whole procedure is. I brought a letter from Dr. Shaw and proof of your being in the army. She told me that there are two forms I have to have filled out — she gave me one for the doctor and one for the hospital saying that the doctor is willing to accept the $50 as payment for his care and the one for the hospital is similar also $50. They are paid after delivery of the baby. Lee — if this works out it will cost us practically nothing, which will be swell.

> *Diana*

Mar 15

Dearest,

I'm glad your chow has been better this series. Regarding the package I realize that the glass jars break, but there are no tins available — should I send the covered candy in a cardboard box? My darling — I had quite a hectic night — out late again and I've been spending two or three afternoons a week at the office and not getting enough sunshine. I've decided to stop coming to the community office. I wrote you that we have a girl to replace me. I've worked it out and I shall leave next week — I think that is best because I'm in the middle of the fifth month and I don't want to take any chances.

> *Your,*
> *Diana*

Mar 16

Dear Diana,

My "Milton" volume is just returned to me by Saul who had it in his barracks bag since January and so it enables me to begin with a little glow of pleasure.

We'll be here 'til April 3 when we say goodbye to Camp Shelby; that day we go to Lake Shelby, the artificial lake for an undetermined number of days and from there we go to Shreveport, Louisiana, the center of our maneuver area. Maneuvers end June 12 after which we'll be on call for overseas shipment.

> *Lenny*

3/17

Dear Diana,

St Paddy's Day — but as usual you'd never know it hereabouts! Your husband is tired. This morning he woke up & was disgusted to learn he was on as latrine orderly today, CQ Saturday & probably guard Sunday. Aside from the burden of detail & the distaste of latrine duty, it leaves me no time to do the many things in regard to care of equipment that are so necessary after 2 weeks rugged field duty.

Lenny

Mar 18

Dearest,

On the $19 windfall — can you put some of it aside for photos — you & "?" — Can you use Lucy's camera? If not, it would be worth buying an inexpensive one for the time being.

Lenny

Mar 18

Dearest Lenny,

My mother agreed to go shopping this morning because there are several things we needed to buy. We bought material for a bed jacket for me. I will need a pretty jacket when I shall have to be in the hospital and people will visit me — my mother will make it for me.

Diana

Mar 19

Dearest Lenny,

Today was an unexpected day for me — I awoke this morning and looked forward to a dreary day of cleaning house. Well, my sister had a ticket to hear Bruno Walter conduct the Philharmonic in Beethoven's 9th Symphony. She gave me the ticket to go to Carnegie Hall. It was magnificent — you know what a blaze of glory the 9th symphony is.

Right now the baby is wiggling a big hello to you also. I'm glad — it's such a funny feeling — I wish I could really describe it to you. Perhaps if you can come home in a few weeks, you will be able to feel it for yourself if you put your hand on my stomach.

Diana

Mar 20

Dear Lenny,

Uman was retaken! Joy in our household!

I understand — a weekend together when the baby comes — I don't dream of it even — I don't want to say that I'd like you to be here until then, because it's not what I mean, but if you could get away from wherever you will be for a few days — well we must fight hard and bring you back soon — to stay when it's all over.

Diana

Mar 22

Dear Diana,

How are you as you round out your fifth month — rounding out?

Lenny

FINALLY THE END IS IN SIGHT—PREPARING TO MOVE ON

Mar 24

Darling,

You will probably receive a batch of packages from me as I unload my excess weight — books & such.[24]

Lenny

Mar 24

Dear Lenny,

And what a night was last night! Well, about 12:45 the phone rang — It was Babe from California calling Lucy. He just came into port (he couldn't say what city he is in). He is fine — He only expects to be here a very short time so, of course, he won't come home. You can just imagine how thrilled Lucy was. She said he sounded as if he were standing next to her even though he was more than 3,000 miles away. Aren't phones wonderful?

Diana

3/25

Dearest,

What I Told My Friend the Would Be Writer

Only he who stands through battle
Only he who breathes in cannon's mouth

---

24. Lenny prepares to leave Camp Shelby.

Only he who hugs the earth and crawls up forward
Daring the enemy machine guns
Braving, the Stuka's fire
Undaunted, the Panzer's bite
He may be the singer of America's future
He may celebrate the freedom we may win.[25]

Lenny

Mar 27

Dearest,

Summer, Mississippi style, is here, with heat, sweat, & sticky midday showers & heavy evening downpours.

I am very glad you liked the "Reverie on Korea."[26] I hope you liked some of the others too. As I've written, these emissions puzzle me a good deal. I can sweat a whole day trying to say something nice about April, & all I can think of is that Chaucer & Browning both did a fine job. And then when I'm leaning on a mop or looking out of a bus anywhere from 3 to 30 lines will come a clamoring to be written down. It never happened to me before.

You say nothing of how you are feeling or progressing — tell me! Your sweetheart loves you — he's been telling the world he's in love, so you know what? The silly dopes; they all say, what will your wife think.

Lenny

Mar 28

Dearest Love,

Happy Birthday, dear —

Latest furlough dope: I am scheduled to leave 4/5 & return 4/15 — 7 days plus 4 day travel time.

Well — now it's April 4, the first day of the furlough — things change every couple of hours.

Now take this business of the baby kicking — what's that all about? What's it kicking for? Tell me everything —

Lenny

---

25. Stuka is a two-man German dive bomber and ground attack aircraft, and a Panzer is a tank.

26. Refers to a poem Lenny wrote and sent to Diana.

For Mar 28

Dearest,

   This is the first time you've been baby having on a birthday! Happy Birthday, Diana, and, may we see many of them together in joy unbounded! Your man what loves you!

For Mar 28, 1944

   Birthday Gift Written March 15, 1944

   Every spring time for your birthday, dear Diana,
   To delight you
   Ransacking thru the treasure bazaars of the caravan lands
   For gardens of Firdusi[27] glimmering on illuminated Persian camel
      bone
   For leafy silvery filigree from the Rialto at Firenze
   For Chunghua's[28] Persian poet poppy blossoms finely veined in
      crimson cinnabar
   For bracelet, necklace, earring,
   This year what shall I but bring my heart home to you?

Lenny

Mar 28

Dear Lenny,

   Yes, dearest — today is my birthday — I cannot say it has been a happy birthday — it couldn't be with you in Mississippi — but you have made me very happy three times today with three letters.

Diana

Mar 29

Dear Diana,

   All night long the storm raged, without rest, the lightning bolts struck & crackled, & the thunder shook our huts, & the flood poured down. So when we reached the Leaf River this morning, it was swollen beyond anything we've seen. Its banks & beaches had disappeared, & it had widened to 200 yard across.

   So in these conditions, the 2nd Battalion made its first attack across a river on a fortified position, making the river crossing in 15 man assault

---

27. Persian poet.

28. City/province in Taiwan.

boats, hand rowed. Naturally inexpert, the 7 oarsmen working in disunity, we managed to drift quite a bit downstream in crossing. Of course this was only for practice — the real attack will be made in blackout about 3 A.M. tonight.

They kept us in the cold, ankle deep in water for a couple of hours more & hiked us in to try to dry & warm up. It'll be colder tonight. But a million times rather be wet, cold & sleepy doing something in training than to be miserable doing nothing as we were earlier this week.

Lenny

Mar 29

Dearest,

I'm so proud that you wrote those love poems to me — so very proud. You make me feel there is so much I have to achieve to be worthy of your love — My darling — I'm glad I'm a fighter's wife!

Diana

3/30

Dear,

So we fell drowsily into line & marched out in battle dress, steel helmet & all, & reached the south shore of the Leaf River at 3 A.M. George, John, & I stood & shivered in the damp cold, & shivered more in anticipation of the cold waters. The water was rising yesterday & we knew we'd wade all the more on the far shore. We waited an age — we didn't cross. The engineer recon boats couldn't find any landing place on the yonder shore, so high had the flood waters gone. So we heaved a sigh, not of disappointment, & marched back.[29]

Can't wait these 5 days 'til I get on the train — I have about $39.00 on me which will about cover travel costs & pay on 3/31 about $23.00 will have to cover our costs at home — that's much better than last time.

Lenny

Mar 30

Darling,

Max just called me — Hurrah! He said I can expect you home next Wednesday, April 5. I realize it can all be changed but I hope it will be OK.

Diana

---

29. Preparing for Normandy landings.

HOMEWARD BOUND AGAIN

3/31–4/2

Dearest,

> As it had come to Mukden, Adowa, Madrid
> As it had come to Linz, Prague and Durazzo,
> Warsaw, Oslo, Leyden, Ghent and Rheims,
> So war came to Brooklyn.
>
> War tore between millions
> Between young husband and wife
> Between young father and firstborn
>
> But war didn't come between us.
> War brought us together.
>
> We knew the war was coming
> We who loved the placid quiet of the sunny park
>
> We who were young and in search of loving
> We saw we had to make a choice.
>
> We chose the turmoil.
> We chose to buck the tide.
> Threw our single strengths against the swastika
>
> Knowing we were not alone
> Knowing we might not succeed,
> Still knowing in the end
> We would succeed.
> So war brought us together.

Lenny

3/31

Dear Diana,

I'm glad you continue to like the lyrics. Somehow I hesitate to call 'em "poems." There's something much too definite about "poem" — it sort of classifies things with Homer and Milton & Shelley — & embarrasses. I prefer lyrics. As to sending them to a paper or magazine, well — you would quickly see how much you love me & how objective other critics are compared to you! Show them to one or two people without mentioning who wrote them & see their reaction. No point in having illusions.

Lenny

4/1

Dear Diana,

This afternoon we got some more tetanus shots; and a call came for immediate overseas in certain qualifications (radio, certain noncoms and others). There were volunteers for each opening and the quota was filled on the spot. That, dearest, is only secondarily an index of good underlying morale. Basically and first it's an indication of the hate the guys have for this place and this outfit.

Lenny

April 1

Lee,

I had your two wonderful letters this morning telling me that you would be home. So now I'm waiting for you and trying to be patient.

Diana

April 3

Dear Lenny,

I went to Dr. Shaw for my monthly check up. I'm fine, he said — he's very pleased with my progress. He signed the authorization for the army to pay him. I registered at Brooklyn Woman's Hospital. I had to answer some routine questions and show proof of your rank and serial no. They accepted me under the army payment plan — so the delivery, etc. won't cost us anything.

Diana

HOME AGAIN

[Furlough—no letters]

4/14, En route

Dearest,

The train is very subdued; in fact everyone slept 'til noon. I've been whiling the time away with Mark Twain's "The Innocents Abroad."

Lenny

April 14

Dearest,

Thank you so much for a wonderful furlough — your every moment with me is so precious until the next time we will be together. Love — it was harder to say "goodnight and so long" than it has been any of the other times. We both felt it — maybe the fact that I am pregnant has made me a little more emotional — but you mustn't be concerned. I shall be strong and do my job well — both the baby and I will do our best while we are working and waiting for you to come home to us.

Diana

April 15

Dearest,

Both the first letter I received yesterday and the post card that came today sounded a little worried about me — There really is no need to be worried — I shall take good care of myself as I promised you. Please be cheerful and happy that we are in love and so lucky to be having a baby.

Diana

April 16

Dear Diana,

Not so good news, promotions are frozen. Looks like a rugged schedule ahead this week — speed marches & distance hikes. It's the 5 mile runs that kill me, mainly on account of breathing trouble.

No doubt you've been waiting for me to recall to you, "What we did on furlough?" — And I've been slow to write it. This has been a subdued furlough, & so shadowed over by the uncertainties of the immediate future, that I hesitated to give it verbal expression. Yet we do want to remember the few hours alone together when I came in on Wednesday — before spending the night between your folks & mine, the Seder.

Dearest, I was so glad to see you in your big bellied sixth month — I so hate to miss all of your pregnancy!

Lenny

4/17

Dear Diana,

The heat indoors is fierce. No one will regret leaving Shelby — a current gag is that "so & so is a coward, he's asking to go "overseas" (implying the greater danger is staying here).

Lenny

ON ALERT

April 18

Dearest,

Today was a real test — there were six silhouette like men in foxholes, at various ranges none known to us except what we could estimate, as it would be in combat; there were men who let you know if you hit it by lowering the target. I had 10 shots to hit 6 enemies & I hit all six with 5 shots; two were in a line so I'm satisfied. I spent a rugged afternoon in heavy rain in the Leaf River swamps & hills in infiltration & scouting good for physical conditioning. I also very viciously bit about 25,000 mosquitoes that were in the area. Also I crawled over the shoulders & hands of several hundred caterpillars. Do I sound confused? So would you coming thru that wilderness of crawling & stinging critters.

Flash! All PVT's & PFC's are "alerted" at once — so it may even be just a matter of hours.

Lenny

4/19, Post No. 5

Dearest,

> Purple-gold-and salmon sky—
> We walk our post together, my gun and I
> Our post — We guard a world, and sons of some yet unborn
> Will owe their freedom, life, the grand songs of their bards,
> All their masterworks
> To my gun and me

Lenny

April 19

Lenny Darling,

What's the matter? I know you were tired when you returned to camp but your letter sounds so disheartened. Well, I'll wait for tomorrow's letter after you've had a night's sleep.

I bought a ticket for the Thurs. night rally on the anniversary of the Warsaw ghetto fight.

Diana

April 20

Dear Diana,

The 69th is busting up for sure, although it's officially "hush, hush" and guys are making ready. I've packed a carton full of stuff to send home. They are not letting us take more than 5 pounds of personal stuff.

Lenny

April 20

Dear Lenny,

You express so well what we both feel but what I cannot always say. I guess we'll know pretty soon now what will happen to you pretty soon now. If you are "shipped out" and do get a chance to come home again even if it's for a few hours — don't spare the money for fare.

Diana

4/21

Dearest,

It's so great to hear that the youngster is on the move — you're right — it makes me happy.

Lenny

April 21

Dearest,

As we discussed on furlough, the name we have decided for our coming baby is:

    If it is a girl Elizabeth Louise Miller   (Hebrew Leah)
    If it is a boy Frederick Douglass Miller (Hebrew Avraham)

With eager expectation, Lenny

April 21

Dearest,

Last night I had a very nice time. There were a number of speakers who spoke as a tribute to the Jews who died in the Warsaw Ghetto last year. Of the group that was present at the gathering, 80 demonstrated their desire to join the antifascist struggle. There was also a Jewish stage entertainer who comes from Warsaw and who lost her father, 2 brothers and 2 sisters last year.

Diana

ALMOST ON HIS WAY

4/22

Dear Diana,

One thing I'd love to do but won't for lack of space, is send home my military library — a real treasure, training material, not available in libraries — some of it I can't send because it's "Restricted" & some of it is just too bulky for you to store.

As to my first two letters after coming back to camp, I was tired & blue, as one always is, coming back. And I am worried — worried that you will be worried in the next 2–3 months when you have such a big job to carry thru, because mail will be very irregular & delayed, & I'll not be able to relieve your worry. And secondly I'm worried about your finances — we know you have the necessities & you have sufficient reserve for emergencies — but you are so tightly squeezed & I want you to have all the comforts.

Lenny

April 22

Darling,

And again we spend Saturday night together my love, and as I sit here writing to you I say to myself — Where is Lenny tonight? Lenny dearest — tomorrow is our anniversary, but if I remember correctly in 1938 we declared our love and watched the sun rise on Fri. night 'til Sat. morn.

Diana

4/23

Dearest,

Thanks, beloved, for your anniversary note. I wish I had your courage! When you write like that, I know I don't have to worry about you — I can only wish that my heart would agree to stop worrying!

The Major made a farewell address which was less inspiring than a sales manager sending out a crew of salesmen to peddle Squibb's Aspirin, & had not a single reference to the enemy we face; and we must sit by & not say a word. Later a man named Doug said he has to leave a 10 year old sow — so I said I have one en route, & so he acknowledged I was missing more — then I told him of my father's family who never had a chance to fight, & at best could expect a quick death rather than lingering misery[30]

---

30. Lenny speaks of those family members who perished during the Holocaust in Germany.

& how much better off we were — and he agreed heartily & his whole outlook changed, he became aggressive & even eager about the shipment.

Six years ago today — gee whiz! I can hardly wait for our 7th anniversary — perhaps we'll be together in the postwar world by then & we'll probably be up all night with a teething baby this time — but that too will be fun!

Lenny

4/23 Song for April 23

> Love came to us in the sunrise
> Love came to us in the dawn
> Love came to us with the lilacs
> And the bird song of the early morn
> Love came to us in the thunder
>   to us in the rain
> Love came to us in the battle
> For Liberty in Spain
> Love lives for us in the struggle
> Love lives for us in the pain
> Love lives for us in our worship
> Of Freedom's hallowed name!
> Love came to us in the sunrise
> Love came to us in the dawn
> Love came to us in the spring time
> With bird song in the early morn

Lenny

For 4/23

Happy anniversary Darling!

'Tis the first time that we have not been together on April 23 and it is hard, but my darling, this April 23 we have more to look forward to then in any other since 1938. The outlook for the people — for the freedom of mankind — surely we have made great strides forward since then. And for us — for you and me — within me beats a new life which is our future!

Yours,
Diana

April 24

Dear Diana,

Day all wasted in petty details — more exchanges of clothing, more stamping of numbers, etc. In the afternoon, we saw two good movies for soldiers only. One was a War Dep't report on the strength of the enemy which rather stressed the long road ahead a bit negatively; but it contained a captured Nazi film on the parachutist "rescue" of Mussolini, who looks like a sad sack. The other showed a guy after trying to evade combat, in the field, haunted by his conscience thereafter.

Lenny

April 25, 8:30 A.M.

Dearest,

The company street looks like a Blake Ave.[31] pushcart day or a bazaar — all the huts are emptied, the cots outside, & all our remaining equipment spread out for display for (we hope) the last inspection.

Lenny

April 25, 7:45 P.M.

Dear Diana,

Hersh, Max & I are at the service club for the last time tonight. We three are leaving by different trains in a matter of hours. While I know where we are going, I'll wait 'til I get there to say — that's best!

Lenny

April 25

Dear Diana,

Well we're packed, dressed & waiting. Waiting is the army's main occupation. It's like graduation day here — autographs being exchanged & such; mostly on the back of the company photo — taken when I was on furlough. There are few regrets at leaving this place.

And how is that youngster within you? I dreamed last night I went home to see the two of you & then had the devil of a time explaining it on return, to the Captain. You see — we can't go "AWOL" now — we can only "desert."

Lenny

---

31. In the East New York section of Brooklyn.

4/25

Hello,

The baby and I are starting this letter off by saying hello to you my darling. Your Fri. letter came today still from Shelby. Since I've had no further word from you, maybe you are still there, although your letter says you are leaving any hour and today is Tues.

Lee, if you will be near Washington — I don't think a trip down there would be too much for me, if I don't take any luggage — I'm sure it won't — let us keep this in mind, in case you cannot come home. I can see you shaking your head, but let us keep it in mind. I love you.

Your, Diana

April 26

Dearest,

I'm sorry — as the saying goes — "There'll be no promotion, this side of the ocean" — but there's the 20 percent raise on overseas service or $10 more for you.

Well, — see you again whenever we can — meanwhile — on my way.

Lenny

On His Way

April 26, En route, still in Mississippi

Dear Diana,

We're riding Pullman, so we'll sleep, which is good. Now 6 of us in our squad are together — As we waited in formation, there was a fellow & his young wife saying goodbye — dragging it out to the last, she clinging, head on his shoulder & sobbing as much as she tried to smile — and we were all angry. A soldier needs to forget such things: by their being there, they made all of us live over all of our partings. As Virgil says, even things that someday will be pleasant to recollect — but not when you are going into greater hardships —

And if I'm not careful I'm going to be very blue soon; for again I'm adrift with no personal perspective — 'tis all very well to say to oneself "be a good soldier" — only meanwhile there's no soldiering to do.

As for my scout training I doubt whether it will ever be used by the army. Well — if we K.O. Hitler & I get a chance to use my M-1 even once — that will be swell.

Lenny

4/26

Dearest Husband,

Gert is interested in a "wives" group and we discussed some of our ideas about it. I'm trying very hard to get a group together in someone's house, some time next week or so, and see if we can't get started.

I received an envelope full of various letters that you want me to keep. I'm still getting daily mail from Shelby, but I sort of expect to get a special delivery or telegram at any time with your new address — unless, of course, you'll be sent somewhere where you cannot let me know immediately.

Love — I realize that you are worried about me and I wish I could help you. You say that I have a big job to carry things in the next few months — well, so do you.

Love, we realized when I became pregnant that you would probably not remain here until the baby is born — as a matter of fact, we thought you would be away much before this — so now we must be strong and have confidence that each of us will do his job well and we must not worry overmuch about each other. I'm sure you'll be happy to know that I received authorization from the Dept. of Health today, that I've been accepted under the Army plan and that they will pay the doctor and hospital — so all is well on that score.

Your Diana, and your?

April 27, Tennessee, somewhere & April 28

Dear Diana,

Today 4/28 we pulled into Fort Meade at dawn. Since then, it's been a perpetual "on line," not without its comic angles: a physical examination in 15 seconds, ditto chow, ditto assignment to present barracks.
(O, my gosh, latrine in the building not ¼ mile away!) All signs point to a very brief stay here. Spirits are high all around.

Lenny

4/27

Lenny,

It's true about not being able to make your heart stop worrying even though you may understand and reason about things out. It's five months since Babe has been in the Pacific — at least Lucy has had some mail.

Diana

FORT MEADE, MARYLAND—THE LONG WAIT CONTINUES

4/28

Dear Diana,

All day gone with endless clothes checking & allied headaches. This place is a tremendous mill, thru which vast numbers are being squeezed under great pressure towards the invasion front. By the way — censorship begins at this point — so consider that in your letters now.[32]

Lenny

4/28

Dearest,

Since I am certain from today's letters that you are no longer at Shelby, I'm waiting anxiously for your new address. I hope there isn't too much of a delay before I get your next letter from the new place. I keep hoping to see you again before you leave for overseas. I wonder?

Diana

4/29

Darling,

There was an under current of excitement at leaving Shelby and going on to new and perhaps more important things. I'm truly glad you don't have to spend another summer in Mississippi. Of course the place you are going to may have its disadvantages, but if you are making a real contribution well, there will be no question of its being worthwhile.

The baby is wiggling a hello to you, and I'm sending you a smile, my love.

Diana and?

ONLY 24 HOURS—BUT HOME AGAIN!

May 1

Dear Diana,

Well, we were lucky again, having the pass, even for just 24 hours — and even though your man's been sleepy all thru — what a time! And silly Diana, got to go to the station — but that's all right, dear — I like you!

---

32. All letters were reviewed by an officer and any references to places or activities deemed sensitive were blacked out. After the war, Lenny added the names of places that had been removed.

And I like you being with me to the last minute too — only a soldier in my position has to be able to lock up his heart in a safe place, and memory with it, so that it will be available when needed, but out of his way for the time being — understand that, beloved, if I acted cool, indifferent — it makes for the best: emotion makes good lyrics but indifferentism makes good soldiers!

Lenny

6:30 P.M.

Dear Diana,

A slow day: going to a teargas chamber to test our new (& greatly improved) gas masks consumed all morning.

They gave us a lecture on what to write in order to have interesting letters & yet abide by censorship & everyone slept through that too, me included.

Lenny

5/2

Dear Lenny,

I went to the doctor today so I could write you what he said. I'm glad that I have such a glowing report to give you. All is swell. I gained 2½ pounds, which is just right.

Diana

May 3

Dear Diana,

Still on call for shipment at any time but nothing more definite just now —

Lenny

May 4

Hello,

Still here — We sat around from 5:30 A.M. 'til 9:30 just waiting.

Lenny

5/4

Dearest Husband,

Boy, has the baby been wiggling in the last hour. I guess it must feel that I'm writing to you and want to make sure I send you its love with mine.

I guess we gals sure keep the post office busy, but our postman always says he enjoys delivering mail from soldiers.

Diana

May 5

Dear Diana,

We get rather less sleep here than at Shelby. I've been in the supply room — sweeping, & sorting stuff that doesn't need to be sorted & counting things that need no count — so I'm taking time out to write to you. Frankly, this delay leaves me extremely unhappy, both at the waste of my time, & the concomitant delay (the big thing) in getting us over & into action. Where the hell is the invasion? (Yeah, I know its coming.)

Lenny

May 5, 10:00 P.M.

Dear Diana,

These days of do nothing waiting here are more than I can bear. Terrible as battle will be, I'll be glad to grip with an enemy I have hated all my life. And the same conscience that led me to pass up a prosperous career in safe academic channels will support me in the face of any fleshing fear of a beastly enemy. But this wasting time, getting soft, doing nothing is unbearable.

Lenny

5/5

Dearest,

Maybe you will again surprise me. Don't misunderstand — I'm not hoping for this because I know all the difficulties even if you are at Meade — but it would be so nice if you could come.

Here's a kiss and a wiggle — the one from me, the second from our youngster.

Diana and?

5/6

Dearest,

Like I told you last week I'm staying at home in case you can come. I keep telling myself not to hope too much, but I guess it's hard for my brain (which is more practical) to tell my heart what to do.

Diana

May 8

Dear Diana,

Now in a foxhole awaiting attack — 'tis a squad in defense problem; & old stuff & petty, compared to our division scale maneuvers, still it is a pleasure compared to sitting around & waiting for nothing. At least I feel like a soldier again.

Again — I'm sorry we had to separate so abruptly last night. It was in many ways the pleasantest weekend — finding you in alone & having all Saturday night together.[33]

Lenny

5/8,

Dearest,

And so again we were extremely lucky and spent Sunday together. My darling — wasn't it nice Sat. night when you came home to me and we were together for about 3 hours before we went over to see your folks. And then later when we said goodnight to them and were together — Whee! I love you so much.

Diana

May 10

Dear Darling,

This soft barracks life — very bad for a field soldier! One wakes from a good mattress — & is not excited by the prospect of work, whereas, rising from a bedroll on the damp ground causes no lingering backward glances!

No word or sign of shipment.

Lenny

5/10

Dear,

I'm so glad that you had some real training — for your sake. Your letter is one of the best I've had from Meade.

Mother's Day card signed "?"

May 11

Dear Diana,

A new shipment in today, so maybe I'll be included when they pull out. With no particular basis, I feel from the general atmosphere that this is my final week at Meade.

Lenny

---

33. Brief weekend furlough.

5/11

Dearest,

Last night I dreamed about you again — I do almost every night now and it was so pleasant. I always awaken smiling and feeling so good.

Well, all the girls who have babies warn me that I should get enough sleep now because you don't while the baby is very young. I'll have to train our baby right, but I guess it's not always a matter of training.

Diana

May 12

Dear Diana,

A nice sweat worked up by a hike this morning — not much, just 3 hours; only I wish I had some dry clothes to put on. A place like this is ruinous to discipline. Except for physical conditioning little or none of the drill really has value.

Such stupidity — they lock up the rifles so we couldn't clean them after they were fired Monday. Now — for inspection — they let us clean them tonight — now that they are saturated with rust — & at that, it was the very devil to get some cleaner & oil from the indifferent supply room.

Lenny

5/12

Dear Lenny,

I went shopping and I bought the first thing for the baby — it may sound funny to you — it's a knitting instruction book which has instructions on how to make many things for the baby. It cost 25 cents.

Your Diana and?

May 13

Darling,

I do hope that I'll see you this evening. After lunch, those of us on the alert were on pins & needles, as we were not told yes or no on passes 'til about 2:00 — when I was called, & told to pack. So I had my pass at 7:30 after being denied it 20 times earlier! A soldier's psychology: I am ready to go anywhere, anytime, for years, if need be, away from home & sweetheart; & never regret it: but to be 4 hours from home, doing nothing & not go home — that would drive him mad.

Lenny

5/13, 11:20 P.M., Saturday

Dearest,

I've decided to wait up for you until midnight because that is when you came home two weeks ago — if you come later you will find me in bed, darling.

There is no point saying I'm not disappointed — because I am. I thought there was a fair chance of your coming. I only hope I will hear from you by Mon. or Tues. so I shall know what's going on. Lenny, there is so much news that's encouraging from the war fronts — the new offensive in Italy by the 5th and 8th armies, the recapture of Sevastopol — these are good things.

Diana

VERY BRIEF LAST FURLOUGH BEFORE SHIPPING OUT

5/15

Dear Lenny,

You can see from my Sat. night letter, I didn't expect you anymore — of course it was all changed when you did come.

I had mail from Eddie who has been assigned to the Marines.

Diana

May 15

Dear Diana,

They're still finding new ways to torment us. For the nth time we unpacked & repacked, lugging the heavy bag a couple of hundred yards and upstairs to & from supply room — & there, as we are getting set to move, they inform me I am an alternate — which means I shall go through all the motions of shipment up to the last minute, & then stay behind, unless someone breaks a leg, to repeat the process all over again.

It is now 2 months since the 69th was declared ready for combat — me included — & it's many, many months since I've been set to go over — & here they continue to piddle & vex & irritate me endlessly.

Lenny

May 16

Dear Diana,

I have been here now 2 weeks & 4 days — & I'm going to hate this

place like Upton. Why in 18 days I could have done the Paradise Regained chapter, or mastered the elements of field artillery.

Lenny

May 17

Dear Diana,

Wednesday morning & the 31 sit in the barracks; orders: "stay in
the barracks." I guess most of the guys figure every day spent is a day
gained — a day less in the combat zone ("let the others win the war"),
a day spent in ease and loafing — only me — I have a sick-all-over
feeling starting in my stomach and radiating thence as I see that here's
another horrid day of inaction.

Oh Dina, how I wish this would be over!

Lenny

May 17, 7 P.M.

Dearest sweetheart,

Well, it looks like this is it at last. All is set, our duffle bags stamped for
shipment. To get away from the doing nothing here is a relief, even if it is
only to P.O.E.[34] and who knows what hell we may endure there — I can
only hope it will be short there and a quick trip & early into action — &
decisive battle before the Fourth of July.

Darling, I know you will continue to be well & take good care of
yourself and "?"; if it will be hard for you these next 2½ months to carry
your job through with one away, it will be also hard for me to do my job
with you so far away — but we'll both do our best, & I am sure that our
baby will be proud of both the parents it has selected.

I look forward to sending you love letters imbued with new atmosphere — the high seas, and who knows what strange countries!

Lenny

May 18

Dear Diana,

Still here at Meade but it's any hour now — After 2 weeks out of
Shelby it's about time.

Lenny

---

34. Port of Embarkation.

May 18, 7 P.M.

Dear Diana,

From all indications we shall leave some time during the night. Darling, darling, darling, we have been so very lucky so far — I am sure we shall continue to be lucky. We can expect our reunion in the post-war world. What a joyful world it will be — with the passing of Hitler & Fascism, & the Japanese empire, it will be like a new sun shining over a new earth — and the way will be open for millions more, in India and Africa and elsewhere to make the greatest advances towards a full, free life. And you & I and "?" will be marching in the victory parade. You can see, sweetheart, how my feelings improve as the moment of motion approaches.

"Dulcissima," rest easy, take care of yourself & "?" & if you feel like crying, go ahead & cry, & then do something for victory, because you are a soldier too, 'tho on special assignment.

Lenny

May 19

Dear Darling,

It seems from these letters that at last you were really leaving and I know how happy you are to go — even your handwriting is better than in the letters from earlier this week. So now I wonder where you are — You say you don't know when you'll be able to write another letter.

Beloved Lenny — the next 10 weeks will be hard for us both, but then so will it be until you are home again, and so has it been for over a year.

Your,
Diana

Censorship in Effect

May 19–20, 1944

Dearest,

I just learned that we're supposed to write on one side of the paper only — and so there's a possibility they will return my previous letters to me since I didn't know about that.

Lenny

5/20

Dear Lenny,

I'm pretty sure that you are no longer at Meade — I'm sending this to the new address since you ask me to in the letter that came this morning.

You write so confidently and well when you feel you are going forward to something important and it makes me happy.

Yes, darling, my feelings also improve as I see you going to decisive places. The tenseness, the anxiety, the uncertainty — all this vanishes as the time for action appears — and I don't feel like crying — no darling — I am not uneasy — I am fully confident that both of us will do our jobs well and earn the right to much happiness when we are together again with our new addition.

Diana

May 21, 1944, Fort Meade

Dearest Diana,

'Tis a beautiful Sunday afternoon, — as the picture postcards say, "Wish you were here" — only we'd better wait 'til after victory.

With no illusions and romantic nonsense about what lies ahead in combat, knowing that we face an enemy to whom killing is as natural as it is alien to us, that we go raw and unprepared into battle, no matter how much training we have as compared to those who saw the bombs fall and the shells roar close at hand, still — if that is what we are here for, if all our training is for the purpose of closing with the enemy, whatever the price to us is individually, well, god dam it, let's do it and not drag out this business in interminable delays.

Lenny

5/22

Dear Lenny,

I guess I must begin to learn to have infrequent mail. I realize that there is still a chance that I shall hear from you before you leave, but I'm not expecting it. I'm trying very hard to be a brave girl and I think I am succeeding. I'm not very worried about you — I know that you will be OK and that you are a good soldier. It's just that I am concerned about you, and mail is so important.

But darling — we've been lucky to be together until now — that is to have been able to see each other as often as we did — when I think of some of our friends who have been apart and not seen each other for more than 2 years — well, I'm glad you are leaving now with the invasion imminent.

Diana

5/23

Dearest,

Since I won't be around to see for myself maybe you can get a profile snapshot to me in about 4 weeks? I had to stop & say "I love you" (That's permitted by the censor — topic # 8)!

Lenny

5/23

Dear Lenny,

The bell just rang — wonderful interruption — it was the mailman with a letter from you. The first letter I've had since you left Ft. Meade and it is censored. As I wrote you yesterday, when I stop receiving mail from you for a few days — then I shall start to use V mail. I gather from your letters that you are OK but getting impatient again. But darling, you are really on your way now, so you should be able to hold out a little longer if necessary.

Diana

5/25

Dear Diana,

Evening mail call of Sunday reads just like a lonesome soldier's wife's letter. Well, 'tis true our wartime separation is now practically definitive, & this time it is for a "duration" length. Even if one comes back as many have before the war's end, one feels that being overseas has been of "duration" length. Dear, so far no solution has presented itself as regards keeping or returning your letters. First of all: please write one side of the paper only, as censors will not pass 2-sides; and second, when next you get stationery, get something much thinner & less bulky, like typing paper.

The company officers today called for all expectant fathers, & took the dates of anticipated arrival. There were about half a dozen. Perhaps there will be some way to smooth the increase of allotment in its time.

Lenny

5/25

Dear Lenny,

As I enter the 8th month this weekend, I've gotten bigger and I'm beginning to find it awkward to sleep face down and to turn around in bed. I'm glad we are settled on "Louise." It's been on my mind — so glad you looked it up.[35]

My Lenny, are you OK? You know your letters from this new place have no postmark at all. It looks funny — they just have the censor's stamp.

Diana

5/26 (Refers to goodbye phone call)

Dear,

Did I tell you what a beautiful voice you have? It was O so sweet, over the phone. Short as it was! You sounded so happy — so of course, I was happy; & smiling still. It was worth standing two hours on line for those few minutes. By the way — it's only fair to be short on the phone, because there were over 100 guys on line behind me trying to get phones in before the place closed down at 10 P.M.

Lenny

5/27

Dear Lenny,

Max called me this morning — he's still at Meade. He told me a very terrible and shocking thing — Meyer has been killed in action in Anzio. Harriet was notified last week. Myra has seen her and she is taking it like a soldier's wife — but it's very difficult to be brave when it hits so close. I don't like to write such things to you, but I know that you would want to know about it.

Diana

5/30 Memorial Day

Dearest,

A letter from Hanna, the latter containing much of pleasant news, but also the melancholy obituaries of two whom I knew in Welfare — who've given their lives in action. The list lengthens: Wilfred[36] was only the first. One almost wishes, for their sake, that there was a heaven.

Nate & I went to the nearest city earlier, & strolled about town. There are average USO facilities — a large center, a small club, & an information centre, all of which we visited. There is also a USO for Negro servicemen;

---

35. "Every little breeze seems to whisper Louise"—Maurice Chevalier in the film *The Innocents of Paris*, 1929.

36. Mendelson, fellow City College student, was killed fighting with the Lincoln Brigade in the Spanish Civil War.

they get around the separate facilities setup delicately — the posters merely say at the bottom "Colored Hostesses." And the friendliness of its girls was rather startling — I'm talking of obviously decent girls, not 'professionals' — one can have a dance date with no effort at all. The contrast to Mississippi hits one very suddenly.

Too bad we cannot mention place names: there's much one could write if that were possible.

Lenny

5/31

Dearest,

In the afternoon we had an interesting half hour of open discussion on war aims & postwar, held by the enlisted men alone. There was a lot of participation. It showed very little questioning of why the war or why we should fight, although this was expressed sometimes as merely "we were attacked and so we must protect our homes." However, there was a lot of questioning of whether the soldier would get a job after the war & what would happen to all the war production, the women workers, etc. Some were cynical & nasty; some pointed with resentment to the wretched treatment extended to soldiers in Mississippi by "civilians & 4F's" & asked wouldn't it be worse after the war; while a substantial number pointed to the repair of plant (railways, utilities), to consumer goods (autos, refrigerators) & to rebuilding the devastated countries as sources of postwar jobs.

Lenny

6/1

Dear Diana,

I am contemplating investing $2 in enrolling for the army's correspondence school, since I guess that, even if I do see combat action, there'll be more spare time than I can provide for. They offer a number of industrial courses like machine shop, but I'm dubious about "learning milling machines by mail" & I might as well take something somewhat related to my previous "paid experience" — So it may be the bookkeeping — accounting — cost accounting series. That's one way of planning for the postwar world; as a family man the problem of supporting the family is — well, a problem.

Lenny

6/1

Dearest, I stopped off at Bennett's to buy stamps. He can sell me half a bottle of vitamins — that is 50 for $3.00, since I don't expect to need more than about 50, its swell. Your wife is OK and so is our heir.

Diana

June 1

My Darling,

Christopher Columbus at least had an idea where he was going, even if he ended up in a different hemisphere; but we, who are sure to be just as surprised at our destination, don't even know where (or when — or if!) we are intended to go.

Lenny

6/2

Dearest,

I came home in time for supper and also because I want to be home this evening in case you can call me. I'm "sorta" hoping.

Diana

6/3

Dearest,

There's a hot rumor around that the big liberation push is on — & it makes one's hands itch for an M-1 & a bayonet. But we'll know soon enough.

Lenny

6/3

Dearest,

You just can't keep up your own place with a child on the allotment. I'm glad I have such a nice place to live. Lee — when I think of how soon it will be now — it's June already. I know it will take a lot of effort, especially until you come home, but I'm so glad we decided to have one. Aren't you?

Diana

6/4

Dear Lenny,

Well I'm beginning to think that you won't talk to me this weekend. I'm still not going to leave the house, though, because I feel there is still a chance and I want to be here.

Diana

Part II

Overseas

4

To the Front

ON THE USS *Wakefield*[1]

JUNE 5–13, 1944

6/5, V

Dear Diana,

This morning brought the glad news of the liberation of Rome. Grand! When this letter reaches you, lots of things will have happened, I guess, which will wait a long time before they can be told.

Lenny

6/5

Darling,

I became so excited when I saw Sgt. Leo Miller on your letters. Of course I was subdued when I opened them and read that it was only a temporary promotion. Here's hoping it sticks.[2]

Diana

6/6, V, D-Day

Dearest,

The censorship restrictions become more stringent, as you will soon see! Heard the news of the liberation offensive reaching France, grand thrill, at long last —

Were you looking up at the moon tonight — as I was? Someday, maybe, we'll look up at the moon together, here where I am.

Lenny

---

1. The USS *Wakefield* was a troop transport with the US Navy during World War II. Before the war, she was a luxury liner, the SS *Manhattan*.

2. Lenny never moved up in rank beyond Pfc while on active duty.

6/6

Dearest,

I'm sure you must know the news too — the invasion forces landed in Normandy this morning or rather during the night. Well, we are on our way — 4,000 ships, 11,000 planes. Those were the first radio reports and there are more reports every few minutes. We have been waiting for this news so long that now that it has actually started, we can only steel ourselves for what we have to do and participate in every way we can to "back the attack."

I know you would want to be there. Well, maybe you will still get your chance. We got the false rumor about the big liberation push over the radio also on Sat. We were kind of disappointed about it — but the real thing today sort of makes up.

Lenny — Roosevelt speaks tonight at 10:00 P.M. I wonder if you will be able to hear him also. It may seem to you that I'm rather calm in this letter considering, but it's not calmness, rather understanding of the tasks ahead.

Diana

6/7, V

Dear Diana,

Another quiet day, between reading and sleeping and chores and chatting the time goes by: it could be more profitably used but it is not being wasted.

Lenny

6/7

Dearest,

I'm fine and so is the baby. There's a feeling of determination among the people and much relief that the liberation push is on. Thousands volunteered for blood donation and bought bonds yesterday. Last night Mayor La Guardia had a special D-day meeting in Madison Square Park which had 50,000 people present.

Diana

6/8, V

Dear Sweetheart,

Still a leisurely life, I'm getting lots of fresh air & sunshine & spending hours in conversation, today, & in more light reading & in loafing. Practically anything else I might say is taboo. Boy, does everyone perk up when the radio brings news bulletins from France!

Lenny

6/8

Dear Lenny,

I spent a pleasant afternoon with my friend, Winnie. She is worried about the possibility of her husband being drafted and worried about money. I really feel sorry for her because she doesn't have what it takes to live today — she won't risk anything that she has, and because of this she is scared and unhappy, even though so far she hasn't really had to risk anything. It's funny for me to say I feel sorry for her — most people would feel it was the other way around right now — but you know what I mean.

Diana

6/9, V

Darling,

My love has traveled far distances and strange new routes, but these days it must be really hard put to find its way back! But it is the same reliable love, and can be trusted to reach you one way or another. Do you know I am getting quite excited at the thought of your approaching big day? Some seven weeks to go! How I wish I could be by to help but you'll do a good job, I know.

After carrying Whitman[3] (the one you gave me last November) thru many months, I read with great pleasure his "Democratic Vistas" & it could not have been saved for a better time.

Lenny

6/10, V

Darling Love,

Last night one could still read a newspaper by daylight at 10:30 P.M., so we continue to be baffled as to where we are.

Lenny

6/10

Dearest,

I had no mail from you today. This is the longest stretch without mail since you've been in the army and it's only the beginning. Now I really don't expect to hear from you for a while. Incidentally, the last mail I had was Tues, the day of the invasion.

---

3. Lenny carried a small volume of Walt Whitman's poems, *Leaves of Grass*, throughout the war. After he was wounded, it was sent home with a few other belongings by a squad mate.

I'm really so happy about the news from the European front. As you once wrote me, we're lucky that you didn't leave America 2 yrs ago and had to sit around waiting for things to happen. Now there are concrete hopes that the last stage of the war is here and that victory is not too far off.

How are you beloved? I'm fine — getting bigger but I don't mind.

Diana

6/11,V

Dear Diana,

The news of Nazi flight in Italy & Russian offensive in Karelin has just come in. The latter is especially to the point because those in Rumania have been asking, "What will Russia do?" It looks like we'll be hitting 'em coming & going now. Good.

Lenny

6/11

Dearest,

Last night I slept in your old room — for the first time alone.[4] Dearest, that room has such wonderful memories for us — we've always had such a good time there. Everyone is taking very good care of me — I am fine — the baby is fine too. I am worried about you, both as a soldier and as my husband but I know you will do a good job as both. Lenny, since the censor permits it, I want to tell you how much I love you.

Diana

6/12,V

Dearest,

There was no mail from you. Tomorrow will be a week.

Diana

6/12,V

Darling,

This is a rewrite, milady — they censored out the rest.

Lenny

6/13,V

Dear Lenny Dear,

I'm feeling fine — just as I have written before, it's uncomfortable

---

4. Diana stayed with Lenny's parents while her parents were on vacation.

now to lug around so much excess. I'll be glad when I'll be able to push it around. How are you, my Lenny? I hope so much that all is well. I really try hard not to worry about you. I know that it will be some time before I receive mail and now it may even be longer because of the fighting in Europe.

Diana

Camp Barton Stacey, England

June 13–July 7, 1944

Camp Barton Stacey, near Basingstoke, was where large numbers of American forces were stationed, especially prior to the June 6th invasion. In 1943, the War Department purchased land for use as a military training area. Lenny enjoyed his time here, often taking excursions into the neighboring countryside and towns.

6/13,V

Dearest,

Last night I again stayed up in the midnight daylight and at least by gosh was able to determine our location — This morning we are sort of sightseers — "and collecting memory souvenirs." Maybe when I get home again, and you have finished your breathless telling me of how you have been, & introducing me to our family, I'll tease you into listening long enough to describe to you some of the things we see today.

Lenny

P.S. We may now say we're here. Mersey River — Liverpool

6/14,V, Somewhere in Great Britain

Dear Diana,

Nate, the Californian says "If this is England, it is well worth fighting for." Most of the countryside I've seen is much like park & garden. The houses are definitely built to last! Not only the homes, but barns and fences are of solid brick wall. No wonder they say an Englishman's home is his castle.

Lenny

6/14, V

Darling,

I haven't received any notice of a new APO number[5] for you yet — I don't know whether I should be sending V-mail. If you haven't left yet, you'll get it anyway and if you have left, it will reach you much faster.

I'm fine — the baby is quite a big baby now from all outward appearance and so active. Well, dearest, I love you very much and here's a kiss for you.

Diana

6/14, Air mail

Dearest,

I wonder where you are.

Your,
Diana

6/15

Dear Diana,

After only V-mail letters for it seems ever so long, & leaving out all the interesting words because of security restrictions I've just got to write a straight letter.

I would never weary of the scenery here & would welcome a tour of the country like anything. As a matter of fact, I've climbed up a nearby knoll a dozen times to see over the horizon, maybe 10 miles away, and let my eyes rove over pastures & hedges, and copses — take a look at Milton's "L'Allegro" — the "hedgerow elms, on hillocks green." Unlike American greenery, though, it is clearly a groomed & gardened landscape, almost like a golf course in its décor. The country lanes are paved for durability (we feel them on our soles under the weight of our packs) and lined with venerable oaks and other trees which I do not recognize. Their trunks have been adding rings since Cromwell's day, no doubt.

The forest land is the most impressive sight of all: all at once I understand a lot of things clearly that I've read before. American woods, even at their densest are friendly from what I've seen. The Adirondack woods invite the hunter & fisher & camper, and in the south the Leaf River forest was dense & almost impassible in spots, but the sun shone through the pines and one felt secure and at home there. But here the forest is

---

5. Army Post Office: address for overseas mail.

dark and sunless, dank, and a solid phalanx abruptly interrupting the open grassland, as a lawn.

We continue to be amazed by the late hours that daylight keeps. It's broad daylight as late as 11 P.M. & after.

Lenny

6/15, V

Dearest,

I have traded in my greenbacks and got four one-pound notes, which are the cipher coupons the British use as legal tender currency and whichever way you fold them don't fit into a dollar-size wallet.

Lenny

6/16, V

Dearest,

Got a chance to play with a rifle again for a while & it was a pleasure. Mostly we have filler classes. Thanks for your handbag mirror — there are none to be had here.

Lenny

6/16, V

Dear Lenny,

The infantry is in for a terrific amount of glorification in the last 10 days since the invasion in Europe. Yesterday there was a parade in honor of the infantry near City Hall. I'm sure this will please you.

How are you my beloved? I'm really very well and so is the baby. So my darling — until my next letter — I kiss your lips.

Diana

6/17, V

Dearest,

Life continues easy but we are advancing, so all is well. We have co-residents of our 6-man tent, a colony of field mice, furry brown little critters who keep burrowing all kinds of tunnel entrances & exits & scoot in and out all the time. While arranging my things for eventualities, I couldn't decide exactly what to do with your photo, the one from our first furlough. It's so sweet to be always able to see the smiling face of the one I love.

A thrill yesterday "Stars & Stripes" reproduced the invasion day front page spreads from the New York papers.

Lenny

6/17, Sat.

Darling,

I think I know why you were asked who was a prospective father. I received in the mail today a letter from the Board of Health thru the War Dept. explaining the Maternity and Child Care Plan and enclosing an application for an increased allotment when the baby is born.

Diana

6/18, V

Dearest,

It's three Sundays today that we spoke to each other — it seems like a long time to me but I have to get used to many, many Sundays alone. I guess I'll feel better when I've had my first letter from you wherever you will be.

Diana

6/19, V

Dear Diana,

Stripping for action — I got a "baldy" haircut. How are my loved ones?

Lenny

6/19

Dear Diana,

We are still restricted to camp — must be always ready to go. However, there is something about a fence that beckons to the world beyond, especially one with gaps in it. So — many take off and wend their way over the pleasant green hills & dales to the little towns that may be found. For example, strolling westward, down the lane, & then to the right, one can enjoy a pleasant two or three hour stroll in the long evening sunlight. One comes to a bridge, on two huge stone arches, built for centuries' use & wear, not like the flimsy shaky structures that are swept away by every spring flood in New York or Mississippi.

There are chateaux, grand mansions, set back behind their private parks, revealing only their uppermost private stories & chimneys. There are the roadside cottages — rough brick or stucco & wood in the Tudor style; no shape, just a box & sloping slate roof. The lane is quiet & placid in the evening, & the steady stream of bicycling women, girls & old men is the only sign that the men are off to the war. The little children call, "Gawt any gawm, chum? Any candy?" One carries some gum on purpose to give them.

Lenny

6/19,V

Dearest Lenny,

In the afternoon we started out for a walk. We passed the Kinema Movie. "Purple Heart" was playing so we decide to go and see it. It was a good war picture. It's the story of the 8 American fliers that were captured in Japan after Doolittle's raid. It is a rather difficult picture to see but worth seeing.

Diana

6/20

Dear,

Another day of inspections and of rifle cleaning, clothes washing, hurrying and waiting.

Lenny

LENNY, WHERE ARE YOU?—WAITING FOR MAIL

6/20,V

Dearest,

Today is just two weeks that I've not had mail from you. It's been funny — writing to you every day not knowing where you are — whether you are on the ocean, still in the United States, whether you have landed anywhere, or whether you are already doing things. I've had to sort of hold on to my emotions and keep them in a separate place in my heart; you understand what I mean. Once in a while I have let go and cried a little, but then I've dried my tears and turned to some concrete way of showing my hatred of fascism.

Diana and?

6/20

Dear Diana,

D Day June 6 and 'til the 12th, I was on USS Wakefield, solo with no convoy. But on the eve of our final night, we received destroyer and flattop escort, off N. Irish coast.

Lenny

6/21,V

Dear Diana,

Some days I miss you so much and I get ever so much more eager for Junior to arrive! First day of summer and I'm still wearing my winter underwear.

Lenny

6/21

Dearest Diana,

There is more sun-shine in New York, in one day in January, than in all northwest Europe in all of July. They say Hitler made a radio speech yesterday ordering us to get out of France. Excuse us, for laughing, please.

Lenny

6/22

Dear Diana,

Day's duty done & chores too, and 5 hours of daylight still ahead at 7 P.M., so three soldiers leaped the low fence of their encampment, & chose a new & unfamiliar lane. The countryside presented a new more familiar face — well-paved lanes tightly set off by holly and privet hedges, pastures of sheep, fields of wheat & hay in the evening sunlight, distant mansions in their groves of ancient trees, nearer cottages of Tudor stucco & timber or rough brick, all bedecked with ivy & flower gardens. One stops to ask a local weather-beaten farmer where one is — he leans on his two-pronged pitchfork & tells the name of the next town.

Lenny

6/22, V

Dear Lenny,

Today is June 22 — an important anniversary in this war[6] and also exactly one year that I went to visit you in Miss. Remember you meeting me early in the morning at the foot of the guest house steps — what a beautiful day we had — and what a week followed. Every time that we've been together ever since you are a soldier has been so packed full of delight and ecstasy and wonder and joy and good fortune — but the next time we see each other — when you come back — it is hard for me to even imagine it. We can only work and wait for it meanwhile.

Diana

---

6. Date of German invasion of the Soviet Union.

6/23, V

Dear Lenny,

Even though we have been separated for the past 14 months — still I feel as though we are together. I feel that way even now — when I've had no mail for over two weeks. I need you with me a lot now, Lenny. There are many things that are troubling me as the time for the birth of the baby approaches. That is why I am so happy at the news from the fronts — I am so happy that you are going across now when the decision is being made, because I hope it won't be too long before you guys will be coming home.

Churchill said last night that Germany will see decisive battles this summer. This is very encouraging.

Diana

6/24

Dearest Lenny,

Now, for the first time since I have been pregnant, I have begun to be impatient about the birth of the baby. I would like to hurry it along for your sake even more than for mine, I know how anxious you must be and I want to be able to let you know that all is well. I guess the fact that I haven't had mail from you in almost three weeks now, has helped the last few weeks drag for me. It's not so much that I'm worried about you because I realize I can't expect mail for about another 10 days to two weeks, it's just that the waiting and uncertainty is so hard.

Diana

6/24, V, Somewhere in England

Dear Diana,

Barracking in an established confinement has its conveniences, especially in toilet & washing facilities, although the dingy old sheds and barren grounds replace the beautiful green valleys. However, the ground is flame-tipped with scattered beds of wild poppies and dandelions, and daisies & buttercups are in profusion. England beats anything I've ever seen for variety of wild-flowers.

Lenny

6/24

Dear Diana,

The lovely hills & long valleys with grazing sheep & cattle are suddenly interrupted by a black shadow in the distance — something one has been searching for: and the girls confirm it is a "colliery" which needs translation into "coal mine" for some of the guys. One soon sees grimy faces & tattered clothes marking the miners as a different group.

At long last one enters the town: this one is sooty — the colliery leaves a mark. The pub, first choice of American soldiers, is a bigger place than some seen before. One experiments: tonight it'll be stout, Whitbread's; a buddy tries Guinness & one exchanges tastes. The former is really enjoyable and well worth the price (shilling for half pint).[7]

Lenny

6/25, V

Dearest,

Time drags. We wait. For our "morale," we have 1½ hours of athletics in the afternoon, while the most interesting places in England lie all around, barred to us for no good reason at all.

And how are you both coming along as you enter your ninth and final inning?

Lenny

June 25, 10:15 P.M.

Dear Diana,

It was a dull day, cloudy & drizzly. But after supper a couple of soldiers started to hike. Finally a jeep, driven by a Negro officer, drew up & 3 of us hopped aboard & tore through the beautiful farm-lands. Regrettably, only an hour was available to take in the city, as the last bus back to camp leaves at 9:00. There is an old cathedral in the town[8] & we walked around under the ancient Gothic buttresses but it seems not to be open at all (a war sign) & so couldn't be entered.

An interesting 20th century innovation is the air raid shelters, which are open. One sees many other indications that once an invasion was momentarily expected; but those details are probably censorable. (Incidentally, there's blackout here, not as in N.Y., once in 3 months for an hour, but every night, all night all over England.) We didn't feel it in our tents, but here in barracks, the windows all have blackout curtains & discipline is strict on this matter.

---

7. A shilling in 1944 was worth eleven American cents.

8. Lenny could not identify his locations during the war, but wrote them in afterward. This is Winchester.

The children ask for gum & American coins — one parts with one's last Lincoln pennies. Then one makes a dash to the bus terminal & rides back on the top tier of a two-deck, very common in England.

Lenny

6/25,V

Dear Lenny,

Today is just a year that we spent our wonderful Sunday together in Mississippi. Remember how we talked of having a baby and how we decided to wait until your furlough before we did anything about it. I didn't really think at that time that we would be able to carry through, because there seemed to be so many obstacles, but I'm glad that we decided as we did and that things worked out for us. It seems funny to me that I ever had any doubt — thanks, darling for understanding and helping me to understand. Here's a kiss because I love you so very much.

Diana

6/26,V

Dear Diana,

We heard combat experiences from men who have been through it.

Lenny

6/26,V

Dear Lenny,

I feel like talking to you, saying I love you. How are you, my darling?

The authorization for the baby allotment, the additional $15, came from the war dept.

Diana

6/27,V

Dearest,

We've been told we'll not get mail for some time to come — I hope at least you get mine.

Studying a bit — a GI book about German infantry weapons and rifle range practice, of which we can never get too much. Although we lay a good deal, in mud, there was a huge double rainbow to help make up for it.

Lenny

6/27,V

Dearest,

Hurrah! Two V-mails from you today! It's three weeks today since I had mail. Of course, the letters don't tell me very much yet. They don't say anything about where you are or of your safe arrival. Since they are dated 6/8 and 6/19, I am assuming they were written en route, and since they are photographed V-mail, I guess they were sent after you arrived, somewhere. I do hope you will be able to say where you are soon. Oh, my beloved, I hope so much that you've had some mail from me.

Diana

6/29, V

Dear Diana,

This is a rugged day — speed march morning, obstacle course afternoon, but of such things no complaining. The countryside hereabouts shows few mansions but runs to large farms. My guess is that the war has brought much unused land back into cultivation, but there's no chance to talk to local folk. The English hide their houses behind big hedges so none of this "thy neighbor on the front porch business" that one finds at home.

Lenny

6/29, V

Dear Lenny,

This bright and sunny morning brought me 8 V-mails from you and now I know where you are and that you have arrived safely. I'm glad that you're in such a beautiful place and that you seem to like England — Darling — write about everything that you are permitted — you know I want to know as much as I can. I wonder — has any of my mail reached you?

Diana

6/30

Dearest Diana,

In your 6/20 letter, you note, how it's hard to visualize me in a strange land. Well, I've tried, & shall continue to describe our surroundings within the limits of military security. Of course, place names & photos are simply out. However, the places I've seen look just like the pictures we see in all standard travel books — the thatched house with trailing rose vines, the gentry's mansions, the narrow lanes, the rugged coast & the busy harbors, the city houses with their second & third floors projecting above the ground floor, & the guildhalls & cathedrals. It's a real country for the historian. On the streets, the khaki-clad Americans, the tweed-dressed British Royal Engineers & Royal Artillery & the blue RAF men exchange carefree banter. There'll always be an England & maybe we'll tour it together.

Lenny

6/30, V

Dear Sweetheart,

Our endless "showdowns" for inspection are futile enough, but what should one say of a "dry run" showdown, like today's, where a whole morning is consumed in arranging a special display of equipment, lugging it all 1/4 mile up & back — without even holding an inspection?

Lenny

6/30

Dear Lenny,

You still don't say much except about the scenery and you write that you expect to be moved. Write me about everything you possibly can.

I went to Dr Shaw today. Since he thinks the baby will come around July 15, he gave me instructions as to what to do. He said for me to call him and he would come to my house and examine me and take me to the hospital when I am ready to deliver.

Diana

7/1, V

Dearest,

I enjoyed a pleasant 10-mile hike this morning, thru lovely farm country and two villages of thatched 2-story houses. This morning we saw a freshly thatched house, so it's not an old-fashioned thing — they pack oak straw, with seeds left on, evenly to about 10 inches, and bind it by other straw, or chicken wire, & use several layers up to 30 inches.

Lenny

7/2, V

Dear Diana,

Curse this blind policy of no passes. There are places near here I am dying to visit — places which were famous & already venerable when Caesar invaded this island — and all around an interesting nation to meet. It was possible to get out hitherto but now KP & guard duty looms big over anyone who chooses to ignore the stupid restrictions. 'Tis curious but I find myself much more familiar with England than I was with Mississippi when I first came there. Probably France will be similarly familiar.

Lenny

7/2,V #2

Dear Diana,

It was bad enough we were gypped when we left the 69th — we had earned the expert infantry badge & it was passed out the week after we left; and now there's a $5 & $10 raise for the badge holders — & I am really sore. Also we've not been issued our good conduct medal ribbons — it's not much but still we have earned it. Between rain & restriction, one is forced to waste the day in sleeping & I don't like it.

Lenny

7/2,V

Lenny,

My mother is home with me because I cannot go to the beach now and she doesn't want to leave me alone. I spent the morning getting all the things ready that I shall need in the hospital.[9]

Darling — how are you? Write me as much as you can now that my kisses know just where to go to reach you.

Diana

7/3,V

Dearest Lenny,

Hurrah again — 10 letters from you this morning. You're spoiling me, beloved — I had 21 letters since last Tues, but oh how I love it, and how I hope it will be able to keep up. I'm so glad that you had mail from me and that my Father's Day card to you came on time.

Lenny, you were right, my mother is getting much more enthusiastic about the baby. We went to buy nightgowns for the baby and they wanted too much money for very poorly made ones so my mother bought some material instead and she made them herself. Darling, the things that you ask for — shave cream, etc, I shall buy and mail to you.

Diana

7/3,V

Dear Diana,

I pray for a cool July for you — wish you could have our temperature here: 'tis like April at home. By now you must have had some mail from me — there's no reason for you to be worried.

---

9. A two-week hospital stay was typical, with complete bed rest after childbirth, which delayed recovery.

The war news has the guys all enthusiastic, although most have a very peculiar idea of just how much we hold in France — because newspaper maps are deceptive.

Lenny

7/4,V

Dearest,

The sky was filled this morning with blue and gold, and a hundred gleaming points of reflected sunshine, and the men smiled, saying that someone would teach Hitler today how we celebrate the Fourth of July. At breakfast tables the buzz went around "Minsk is taken!" Never has there been such interest in the war news, and rushing to buy papers.

Look to the moon beloved, it is near full.

Lenny

ANTICIPATING THE BABY'S ARRIVAL

7/4,V

Darling,

I spent the morning getting my drawers in shape so that I could empty out some for the baby's things. The bassinette which your cousin Edith sent arrived today. The Railway Express delivered it even on the 4th of July — they are so busy. It is very nice and will be swell until I get a crib. I also arranged with Babe's father to let me use his camera to take pictures of the baby — now I'll try to get film.[10]

Diana

7/5,V

Darling,

I love your V-mail letters — I gobble them up and watch the dates so eagerly — but I love your long letters too — they are the real meat — they give me a feeling of where you are and what you are doing. Please continue to send me both kinds as long as you possibly can have time to.

Diana

7/5,V

Dear Diana,

Tonight passed the third mail call with your letters still delayed some-

10. There was a wartime shortage.

where — I pray you have had some of mine. And you have less than a month to go! Happy?

Lenny

7/6,V

Dearest,

I arranged with Lucy about mailing you a cablegram, as soon as the baby is born. She will also write you a V-mail immediately. I'll write, myself, as soon as I can. We shall also see if we can have you notified thru the Red Cross, but I don't know if they do those things.

Diana

7/6,V

Dearest Diana,

We won another battle this afternoon by holding showdown inspection number 41,395. It would take a Gilbert & Sullivan to do it justice. Strange — this is one of those occasions when there's nothing to say that can be said in an open letter subject to restrictions. It's also hard to keep writing when there's no response as you've already observed.

Lenny

7/7,V

Darling Lenny,

I'm doing very well and so is the baby. I'm all ready now. I have the things to bring the baby home, a bassinette for it to sleep in and all the things, I shall need in the hospital so I'm just waiting.

Diana

5

Somewhere in France, Somewhere in Belgium

BETTY LOU AND THE BREAKOUT FROM NORMANDY
JULY 9–SEPTEMBER 11, 1944

On July 9, 1944, Lenny landed in Normandy on Utah Beach at St. Germain de Varreville. The 69th Division, famous from World War I, finally disappeared from history while Lenny was in England. Lenny was to be one of the thousands of replacement soldiers to fill in the ranks of the divisions depleted from the Normandy losses.

He joined the 3rd Infantry Battalion, 120th Infantry Regiment, 30th Infantry Division, First Army. On July 19, in the midst of the 29th, 30th, and 35th Infantry Division's two-week battle for St. Lô, which left 95 percent of the town in rubble, Lenny suffered a badly sprained ankle when he dived to avoid a sudden German Stuka (two man dive-bomber) attack.

He was laid up in the hospital in La Cambe, an army convalescent hospital, long enough to miss the 30th Division leading the advance in the first day of the Normandy breakout (Operation Cobra) July 25 through 31. Cobra immediately commenced after the battle for the high ground in St. Lô. Many American troops were killed, also suffering casualties from their own air force, due to the overcast weather, last minutes changes in plans, and miscommunications characteristic of the immature technology of this early phase of joint air-ground operations. Seven weeks after D-Day, the breakout from the hedgerow country of Normandy had finally begun.

One week after the breakout, with the Third Army armor and First Army infantry streaming along the southern flank of the German forces in Normandy, the 2nd Battalion, 120th Infantry

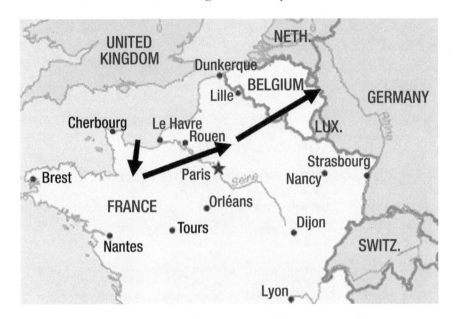

France and Belgium

Regiment of the 30th Infantry Division blocked key elements of the German counterattack by four to six Panzer Divisions, ordered by Hitler into the fray, by stubbornly holding on to the high ground of Hill #314, west of Mortain. The resistance at Mortain and by the 30th Division, overall, helped lead to the collapse of German forces in France and their retreat back to Germany.[1]

During this period while Diana was awaiting the arrival of the baby, their mail was significantly delayed so that neither knew what was happening to the other.

From August 7 to August 13, mail was cut off during the strong German counterattack in response to the Allied breakout. Betty Lou was two weeks late. By the time Lenny received the cablegram about

---

1. Isolated from their division and regiment, the wounded of the "Lost Battalion" were noted as some of the most vocal voices against any surrender to the Germans. The officers mentioned in a reprint of the *Stars & Stripes* article on "The Lost Battalion" that Lenny sent home in November were still leading the 120th Regiment during the Battle of the Bulge. One of them, he noted later, was killed there at Malmédy in December 1944.

the baby, delayed because it was sent to his address in England, Lenny had rejoined his unit at Domfront.[2]

From here on in, mixed in with all this "baby" talk and Diana sorting out just where Lenny was, was the story of Lenny's and the American forces' rapid advance through France toward the Seine and Paris. Assigned to S-3 (Intelligence/Interrogation), Lenny initially went ahead by vehicle, with two colonels, acting as interpreter since he spoke French and German, as the officers made their way through the newly liberated French towns.

By the time Lenny reached the River Seine, he had resumed this "intelligence" role with his regular unit, in the 3rd Battalion, 120th Infantry and joined in interrogations of large numbers of prisoners. These sometimes hair-raising interrogations took place on the open road, in the midst of the intense traffic of the large convergence of American units crowding the roads along the Seine River, heading for Paris, interspersed with the sound effects of daily artillery and machine gun assaults by the fleeing Germans.

Just as Lenny's unit came in sight of the Eiffel Tower in the distance, the week-long liberation of Paris by the Resistance finally ended on August 25 and the First Army was ordered to turn north toward Belgium and Germany in the race to the Siegfried Line.

LENNY LANDS AT UTAH BEACH — ONE MONTH AFTER D-DAY

7/9

Dear Diana,

Mail from me is bound to be uncertain. I am taking good care of myself for your sake and for the sake of all that there is to do, after this war is won. It is hard, of course, when you do not know where I am,[3]

---

2. Still recovering from his injury at St. Lô, Lenny was separated from his own unit during the action at Mortain. With the article he sent to Diana in November, he wrote: "I deeply regret that during this week I was only able to set back at the Service Co with one cook & our mail clerk, we 3 wondering all the while if we were to be the Company's only survivors."

3. This is the first reference to Lenny being in France near Utah Beach, Lower Normandy. When he landed in Normandy, he was assigned to the 30th Division, Old Hickory. The 29th and 30th Divisions saw action in the fierce battles around St. Lô.

except in a general way, but as a rule I know where I am and you know you can rely on me!

Lenny

7/10,V

Dearest,

Language is no barrier at St. Germain de Varreville. All the time I was training I asked for examples of captured German material and now our invasion has made a lot of it available.

Read my Whitman awhile today — it's beginning to show signs of field use!

Lenny

7/10,V

Dear Diana,

Love, I'm extremely pleased about the bond allotment. Are you sure you'll be able to manage on $13.40 per month? If you need more, I shall send it to you. I'm so pleased because it means buying bonds and saving, both of which we have not been able to do since I stopped working. I hope with $95 I shall not have to use any of our savings except for initial expenses.

Lenny

7/10

Dear Lenny,

Last night I went to the movies with Lucy — the first time I have been anywhere in 10 days. You see I stay home mostly now because it is best for me to take it easy. My darling — I'm fine and so is kid activity — boy what a kicker.

You should see me — I think you would laugh — I'm really so round and I stick out in front and I waddle like a duck. And in this heat, I'd be so glad to push the baby around instead of lugging it around.

Diana and?

7/12,V

Dear Diana,

At last some sun, but with a vengeance, for we hiked under a heavy load this afternoon, seeing some piece of the country. Hereabouts roads are extremely narrow, one-way affairs, locked in by high hedges (often solid rows of trees, with earth banked up like walls) and by stone walls.

War economy shows up in clothes here; food in a farming area seems a small problem; but clothes are ragged & discolored by age.

Lenny

7/13, V

Dearest,

Every passing day, I count the hours and the minutes to your big day — dearest, how are you??? And your last letter was dated 6/22, so that 21 of your letters, lie in mail pouches between Brooklyn and this apple tree under which I write. Gee, gosh, oh well. Blasted Nazis!

Lenny

7/13, V

Darling,

Most of our friends, who have children, have told me that the last few weeks before the baby is born seem the longest, and that is just how I feel. I'm terribly impatient. I guess this waiting must be difficult for you too because it will take even longer before you know.

Yours,
Diana

7/14, V

Dearest,

I just came home from the doctor a little while ago. All is well with me and he told me, the next he expects to hear, is when he will be called to take me to the hospital. My darling, I love you so — I do look at the moon at night and know you do.

Diana

7/15, V

Dear Lenny,

Today is the day that Dr. Shaw said, but I'm figuring as you and I did — towards the end of the month.

Diana and?

Somewhere in France

7/17

Dearest Darling,

I'm writing this slow mail on purpose — it should·reach you after the baby arrives. First of all, I am "somewhere in France" and have been for some time. The first day, when we waded ashore & began to taste the war as a real thing, was the most interesting day of my life.

At present I expect to see an even more interesting day before the week is out and since it may be some time before I can write again this should explain matters for a while.

Beloved, as I approach the real test of tests, having undergone some small ones already over here, I find that I have the confidence of a well-trained soldier on top of the serene, confidence of one who is sure of his cause and ready to do anything for it.

Lenny

7/18

Dear Dena,

By the time you get this, you're either about to or already have given birth. Gee! Well, & now I have my new address. Please contact the Red Cross to let me know the news.

Good luck, beloved, I pray you have an easy time of it, at least as easy as can be.

Lenny

7/18

Dear,

Yesterday it was "hurry up", and today it is "wait." Time is occupied and we are prepared.

Lenny

7/18

Dear Diana,

A little 9-year-old, undersized French kid, in a pasture where we stopped a while yesterday told me that the Germans stole all the "food" and their troops occupied local homes sleeping on the beds, while the residents had the floor.

The few adults I've met reflect the different attitudes that the press has reported. Just like New York, some people believe in democracy & some don't give a damn.

Lenny

7/18, V

Dearest,

Since I have a little extra money this month, I think I shall use it to make a contribution to the war cause.

Diana

ASSUMES BABY IS BORN

7/19

Darling Diana,

May I be the first to congratulate you? Maybe this will reach you sooner, but you can see from the date I was first! As soon as possible, let me know all the details and don't leave anything out.

Lenny

7/19,V

Dear Lenny,

It seems to me when you get home, we'll talk for months and months and then still have much to say. Even though, it is not yet two months, since last time I saw you and even though we write every day.

Diana

7/20

Dearest,

While I still have no special preference, it begins to be a matter of interest whether it is a boy or a girl.

Lenny

7/21,V

Dearest,

Every day I get at least two or three phone calls asking how I am. My folks don't leave me alone for a minute now.

Diana

7/22,V

Dear Lenny,

Your brother Eddie got a pass and is fine. He is much more mature, Lenny — both in appearance and in his attitude towards things. He is a little one sided and said, "Outside of his brother, no one else is a real fighter unless he is a marine." but I think he can be forgiven.

Diana

7/23,V

Dearest,

My mother is home with me but nothing I can say will persuade her to leave me alone. Now, unless her vacation will be over before the baby is born and she will have to go back to work. Well, there's a whole week to go yet, so I won't worry about it now.

Diana

No Mail for a Month

7/24

Dearest,

It's more than a month since the date of your last mail, and there's no prospect of getting any, either, and one gets to be lonesome sometimes.

The German prisoners we saw at Shelby were men, adults. Here we see the full "flower of the Hitler youth" — kids of 16–17–18, looking 13–15.

Lenny

7/24,V

Dearest,

I had two V-mails from you today, in which, you still haven't heard from me. My darling, it must be so difficult for you even though you say you aren't worried. There must be 30 letters at least that are on their way to you. Dearest, I'm well and so is #2.

Diana

7/25

Dearest,

If this paper recorded like a phonograph record, it would not sound so remote from the war. Have no fear, I'm having my fill of soldiering.[4]

Lenny

7/25,V

Dearest,

I had 3 letters from you today from 7/14 and 7/16. Darling, since to-day is the 25th of the month, the baby should really come very soon now. I'm really quite concerned about letting you know because no mail seems to be reaching you at this place. I haven't your new address yet.

One of your V-mails today had your poem entitled, "France." I like it very much and I was happy to see it. I've been looking forward to some poetry from you.

---

4. From July 9 through 24, the Allies broke through the German lines west of St. Lô. This is the first indication he is seeing action.

Lenny, sweetheart — I'm impatient too but we have to wait until the baby is ready. Next baby we shall wait for together and it will be easier.

Diana

7/26

Dear Darling,

Becoming a papa at long distance without benefit of bulletins, of any sort, leaves one not knowing what to say. Of course, my hunger for the news, as you may expect, is shared by several hundred troops out here.

Lenny

7/27,V

Dearest,

Of course you and I know that the baby is due now — that it wasn't due in the middle of July, but the Dr. confused us. However, since it is due now, I wish it would hurry up and not keep us waiting much longer.

Diana

7/28,V

Dear Lenny,

These days now are quite uninteresting because there is so little I can do. I know that my letters to you must reflect this, darling, but soon, very soon, I hope, a new personality will appear in my letter. And there should be so much that is interesting and wonderful to observe. I'm so very anxious to start having the responsibility of developing this new little person.

Diana

7/29,V

Dear Lenny,

Today I received your new address darling. Can you write me where you are? I wonder, are you still in England?[5] Take care of yourself. Darling, I feel fine — just so very big and clumsy.

Diana

7/29

Dearest,

We shall do our best to let you know as quickly as possible — I only hope the message is not held up like my letters of the past 5 weeks.

I'm glad that you seem to be satisfied with what you are doing

---

5. Lenny has been in action for almost a month. Diana has no news of that yet.

although I can only guess what it is. Since you are in the same type of an outfit as in Mississippi, I'm glad of all the training you had. Dearest, you don't write where you are — I guess you would if you were able to. I did read about the 120th Infantry in the newspaper, though, and they seem to be quite busy. I wish I could know if you are with that particular group.

Diana

7/30, V

Dear Darling,

Here it is practically the end of July and I'm still waiting for the big day. Darling, it must be even more difficult for you to wait not knowing what is going on here.

Diana

7/30

Dearest Diana,

How has the housing situation been worked out? I hope it hasn't been too hard on Lucy, but I'm afraid it may have. And tell me, Dina, how are our parents holding up to suddenly becoming grandma and grandpa & aunts and such? Do they appreciate what we have done for them?

Lenny

7/31

Dearest,

And so — the kid has come and all is well[6] — and you are happy, aren't you? It was tough, those last hours in labor — we knew they would be — but that's over now. After waiting six years for this happiness, now it is really a strain till the actual word comes through.

"Dininka," would you trace me the outline of the kid's hands & feet on paper — get fingerprints — anything else that can legally be mailed — as well as a photo as soon as can be?

O, Dina, these great times of the liberation offensive are a grand time for great love, and soon millions more will be able to enjoy the same outlets as today we look forward to.

Lenny

---

6. Lenny assumes the baby is born, based on the expected due date.

SHE KNOWS HE'S IN FRANCE

7/31,V

Darling,

Today's V-mails confirmed what I thought when I first received your new address. Also, darling, I had read in the newspaper that the 120th Infantry is in France. I was just surprised that you hadn't written it.

You will probably be a bit disappointed that the news reached me before you intended it to, that is before the baby was born, but don't mind, my darling. Your wife tries hard to be as good a soldier as her husband, and I know that you weren't sent overseas to sit around. I won't say that I'm not worried — I am sad. I shall be until you come home after victory — but I shall try to turn my anxiety into the fighting kind, so that I shall do a good job with our baby and make a contribution to help win the war in whatever way I shall be able to.

Yes, dearest, you are the first to congratulate me — I'm glad you are the first even though it is a little early. I love you so, Lenny — I'm glad I know where you are — but I do understand your motive in not telling me immediately. Try not to keep things from me, though, because you know I want to know as much as I can.

Diana

8/1

Dearest,

I had a long letter, extremely interesting because it was the account of your trip over. Yes, the censors passed the whole thing, not even cutting out a single word.

Love, don't be too worried about me, please. You be OK and all will be well with me. My darling — you'll write, of course, as soon as you hear from me. Here's a kiss for my special soldier whom I love very much.

Diana

8/2

Dearest Diana,

I see by "Stars & Stripes" that it is publicly announced that my regiment is in action in France so it's no use my covering up that fact. Actually I already owned up to that fact in a slow mail letter of July 19, but I wanted to spare you unnecessary anxiety during the last weeks of your pregnancy. It will be a load off my mind to be able to write freely again, without watching every word. But, sweetheart, don't let it be a load on your mind.

The face of war is something very dreadful, indeed, but far less dreadful than a conscience, uneasy because of not doing enough in the holy cause of freedom. So far, in the sense of personal safety, we have been rather lucky, although I would be happier if luck had also permitted me to do more than so far has been possible. To you, of all people, there is no need to explain that coming to grips in direct physical combat with the Nazis is the goal of all the training time spent in the army at home — not to speak of all that we have said & done in the years that came before. And if you and our family are well, all is well.

Blasted Nazis — Six weeks no mail.

Lenny

8/2,V

Dearest,

I'm still around and getting more impatient every minute. Dearest, I guess I must have conceived towards the end of the two weeks we spent together or perhaps it is because the full term is 280 days which is one week more than nine months.

Diana

8/3,V

Dearest Lenny,

My darling, we can't have much longer to wait so let us try to be patient. I know that's easier said than done for both of us, but let's try. All my love —

Diana

THE BABY ARRIVES

8/6,V

Dear Lenny,

Hurrah! You have a big, baby daughter weighing 8 lbs, 12 ounces. You can be proud of Diana & "?." Diana took it like a trooper. Mama and Daddy saw her soon after and said she's fine. Saw the baby, too, when she was 15 minutes old. They're already prejudiced — they called her beautiful. I hope this gets to you soon, Lenny. I also sent you a cable earlier this evening. I also hope you're home to celebrate your daughter's first birthday. Do a good and fast job on the front. There's so much for you to fight for now!

Lucy

8/6

Dearest,

Today is the second month of the Second Front in France — the door is just opening and we've got a foot in — but we're pushing. No one really enjoys the prospect of returning to the front, but it is fearfully dull here.

Lenny

August 7, Western Union Cablegram

HURRAH YOU ARE A FATHER DIANA AND DAUGHTER DOING FINE

LUCY[7]

8/7

Dearest,

I hunger so much for mail.

Lenny

8/7, V

Dearest,

Mazel Tov and congratulations, daddy Lenny! We have a new daughter, born just before 7 P.M. last night, Sun. Aug 6, weighing 8 lbs, 12 oz. Isn't it wonderful? Darling, it is hard for me to write because I am flat on my back although I feel fine so don't mind my handwriting.

I just saw Betty Lou and she's perfectly fine. Dr. Shaw says she's perfectly normal. Aren't you happy? I am and I'm glad it's over. Love from your two girls —

Diana

8/8

Dear Diana,

And how are "my darlings" this morning? Right now I'd walk from here to anywhere if only I know there was word to be found there —

---

7. The cablegram sent by Diana's sister, Lucy, was delayed because it was sent to Lenny's address in England and also, from August 7 to August 13, mail was cut off during the strong German counterattack in response to the Allied breakout during the Battle of Normandy.

46 days without a letter. How long does a maternity case stay in the hospital these days? Have you been very lonely? You shouldn't be — you have the family (our family) with you 'til I come home to join you again.

Lenny

Aug 8, V

Dear Lenny,

Gosh, darling, I just saw Betty Lou again. I'm so very thrilled. I don't know but she's a little like you and a little like me and she's wonderful. Or am I prejudiced?

Diana

8/8

Dearest Lenny,

The pains started Sat. during the night. Gosh, dearest, the first letter that I get from you in which you know about the baby — I just can't wait for it. I've been very comfortable in the hospital. You should see my bed — it's all decorated with flowers — roses from your folks and Lucy and a bouquet from my father's society.[8] Everyone is so excited about our baby. The folks are thrilled. My goodness, I never saw them so excited about anything —

Your,
Diana

8/9, V

Dearest Lenny,

I think that I'll devote this letter to telling you about our folks' reaction to the baby. It's really unbelievable — just like you said. They are all so thrilled, you can hardly talk to them. Your folks are buying the crib for the baby and mine are buying the baby's carriage so that takes care of the big items.

It's funny to me now that I could ever have thought that they weren't pleased about the baby. Now all we want is that the war be won soon, so we can all be happy together. I haven't seen the baby today because they only show them to mothers that aren't nursing every three days.[9]

Dr. Shaw comes to see me every day and he was swell to me when I was in labor, but I'll write to you about that when I describe the whole

---

8. Organization of folks from the same town in Eastern Europe.

9. Diana didn't nurse because of the strain she was under with her husband at the front.

thing. I feel OK dearest, better every day and now I can turn and my bed is raised higher every day too.

Diana

8/10,V

Darling,

I have people come to see me everyday. Your folks, my folks, etc., everyone tries so hard for me not to be lonely. I didn't see the baby today because they only show them twice a week but Dr. Shaw came in to see me after he saw her and he said she's fine.

Diana

8/11

Dearest,

At last I've found a chaplain who promises results and gives me hope of some mail reaching you — a cable, information at an early date. Here's hoping. Meanwhile I trust that all's well with you.

Lenny

8/11

Dearest Lenny,

I am in a room with 5 other girls — 3 plus me are servicemen's wives — the other two are civilians and paying $70 for the 9 days. I am the only one with a husband overseas — the other soldiers are all on furlough, which makes it a little hard for me. It's funny you're assuming that the baby's birthday is July 31. I sort of expected it to be then also, but since it is Aug. 6, I guess that I conceived during the second week of our stay together.

Darling, in your letters you ask for pictures — we shall take them as soon as I bring the baby home — also an outline of her hands and feet. Betty Lou and I are the proudest ones here because our man is away fighting for us and making the world a better place for us to live in. I would like us to have another baby when you come home and after you get to know Betty Lou — you missed so much with this one. Well, we shall see — huh, darling?

Diana

8/11

Dearest,

Well, today I shall attempt to write telling you of the birth of the baby. Sat. night, Aug. 5 I went to bed feeling fine and chipper and with no indication anything would happen. At 5 A.M. I was awakened. I had to go to the bathroom so I stood up and as I did — water started to flow out of me. I realized that my water had broken so I awoke Lucy.

By 6:30 A.M. the pains were coming every 10 minutes. My mother called Dr. Shaw and he came right over. He took me to the hospital in his car. When we got there, he examined me and decided that it was just beginning. He took me home again. He came over every 1½ hours to examine me. The real bad pain was from 3 P.M. to 6 P.M. He decided I was ready and took me to the hospital and she was born a few minutes before 7 P.M., Sun. Aug. 6.

I awoke at 7 P.M. and Dr. Shaw said "You have a wonderful baby girl." They showed her to me immediately.

Your,
Girls

8/11, Fri., V

Beloved Daddy Lenny —

I just had Betty Lou with me again — the first time I've seen her since Tues. She looks fine — the nursery nurse says she eats well but she cries a little and she's very active. While she was with me, she cried a little so I started to talk to her and tell her all about her wonderful Daddy so she quieted down and listened and wiggled a little. All the nurses say she looks like me but she has your mouth.

Dearest, it's a wonderful feeling to have her with me. Today for the first time, I got the nerve to pick her up a little off the bed — the first two times I was afraid to touch her. I guess I'll get used to it.

Betty Lou and Diana

8/12

Dearest Diana,

I reached the Red Cross rep for my division tonight & he had received no cable yet.

Lenny

8/12

Dearest,

Gosh, darling, you are excited about the baby and I'm so happy and proud — and this is without you even knowing definitely about her being born yet. I can't wait for your letters after you know about her and you hear all about everything.

You probably want to know how I feel about being a mother. I really find it hard to say right now. You see dearest I've only had the baby 3 times and I haven't done anything for her yet, so I hardly know her. I haven't even held her in my arms yet.

Diana

8/13, Sat., V

Dearest,

I feel stronger every day. Today I sat up in bed for the first time with my feet dangling over the side and it felt pretty good. I was a little dizzy but it cleared up quickly. Tomorrow I hope to get off the bed and Monday — Betty Lou and I'll go home. I can't see her again until Monday because they only show the baby's to the non-nursing mothers on Tues. & Fri.

All my Love,
Diana

8/13 Sun, V

Dearest Lenny,

I hope to go home tomorrow morning. Your mother is coming to take me home so my mother won't have to take off from work. The best news of today is that I got off the bed and walked. I was a little dizzy at first but I made it to a chair and as soon as I sat for a while I felt better and later I was able to walk around.

The baby is just a week old now since it's 6:50 P.M. so happy birthday to our daughter.

Diana

8/15

Dearest,

About 3 weeks ago I commented in a letter that we were in a position to see the news before you do — that was the day the push began with a great air armada blasting the German lines hard. Now it's the opposite. None of us knows where or what's going on beyond our range of eyesight right here, and as for other fronts, they might as well be on Mars!

Lenny

8/15

Dearest Lenny,

I came home yesterday, dearest, but it was such an exciting day and I was so tired that I couldn't write to you.

Your mother took me home. A taxi brought us right to the door. The doctor didn't discharge me until noon. There was so much he had to tell me about taking care of the baby and he was also here this morning to show me how to sterilize and make the formula. I did feed the baby for the rest of the day and I held her and got used to her.

Dearest, now I really begin to feel like a momma and it's so thrilling. Our folks are trying to take good care of me — my mother is giving her the 2 A.M. feeding this week so I can sleep — she is staying home from work until noon every day to help me out in the morning and your mother is coming to spend the afternoons with me. I find, beloved, that even though I'm a little scared, I can handle her nicely — maybe because I love her so.

Diana

DIANA FINALLY LEARNS LENNY WAS INJURED ON JULY 19TH

8/15

Lenny — oh my Lenny,

My father gave me the telegram last night saying that you were slightly wounded on July 19. They kept it from me until I came home from the hospital yesterday, although they received it last Wed.

Dearest what happened?[10] I'm so anxious to know. You hardly mention it in any of your letters since July 19 except to say casually that you are in a rest camp. Of course, when the folks told me last night, it was a terrific shock and it took me a little while to collect my wits, but then I realized I've received mail from you every day since then, that you've written yourself and that you write of going for walks and to the movies — so I hope you are fairly OK.

My family also told me that a Red Cross worker had been here to find out if I had had the baby in answer to your inquiry on the other side. She said you would know in two or three days so I'm hoping you know by now.

Betty's formula has 16 oz certified milk and 8 oz of boiled water and 5

---

10. Diana is referring to Lenny's suffering a badly sprained ankle when he dived to avoid a sudden German Stuka (two-man dive bomber) attack. He was laid up in the hospital in La Cambe, an army convalescent hospital, long enough to miss the 30th Division Normandy breakout, which may have been fortunate, because many American troops were killed.

tablespoons of maltose. These 24 oz are divided evenly into 6 bottles — 4 oz each and she is fed every 4 hours.

Diana

8/16, V

Dearest,

Our daughter is resting and so am I. She's really so sweet and good, dearest — not much trouble at all, but I'm not so strong yet. I want to get my strength back as soon as possible so my mother won't have to stay home with me mornings and your mother won't have to come for the afternoon.

Diana

News of the Baby's Birth Finally Reaches Lenny

8/16

Darling,

Hurrah — GOT THE TELEGRAM. THANKS LUCY.

We got a brief report of the invasion of South France yesterday — but the details I'll probably see weeks hence. Some French folk with a son who is prisoner of war since '40 celebrated Assumption Day yesterday by passing out cider to all the Americans passing by — but, like a necessary surgical operation, there's a lot of French suffering going on as a by-product of the war. Believe me it's cheaper to fight the aggressor in someone else's country — that's a frequent comment.

Lenny

8/16

Dearly Beloved,

Today was as in many ways as interesting as my first day in France, but very pleasantly so. Then the cable came with the happy news; and then the biggest batch of mail since I left the U.S.

If anyone wants to know, I'm glad it's a girl just as if it were a boy I'd be glad. And I'm glad, too, you are spared a bit of ceremony[11] and also have it easier in the name business, too (I hope). Of course I can't wait for all the details but it is so good to know you've come through. Was it very hard?

---

11. Lenny refers to the "bris" — Jewish circumcision ceremony.

Today I spent as translator with my S-2 (security officer) in the morning & my B. CO captain in the afternoon riding around freshly liberated areas and talking to civilians for information — and relaxation. Met some of the De Gaullist underground and visited a dungeon tower built in the 11th century.

Tell Lucy thanks a million for the cable. What did Betty Lou say when you saw her? And did you explain I was unavoidably detained, but was very eager to meet her as soon as possible — & also her mother?

Lenny

8/17, V

Dear Diana,

The officers visited a well-to-do farmer & I interviewed him.[12] He said that while those personally hit naturally felt bad (in the ruined areas) 80 to 90 percent of the French understood that to make an omelet you must break the eggs. Paris, starving, center of the Resistance, still is the same Paris.

Lenny

8/17, V

Dearest Darling Love,

How are you and Baby Betty today? By now she must be out of the frankfurter, looking stage — and are you coming back to shape? It's funny but I have to make an effort to memorize August 6 as the birthday, because for my own peace of mind I'd set July 31st as the day.

I'm parked on a sort of rough lawn of a farmhouse — the occupants have just come back from their flight away and are staying at a neighbor's. We traded some soap for fresh eggs, which will presently grace my squad's lunch. It's wonderful to speak the language.

Excuse, please, they're yelling, "Miller to the CP" which means an interpreter is needed.

Lenny

8/17, M

Dearest,

Here is a copy of the announcement card. We sent out 100. They cost

---

12. Lenny was often sent ahead with an officer by vehicle, especially when contacting locals or units of the Resistance, since he spoke French and German and later taught himself some Flemish and Dutch.

$7.50 for the 100 cards, which is quite expensive, but I think they are very nice.

Diana

8/17,V

Dearest Lenny,

You still don't mention in any of your letters what is wrong with you, but since you seem to be able to get around, I'm hoping it's nothing serious. I'm waiting for the War Dept. to let me know further details but so far they haven't.

Your mother gave me a carriage cover which was yours. It is quite lovely and was embroidered by your grandma. I'm going to use it to take the baby out the first time.[13]

Diana

8/18,V

Dear Diana,

This morning we had a speech by our commanding general, routine, pedestrian business. A little livelier was a complaint by a very charming young lady, on behalf of the family whose property we by force of circumstances are occupying, which I had to transmit to & translate to the proper authority. It wasn't any objection to our being there, but a valid detail about maintenance. She was curious to know whether we had any trouble with traitors among the French, and hoped we'd shoot any who we caught. She said there were traitors among those who smiled the most ardent welcome to us but generally we find the French handle their own.

Lenny

8/18,V

Dearest,

It's very amazing to see the folks' reaction to the baby. They are just crazy about her. My folks think she is out of this world and my mother — she doesn't like small children, but this one is different. You should see them talk to her. And your folks — they are over every day and they are practically afraid to look at her, they think she's so wonderful. I'm really glad that they are so pleased.

Diana

---

13. I have the cover and used it for my three children.

8/18, written on American Red Cross paper

Dear Diana,

’Tis just like my Diana to be so full of what to say that pages are filled with hospital routine, but the essentials — How long in labor? — How was it? — How do you feel? — How did you get to the hospital? Are Baby’s eyes brown, is she blond or brunette? — All the vital things — where are they?

There passed me here in the farmyard, a pair of women and 6 little children ranging from about 6–12. They were thirsty, very thirsty, but no one understood them — they were refugees from a city in German hands who somehow had got through, on foot or by chance lifts (car rides) and have been walking, with a few shopping bags of possessions, ’til they came to the town near here looking for a relative, but the town is in ruins, and their relative also a refugee housed in a neighboring farm.

Well, before they were able to tell their story, we got them some water from our “kitchen” & some bread, & I gave them a leftover K ration I had. Their husbands are both prisoners of war in Germany since 1940. The little girls assured me gravely that the Germans were wicked men. The women were rather surprised to find us in place of the normal residents, their relatives, at the farm (their relatives are at a neighbor’s) but assured me we were very welcome, so long as we get the Germans out of France.

So dearest — I am happy with you & because of you — but in the midst of the painful job here, emotions conflict. It’s easy to say we are rolling back the black night from Europe, daily more people breathe freedom’s air — but it’s a brave thing to say that in the middle of war’s desolation, not as easy as in New York. The fight for freedom there was, & is, a conflict of ideas, still, but here it is a conflict in stark brutal physical terms, not nearly as beautiful as the ideal picture we cultivate!

But to return: 8 pounds 12 ounces! Golly! O my, gosh! No kidding? Tell me more quickly. It’s almost like twins!

Lenny

8/19, V

Dearest,

You would be surprised to see how busy a little one like our Betty Lou can keep 4 adults — my mother, my father, Lucy and me. It’s really amazing how much attention she requires.

My dearest, I'm OK — just concerned about you — I do so want to hear what is wrong with you and how you are and that you know about the baby.

Diana

8/19

Dear Diana,

In the woods, somewhere in France — It is a pleasant thing to go through villages we took without a fight — where the people turn out to shout "Viva L'Amerique," joy and enthusiasm undimmed by personal losses. I speak to whom I can — women whose men are prisoners, men who are of the "Resistance" who cooperate with us in a hundred ways, French African troops, etc.

Lenny

8/20, V

Dearest Darling,

Betty Lou is 2 weeks old today — quite a lady and so cute. Today I went out for the first time. My mother teases me that I ought to save some of the gift money for "naden"[14] but I keep insisting she'll use the same "naden" that her mother used and I hope she'll get as nice a guy as her mother has and be as happy as her mother is and so much in love.

Diana

8/21

Dearest Lenny,

The Red Cross has already inquired about me and they have all the information which they say was forwarded to you. You see, they called while I was in the hospital in response to your inquiry in France.

I'm so very, very thrilled and happy that you finally heard from me — I've been waiting so long for a letter that says that. Even though you still don't mention knowing about the baby, now I hope you will soon know about her.

My cousin Ben sent the baby $10 in a letter today. I swear our daughter will soon be richer than we are.

Diana

---

14. Betty's future dowry.

8/21, in an oat-field, somewhere in France

Dear Diana,

When we come into a town fresh after the Nazis, or after cleaning them out, it is most interesting to meet the townspeople. Today, I had a delicious cup of hot tea while we held up for a few minutes by the roadside, the children had to be reassured by the mothers that they could accept candy from us — they had forbidden them to take anything from the Germans.

We picked up a scattering of prisoners during the morning whom I questioned in German. One assured me he was Sudeten, "more Czech than German"; another, a "West Prussian," that he was Polish. Sudden changes in nationality! Those from Germany proper extremely depressed, especially when they heard the state of the Eastern front. And do the French show hate to the prisoners & mock them as they pass!

Lenny

8/22

Dearest Lee,

I had 3 V-mails from you today. Don't worry about a job for after the war — we'll manage as we have always done — I'm not in the least worried.

I had an appointment with your brother-in-law Mike to take pictures of Betty Lou and me last Sun. but he had a cold. If he's better we'll take them this Sun.

Diana

8/22, V

Dear,

Mail this morning — It was good to know the details of the delivery, but it seems you have somewhat skipped, either the delicacy or not wanting to trouble me, the pain — It doesn't seem to have been an "easy" case at all; but it is good to know you are OK now.

I keep writing while I can though no mail has been collected for 3 days now — we move too much, I guess.

The newly liberated towns still have the German & Vichy posters — Vichy urging French to accept the Nazi labor draft "to build defense of France" and a cartoon poster saying the Americans cannot land in France because of submarines and they have to dig an oceanic tunnel.

Some souvenirs which my S-2 says I can send you:

1. Two leaflets dropped to Germans urging surrender.

2. Some snapshots

3. German letter from Landshut, July 29, from a father to his children with final salutation, "Heil Hitler!"

Lenny

8/23

Darling,

When I get lonely, and I do in spite of all the people I have around me, then I talk to the baby. Darling, I miss you so much, especially now when I often feel very helpless. I've never been a mama before and there are so many things I don't know and that I don't understand.

It has been so many years that you helped with all my problems and that we talked everything over together — it's hard for me to decide what to do alone.

Ever since 8/14 when I learned about the telegram saying you were wounded, I've been so anxious to know what happened to you. Also, if possible, write me what you are doing. You write you were in a rest camp in France. Are you still there or are you back in action?[15]

Diana

8/24, V

Dearest,

We entered a town where even the cops wore the De Gaullist armbands of the underground and we got a grand reception. There was a swastika flag on a house midst many French tricolors, and when I asked why not tear it down, the neighbors said they'd put it up to mark the "one collaborator."

Yesterday in the course of operations, we captured a big Nazi swastika. I had the pleasure of trampling on it on the ground for the edification of our fresh caught prisoners, Berliners & Nazis who cringed like jellyfish, because they were sure we were going to shoot them.

I finished our anniversary day by digging the biggest hole yet in

---

15. Due to the delay in letters, one month after he is back in action, she is still wondering if he has returned to his unit.

France, & it has a grand view overlooking a pleasant river valley and a Cathedral city which will be in the headlines, no doubt, shortly!

Lenny

8/24

Dearest Love,

I received your letters from 8/14 & 8/15 today. You still don't know about the baby as of 8/15 nine days after we sent you the cablegram — I only hope that you know by now.

You ask how it is working out living with my folks? Dearest, all I can say is that they are certainly doing all they can to help me as much as possible. It isn't easy on them at all, especially because I'm really just beginning to get my strength back.

Well, with Paris freed yesterday and the news as encouraging as it has been in the last few weeks, let us hope that soon Betty and I will be able to move into our own place with you, darling. We both do need you, so very much as soon as you have finished the job you are doing now, and we are waiting for you so eagerly.

Diana

8/25, V

Dear Diana,

Yesterday when I was out on a big deal, I rode in a jeep (for a change) with one of our chaplains and a "chief" of the local Resistance, a local commander & a French liaison officer & me as interpreter, out on reconnaissance, in force, directed against a pocket of German troops reported to us by a French patrol. All goes A-1 with me — I hope you are equally well. The fear which was naturally all present weeks ago is hardly felt now, & what made me sick to my stomach at first is now a matter of curiosity, so spare yourself any worry, and kiss Betty Lou for me.

Lenny

8/25

Dearest,

Our sweet little Betty has a carriage already. My father and I went and bought it last night. The carriage costs $70 which is a great deal of money. I intend to take the baby out tomorrow.

Diana

8/26

Dear Lenny,

So I took the baby out today for the first time. It was such a thrill. Since it is Sat., my mother and Lucy were very busy, so my father and I took the baby out. We walked over to your mother's house with her and visited for about five minutes. You see, I was only allowed to keep her out for ½ hour in the morning and ½ hr. in the afternoon. My aunt from Boston is visiting. She gave me $10 for the baby — so Betty now has $55 plus 1 $25 war bond.

Diana

8/26, Airmail with mud

Dear Diana,

I seize a momentary lull to be domestic and do some washing, & take a helmet bath — luckily there is a fire handy to dry it over.

Well, how is the family? What does Betty Lou think of Shepherd Ave? Has she been out yet?

Yesterday I sent you some souvenirs: 1) the armband of the French underground, given me by the "chief" of this region; I gave him a pile of cigarettes, having nothing else, but they were welcome, 2) copies of American publications issued to the French in advance of the invasion, 3) a leaflet to German soldiers.

Lenny

8/26, V

Dearest Diana,

I am OK — but horrified by the V-mails just here — some missing — but references to a War Dept. telegram & as such seem to indicate a snafu — miserable curses, what the devil happened at your end — I mean, what did they tell you?[16]

Very simply, the third day after reaching my division, I sprained my left ankle and banged up the leg — while diving into a hedgerow ditch on one of the last times the Germans had any planes to send over, so the medics sent me back to the hospital because I couldn't walk. The doctors assured me there would be no report home. I got out about ½ week later

---

16. Lenny is upset that the War Department notified the family of his minor injury, in spite of his request that they hold the news because Diana was expecting.

and have been on the job since. There was nothing serious — honest.

Lenny

8/26,V

Dena,

Scene in a dense thicket, somewhere in the woods in France, a late Saturday afternoon — On the perimeter are the dugouts with their roofs of fagots and branches.

Lenny

Diana Wonders If He Knows Their Baby Is Born

8/27,V

Dearest Lenny Daddy,

The baby is three weeks old today and still I have no word from you that you know about her. I hope so much that soon you will write me that — these are hard times for us as for thousands of people — well, it looks as though soon the Nazi beast will be beaten and then when we've destroyed the Japanese fascists — the world will breathe free again and people like you and I will be able to be together.

We took pictures this afternoon — some outside and some inside. Harriet is having them developed and I'll send them to you as soon as they are ready.

Diana

8/27,V

Dearest,

Just saw "Stars & Stripes" of Aug 24 with the grand story of Paris' self-liberation: as had been promised by various Frenchmen with whom I'd spoken earlier. It was good after a sickening mess I had to handle last night involving a fight between collaborators, some willing & some supposedly under duress. Alas good to hear Rumania threw in the towel.

Lenny

8/28,V

Dear Lenny,

By the way, everyone says Betty Lou looks just like you — I'm so glad about that. She slept through the pictures we took yesterday so I hope you'll see part of her at least.

Your Diana and Betty Lou

8/28

Dearest Sweetheart,

Got your long letter about coming home to that miserable telegram — Poor Diana, it must have been terrible.

I spent a couple of hours studying a certain village (part of my job), speaking to most everyone, stepped into a 18th century church where mass was being celebrated and there was a woman with a little girl a week older than ours, named Therese — so I held Betty Lou by proxy a little while to get the feel of being a poppa.

And an interesting evening with a family in refuge here from elsewhere, a well-to-do man in the auto business, whose country home was more beautiful than the Friedman's luxurious home. He spoke perfect English, but we spoke in French about a world of things, 'til time came for me to rejoin my squad out on guard where it counts.

Your package came. There's a lot — it will do almost for the duration! But you could put Band-aids, 2–3, in a letter every month or so?

Lenny

8/29,V

Dearest Lenny,

In your V-mail of 8/16 that came today, you ask if I have told Betty Lou that you are unavoidably detained. Yes, darling, I have told her where you are and I'm sure she feels the same about it that I do — so proud of her daddy. You know I talk to her all the time about her daddy.

Darling — it's a wonderful thing to have a baby — we have so much to look forward to after the war is over — you and Betty Lou and me.

Diana

8/29

Dearest,

Betty Lou is getting to be a little devil and so cute. She begins to hold her head up a little and is beginning to see and to hear. It's very interesting to watch her as she develops day by day.

It's hard for me to decide if she is a hard baby to care for or not. I guess like all of us, she has her moods. The wonderful thing so far is that she sleeps at night very well. I've cut out the 2 A.M. bottle this week because she didn't wake for it so the Dr. said I should divide that milk into the other bottles and not bother her during the night.

I have followed the policy of not letting her cry too long. This is the latest thing in child psychology — children as young as Betty Lou cannot be spoiled and need a certain amount of loving and holding and cuddling. I don't know, darling, I hope I'm doing right.

I've started to give her orange juice yesterday ¼ teaspoon — You should have seen her — she made such a funny face but then she swallowed it and opened her mouth for more. At 1 month she will be getting zwieback.

Love — the mailman just brought me a V-mail from 8/16 and you know about the baby — hurrah and more hurrahs — I'm so happy!

Darling — how are you? Are you still in the rest camp? Write me how you feel, if it is allowed.

Diana

8/29, V

Dearest Diana,

Spent the night on guard by the banks of a river famous in legend & history — but what is called a river in Europe wouldn't be a creek at home! I find myself digging even deeper now, on occasion, account of Betty Lou — and yesterday as we advanced we also had to do a lot of digging also — spent the night, although, in a very deep trench left behind by our predecessors, the Germans, & was glad they'd dug it, too!

Had a delicious tomato-onion salad given us by friendly French on the road yesterday — also blackberries, apples begin to be ripe.

Dearest, all is well — you can read the headlines as we make them, smile & tell the world.

Lenny

8/30

Dearest Lenny,

My days are beginning to have a routine although I still don't have a very good one. You see, what I get done depends so much on Betty Lou that it is very hard for me to get a good system. I still don't have her adjusted, so that her sleeping periods are not regular, and because of that, it's hard for me to plan. I don't like her to cry long — so I try to distract her and play with her until she falls asleep again. Of course that takes up a lot of my time, but then right now I have only one job to do and I want to do it well. Write me what you think of this crying business if you have the time. And as I have written you before, I do feel so inadequate at times and at a loss because as far as I'm concerned it's mostly guessing.

Diana

The Race across France and Belgium:
August through Early September 1944

The Allies were pinned down for two months in Normandy. After the collapse of the Falaise Pocket and the fall of Paris to the French Resistance, the remaining German units retreated rapidly to more secure lines in Holland and, finally, behind the Siegfried Line, the Roer and the Rhine Rivers. Bypassing free Paris, the 30th Division of General Hodge's First Army rapidly advanced through northern France and Belgium, sometimes only less than a day behind the fleeing Germans.

The Allied units had to be careful not to outrun their fellow units and especially their supply lines, which stretched, until the capture of Antwerp, back to the Normandy Beaches. This explains Lenny's unit's brief stops in Belgium.

The objective of the 30th Division, First Army, was southern Holland, opposite the Roer, behind which lay the Rhine River and Cologne. The Allies pushed forward toward these rivers and the Siegfried Line. German resistance stiffened, and fierce fighting ensued, as they approached Germany proper.

In the middle of the First Army's front was Aachen. Fierce urban fighting to take this largest German city on the Siegfried Line, a city dating back to Charlemagne the Great, whose capital it had been, would have to wait.

8/30,V

Dear Diana,

Yesterday hectic; busy as hell — managed to begin the day with a good conversation with some Frenchmen — But a really hectic day after, one of the most — In the middle of a hot moving action,[17] I was busy with the fresh prisoners, interrogating, searching, and arranging for guards &

---

17. Lenny, the only one able to speak German, "was lying down in the unsheltered open with his rifle trained on 12 Nazi prisoners who were trying to run out from under a terrific mortar barrage, from which I too would gladly have sought shelter — and there we were with our company commander yelling from his position in the chateau 'Miller don't let the prisoners escape.' It was really funny despite the danger." (From the summary letter—#4, October 21, 1944—to Diana, reviewing in detail the events of the past four months.)

transmittal, under conditions which made it really a job. Not even time to eat — saying a lot for me!

Dear, it is impossible to send mail out as we advance (I write, but officers can't take time to censor). On guard last night at a real genuine chateau, towers & all, with the beautiful Nazi slogans on the wall outside, & signs of their vandalism & carousing inside.

A la Johnny Appleseed, when we pass French folk whose surprise at our arrival exceeds their usual spontaneous gifts of fruit & cider & wine, I greet them & tell them the group, farther back are thirsty, and they respond handsomely — so at least behind us no one need go thirsty! It's fun to be able to talk French, in 100 ways.

Lenny

8/31,V

Dearest,

Again the rate of our activity permits writing only at one of our rare halts. This morning we entered a town hot on the heels as it were of the retreating Germans — what a reception we got — joy, enthusiasm, happiness — we got banqueted and wined — and bread with jam and cheers and kisses — even I got kissed twice before I got my guard up.

Yesterday was one of those days an infantryman dreads — rain, knee deep mud and after an all-day killer of a march uphill, through woods, no rest pauses, a night of rain in the open. It is the "toil and sweat" which is much more with us.

I get a big rise out of the crowd as we march by, when they hold their babies up, by saying — "I too have a baby girl, who is today 25 days old." So Betty Lou is cheered in France!

Lenny

8/31,V

Dear Lenny,

Your sister Rose mailed the watch strap and two pens to you this morning and I also put in a few packages of Life-savers.

Diana

9/1,V

Dearest Darling,

It's great to be welcomed wildly as we come through town after town — but oh, our aching feet, our burning soles! We are being issued new sox about once a week now! In larger places the crowds grab your hands to squeeze & it's all you can do to keep going. In smaller settlements they are quieter, stand smiling, waving tricolor flags & calling "Bon Jour" — so I usually bat out a phrase of French, like "Hurrah for free France" (Vive La France Libre) which gets a big rise out of them — a shrill chorus of "Hurrah for America" and they applaud and others cheer. Many say, "Four long years we have suffered" or "Four years we have waited."

Lenny

9/1, V

Dearest Lenny,

I had two more letters from Aug 16 today. In these you write of having the cablegram. I'm so very, very happy that you know of our daughter already even though it was 10 days after her birth before you found out. I know you are glad it is a girl — so am I and I would have been glad for a boy too — but it does save me a number of headaches as you mention. I had no trouble about the name — everyone accepted it and liked it — yes, darling we'll have a son when you come home — at least we can try.

I'm glad your knowledge of French is proving so useful. I guess you are no longer in a rest camp from what you write. Dearest, are you really OK?

Diana

9/2, V, Somewhere in France

Darling Diana,

Since I am here I have been able to supplement my K rations with something fresh from a garden either asking, or swapping cigarettes, etc. We are moving very fast. Today we passed through several cities, one very historic, with 12th century gates & still smoldering Nazi tanks, and at last I got a fleeting glimpse of industrial France — a coal area, dingy, slums, like our Pennsylvania coal towns.

Lenny

9/2, V, Somewhere in France

Dearest,

Rested a bit after a half day of lolling in the sun — and then under a great full moon we rolled — through long plains & fields — making history is a good experience for a historian to live through! Folks stayed up all night to greet us as we came through — they knew from the German retreat, that we were coming. Still, as we park awhile here, it's fun to see the surprise on the kids faces as they discover it's Americans here now and the awed pleasure of the adults as they see our arrived might stretching out.

Beloved, you can see, much as one suffers the fatigue of the campaign, the everlasting rain, the K rations, and a million discomforts, this past night was one of the happiest I've spent — we matched some of the fastest Russian advances, I guess.

Tough days still ahead, of course, still a job to be done. My mail will be delayed a good deal, these days.

Lenny

9/2

Dearest Lenny,

I got the pictures today and there are four which are good enough to send to you. I shall put one in each letter for the next few days so that you will be sure to get one. Write me, dearest, just what you think of your daughter. I think she's very cute. Don't you think she looks like you?

Diana

9/3, V

Dear Diana,

It is grand and thrilling to be part of the great liberation offensive, even with all the hardships we suffer, that I want to write some more today. We have been occupying more places, & the joy of the people is something to see. As a matter of fact, we came in by surprise last night to one town and folks were amazed we were not Germans. And today when they heard Paris is free they began to make all the flags we see everywhere saved from scraps in secrecy. Now a kid's giving me the details of the Germans' sorry state the last weeks, & I gave him a Lincoln penny souvenir telling him the story of Lincoln, as I rest a while.

Lenny

In Belgium through September 10

9/3, Somewhere in Belgium

Dearest,

As you can see in the headlines, here we are — came in during the night. I found refuge from the rain in a garage of a private house (it's great to speak the language), so we got an hour's sleep by this morning, had chicory coffee & warmed by breakfast, & chatted with the old couple who said they were honored to receive Americans in their arrival, and we went out for a patrol.

The underground were at work rounding up Rexists[18] pulling down their signs, & everywhere go up the Belgium flag & pendants — it's beautiful.

One thing is noticeable — there is greater emphasis on the Allies here by the Belgians; in France, they welcomed Americans, but here they have the flags of USSR, Britain and US together everywhere. I kiss you and Betty from Belgium.

Lenny

9/4

Dear Diana,

Out this morning to accompany Belgium Interior forces in picking up some German stragglers — and some Rexists on the way. There were 6 Russians among the Germans, taken prisoner in 1942 & impressed into the German army. Too bad I can't do anything in Russian but my knowledge of music served to prove them really Russian, not pretenders. Some such Russians have surrendered to us, asking to go at once into action, and one got me to say his head was Russian, though his uniform German. He's ready to serve in the Russian army. I've seen too many German uniforms to trust anyone in it, but some such Russians have surrendered to us asking to go at once into action against Germany (so says YANK).[19]

Dear, tell Betty Lou but not to make her swell headed, that Belgian as well as French crowds who greet us have cheered her as I proudly announced her arrival — & her age — when I say in French — "she has today 28 days," pausing after the number, it always gets a laugh, & a cheer.

One is embarrassed by the eagerness of the people here, to fete & feed us, since we know how meager their own fare is, & how chicory is their coffee. The walls here all have leaflets posted by the Belgium Front of Resistance in the Interior calling on farmers to prevent Nazis getting their products but to produce more for Belgian use. Thanks a million for the announcement of Betty Lou's arrival, the bow at the bottom was swell.

Lenny

---

18. Rexist was a fascist political movement in Belgium in the first half of the twentieth century, mostly supported by the Walloons, some other Belgians, and Nazis.

19. *Yank* was the weekly magazine published by the U.S. Army during World War II.

Sept 4, Labor Day

Dear Diana,

On captured German stationery with ink from a Belgian friend — here's greetings! Enclosed are some of your letters which I return according to our usual practice, also, a captured photo — the Hitler Youth Group "Pathfinders," and a U.S. air-borne leaflet dropped over France. Note news of Dobromil, page 2.[20]

Lenny

9/4, V,

Dearest,

Today is Labor Day. This morning I went to buy a crib with your mother and father. It is a present from them to the baby. We bought a very beautiful crib — light birch wood — solid back and front like our bedroom set with a small painted floral design.

Diana

9/5, V

Dear Darling,

There is no photographer in town. I inquired where all their fine pictures come from and was told there is a young man, Henri whose hobby is photography. An appointment was arranged and I arrived at their chateau and met the family. Their home was really elegant — full of genuine heirlooms, antique furniture, 17th–18th centuries, family portraits, grand salons. Henri's father broke out a bottle of Madeira wine, later showed me his cellar—apparently his dearest loss, left as the Nazis left it in 1940, when they drank out 3,000 bottles (3,000, yes, and left them smashed in the cellar.) They have been bringing out their belongings, rugs, statues etc., out of hiding since we are here, so the house looks half-way set up. We are sleeping in his plant's buildings.

Lenny

9/5

Dearest Lenny —

You write of your acting as an interpreter. I'm glad of this — you

---

20. Dobromil, Poland, is the town my father's parents came from. "A l'ouest de Sambor, ville situe au sud-ouest de Lvov, les Russes ont pris Chyrov et Dobromil." The translation: "To the west of Sambor, a city situated southwest of Lvov, the Russians have taken Chyrov and Dobromil."

Lenny in Belgium, September 5, 1944

aren't doing your job as a scout now? Maybe you can't write me this. I also received the German leaflets and letters you sent by regular mail. The snapshots must have been taken out because they didn't come.

Diana

9/6

Dear Diana,

Much as I like to keep down the souvenir business, sometimes a few small items insist on coming in — here is the family of M. Lotan, Mme. & their 3 kids at the communion of Analiese. They have been very pleasant to us — introduced me to the camera fan who took my photo —filled

Lenny with a Belgian family

me with coffee & waffles. M. works in the cement plant here. I gave them some chocolate, a German (captured) blanket, & some castoff G.I. clothes — so of course the photo enclosed came in exchange.

Lenny

9/6

Dearest,

A pleasant afternoon with Rudy, of my squad, spent visiting the charming family of M Desablens. He is a tailor, pretty successful at the trade. We chatted of family, of the war, our experiences; their life under the Germans, the system of hiding young men from the German labor draft, really amazing stories, why we find so many here, to swell the White Army of Liberation, the underground.

Still with the family — They insisted on giving us coffee and tartines 'tho we protested since rationing is severe. My French naturally improves with all this use and I've picked up a lot of Belgian idioms.

On your question, well, all should be clear to you by now — that I'm all OK — & on the job — even if "rest camp" was a euphemism for convalescent hospital — It was only a rest camp, really, no medical care being necessary any longer — after the first week was over.

Did you get the armbands I sent you of the French and Belgian undergrounds? Saw the first free Belgian paper today but restrained myself from sending too — somehow it's got place names on it and won't pass.

Lenny

BETTY IS ONE MONTH OLD

Sept 6

Dear Diana, and Betty Lou,

Happy birthday, Betty — and many happy returns of the day — When I see the rickets ridden kids of Belgium hereabout, I am glad I came here — for Betty's sake as much as for theirs — we never doubted the value of our sacrifices, "the price we have to pay," but here we see it proved. Enclosed is a souvenir card given me by the local family who took my picture. There are no place names on it, so it should pass the censor: the inscription says — "Our most cordial welcome to the valiant American soldiers and especially to Mr. Leo Miller, 5 Sept. 1944." 'Tis really a magnificent place inside, garden outside, the "chateau" of this region — All my love, my darlings

Lenny

P.S. I delight to write on this stationery which we took from a Nazi paratroop officer as I delight to turn over their blankets etc. to the Belgians.

9/6

Dearest,

Happy Birthday to our daughter — one month old today — I took her to the Dr. this morning. She is fine and weighs 9 lbs 10 oz. — very good for one month. She will start getting zwieback tomorrow and also cod liver oil. I'll write you what she thinks of the zwieback — her first solid food.

What you write me of the children that you see — I think of our well protected and taken care of little girl and the thought of anything like that for her is unbearable — just as these French, children's mothers must feel. We are so lucky — we, Americans.

Diana

9/7

Dear Diana,

In line of duty had a delightful visit to a nearby town — I came to question prisoners in a military hospital run by the Belgian Interior forces, the

White army. The prisoners are a sorry lot, but one still, one alone, believed Germany can win. In addition, we captured one Hitler Youth, the toughest Nazi I've yet met, one still not broken in spirit, son of a city official and student, who yielded no information. He denied that Germans shoot prisoners (being afraid we or the Belgians would shoot him) but admitted they shoot prisoners in Poland, Yugoslavia, etc., as "bandits." A real Nazi!

Lenny

9/7

Dearest Lenny,

We had a wonderful surprise today. Eddie came home on furlough unexpectedly. Betty wasn't impressed at all and just slept.

They delivered the crib today. It is a really nice one. It doesn't show up too well in this room because the room is quite crowded. I hope when we have a baby's room, we shall be able to fix it up nicely.

Betty Lou started to eat zwieback today. She didn't know just what to do with it so she spit a lot of it instead of swallowing it.

There is one thing that worries me a lot and I want to talk to you about it. I know you are very busy and have a good deal on your mind, but I'm trying to develop habits in her that are regular and good. So far she eats well and has gained nicely, but her sleeping habits are very unpredictable. Sometimes she sleeps for 24 hours straight and just gets up to take the bottle and then some days she doesn't sleep at all.

When she doesn't sleep, I have such a problem, she cries a great deal because she is too small to play, and I don't know what to do. I don't like to let her just scream — the more she cries, the more hysterical she gets. I try to calm her until she gets relaxed and I try to put her to sleep. It sounds very simple, but I often take several hours until I get her really asleep. The latest thing to do is what I am doing, but I wonder if it isn't spoiling her.

Love, I'm sorry to trouble you with these problems, but I just felt I had to talk to someone who would understand. I guess the strain that I'm living under doesn't help Betty Lou too much either. If you have any time to think about it — write me how you would handle it.

Your,

Diana

9/8

Dear Sweetheart,

Last night, on duty — Later visited a batch of Belgian-held prisoners, all Polish and Soviet — the Soviet were Russians & also Mongolians, that is, not Germans faking.

Lenny

9/8

Dearest Lenny,

    I'm so relieved. I had the letter from you this morning in which you explain about the telegram I got. I'm so glad it wasn't anything more serious than a sprained ankle.[21] Lee — please dearest, now that I am no longer pregnant, don't keep anything from me. Please write me if anything happens.

    These four weeks of guessing since I had the telegram were not easy ones. Only after I had your letters saying you were back on the job, did I begin to feel it couldn't have been too bad. So my darling — let's go back to our old policy of not keeping things from each other.

    Betty Lou sends you a smile. She looks so much like you when she smiles and she wrinkles her brow just as you do even as young as she is.

Diana

9/9

Dearest,

    Moving — pushing on through Belgium — a roadside halt. My friend, Pierre, thinks I waste time to learn a "mere dialect" — he doesn't see the grand effect it has on the people. He is a Parisian law student, from the Maquis, a rural guerilla band of French Resistance, whose outfit finished its work — so he joined us to see action against Germany instead of waiting for the draft in France. Of course, we disagree on plenty of things — he does not see that the French overseas possessions may want — or deserve — the same freedom as he wants for France. It's Indian summer in New York but here we begin to feel the morning chill — I pray for victory before winter.

Lenny

9/9

Lee,

    Betty Lou has learned something new. Today she played with a rattle the first time. I tried to give her one two days ago but she couldn't hold it yet. Today she held it and was interested for a few minutes.

Diana

---

21. Two months after the ankle injury occurred and a month after the telegram arrived, Diana finally understands Lenny's injury.

9/10

Dearest,

It is cool here, as in our late October, but I slept well in a bed of "deep wheat straw" outside of my 3 A.M. tour of guard duty. Spent time talking politics with locals —

Lenny

9/10,V

Dear Lenny,

Will try to take pictures next weekend when Betty Lou is awake. My cousins Blanche and Seymour were here this evening and they gave Betty Lou $15 as a gift. She now has $95 plus a bond. Isn't she a rich little girl?

Diana

MAKING HEADLINES: FORT EBEN-EMAEL

Ft. Eben-Emael, whose capture from the Allies astounded the military world in 1940, fell without a shot to Lt. Col. Paul W. McCollum, of High Point, N.C.

—*Star and Stripes*, September 13, 1944

Eben-Emael was one of many defensive forts built by the Belgians before World War II to guard against a possible repeat of the German invasion during World War I. It was the most important, because of its strategic position overlooking the Albert Canal and Meuse River crossings. Its capture by the Germans with a daring raid from above, using gliders, at the beginning of World War II, paved the way for the German end run through Belgium, leading to Dunkirk. The fort is a huge underground complex, with long tunnels and multiple levels buried into the side of a hill, with only the entrance visible from the outside. In this excerpt from his unpublished memoir, Lenny describes how he, his captain, and their jeep driver were the first Americans to enter the fort immediately after the Belgian Resistance took over the fort from the fleeing Germans. He sent home four Nazi flags from here, one of which my family still has.

The Captain summoned the jeep driver and myself and took off in advance of the marching men. Our jeep cut deep furrows through the turnips, roared over hills and careened down steep inclines . . . as we approached the crest above the fort the captain said, referring to the possibility of being shot as we silhouetted across the summit, "To hell with it, we're taking a chance on mines in the ground anyhow." We tore down the path emerging on the smooth ground before the main pillbox.

To our surprise the (Belgian) Armée Blanche was there already, having beat us by about ten minutes, dragging out some wretched bedraggled prisoners.[22]

9/11

Dearly Beloved,

Yesterday we made headlines again, big headlines, quite likely! When I saw our objective marked on the operations map in the morning, I felt the cold shivers up my spine; not of fear but of excitement — because the name is one already celebrated in the war. When I studied accounts of the battle here, I never dreamed that one day in the setting sun I'd stand in the tremendous casements & question prisoners & chat with Belgian fighters, nurses of the underground.

The Fleming-Walloon business is curious, Belgium is half-Flemish speaking and half-French, and there are islands within islands.

At the farm yesterday, Mme told me how 2 weeks ago with the Germans still on her property she hid in her room & sewed the handsome U.S. flag she greeted us with. Many of these handmade flags have an odd number of stars but she carefully consulted Larousse & copied it faithfully. The kids here are collecting the shrapnel sent over yesterday by the retreating Nazis. Funny how indifferent I have become to what would have really terrified me 2 months ago.

Lenny

9/11

Dear Diana,

Under separate cover, I plan to send my first & last bulky souvenir to you — a trophy, a captured Nazi flag, taken by me yesterday.[23] It is one of 4 you will receive. Please ask my father to deliver one in my name to Pat, to use in his bond campaign, etc. Tell them all that they were captured by the Americans and Belgian underground forces together, & that I hope

---

22. From "Rifleman's Road," an unpublished memoir written by Lenny based on his wartime experiences.

23. The words Fort Eben-Emael were blacked out by the censors.

they can use these trophies to raise funds and enthusiasm generally, as I know they well can. Soon I hope we will be capturing the flags of Berlin itself!

The flags are coming in 2 ration cartons which I hope will stand the voyage — also I hope the situation will allow me to send them because they can't be carried on me! The flags were found in a large room in Fort Eben-Emael, strategically located on the Albert Canal, at the eastern edge of Belgium.

Lenny

9/11, V

Dear Lenny,

I spent this afternoon in the little playground. The more I observe, the more I realize what a difference there is when a child understands. Louis is 17 months old and it's a pleasure to be with him. The difficult thing with Betty Lou is that when she isn't asleep, she gets bored quickly even when you try to play with her and she cries a great deal.

Diana

6

Somewhere in Holland, Somewhere in Germany

MID-SEPTEMBER THROUGH MID-DECEMBER 1944

From Fort Eben-Emael, Lenny's 30th Division entered the Dutch Province of Limburg in southern Holland, sandwiched in between Belgium and Germany. Intense tank battles and artillery barrages took place as the Germans put up a fierce resistance, so close were the Allies to German soil.

For the next three months, the Americans were moving back and forth between Holland and Germany, the battles of Aachen and surrounding areas, and probing the territory toward the Roer River. Periods of intense activity alternated with welcome breaks and news from Diana and Betty Lou.

9/12, Somewhere in Holland

Dearest Diana,

Was welcomed into Holland today! Now in a Gestapo headquarters, & leaning this paper on a book marked "confidential," being a list of Jews, political suspects, people with records, and the like in Holland. There is also one here for France.

Lenny

9/13, V

Dearest,

Still no mail today — the 5th day — are you all right, darling? It's very hard when there is no mail — I can imagine how you felt for the seven weeks when you didn't have any from me.

Diana

Netherlands, Germany, and Belgium

9/14

Dear Diana,

I am trying to talk Dutch & with a little French, German & Flemish, I manage. Dutch is as distant from German as English but close to Flemish. Received the first photo of Betty — thanks a million — reserving comment. Already I have shown it to my new Dutch friends.

Lenny

9/14, V

Dearest,

So it is still raining and Betty Lou and I are again confined to the house. And still there is no mail from you. Tomorrow is a week since I've had a letter. Are you OK, my darling?

Yours, Diana

9/15

Dearest,

By fading daylight, I joyously received the biggest batch of letters from you in a long time & 3 more photos of my two girls — the only one who can match me tonight is my Co-commander who also got word of his daughter's arrival today. My thanks to your folks for the carriage, gold plated — $80!!! On Betty's crying, damn if I know what to do.

Lenny

9/15

Dearest Diana,

While we have been in Holland we've met patriotic folk, who display national colors & such but have not been in a position to meet active underground forces so far. Love to all — kisses to Betty & her mother.

Lenny

9/15

Dear Diana,

It was well to learn that Betty has more sense than to keep up that 2 A.M. feeding business, and your description of her discovery of orange juice really made me laugh. The war which was vehemently present with us only a few days ago, is less assertive here, where the loud "bawing" of the sheep prevails over all other sounds.

Lenny

9/15

Dearest,

Still no mail — I'm really getting impatient. Last night we had one of the worst storms that I even remember — it was a terrific hurricane and it lasted several hours. Lucy was at school and we were very worried until she came home at 10:30 P.M. The 8th Ave & BMT subways weren't running — all the trolleys and buses had to stop — the electricity went off at 8 P.M. and still isn't on yet, and the phone is out of order. I don't know the extent of the damage because I can't hear the radio.

I walked to the butcher shop this morning and all along Belmont Ave the trees are turned over on the houses — branches fell and even whole trees — the victory garden in back of my house — there is nothing left of it. I'm very grateful that our Frigidaire is on gas because of the baby's milk.

Dearest — I wonder why there is such a delay in the mail — I hope nothing is wrong.

Diana

9/16, 17, Holland

Dear Darling,

Yesterday was an awful lot of war, everything except battleships, so no chance to write — but all goes well. Since I don't keep any diary, all these days run one into another & one can't distinguish but it was one of the liveliest. It was followed by a night of guarding a big batch of prisoners, whom earlier I interrogated.

Yesterday we met some of the Dutch underground, wearing a white armband with orange stripes. Here we see kids whose growth stopped 5 years ago — a 16-year-old boy looks like an 11-year-old, and sickly at that, & so on. Their stories are unbelievable when you talk with them.

Lenny

9/16, V

Dearest,

It may take a few days before we will have electricity. Betty Lou and I are both fine but it's more than a week since we heard from our fellow and we are getting a little concerned. Are you OK, darling?

Diana

9/18, V

Dear Lenny,

We took pictures of Betty Lou again today. I hope so much that they come out well because she had her eyes open in these.

Tonight starts Rosh Hashanah. I had supper at your folks. I left Betty Lou with my mother after her 6 P.M. bottle. She started to get "Pablum" today which is prepared children's cereal and she liked it very well. Today she is six weeks old.

Diana

Mail Gets Through

9/18

Dearest Lenny,

Well, today was the real bonanza — <u>after a week of waiting for mail, I had 24 letters, 19 V-mails and 5 straight mail up til Sept 5</u>. I'm so glad that you are OK and that you seem happy at what you are doing. I realize how you are restraining yourself in regard to trophies — I'm always very pleased to get one from you especially something like the armband. Don't

Diana with Betty Lou, age six weeks

restrain yourself too much on the things you really want — I'll find place for them crowded as we are and when you and Betty Lou and I move together — we'll take a big apartment.

It's fine to have our daughter cheered in strange places — I think her Daddy should be cheered too, but I don't know about this kissing business. Maybe you should get your guard up a little faster, darling.

I realize now why your letters were delayed — well — I won't be as concerned should it happen again. So you are in Belgium now. Darling, I'm so thrilled about the picture that the Belgium boy took of you. I hope so much that it will come out so he can send it.

Diana

9/18

Darling,

If you read the headlines, you know we're busy! And my, how the prisoners roll in — yesterday there was hardly time to catch my breath.

Lenny

9/19

Beloved,

So we zigzag around thru Holland. Whoever named these the Low Countries was a darn liar — they go upwards whenever we have to advance.

National psychology is a curious thing. Here, when we come thru a town, flags are out, girls wear ribbons, but nary a cheer or acclamation. They sit quietly outside their houses & watch us with blank faces, & don't offer us the fruit & drink so freely given in France & especially Belgium. When I call "live Nederland," they repeat it — whereas France & Belgium always answered "Hooray, America."

I saw a Nazi collaborator woman's hair cut off — the barber did it thoroughly & neatly, — and privately — & she walked away quietly, only bursting into tears into her handkerchief after a while — and people lifted their eyebrows as she passed — where in France it was done with much excitement and public attention & ballyhoo.

Last night I slept deliciously in a foxhole left behind by retreating Nazis, which I lined with straw. Tom & I agreed it was about the best all around 2-man foxhole we'd ever dug — in the easy Dutch loess, all dirt, no rock, & a fine barn door for cover on top of which we had 6 inches of sod — but in the middle of the night a couple of big Holstein cows walked in on us, to eat the straw we lined the hole with, & their weight brought the roof down on Tom's chest, so we had to get out, & of course it rained cats & dogs, & we are all covered with mud.

Lenny

9/19

Dearest,

Enclosed is a clipping from "Stars & Stripes," 9/13/44[1] to hold for me. Also enclosed is a flyer in German and English. It reads, "The German soldier who carries this safe conduct is using it as a sign of his genuine wish to give himself up. He is to be disarmed, to be well looked after, to receive food and medical attention as required, and to be removed from the danger zone as soon as possible."
(Signed) Dwight D. Eisenhower

Lenny

---

1. The *Stars and Stripes* article refers to Lenny's arrival at Fort Eben-Emael.

9/19

Dear Lenny,

Today is the second day of Rosh Hashanah. I'm not so clear on what you are doing — maybe I'm not supposed to be. Aren't you a scout any more? Were you even one in France?

I'm so glad to have visitors now — that's really my only form of entertainment at present.

A happy New Year, dearest — Let us hope that this New Year will see the end of fascism and the beginning of a new life for the people.

Diana

9/20

Dear,

The soldier in action, as you know, has to school himself into a stoic indifference which becomes second nature after a while. It is not good to think often of home or sweetheart or family so it is only at odd moments that almost by chance a trifling incident reveals to him what is really uppermost in his thoughts & only masked: I take out something from my pocket and your picture comes out first or we pass a pink "ribboned" baby carriage with the infant all but invisible, to whom I throw a kiss as we march on.

Our separation which still must continue ever so long will be one day, although it feels like eternity, when we are together again and can forget the long waiting. Meanwhile you shall have my love from more new places, strange countries.

Lenny

9/20

Lenny,

Today brought three more letters — the one with the Belgium underground armband. I'm glad you thought the birth announcement was cute.

Talking of trophies, Lucy's brother-in-law Paul — you know, the submarine sailor — asked if you could send him a German pistol.

Betty Lou continues to get cuter every day. She looks straight at you now when you talk to her and she opens her mouth and tries to make motions as though to imitate you.

Diana

9/21

Dear Sweetheart,

Last night I saw the first issue of (probably) the first free newspaper in free Holland, which was a welcome sight — but one notes the farmers here, as in Normandy, worry so much about a few holes in their orchards, a cheap enough price for them.

Dearest, would you please write me in big detail, the latest news from the folks back home about these matters: 1) What kind of treatment should we give Germany, the war prisoners, & the civilians? 2) What is the status of Russian-Polish relations? 3) What concept of post-war world organization & peace machinery seems to be most likely now?

Lenny

9/21 V

Dear Lenny,

I think she is beginning to know me — I can usually make her smile quite quickly and she looks at me quite as though she knows me — maybe it's my imagination but I think so.

Diana

9/22, Holland

Dearest,

Waiting is also necessary, but it leaves me very dissatisfied, especially since we are stuck in a dull out-of-the-way place. However, it made possible a delicious hot shower, even though I had to hike a rugged mile to the maternity hospital where it was available. While there I saw 2 young couples leaving with newborn infants. I'm glad the children were born in freedom & already wore orange rosettes on their bonnets.

I hate to ask you to send me stuff because you're so tied up — but if you could manage, please send me the pair of leggings I left, 5 peppermint Lifesaver packs and a Colgate — medium size toothpaste. And I would not say no to a tin of cookies. Thanks again.

Lenny

9/22, V

Dear Sweetheart,

In a way I miss Friday night supper in your mother's house — They were sort of a milestone in the week and they were enjoyable. Maybe when Betty Lou gets a little older, we can go there again with her. It will be nice when we can take her places — right now I'm really confined to the house.

Diana

9/23

Dear Diana,

Less these stretches of guard & waiting become too boring, the Germans on occasion like to send us reminders that they are still around — which we just sweat out like everything else in the army.

Lenny

9/24

Darling,

Betty Lou has another accomplishment. Today she learned how to hit the rattles I have hung up over her crib. The noise fascinates her. She got so excited when she first did it. The last letter I had from our friend Rona she wrote, "Too bad you cannot have your second baby first — it would be so much easier."

Diana

9/24

Dear Diana,

We've seen them often enough in the movies, the tragic pictures of burning farmhouses, of panicky horses & cattle in stampede, of families pitifully trying to rescue a few belongings, or the steady trickle of refugees down the dirt roads, on foot, by bicycle, drawing babies in children's play wagons, in terror of the bursting artillery shells bursting all around.

This is the third country where I have seen that happening. It makes it very vivid to me that I am protecting you & Betty Lou on Shepherd Avenue. I've seen men going at the risk of their lives through fighting lines to bring back a bottle of milk or a bag of potatoes, and the heartbreaking look when, startled by a Nazi shell explosion, he drops the bottle and sees it break on the ground.

Lenny

9/25

Dear Diana,

No wonder the Europeans were so lit up about discovering America. If I had to live in this climate all my life, I'd also want to discover America. Forever raining, forever drizzling, cold nasty November weather but a foxhole is warm, when dry, but the soil is not that weatherproof. Thank goodness for the nearby barn! We have eaten well, on the whole, but this past week, we've had a spell of inadequate rations & only the orchard to supplement them.

The civilian exodus continues to be the most piteous sight, and incidentally creates some additional odd jobs for me as translator.

Lenny

9/25,V

Dear Lenny,

I'm sitting out in front of the house. The mailman hasn't been here yet — he's a little late so every few minutes another woman sticks her head out of the window and asks if the mailman has passed. There isn't one house on our block where there isn't someone waiting for mail.

Your,

Diana

"The Face of War Is Not for the Young"

9/26

Dearest,

There are scenes one never forgets, and crimes one never forgives. The soldier who goes into action expects to take it because he is prepared to dish it out, and in "total war" civilians in war plants can't be exempt — but there are still some criteria of humanity somewhere.

When the Germans compel a town to evacuate, driving the people down a road in confusion, and then turn loose an artillery barrage on the road — well, that's the Nazis. As interpreter, I was called in by the medics to speak with the wounded (where they could still talk) about where they were injured, to help keep families together, where only some needed to be sent to rear hospitals, etc. There was one woman with 3 kids, two injured, whom we got together, but couldn't locate her husband. In another case we found the wife & 2 kids to go along with the injured father.

Of course, there were some very critical cases & some beyond all help. Our boys have seen much but this shocked them into speechlessness — in complete silence they broke out what reserve K rations we've picked up to feed these kids. The medic captain went out to help the inevitable woman in premature labor on the road. Remember Marina, in the "North Star" & her reply to the old farmer? She says, "The face of war is not for the young" & she says "We are no longer young." There were 4 year olds there yesterday who will never be young.

Lenny

Lenny's squad and buddies

9/26

Dear Diana,

Today the sun shines beautifully again (a rarity!) and chow was A-1 & there's a movie being shown at the dairy barn, and one tries to forget what happened yesterday. I held a little Dutch kid (about 5) on my knee thru the show and both enjoyed the performance.

There's been no mail for a while — I eagerly await the latest achievements of Betty Lou and her mother.

9/26,

Dearest,

It is in accordance with my usual luck to be in a forgotten corner of Holland and miss all that's really of interest. Here is neither windmill country nor the tulip country — as ever, we miss the large cities and cultural centers. There are mines rather nearby, no trace of Rembrandt here, or Vondel (most prominent Dutch writer & playwright of 17th C), nor the Rabbis whose treatises I've studied.

Of course, as the Dutch regard the royal house as a resistance symbol (different from Leopold of Belgium!), so we accord them like recognition.

Lenny

9/26,V

Dearest,

Lenny darling, how are you? The newspapers report strong German resistance.

Diana

9/27 Yom Kippur in Holland

Dear Diana,

This morning I attended with 5 others from my company the Yom Kippur services held for the Jewish men in this region — several hundred assembling in the elegant schoolhouse in a pretty Dutch city. Also amusing to us front soldiers was the way corps & division echelon personnel ducked when ack guns opened up on some passing German planes, while we stood unperturbed — some of those rear echelon personnel being officers. Not to worry you — but to show you that I'm OK & can take care of myself, no longer a new recruit. I've already been thru airplane strafing four times, bombing once, any number of utility barrages, as well as machine gun, "burp" gun, rifle & sniper fire, also mortar fire. After a while one goes about one's duties, or eats, or sleeps, quite nonchalantly, maybe counting the shell bursts for statistical comparison.

While I'm fully confident of your ability to manage on whatever our resources are, I'd like to know the details, because I might be able to help plan for the future. There's much confusion on the $10 infantry combat pay & none of us has yet received any. If it comes through, there's another $10 a month for you.

Continuing about the financial business — Now for our situation the day I get my discharge (happy day!) — We'll have $300 in three monthly allotments of $100. Our expenses — well, I'll want to spend say 2 weeks on vacation with you & getting acquainted with Betty, we'll need rent money for a new apartment, moving out of storage dough, linoleum, etc & some civilian clothes for me: easily we'll need at least $200 cash on my discharge day & we won't want to touch what we have put away in the bank (with Betty we need a bigger reserve than $200). So in figuring your budget we also have to plan on saving a minimum of $200 in the next 12 months but only after your needs are fully met. At present we must plan on my returning to my old job as soon as possible, say 30 days after discharge at most.

After settling your current budget and our expenses for discharge day, I want to do some thinking about the future — in general. The biggest job is making up our minds as to my job, whether to stay on at my present job, at $2,100, or to start looking for something paying better, which is a darn sight easier said than done. Barring an unpredictable lucky break, or an opening of opportunities not now open, that almost inevitably demands some specialized training. There's always that PhD at Columbia hanging on.[2] There's social work courses, also very distasteful, but almost sine qua now for a job with a private agency, where the good-paying jobs are etc. Or I could break out entirely & try a technical line, as you did so well. And needless to say, I want to resume my Milton & other manuscripts. Let's discuss this in a couple of letters & see what we can figure out.

Lenny

9/28

Lee,

I had pretty much of a scare again today — thank goodness it was only a scare. I had another telegram from the War Dept. telling me you are OK and back in action. I wish they used another method of letting me know — so much can flash thru your mind before you open a telegram these days.

Diana

9/29

Dear Diana,

Mail from my friend, Sam, somewhere in France, and he says he met a Jewish woman, just out of Gestapo hands, who today saw her 12-year-old daughter for the first time in 20 months & still can't find her husband & 2 other children who are elsewhere in Nazi hands.

Lenny

10/1

Dear Diana,

I am very happy in doing my job in winning the war — but not happy when we just sit around. By all means I'm still in the same job that I was trained for, & served that way in France only there's the censorship on such matters. Enclosed is the safe conduct pass we send by plane & artillery into German lines. I've not sent a Dutch armband because I have not yet got an authentic underground one.

Sorry, but please tell Paul it's impossible to send him a pistol — weapons cannot be sent. Secondly, I have yet to get me "my" captured pistol.

---

2. Lenny had completed all the course work, but not his thesis.

Officers are offering $100 flat cash for pistols, but have no takers. Most pistols are captured by line company riflemen — you see, you get it either by killing or capturing a German, or getting there soon enough to search him or the corpse first. In my job it's not been yet my luck to get one with a pistol, or to get there first. In my job I can use a pistol, so I'm on the lookout (as everyone is!) especially for the 22 caliber vest pocket size one, which suits my job more than the famous but big sized Lugers and Walthers.

Lastly & most of all — thanks a million for the newsy notes of Betty — which I have to study a bit before I comment — and I can't wait for the next photos! Today I spent about 3 hours just looking at the two of you, at your photos. Be well, all my love —

Lenny

10/1, V

Dearest,

Feeling very comfortable just now, after a hot cup of coffee topping off a K-ration dinner Only I'm more & more annoyed at this taking it easy. It will be tough finishing this war but I for one want to see the war finish. I've said as before, and here where I can't do anything but my simple soldier's duty, it is felt more & more, especially when things are so quiet. Given free choice, I wouldn't trade these last 4 months experience in the European Theater of Operations for anything: only I wish I could see some sort of future for us in the present postwar prospects. Pierre, my French friend, is very ambitious and rich. He intends to hitch up with the biggest political party in France & carve out a big career — it's so easy for him!

Lenny

Oct 1

Dearest,

I went to the doctor last night for my post-natal check up and he was very pleased. I'm all healed up and he said I was fine.

Well — I have something new to say about our daughter. She has become a thumb sucker. She always used to try to get her thumb in her mouth ever since she was born but her muscles were not coordinated so she used to miss. Now she no longer misses. Everyone including the Dr. says for me to leave her alone — that's the latest theory. I'm not really pleased about this at all. I did try to take her finger out of her mouth for a few days, but she always managed to put it back. Lenny — it's a hard job to raise a little girl — every few days there are new problems — but she is a lot of fun.

The election campaign is now going full swing here at home. This past Thurs., Mrs. Roosevelt spoke at the Parkway Theater. There were 4,000 people listening outside to loudspeakers. I would have liked to go. Well, maybe in another month or two, I'll be freer in the evening. I do miss the things I used to do — but right now Betty Lou is a full time project. I love you.

Diana

Oct 2, V

Darling Diana,

Last night we saw the moon while on guard, a rare sight & it was the full moon — which you most likely looked to also — 'tis the Succoth full moon that's so clear in New York. This morning we got an orange for breakfast, the first since I left the hospital back in July.

Lenny

Oct 2, 1944

Dearest,

Thank you so much for the anniversary letter. I haven't had a letter like that from you in a long time and I felt good to read it. Mostly your letters now are quite impersonal and I can understand how you feel. Still it was swell to receive a letter that was just special for me and I'm glad you wrote it.

I realize my darling, that you can hardly advise on the care of a baby under the present circumstances but I know that you want to know about my problems and also it helps me just to write to you. In any case I am much calmer now than I was when I wrote the first letters about her. You see I was very scared when I brought her home — I thought she would break any minute and that I must do everything just perfectly or something serious would happen. Well, by now, I'm much more accustomed to handling her. I know that she won't break or fall apart even if I make a mistake.

Diana

Oct 3, V

Dear Diana,

I'm authorized to get the Combat Infantry Badge as of September 1st — which is swell news. There is no decoration — none at all — that I would rather wear. And of course, it means $10 more dough a month. The theory is you first prove yourself in combat — but that doesn't include the retroactive principle!

Impatiently awaiting the new photos of Betty — what color are her eyes now?

Lenny

Oct 3, 1944

Dearest Lenny,

There were eight letters from you today — the ones that were missing up to Sept 23.

Lenny darling — one thing upset me a little. You ask me to let your folks read your letters. I may be wrong, but I feel that your letters to me are very personal things only to be shown when I feel like showing them because they are mine.

I've written you where Lucy is staying. We put one of the metal beds into the living room and she sleeps on it. Someday we'll try to make up to my family all they are doing for us now — I don't really know how we'll ever be able to.

Yes, darling — I can get into the red dress with the heart-shaped neck-line. All my former clothes fit me very well. I am now 5 lbs less then when I became pregnant.

You ask me what work there is for me to do with Betty Lou. Don't you get the feeling from my letters that I am busy all day long with her — and so am I.

Darling, your mother often mentions to me that she knows how I feel because she was separated from your father when he worked out of town — of course it is hardly comparable — she had much less to worry about — but I'm sure she would not have wanted to share his letters to her. Did your father or mother complain about me not showing the letters? By the way, I see your mother almost daily and your father 2 or 3 times a week and I do tell them about most of your mail.

Diana

Oct 4, V

Dearest,

Some days back "Stars and Stripes" printed a not-too-well-thought-out editorial "So You Wanna Go Home" — a sore nerve in any GI's makeup and provoked a pile of letters with a common idea. "Sure we wanna go home — when Hitler and the rest of his mob are completely rubbed out."

In fact so many letters that the paper is sending them in scrapbook form to Gen. Eisenhower and the War Dept.

Few things bother us more than 1) point plans for seniority in re-turn home, which we know won't hold, 2) gripes by special groups, the over-28's, and married men, for special consideration, 3) talk of discharg-ing so many after Germany's advances, 4) talking of conversion to peace-time economy at home, 5) talk that it will take 2 ...3 ...4 ...years to finish Japan. Everyone here says that those who've been over longest should go home first, & especially guys who've been in action here since 1942–43, but no one wants a fighting division stripped of its veteran personnel until the Nazis throw in the towel.

Lenny

Oct 4

Dear Lenny,

You ask about the attitude of the people back home on the treat-ment of German prisoners and civilians. Well, it depends to a large extent on how closely the war has affected these people. There is a good deal of controversy. The prisoners in the camps in the U.S. are being treated very leniently — given much freedom and treated much better than some of our own troops. This has caused much resentment among certain sections of the people, but there are still very many people who feel that we should be kind.

I know how this must sound to you and how the other men with you must feel, and how the majority of the people you have met in the occupied countries must feel — but many people at home still feel very far away from it all — there is so much talk now in the press of a winter stalemate. I'm certain that Eisenhower and you men who are fighting are thinking much to the contrary — but the local setback at Arnhem, Netherlands last week gave many newspapers and commentators just the opportunity they were looking for to begin such talk.

Diana

Oct 5, V

Dearest,

Yesterday, in moving on, my squad as usual drew the dreariest area, as guard, but glory to the knowledge of languages — talking to the local vol-unteer patriot group, I was able to get for us a little brick cottage, just evacu-ated by a Nazi family who was part of the local occupation machinery &

who beat it back to Germany. It's the first night I've spent in a home since arriving in Europe. I picked up a batch of German books that I bitterly regret leaving.

Lenny

In the Thick of It

Lenny's 30th Division took part in the Battle of Aachen, fought both in and around Aachen, from October 2 to October 21. The 29th, 30th, and the 1st Infantry Divisions took leading parts in the siege by the First Army in this fierce conflict.

The city was part of the Siegfried Line, the main defensive network on Germany's western border. Although most of the civilian population was evacuated, much of the city was destroyed and both sides suffered heavy losses. This was one of the largest urban battles fought by the U.S. troops, and Aachen was the first city on German soil to be captured by the Allies. The battle, though necessary, further delayed Allied plans to advance in Germany.

Though the German forces eventually surrendered in the actual city of Aachen, they continued a fierce resistance in the outlying towns north of Aachen, with intense close fighting and artillery barrages. Lenny's unit, in the intelligence section of the battalion, included guarding and interrogating prisoners and dealing with local civilians, roles that became increasingly important, as well as dangerous.

Oct 6,V

Dearest,

Well, sweetheart, the deciding phase of the war is on, & your husband is not in a ringside seat — he's in the ring, and the punches are flying fast & furious. Things are now in such an interesting stage that all that happens must wait 'til after times to be told. In new, strange, & still hateful places, still my love goes homeward to you & all I hold dear. It is regrettable now above all that my letters must wait, but I pray the ones sent in the past week keep reaching you gradually. When in years gone by I saw, or read of freedom fighters locked in battle, it was easy to exult: when you're in the middle of it, you don't think that way — there's too much tragedy close at hand.

Lenny

Oct 8, V, Somewhere in Germany

Dear Darling Wife,

This is being written 10/8, as yesterday we were too busy to write & only a lucky break allows me to snatch a few minutes to write. They are all out, only I am left by the phone. This is not the first time I'm in Germany: although I couldn't write it before, I made 3 trips into this hateful land (once so different in our thoughts!) in line of duty. Right now I write on a copy of "Mein Kampf," taken from a German.

The last 72 hours have been the severest I've had to go through, & gave me rather more chances to laugh, after holding my breath, than one likes, in one day. But of course, there's a black lining to the silver cloud, some of our losses have been painful in the extreme. And are we kept busy. By gosh, how the prisoners roll in, practically a belt-line system is needed to process them, and it's really a headache now that we are in enemy territory surrounded by enemy civilians.

Yesterday I spoke to some civilians. They tried to exonerate themselves from blame, tried to show a separation between them & the Nazi party, but they wouldn't point to any evidence of doing anything about it! They made no denial, rather admitted, what most German soldiers pretend to deny, the atrocities in their land. They are very afraid, as afraid of us, as they say they were of the Nazi party — although fear didn't prevent the French or Yugoslavs from resisting.

Yesterday was Betty Lou day, two months old — I had no time to write about it separately as I had intended.

Lenny

Oct 8, V, Somewhere in Germany

Dear Diana,

Among interesting characters I've met, a number of German officers including a regiment commander (Lt. Co), some standing on their Nazi honor, others as morale-broken as their soldiers and a Russian peasant from Konotop, a city in Northern Ukraine just escaped from a German concentration camp, who capered around happily barefoot, & wanted to strangle the German PW's, and who gave us no end of amusing difficulties because he couldn't understand why he couldn't be turned loose upon them and had to march with them to be evacuated. Of course he wasn't handled as a German.

We're picking up more guys who claim to be non-Nazi or anti but no one who says he was not too scared to stand against them.

Well, beloved, I am happy. All goes well. Just you be well too with Betty.

Just saw the whole front of a newspaper map — we are making head-lines — boy, oh boy!

Lenny

Oct 9, V, Somewhere in Germany

Dearest,

Today new tasks — civilians, a problem — The Germans had simple methods, which we won't use & we're in no position to administer a vil-lage while we do our main job — so it means more interpreting work — more complications. We appointed a new mayor, an old guy from before '32, & he's in charge along with the local priest!

Gosh, do I want this war to end — Too god-damn much work and too much noise & excitement. It's swell to think of it all when it's quiet, but other times, wow.

Lenny

October 10, Somewhere in Germany

Dearest,

Midst of the "routine" other things come up, like receiving a couple of old & sick nuns from a danger zone (they had thought the Germans would spare a German church & town from shelling — of course, in er-ror) & bringing them to a dugout safely, and 2 pretty 19-year-old girls were brought in under suspicion, & turn out to be Ukrainians brought here as slave labor.

The civilians here keep pleading innocence, claiming compulsion by the Nazi party & claiming to distinguish between "Nazi" & "German." The priest was the one who kept saying that the Nazis were no friend to the church & our respect for their religious feelings has helped the situ-ation a lot. They told me before Hitler there were 23 political parties but mostly here were Catholic Centrum & Social Democrat.

Lenny

Oct 11, V Somewhere in Germany

Dearest,

Spent the night in a cottage cellar, except for 5 hours on guard & breakfasted at a table, on porcelain dishes & tablecloth, with hot K-rations & coffee, plus from the garden, fresh carrots, onions, tomatoes, pears, & applesauce & jam from the cupboard. All Nazis have fled, so perishables might as well be used. The wretched Germans really wrecked the last town, shelling their own people. I had gone to the central shelter, deep underground, and worked out a plan with the priest (quoting him out of St. Paul to his amazement, & the by-stander's amusement) and the new mayor on handling the 1,000 or so remaining civilians, but we moved on before we could put it into effect.

Chatted much with Pierre who's rejoined us again — Poor guy is not able to be in contact with his folks.[3]

Lenny

Oct 11

Dear Diana,

Here are a few little souvenir items:

1. Sternenbanner, a U.S. issued paper sent to German soldiers by our Air Force.

2. A Bill Mauldin cartoon — highly appropriate — he always clicks

3. A specimen of Russian currency, souvenirs of the Russian front, later abandoned by a German soldier.

4. "Surrender Now" leaflet to German troops from U.S.

Lenny

HOLDING OUR BREATH

Oct 12, V, Somewhere in Germany

Darling,

On guard duty 5 hours each night, so tired — However, food is swell: we have our good K-rations, plus the garden's fruit & vegetables. Tomatoes, onions, carrots, potatoes, cabbage, peas — Apples & the cellar preserves: green peas, cherries, pears, jam and so on; we can heat it, & eat at a table out of dishes.

Meanwhile the cannon thunders & the earth trembles, shells scream & crash, small arms rattle, planes groan & hum; the world reels from the tremendous wrestling of the giants. We have no doubt of the finish outcome

---

3. Lenny asked Diana to contact Pierre's father, who was working on Wall Street as a broker. In 1961, Lenny used long-delayed back pay owed to him, to finance a family trip to Paris. We were met at the airport by Pierre, who kissed my mother's hand, as only a Frenchman can, and she didn't wash her hand for days.

but from round to round we hold our breath — being in the ring ourselves gives double cause to wonder at the outcome of each round.

Very happy to have got some mail out to you this A.M. & hope it
reaches you soon. Kiss our Betty Lou and tell her all goes well.

Lenny

Oct 12,V, Germany

Dearest Diana,

Germany is a picture postcard country, & when I'm permitted I'll
send you some showing the places or some of them. Rich, my friend, has
the most beautiful shots of the very buildings & streets we have survived
through. As one remarked, "In New York a building like this would be
roped off, & a police guard posted to keep you away. Here we set up
housekeeping in it."

Lenny

Oct 13

Dearest,

Scurrying around a bit so we had to leave our grand little "victory
garden" & preserves cellar, but we shall manage!

Chatting further with Pierre, one learns he has a brother in the R.A.F.
We discussed the future of France and the post war-world & Indochina
last night.

Lenny

10/14

Dearest,

We had a sort of farewell party for Lucy. She leaves tomorrow for her
new job. Lucy seemed pleased. I hope this job works out for her.

Diana

Oct 14,V

Dearest Diana,

The enemy is a wounded beast, like a monster his artillery snarls in
anger, growls, barks, roars, his claws strike wildly at steeples and rooftops, at
walls & fences, tearing huge gaps, big ugly wounds in homes and churches.
But all unconcerned with his lashing paws, we stand perched way up on a
high tower observing his every move & phoning them in. Let him thrash
and beat as he will, his wounds will soon be mortal.

Glad to hear of your postnatal checkup and disappointed that the second batch of Betty's photos weren't developed yet.

Lenny

Oct 14

Dearest,

Some "Stars & Stripes" of special interest — see the note on the Old Hickory Division (mine) in "Somewhere in Europe" — and much else that reflects my present experience.

From "Stars & Stripes," Oct 11 ("With all roads running to Aachen cut off and all terrain surrounding it commanded by American guns, the city was warned yesterday to surrender unconditionally within 24 hours or be destroyed. While the First Army massed before Aachen, and according to front-line reports, narrowed the city's escape gap to one mile, it was announced yesterday that the First Army was holding down the southern sector of the West Front.")

From "Stars & Stripes," Oct 12: "Besieged Aachen, first German city to be condemned to death. The promised destruction of the city of 165,000 got underway soon after the expiration of the U.S. First Army's unconditional surrender ultimatum."

Lenny

Oct 15, V

Dearest Diana,

The battle goes on but here are a few free minutes. It's good to hear you mention reading — while it has been pleasant to see you so fully occupied with Betty Lou, it is pleasanter to see you continuing the vast range of interests we valued so highly. And you will have a full-time job, when I get home, beating some civility back into me who have become such a savage and uncivilized critter over here.

Thanks to the persistence of one guy here who is much less hesitant than I about shoving mail forward to be censored no matter how many shells are falling, maybe they'll be shorter intervals between batches of letters. We do not look too cheerfully at the prospect of more months over here but hopefully, we'll make more progress in Japan.

Lenny

10/16, V

Dearest Lenny,

Your mother was just here. She is making Betty Lou some little flannel jackets — so cute and useful in the cold weather. Between her two grandmas Betty Lou will be well clothed.

Lenny, I am still hoping to get the picture that the Belgian boy took, but if you come across another opportunity, please take another one. I'd so like to have one of you that is more recent than those I have.

Diana

10/16,V

Dear,

Writing you, and loving you, from the cellar of a beer hall in a little town somewhere in Germany. Handling some P W's — why we are so lucky, when all hell rages around you day & night and you can still go on and on. These prisoners, they give cause for wonder: there's no mistake about the fierce resistance the German army is putting up; and then you look at a baby face of 18, inducted on August 8, 1944, captured on his first day of combat because he slept on guard; or else you run up against the devilish kind — a 24-year-old guy who speaks English, French, Italian and Latin, if you please — and who coolly explains why it is "wrong" for the U.S. to invade Germany, why we should seek war against the "Bolshevist danger" — and cleverly begins to spin the web of World War III on the basis of splitting us & our allies. He was 3 years in Russia on the front & speaks with the voice of experience. Pierre asked me why I got so angry with him, as sometimes I do, with some, though mostly I handle the P W's with no outward display of anger.

Lenny

Oct 16

Dear Diana,

I mentioned reading "The Nazi State" by William Ebenstein, published by "Infantry Journal." It is a very good academic study of the Nazi set up — politics, government, local government, the party, justice & law, propaganda, art & literature, education, youth, religion, economy, labor & foreign policy.

Lenny

10/17

Dearest Diana,

Happy with your oh-so-happy letters of 9/29–30 telling of your joys, & my mother's with our little Betty Lou.

At last I have a pistol — at least the use of one — a fine P-38 Walther, the latest standard German model — from a friend in M company. Maybe I'll be able to keep it — meanwhile I have it. It's very good for close-in work, like handling prisoners, where a rifle is too bulky. Only it's damn heavy on my belt. I'd rather have an Italian Berretta.

When I first came to France I observed the strange look in the eyes of the men first out of combat — a look of intentness, of waiting expectancy, of grimness & things one doesn't speak about — and I wondered if I'd ever wear that look. Well, I don't know if I've worn the look, but I've felt it on occasion recently.

Fear is a funny thing — I find it more a physical instinct — for example, one shivers with cold, & the shivering induces the shiver of fear. Sometimes I find I hate the idea of being out alone on guard, but never gave it a thought when I had to run out to check on a tank coming thru (it was ours but could have been German). Strange what one learns to endure!

Lenny

10/17, V

Dear Lenny,

Two of the Nazi flags that you sent came today. I guess the other two will come shortly. Boy, they are tremendous! I didn't think they would be anywhere near that size when you wrote about them. I got a very peculiar feeling when I opened them up. I felt just like tearing them to shreds, then I thought it over and I realized that they are just symbols and not the enemy.[4]

Diana

10/18

Dear Diana,

The information about your routine (15–20 diapers per day) is exactly what I want to read. I understand your situation but want the details very much. I can see from your letters how tired & strained you are. As to my letters, I understand how you feel, but must disagree & repeat: now I insist you give my letters to be read by my folks, no they did not complain, not at all, but I want it.

'Tis true you are under strain, but believe me — it's strained here! As I write, shells are exploding within 50 & 100 yards, while I must stay in this cellar entrance: so if I ask a little thing like that, please honor my request,

---

4. The family story is that the flags were musty and dirty from use. My grandmother usually hung clothes outside, to dry or air out, on a clothesline operated by a pulley from the bedroom window, attached to the building across the way. She took the flag and began to hang it out. My mother started screaming, "Mama, stop, stop, are you crazy? You can't hang a Nazi flag out the window in Brooklyn!"

huh? Please tell my father about my checking on Dobromil.[5] I have asked many prisoners of war whether they passed there, and also when we find Poles & Ukrainians, I always ask, but so far no luck.

We GI's do not want any winter stalemate! Hell no! As to civilians, they are more & more "beaten" in attitude. They are a big problem, since they tangle up in the fighting lines in search of food & missing kin, & we have to deal with them.

Beloved, when you are tired & worn out with the grunt work, please remember our joyous years of love together, past & yet to come.

Lenny

10/18, V

Dearest Lenny,

You should see your daughter in the morning — she is the cutest thing. She laughs and plays and is so happy after the night's rest and the 6 A.M. bottle. I'm usually so tired at that hour and busy with the formula, but it's such a pleasure to watch her having fun.

Diana

10/19, V

Dear Diana,

Things continue severe here: it is a heck of an experience to watch the enemy from an observation post when he is gunning for you all out — and I can add a few more hair raisers to the postwar story collection. And midst it all, a miserable batch of civilians to handle, a real headache — sick & injured old folks, pregnant girls, men who should stay in their cellars but come out for food or for curiosity & once they see our positions have to be detained regardless of their families & so on — and a thousand conflicting orders, on each case, most of them impossible. And having to escort old ladies to the toilet, under fire, & back, imagine!!!

As civilians they continue to affirm their dislike of the Nazis & welcome for us, but I feel no German is to be trusted until they take up armed resistance to the Nazis.

Lenny

10/20

Dear Diana,

My V-mails are with my pack & other stuff "back" with the company — I'm a little further forward carrying & handling a radio (back-carry

---

5. Lenny is asking for news about the town his father came from.

type) with the Lt. It is noisy here, & the Germans continue to be a troublesome lot, but it is one of the ironies of war that it is more comfortable here in the front lines than in some rear areas we have been.

We have taken up lodgings in a very secure cellar shelter of a ruined row of apartment houses; we have a stove, good mattresses & pillows & quilts, tables & chairs, a supply of preserved strawberries. The cellar is quite dry & secure, although the rooms upstairs are shot all to pieces — walls gone, furnishings a shambles. When one looks at the furniture, recently so well kept, at the linen neatly piled in chests, at the wedding pictures fallen on the floor, at the popular scenic photos of Germany one sees everywhere, it hurts that such a people should have fallen so far from their human duties & still persist in this insane course of ruin, wrecked by Germany's own shells & pillaged by her own civilians & soldiers. Do you know, all along the border towns there are circulars posted up appealing to the German soldiers not to pillage the homes & gardens of German families?

Of course these comforts can't last! Soon we're off again — & the sooner we k.o. the enemy the better. Meanwhile all my love to my Dina & Betty — and you'll see that my folks read this letter, perhaps? It's been more than 2 weeks since I could write them.

Lenny

10/21, V

Dearest,

Our little daughter is so sweet. I could eat her up. Remember the little Dutch decals my mother has in the kitchen? Well, Betty Lou has picked herself a little boyfriend one of the little Dutch boys. It's so cute — every time she sees him she smiles and is so happy. I guess it is his red jacket that attracts her because she doesn't like the little girl, who is dressed in blue, half as much.

Diana

Oct 21

Dear Darling,

Writing with one hand & handling the radio with the other — maybe too busy to write later! Infernal Germans kicked up quite a racket last night, & interrupted sleep a number of times. This morning a lucky find — a dozen fresh eggs in this cellar's recesses — so, they were fried & heartily eaten: delicious! Especially since we are away from our company, & so short of rations: but not hungry while the preserves last! Tomorrow I am 29 and it is good that I am too busy to reflect on it!

All my love — Lenny

Oct 22

Dear Diana,

Happy birthday to me! Regardless of any lugubrious reflections I may have expressed on various anniversary dates passed, your husband is quite happy to register this birthday — considering what we've been through since leaving America. Thanks to the guys, who ran the gauntlet of enemy shells & tank fire, new rations & mail reached us last night at this advanced out-post. Your letter of 10/13 (only 8 days old), plus 2 more of the first Betty Lou snapshots arrived.

Your present routine: geez, 9 feedings a day poured into our "Gargantuan!"

As to your questions, my stomach has been better than at any time in 6 or 7 years: we had a 2-day scare in Holland, when the doctors thought my appendix was acting up, but one dose of mineral oil cleared that up, & that's been the only incident since I'm in Europe. It seems the K-ration combination suits my interior fine. My feet are fair: the left leg is OK, only when we hike 20–25 miles several days in a row, it reminds me of St. Lô, where I sprained my ankle, and my acquired swollen Achilles tendon on the march in France in my right foot, which was very crippling. Rather than go to the hospital again I got permission from my Lt. to ride a couple of days. It's not too serious now as we walk very much less since we are in Germany.

As a soldier, I continue to accumulate veteran experience all to the good. Since the last enumeration of enemy weapons I've experienced, add: tanks — screaming meemies and grenades fired by rifle, as well as some more air raid bombs.

"The house we live in" here has been altered considerably, since we moved in, by the "Jerries"; some more rooms have been given air & light beyond the original architect's ideas, and a lot of the furniture has been moved around but our cellar shelter is snug as ever. Only — last night, the blast from a dive bomber blew our door open, no damage, really, but it made me nervous for the first time in a long while: but after inspecting the situation it only served to show how secure our set-up is here.

Do you see the point I'm driving at? Simply this: there's no point in being blind to the perils around here, but it is foolish to worry — you take all precautions possible so as to be able to perform your mission and keep your mind at ease. And as you pass each day, your chances are better. The only way out is to finish the war as fast as possible.

Be well, my love: take care of yourself and Betty — and have as serene and calm a mind as your husband enjoys, & all will be well.

Lenny

10/22

Darling,

Happy birthday, darling and many, many returns — I sang you a happy birthday this morning when I awoke — did you hear me?

I do hope that next year we'll spend your birthday together with Betty Lou. Twenty-nine years old, my darling — gosh — Today is also Betty Lou's birthday — 11 weeks old — getting to be such a big girl.

Diana

Oct 23, Somewhere in Germany

· *Dearest,*

> Far from home and warm love's embrace,
> Every moment life teetering on the vast abyss,
> Midst the ghastly city-cadavers, skeletons of towns,
> Falling walls and crumbling ruin,
> Where the war-monster screams as he lashes
> His cruel claw at men and gnashes his jagged teeth.
> At man's monuments and man's best memories
> Where no butterfly thoughts come flitting, and
> Winds racked by rocket bombs
> Are rugged roads for love's dreams to travel
> Still there's a moment's breath to remember
> A star sparkling eye and a tear brushed aside,
> And a parting smile so tender.
> No more, for
> Here where, the bravest man trembles
> At the furies his won hand sets free,
> Home thoughts are blinding, and the eager yearning glance,
> At days to come, makes the fighter turn and falter.
> First blot off the earth this cancerous blight,
> Roll back this oppressive night, the somber glooms
> Of the Bushido[6] shadow and the swastika,
> 'Til rosy the dawn comes up with the liberty light

---

6. Samurai way of the warrior.

Bright once more on Rhine, and China's shore,
Then, only then, we may relax, and rest, and seek
Visions of home, and wife, and child, in pure delight

Dear, we shall have a pleasanter anniversary day a year from now, no doubt.

Lenny

Overseas Five Months

10/23

Lenny,

Again I have had no mail for a while — my most recent letter is 10/3. I await some eagerly. Lenny dear — how are you? Soon it will be five months that you are away — the longest time that we have been apart — and it will be a while again 'til we are together. I think I understand better what people mean when they say you get used to being separated. You don't get used to it — you just have to not think of it and put it out of your mind.

I know that often some of the people are surprised that I don't talk more about you and about you not knowing Betty Lou personally. I can't talk about it to anyone — not even those who are very close to me. I have to keep that in the back of my mind and only think about it when I am alone or when I am writing. I'm so happy that we did decide what we spoke about when I visited you in Mississippi. She is really wonderful and such a help to me even though she doesn't realize it. And the great decision — wasn't it a nice cubby-hole in the Chinese restaurant on that very rainy Tues. evening? You were so right, darling, to convince me. I love you so —

Diana

Oct 24, V

Dear Dena,

Came back to the company today with our Lt. from our forward position. Rugged as it was up there, especially during two days of German counterattack, it was so homey with stove & frying pan & pots & eats galore to make our rations swell!

Thanks for the second batch of snapshots. Thanks for what you are sending me; but don't send salami or canned goods, we have nothing but canned stuff, every meal & too much to carry as is. Don't worry: we never go hungry for lack of food.

Lenny

Oct 25, German paper with envelope taken from a soldier

Dearest,

I had a "quiet" day back with the company: here there are intervals between the German shelling & had 3 hours of guard instead of all day alert. Got the news, on return, of MacArthur's force landing in the Philippines (grand!) but would have preferred "we" to "I" in his announcement. Also good to hear of Belgrade being free: one country that's earned its freedom.

Had occasion to speak with a German civilian woman: much self-pity for having had to work 10 hours & Sundays on munitions, crocodile tears for the Jews (property losses was all she seemed to think they endured) but no ability to understand that Germans might have done something against Hitler when all Europe rose, & that they still must earn a place among civilized peoples. As one American soldier said, "They are friendly & servile — to us, when we are here with the guns, as they were when the Nazis were." That sort of friendliness is only repelling.

Lenny

10/25, V

Dearest,

All last night I dreamed of you and I was so sorry to awaken this morning. You see during the day I thought several times that it is just a year that you had the wonderful furlough.

Diana

Oct 25/26

Dear Diana,

It is a curious feeling to return, for the first time since we are in action, to a place we were in formerly & set up in a house a few doors from where we had our victory garden some weeks ago — we are here for a much-needed rest, since we have had the most rugged time since the Normandy hedgerows.

I've about 30 people to answer, since it was impossible to write more than to you since we bucked into Germany. I can't mention names of places, but you can see the maps in the papers & judge for yourself where we've been & what we've had to go through.

Lenny

Oct 26, V

Dearest,

Arriving here for the breather, I got issued free: Colgate's toothpaste, Mennon's shave cream, Lux soap & Gillette blades. What more can one ask? Also 3 swell, hot meals prepared by the kitchen & we are promised a shower tomorrow. Also I have my bedroll from the kitchen & so my 1st change of underwear in 7 weeks. Of course, one can hear the artillery (enemy) and see the towns where we were sweating it out, last week from here, but here it is almost like a furlough. We ate around the table and laughed & joked — we were all scattered apart last week & had a lot of experiences to exchange.

Wrote a pile of letters to all who write to me, since in the past weeks it was impossible to write to them. Dear, again, let me ask you to show my letters to my parents & family. Many days elapse between my letters directly to them, & I intend these, which go to you, for all.

Lenny

10/26

Diana,

Enclosed I sent 2 little pamphlets of interest to me that I'd like to keep here but have no room: 1) A German soldier songbook, 2) A copy of the Weimar constitution — a very interesting document in many ways.

Lenny

SOMEWHERE IN HOLLAND

Oct 27, Red Cross stationery (Enclosed is copy of "A Dirge for Germany")

Dearest,

> Deutschland, Deutschland, toll the bell
> A people is dying,
> Your people are dying.
> In Aachen, in Aachen, where Charlemagne is tombed
> The bells clanged night and day when Paris fell
> In Aachen the bells rang, rang loud, rang long,
> Twenty-four hours long, day and night, when Paris fell
> Now clang your bells again, for Aachen is fallen.

Lenny

Oct 27,V, Somewhere in Holland

Dearest,

Strange & unbelievable (almost uncomfortable) we are on a holiday — writing you from the Red Cross Recreation Center here. The schedule isn't set but showers & movies are promised.

Hurried as this day has been, and suited most to the least common denominator taste still it's been a holiday — beer — 5% beer, and ping-pong, although the guns boomed every so often through the performance. Of course, we know they are ours without listening the way we do at the front. "At the front," it sounds so peculiar to say that. France is as distant as New York as far as the war is concerned (of course I mean Paris & the beach, not where the fighting is still on). But at the front is where we have been continuously since D+6,[7] as far as my own division goes and 8/16 for me (my second arrival at the company, at a point between Domfrait and St. Bomer des Forges).[8]

Lenny

10/27

Dearest,

I write this as I am listening to Pres. Roosevelt making a campaign speech. Today is Navy Day and he says that today our Navy is bigger than all the navies of the world put together. We have just won a terrific victory over the Japanese Fleet in the Philippines.

Lenny, Roosevelt is answering Dewey's false attacks by showing how well the war is going. He says there were 27 D days in the past year — that is landings in various parts of the world.

Diana

Oct 27

Dear Diana,

It was nice to ride (truck) thru several Dutch cities I passed thru before & see the debris cleaned up & patching & repairs going on, & Dutch authorities in charge.

No sign of the flags I sent, is there?

Lenny

---

7. Lenny refers to the day he landed at Utah Beach.

8. He is remembering back to Normandy, when he was separated from his company after he sprained his ankle during the Battle of St. Lô, sometime during the week of July 3 and was recuperating in the hospital.

10/28,V

Dear Lenny,

Here it is Sat night and I'm sitting here alone writing to you. My mother & father are out as is Lucy, so Betty Lou and I are alone — she is asleep and I'm writing.

I received the other two Nazi flags that you sent.

Did I write you that Betty Lou's latest trick is to follow me around, with her eyes, whenever I go in the room and follow me as I walk out? She seems to know me already.

Diana

Oct 28,V

Dearest,

A fine breakfast was followed by a stroll thru the cloisters & gardens of this monastery where we were — Now we've gone elsewhere, and are quartered in a garage of a 3-story Dutch tenement. There is a young couple here on the floor, the parents of the husband on the floor below, who cannot do enough for our comfort — we are embarrassed by their attention. They're listening to the radio which for 4 years was hidden behind a stone block in the cellar wall.

Lenny

Oct 28,V

Dear Diana,

Just in to warm up — It's a cool October here — although pleasant for an afternoon stroll in the sunlight. Germany was pretty sunless, & we spent our time either in cellars or blacked out houses. The Dutch family with whom we are spending a pleasant evening are admiring the photos of Betty & her mother & calling me "papa."

Lenny

Oct 28

Dear Diana,

These little Nazi insignia arm-bands are slight compared to the battle flags I've sent — which I hope can be widely used — but even these little trophies should serve as some incentives to the folks in East New York. Keep one, if you like, & give the other 2 away — they were torn down from German walls during battle in Germany.

Lenny

Oct 29

Dear Diana,

Today sent you the following items: 1) A book on submarines, the German kind, for Lucy's brother-in-law, Paul, since he is on a submarine, 2) A Dutch armband of the interior forces, authentic in every way — you'll see the ink markings still — given me by my host, formerly in the underground here & now in the Ordedienst, resistance forces, 3) Copies of 4 Belgian newspapers from the first week of their freedom. You can judge their content from the headlines. They're real documents.

A few days ago I saw a book which regrettably was impossible to carry along because of the tactical situation but if I can get another I'll mail it to you: "Das Land Madil" by Gavriele Kreiger & Maria Muller Kemler, 1943. It is a very inclusive book designed as a textbook for girls, containing practical material like recipes, personal hygiene of girls & mothers, baby care, and above all praise of rural life. There are chapters on Der Fuhrer, his life & struggle for peace (yes, that's what it says) and the history of the Nazi party; & the story of the war since '39. But best of all the chapters is one on race. It begins by drawing analogies to breeds of chickens & horses & then proceeds to draw such conclusions: p. 44 "A Negro can have the same religion as a white, and remains still Negro. A Jew may be baptized, live in Germany but he remains a Jew. Race is a blood community, which by race-care and prevention of race-mixture is to be shielded from danger thru centuries." There's a table on p.47 as follows:

	ARYANS	JEWS
Build:	upright, straight & proud, tall	most small, bent
Walk:	elastic & harmonious	flatfooted, heavy & un-harmonic
Behavior:	calm, masterful, sure of goal	uneasy, gesticulating with hand & arm
Hair:	blond or brown *(revised classification of Arians to admit brown-haired Hitler)*	black & curly as Negroes
Eyes:	blue or brown with clear, calm look	dark with piercing uneasy look
Character:	loving honor & honorable, heroic & ready for battle, ...has national pride community spirit	without honor or dishonorable, egotistic & "internationalistic"

Many times I've come across Nazi propaganda & been tempted to keep the samples but these two were too good to pass up. One is the Labor Front leader, Robert Ley's discussion of "The Greatest Socialist Construction of the German People," with his theory of the enterprise-community based on complete equality (of racial origin) and led by the employer — Fuhrer. The other, with the Michelangelo head of David, is a sample of Nazi glorification techniques: notice the 6 former military heroes with the pictures of Hitler, Sgt. Hess, Lt. Goering & Sgt. Ley & the mocking of the British & African groups pictured.

Lenny

10/29, V

Dear Lenny,

Today was a real brisk day and Betty Lou had nice red cheeks when I took her upstairs. She slept like a log outside — I guess the cold air did it.

Diana

Oct 29, V

Dear,

I sit by the window and read my Whitman aloud. Over yonder, eastward, I can hear clearly the sounds of battle, and you can guess I am impatient to be there, but our boys have earned their rest.

Later on guard on the cold, windy street, bathed in bright moonlight, and one cursed a double curse at the German recon planes droning above. Last night we spent in the rooms of the family with whom we stay. We carry on our conversation in German, with me translating for the group, but their German is very much a Dutch edition as mine is a Yiddish one. We have a change of officers this week. Our Lt. has been reassigned & I have yet to meet our new one.

Lenny

10/30, M

Dear Lee,

I called the union and spoke to Pete about the flag you sent and he was very enthusiastic.[9]

Diana

---

9. At union rallies, the huge Nazi flags were covered with war bonds or dollar bills, raising money for the war effort.

Oct 30, V, Holland

Dearest,

Just burned a big batch of mail from friends, to clear out my gas mask, just in case[10] — 'Tis Halloween & it gets to be wintry cold here, especially on guard. Over in Europe no one believes (that is the Europeans) in the possibility of Dewey winning — but they don't know America, or the electoral system.

Lenny

Oct 30

Dear Diana,

Last night I spent a few hours visiting a different family, a rather poor one, in an ill furnished apartment: a thin, careworn miner of years ago, now on invalid pension, his small but apparently healthy wife, & their 8 kids, ranging from boys in their late teen years and some charming girls down to a babe-in-arms. Although a Hollander, he did time as a political in Germany for 7 months in 1935, and recently was taken by the Gestapo again into Germany, but got away in the general havoc. He spoke a mixed dialect, rather more unpolished Dutch & a little German, but we understood each other well.

I asked why they had no national flags or Wilhelmina photos in their front window, pointing out that as an American democrat with decidedly no preference for monarchy I nevertheless showed my solidarity with the Dutch by wearing their popular emblem (crossed flags, orange, and red-white-blue, with the Queen's picture in the center). And they agreed they ought to.

They went down the list of names of the formerly well known leaders — all dead, or missing in Germany. From this province 30 died & 100 went to concentration camps in Germany. This family really suffered. In the recent evacuation they had to burn whatever books or papers still survived. So they had nothing to show me, but they had had a splendid library, mentioning titles. Most interesting was the news that he had contact with a similar outfit in Germany, a group of 12 in a town near which I've passed. He has helped by delivering their local paper in various devious methods to evade the Gestapo.

Lenny

---

10. Lenny stored letters in his gas mask, when he wasn't using it, before sending them home.

ACROSS THE BORDER: SOMEWHERE IN GERMANY

Oct 30, Somewhere in Germany

Dearest Diana,

When we left the house today, the younger, Mrs. actually had tears streaming — we'd all become great friends — but it was really something in the way of a tribute to behavior, when civilians, strangers, are so moved at the going of soldiers quartered with them.

Well, now we're back in this wretched land but for the moment well set up in the cellar of some Countess's chateau. It's pretty much messed up, but they had taste here! Kid mohair couches as well as various fine woods with inlay, lace tablecloths, photo albums made by the finest of photographers, books — and in the midst of all a little snapshot of a boulder marked in memory of a young fellow who died at the age of 22 in Russia. So it goes!

Lenny

Oct 30

Dear Diana,

See page 4 of "War Week," Oct 28 — some day I'll tell you more about that place & that river crossing.[11]

Lenny

10/31

Dearest,

Still snug in this chateau cellar —

Dear, why & what is this anointing of Betty with oil? What kind of oil? I have to oil my baby M-1 every so often against rust & our jeep gets oiled to run smoothly; but Betty surely needs neither lubrication nor unction. Explicate please!

Regarding the first Nazi flag I captured. I trampled it into the mud before the eyes of the German soldiers who were surprised to see guys take it as a souvenir. Personally I'm still fighting off the souvenir bug, but

---

11. During a river crossing the advancing infantry often came under an all-out artillery barrage from the enemy. Such a crossing was made by members of Lenny's division. The men hand-carried sections of a footbridge with them, to throw across a narrow stream. They were then confronted with a steep and slippery far bank and, beyond, with a fortified woods and an old castle, from which the Germans used heavy small arms and machine guns to fire on them.

weakening fast. They say the other countries are in the war for freedom, the American soldiers for souvenirs. I'm definitely not going to send home the kid mohair divan they have here, but it's hurting not to!!! Also I've passed up beautiful cutlery, glassware, bookends, prints, etc. By the way, looting is strictly forbidden — these are all abandoned things.

Lenny

Oct 31, Germany

Darling,

'Tis cold & dreary, but I'm pretty snug here, reading William Tell in the original & Grimm's Fairy Tales. Also found a copy of a very common type of Nazi propaganda, "Exposure of the Soviet Paradise," a book of critical cartoons from the Soviet press which the Nazis try to use points to discredit Russia. I have also seen similar booklets of letters, from German soldiers, on the Russian front, sponsored by Goebbels. A friend also brought me a copy of "Socialism Betrayed" by K I Albrecht, 652 "exposures" of one who claims to have been an official of the German Communists & held some positions in Russia, escaping punishment for said crimes by invoking his German citizenship — he writes from Switzerland but the book is printed in Berlin, in 10 editions of 10,000 & a people's edition of 250,000 in '41, when it was needed. In the preface he writes, "We fight under the genial leadership of Adolf Hitler, who is not only the greatest commander and statesman but also the greatest Socialist of all times."

Lenny

10/31 Halloween

Dear Lenny,

First I must tell you Betty Lou's latest trick. This morning as I was oiling her, I put some under her chin and she laughed real laughter — not just a smile. I guess it must have tickled her. It was the first time she laughed and I was so pleased.

Lenny, I'm sorry that my letters have been tired and strained. I guess I couldn't hide it as much as I tried. You see, darling, when I first brought Betty Lou home, I was terribly scared and very tired and worried. Now I feel much better — I'm not so tired although I still don't get enough sleep, and I'm not scared any longer. I can handle Betty Lou pretty well now and she is really a good little girl.

Of course, I still have a great deal to think of regarding Betty Lou's daddy, but I'm doing my best to think cheerfully.

Darling, one more word regarding your letters, I shall show them to your folks when I have the opportunity but it is only because you are insisting I do it. I certainly am not doing it willingly. I'm sorry, darling, but I don't want to share your letters with anyone and it will hurt me very much to do it.

And dearest — I know what you are living thru — first because you write me and because I read and am well aware of the situation at the front. If I don't write of it, it is not because I don't think about it constantly.

Diana

Nov 1, V, Germany

Dearest,

Things are not too rugged for me just now — supposed to handle some prisoners but so far zero. So I will work on improving my command of German. By the way, for once, I've got picture cards of our location, to send you when censorship lifts in a couple of months.

Lenny

CLOSE CALL

Nov 1, evening, V

Diana,

Well my love, as our Capt. said "That was close." A couple of Germans in civilian clothes had been arrested for returning to a forbidden zone, after being warned to stay away, and they were being turned over to my custody, as is usually the procedure. One of them was either out of his mind or desperate, or both — anyhow he jumped me & tried to tear the pistol I was using out of my hands. A second later our wrestling match was surrounded by half a dozen buddies with pistols, but happily they didn't take the chance of shooting and I was able to knock the — down to the ground and (how we remain governed by American ideas of fairness) couldn't get myself to shoot an unarmed man who was down, but that pair went back under special guard after we took knives off of them. But these disgustingly, wretched Germans — this same "daredevil desperado" who tried this stunt so blazingly not five minutes later went down on his knees pleading to me for mercy and forgiveness. It infuriates me to see human beings so utterly devoid of moral courage.

Discover in tonight's paper that a castle we fought over, & I passed at least a dozen times, is full of priceless Vermeers and Bruegels, & is now under special guard, it was very hot when we were there but I'd have gone in to look anyhow, if I could — geez!!! All my love — all still goes well.

Lenny

11/2,V

Dear Diana,

I am sending by slow mail two envelopes — One containing some lines written in France before the liberation of Paris, and one with some small but significant samples of Nazi propaganda.

It is now two months since we took off on the big drive that carried us from the Paris region across the Belgian line, and guys begin to wonder if the war will end as quickly as we then anticipated. Of course at that time we didn't know whether the Siegfried line was fact or fable. Since then from personal observation, I am satisfied as it is fact, although by no means impregnable. They are slick pillboxes[12] camouflaged into houses, into forest boulders, into flat plains, & they are snug within & have marvelous systems of periscopes for vision. I've been in some we've used after capture — but just the same we've pushed them, piled up dirt into the entrances, or blasted 50-ton concrete domes off. Even if the Germans lack troops, they still have some A-1 pieces of equipment like the SS gun and their big Mark V and Mark VI tanks.

Lenny

Nov 3

Dearest,

I volunteered for a night shift observation post — & what a night, & what a place — a fit scene for wild fantastic & macabre deeds — a killing climb up to this location, black desolate and windswept. At first it was black as can be, only on the horizon smoldering embers of ruined houses. And the moan of places filled the winds, one afire crossing clear across the sky, then the "ack, ack" boom broke loose in pale luminous starbursts — and Halloween gave way to Christmas, red & green lights and flares.

The Germans picked that night for a special show. Off to the left a machine gun coughed and grumbled — and about 30 times an hour a shell came a whooping by and crashed below in the valley and our mortars beat a sparking path out to forward.

Lenny

---

12. Wartime bunkers and anti-tank defenses.

11/4

Darling Lenny,

   Your folks were here a little while ago and they played with Betty Lou before she went to bed. She looked very cute tonight because she wore pajamas for the first time. You know her crib is adjustable — I can move the mattress up and down. Up to now I had it on the highest rung because it was easiest for me to handle her, but today I moved it down because I wanted to hang up her cradle gym. The cradle gym is a toy which you string across the crib and it has handle bars, a trapeze, rings and balls suspended.

Diana

Nov 4

Dearest Diana,

   I'm in the foxhole, and sprawled out on the rim of this place I can see many places I've been in the town where we set up the new civilian administration, a corner where we had one of our closest shaves, the place where the lieutenant and I spent 5 days & the town around, or what's left — and the place where we had our victory garden but not any more. But what is important is we can look right down into "Jerry's" throat, and see his tonsils and that's why we're here.[13] By the way "Jerry" is slang for "German," corresponding on our side to Yank and Tommy.

   Overheard on the phone (we have one in our lookout here), they are checking up on balloting in the U.S. election — considering that I can practically spit the German soldiers in the eye, that's pretty good, reaching the fighting front!

Lenny

11/5

Lenny Dearest,

   There is a great deal that I want to write you regarding our daughter. I could just about fill up every letter with her. She does such tricks. She has just begun to pick up her hands when I stick mine out to lift her as though she asks to be lifted.

Diana

---

13. Lenny is referring to his volunteering to man an observation post on a slag heap, at Alsdorf (see November 3 letter). He took Diana back here in 1978.

Nov 5, V

Dear Diana,

I am all packed as is my unit, ready for anything, but before I can shave I want to write good morning to you. All packed means including my library — which is a little problem! I have had to give out with a plea to my friends on that score — recognizing my interest, everyone has been bringing me choice items, some of which are too good to leave — yet I am leaving behind a beautiful edition of Homer's Iliad, an excellent collection of German school readers, no end of German grammars and dictionaries of other languages — Spanish, Danish, Polish, etc. These books are usually lying out in the debris of ruined houses — most are weather-ruined but some escape. If I had an artillery man's or tanker's transportation!!! There have been whole sets of Goethe, for example, in some wrecked houses we've occupied. Oh, well!!!!

Betty does smile swell, doesn't she!!! This latest set of snapshots is grand, if only they were clearer. Where is her mom, though? Let's see you too, huh???? And some of our other folks too, once in a little while — Am I too demanding? Excuse me.

Lenny

Nov 5, V

Dear Diana,

We are again in the little farm cottage where we were before we went for that break in Holland. We regret that the tenants who were here in between left quite an untidy mess, & so we put in a few hours, cleaning up again, repairing the stove chimney etc. & also had quite a rifle cleaning session. We were sorry to leave the electric lights and warm cellar of the castle but this is fair while our candles last — only it's hard to read German Gothic type in dim light. The big advantage here is the carrots are still good in the garden.

Lenny

Nov 5, evening

Diana,

Am glad you like the division's insignia — I'm trying to get more. I couldn't explain then but can now, that the XXX stands for the 30th division and that we were at Eben-Emael.

My friend Pierre was recalled to Paris, by the French liaison officer, while I was spending those 5 days in that hot corner with my Lt.

As to photos from me, I had some civilians take some once in Belgium and in Holland, but I guess the mails don't work or censors hold them back — I told them in each case not to include any indication of where they were taken but censors are rigid. Also, there's no corner drugstore to develop the films.

The photos of Betty are good to get. By the way, doesn't she have any more hair on her head than that???!!! You know I study the snapshots with the aerial photograph magnifying glass?

Lenny

BETTY IS THREE MONTHS OLD

11/6

Dearest,

I took Betty Lou to the doctor today. She is fine — weighs 13 lb, 13 oz. and is doing splendidly. He increased her diet — gave her vegetables — carrots, spinach, potatoes, also banana, peaches, tomato juice and prune juice — quite a variety, no? Today is her three-month birthday.

Diana and Betty Lou

Nov 6–7

Dearest,

The German propaganda books are very interesting — but of course, there are limits on what we can hold. Coincidentally, we got a dose of their propaganda by air artillery shell this afternoon — the wind tore most of the circulars to shreds but I got a look at them, being sent out to round up copies for the chiefs. Both were cunning takeoffs on tomorrow's election. It's Election Day. Beloved, Election Day makes your husband a wee nostalgic for the sidewalks of East New York — soon again, who can say.

Lenny

11/7, V, Election Day

Dear Lenny,

Today is certainly an exciting day for us. I'm writing this in the late afternoon — voting is still going on. I voted about an hour ago and 2/3 had already voted in our E.D.

Diana

11/8

Lenny Dearest,

Congratulations on our victory. Now we can go on to the business of finishing the war and making the peace with confidence. The counting of the votes is still not complete and in some states the soldier vote has not been counted but Roosevelt already had 36 states.

Pierre's dad called me today.[14] Pierre's mother and sister are fine. His brother is a prisoner in Germany. His father has had mail from Pierre.

I'm so glad you are getting a rest finally. I know how badly you need it, and boy, I'm certainly looking forward to the mail you promised. My darling — is there any special reason that you were given this rest? You are OK, aren't you?

Diana

Nov 8, Germany

Dear Diana,

Back to the barn, but by now it is all the same whether one is out in front of our front lines or a cat's whiskers behind, except in the former case I don't take my shoes off when I sleep. Everyone is talking about the election but of course we won't have any results for some time here. The sentiment is clearly pro FDR here, by the way, very few Dewey men. Curiously, before election one heard grumbling that FDR shouldn't have said "unconditional surrender" because it (supposedly) makes it harder for us (supposedly the Germans fight harder) but in the cold grey morning after, the sober good sense comes out, "If Dewey wins, Hitler will hold out for easier terms & that'll be no good."

You made me smile when you wrote on learning I'm in Germany, "take care of yourself." So far, praise the Lord, the ammunition has passed me — I don't worry about it. Some of the most cautious guys have got it, & some of the most indifferent are still here. No, dear, no point in worrying — in fact I'm looking for a place to store up K ration tops — there's a rumor that with one million box tops or facsimile and 10 cents in stamps you can get a furlough home. Be well, beloved. If all is well with you, all is well.

Lenny

---

14. Pierre's dad called in response to Diana calling him, at Lenny's request, to get news of the family for Pierre.

Nov 9,V

Dear Diana,

The guys are laying 10–1 there will not be a repeat of Armistice Day on this 11th — but the news of FDR's reelection (still in the probably class here since we have no definite word, only word of mouth from radio) is well received. Needless to say I expect you will send me the complete vote figures. On the election, of course, Congress & Governor results mean a lot too — Hope you clip them out of the paper and send them on.

Now to scrape a few inches of grime off my hands & face tonight —
Lenny

11/9,V

Dearest Lenny,

The results of the election are still coming in and it looks as though Dewey will have 99 electoral votes from 12 states.
Diana

SNOW COMES EARLY

Nov 9/10,V

Dearest,

Ruefully we look at the swirling snow, whose coming we've been expecting, and the Southern born boys are ragging the Yankees because of the stuff. But best of all, came yesterday into the area a young fellow, just arrived overseas, who's in another division but who will have duties like mine, and he asked me to give him a hand on how the ropes go. He turns out to be the author of "The Six Weeks War," a book recently reviewed very favorably by the "Infantry Journal" and a very interesting fellow. His name is Pfc. Theodore Draper.

Days without mail are like months — are they so with you?
Lenny

Nov 11

Dear Diana,

Armistice Day is here again! No cynical comments are necessary but one hears a few.

We're not in a barn now but in a big place used 'til recently as a shelter by German civilians, and for the first time since I've been in the ETO,[15] I slept on a bed with mattress and springs. These civilians had to move out as we came in, and the family which occupied this room went to some kinfolk — they had to (or rather we permitted them to) take their belongings, clothes, food (preserves in jars mainly), some furniture, etc.

We stood by, hands-off policy: it is the first time I let a middle-aged man, woman & two late teenage girls lug a lot of heavy and bulky stuff, without lending a hand, but as I told them it is justice — and they're being evacuated in a much more tolerant fashion than the Germans showed to the Poles & French. We have found that to show them common decency or politeness — like offering to help with the load — would be to be sneered at for suckers by them. They revert from cringing to arrogance in a moment. I've seen Germans pack an alarm clock into a sock and leave food behind and what's more we have unbelievably idiotic Germans coming back under fire to feed pigeons or milk cows out in no-man's-land. It's one of the problems that usually comes through my hands, what to do with them.

Lenny

Nov 11

Dear,

Your husband is fresh & clean from a hot shower in a coal mine close by, which is now operated by the Germans under our auspices. Some of the miners were using the showers. One in the stall next to me was a typical cartoon of a German worker of former years — skinny and wizened in the raw, and dressed later in the visor cap and rough jacket. Like so many others, he said he was always against the Nazis, that the 99% votes were frauds; that he opposed the persecution of Jews, that he knew the war would be the ruin of Germany.

When I asked him what he had done about it, he came back with the old refrain, "wir konnen nichts" (we couldn't do anything). He was 50 years old, & recalled the days of the 8-hour day and free speech under the Republic. He said he was never a member of the Centrist & Social Democratic parties but praised the comparative good times under the administration of the latter. He said that he lived in Cologne and that city is now in ruins. As to the future, he expects to see Germany cut up, & especially cut down in size. Otherwise, he says, there will be another war in 30 years,

---

15. European Theater of Operations.

& so he's not opposed to an independent Rhineland or even to annexation by France, Belgium or Holland. He also gave out some idealist ideas of a world language & eternal peace. But of anti-Hitler movement, zero!

The lavatory & shower attendant was 65 years old & 47 years employed in this mine. He is an ex Stahlhelm (Steel Helmet) member & when that veteran's organization was dissolved, he declined to join the Nazis. Leaving the place, we asked the Fraulein at the information desk for a lapel pin of the Labor Front. She hastened to say she had never belonged to it, & so did the by standing workmen. But then one brought a couple out of a drawer. It is a swastika in a cogwheel, of cheap metal. I also have a Nazi party pin & Hitler Jugend (Youth) pin, & am on the lookout for their women's organization pin. In taking the pins, I remarked in German, "I am preparing materials for a museum of barbarism, in America." They laughed and repeated it appreciatively, but drat their "hides," they don't do anything to show that they mean it when they say they're not Nazis.

Lenny

11/11–12, Midnight

Dear Diana,

Ought to be sleeping but there's a table & electric light down here & I've just come off guard out in the cold dark, with only the stars for company — and Jerry machine guns burping off somewhere down that away — and once in a while their artillery laying on a barrage & then our counter battery and that whole mysterious panorama of flares & searchlights always appearing at night, that one never quite knows the meaning of — and the hum of planes, some of ours & one of Jerry's — that's one way to tell them apart, ours come as many, theirs as single, very often. So you can see when I came down from the post into this shelter & munched a snack of D-ration chocolate, why I feel first of all like saying "good night-hello" to you before I kick off my shoes & turn in. You know, since I'm in action I only take off my helmet & shoes to sleep — & of course there are many nights when they stay on too!!

Thanks for contacting M. Le Bailly. Although Pierre & I were friends about 7 weeks, & much of that time we were apart, in combat one makes deep friendships fast, & covers lots of ground in the long hours together — on the march — on guard at night, questioning civilians in Belgium — lying pinned down by machine gun fire in Holland, when the tanks made a spectacular push & flaming planes made a swirling exit from the dog fights 20,000 feet up in the air — standing side by side, in a beer joint in Germany, our temporary shelter, circumstances which make men very close. He's the only guy I've met in the army, with whom to exchange philosophic ideas with.

Well, maybe more tomorrow. Now must sleep — The war demands it.

Lenny

Nov 11

Dearest,

Some odds & ends for your curiosity & file: 1) "Three Speeches" — leaflet sent us by Germans via shells day before election, 2) Fragment of another that got shot to pieces as it came, "Be a Patriot," 3) 3 Russian money notes — one ruble and 2 of 3 rubles, 4) "Stars & Stripes" clipping about the 442nd Regimental Combat Team we trained with in our Mississippi maneuvers, 5) "Holy Letter" sent me by a friend's mother — it guarantees against small arms fire — but I don't have any concern about German small arms marksmanship, it's their mortars & 88's that hurt.

Lenny

11/12, V

Dear Lenny,

Even though today is Sunday, I have spent the day alone because my folks and Lucy went to the movie house to see the "Rainbow." Betty Lou is fine company but it does get lonely every once in a while because it's a little difficult to carry on a conversation with her.

Diana

11/13

Dear Lenny,

I'm very glad for your letter written on your birthday. You sound most cheerful in it. Some of the things you wrote made me laugh. If you insist on comparing our daughter to a horse — well, I guess there is little I can do but register my protest. You are free to continue the comparison, however, Lenny — she does eat nice-sized meals for a little girl — it's a pleasure to see her eat.

Diana

Nov 13, V

Dearest,

They say we can write all things up to Oct 23, but there seem to be a 35-mile distance limit which crimps the first. However, by now you must have seen by the newspapers that we were the boys that put the iron ring around Aachen — and it was hot because, until the city surrendered, we were as much surrounded as we were encircling.

We happen to be within easy grasp of a fine library, a private one belonging to a Nazi who has fled to interior Germany, but no can avail myself of its riches.

Finally got my new winter coat and field jacket & will be happy in both.

Lenny

11/14

Dearest,

I intend to go out this evening to a victory celebration for Roosevelt's election.

Diana

Nov 14, letter

Dear Diana,

I have a souvenir book which I may be able to send home. "(name of the town) under the Swastika," commemorating 9/9–9/17, 1933 Nazi week here. Greetings, verse, photos, program for the week. Turning the pages, reading its account of the rise of the Nazi movement here from 1927 to 1933, you can see how they cheered the Nazis there. It recounts how in March 1928, they first raised the placard "Jews May Not Enter" — great day!

While the things I've observed and written of as regards to how German's stand, I still am looking (Diogenes seeking an honest man!) for some basis of a future democratic Germany. Of several attendants & bystanders in the showers, all of 20 to 30 years service there, one was the usual, "I never meddled in politics … we could do nothing," one recognized a couple of songs — but came out with the same comments. He made it a little stronger, said the German working men (he of course is one) were "idiots;" that when a 95% or 99% vote was reported by the Nazis it was really 30. But still nothing was done. He mentioned that they still fear to speak & that a pistol shot would come for singing those songs.

A rugged errand tonight — Germany, in wet snowfall and blackout, is dark as the inside of an inkwell, & you can't see 6 feet or 6 inches away — but one occasionally has to make a jeep trip on duty — and one is glad there is no illumination from enemy shells — as some nights!

Lenny

Nov 15, V

Dearest,

We are again in the little farm cottage where we were before we went for that break in Holland. We regret to notice that the "Krauts" who were in here in between left quite an untidy mess, and so we put in a few hours cleaning up again.

The moon came out, & Orion very resplendent, for a while last night — but the serene beauty of the night was jarred by the discordant rasping and glare of planes going down, often in clear view.

Lenny

11/15

Dear Lenny,

There is much developing in the community as a result of the election. There is a new plant of 800 workers on Atlantic Avenue which is going to sponsor a clubroom of a non-partisan character in that neighborhood.

Diana

Nov 15, V

Dearest,

All in a day's work — We were detailed to reconnoiter for a particular type of coal & I volunteered to go because with the language one can save endless time, & after a while we located a supply after touring the region, back a couple of towns. Well, the town is far enough back to be in the Allied Military Government rule & I was interested to catch a fleeting glimpse at some of the latest ordinances & laws, especially the one which outlaws the Nazi party and about subsidiary organizations — posted in prominent places.

Lenny

Nov 15, V

Diana,

Your all-too-short V-mails of 11/2 & 11/3 came tonight, and also the tin of cookies — very good, grand!!! Thanks!

Your husband is getting again a mite restless things are a mite too quiet. But soon they'll be hot enough.

Lenny

11/16

Dear Lenny,

I had 4 letters from you today from 10/31, 11/1, 11/2, and 11/3. There are some letters missing — but I gather you are back in Germany.

The baby has had no reaction to the smallpox vaccination yet and there is no mark. She's perfectly happy and comfortable and her usual self.

Diana

Nov 17, V

Dearly Beloved,

Things are humming again, so all is well.

By the way, I was expecting to write you a detailed review of our experiences in Holland & Germany because we can now write "Up to Oct 22" — but that is nullified by distance limitations until some time in the future. I have a set of photographs & postcards of places we've been to send you when censorship will permit it.

Lenny

11/17

Lenny,

That was some close shave you had with that German prisoner — I hate those —.

I'm glad you are all right. I can see by the newspapers that you are very busy again. The papers say that a big offensive has been launched on the western front and the First Army is participating. Good luck, my darling.

Diana

An Awful Lot of War

Nov 17/18, V, Germany

Dear Diana,

Yesterday was one of those "awful lot of war" days, of which I've had occasion to write before. Excuse me, please — Jerry just came knocking at our door, & having nothing but some clouds overhead, I've followed the gang downstairs to the cellar. For a guy who disliked noise in civilian life, the savage balk of enemy shells does not bother me. I have a decent respect for enemy artillery & shrapnel, but it doesn't scare me. The city in which I spent yesterday and where I've come back to, after spending the night farther forward is the most beat-up place I've seen since St. Lô in

France, although not equally in ruin. Here some walls still stand.

Yesterday I also handled a big mess of prisoners, one of our largest batches.

Lenny

11/18

Dearest Lenny,

Your sister, Harriet brought the latest set of pictures that she took and they are the best we've taken. You can really meet your daughter on them. You asked me to explain about "oiling" Betty Lou. Well, I shall. I rub olive oil all over her body every morning as a means of lubricating her skin. I oil her and put cornstarch on it so that it is dry and clean and the skin is soft. It is similar to a bath, but I use oil instead. She also gets bathed in water.

Diana

Nov 19,V

Dear Diana,

Pay day — $32.60 — and in a couple of days a money order for $40.00 will be going your way. Outside of a dollar's worth of air mail stamps, I've bought as an emergency reserve I've spent nary a cent from last pay day to this.

Still having it pretty easy — We only had to do a little sweeping up in the corridor today. Still hungering for some real mail from you, not just one or two little V-mails a week.

Lenny

11/19

Dearest Lenny,

Today was the first day Betty Lou began to have a reaction to her vaccination and she fussed quite a bit all day. It is inflamed now and full of pus. This will probably last a few days, then it dries up and the scab falls off and it's all over.

My father was a delegate to a Russian War Relief Conference today. The "Justingrader" sent him. Your father was a delegate from the "Dobrimilar."[16]

Diana

---

16. Diana refers to fraternal organizations for those from the same community in Eastern Europe.

Nov 19,V

Dear Diana,

The weather is fine for a change and you can see by the papers what's happening to the Germans. Except for a few diehards, young officers & such, civilians & soldiers are hollering "uncle," and if they want to have all Germany leveled the way these towns are, before all of them holler uncle, they'll have it so. Saw [name blacked out by censor] today, he's over [words blacked out] and he said a few words of encouragement to us [words blacked out]. First time I've seen him.

The excitement of the last 96 hours has let up for a bit & all of a sudden one feels so tired one doesn't notice when the shells are coming in. By grapevine, I heard the regimental Colonel had some nice things to say about the soldiers names unknown, of course, as usual — who guarded a batch of prisoners under "shellfire" — that was me the other day, and thanks to the colonel were with me because he finally got some others out of their cellars to carry on with the job I had been doing solo.

Lenny

Nov 20,V

Dearest Diana,

Last night my supper was delayed a little — not that is anything unusual! Only it was a bit rugged at moments. First I got pulled away to handle a business of a young civilian girl, who turned out to be one of the Ukrainian forced labor importees, & had to go a ways to get her sister & friend, the same nationalities & convey them to a shelter.

Coming back I sat down in the cellar & heated my "C" ration & coffee a second time when along came a batch of 5 dozen prisoners to be handled — which wouldn't be much, even in this blasted inky German night — only the Germans proceeded to furnish illumination by giant firecrackers, and not only illumination.

Lenny

Nov 20,V

Dearest,

Thanks for arranging for the delivery of the Nazi flags — but I am curious what each recipient had to say, & if real use may be made of them.

Lenny

11/20

Dear Lee,

You are not at all demanding when you ask for pictures of the baby and us. Darling, that is the least we can do until you can see her in person.

My darling — that is all the hair Betty Lou has. Whatever she does have in the back of her head — the front is practically bald. It is not unusual for an infant of her age.

I'm enclosing the last two pictures with this letter. One you can get a fairly good idea of the baby's crib. The thing lining it is called a bumper. That is to prevent her from hitting her head on the wood or getting her hands through the slats while she is so small. The little toy head underneath her hand is called a duck pin. It has a spring and the mouth opens to hold her covers on at night.

Diana

11/21

Dear Lenny,

I think that Betty Lou is taking the vaccination like a Major — she seems OK — no temperature — she is her usual self. Her arm is all enflamed, though, and full of pus.

Diana

Nov 21–22, V not photographed

Dear Diana,

Writing this the 22nd as yesterday it was impossible to write — another one of those "awful lot of war" days — a headline date very likely! Rain, rain, and endless soupy mud but on we go — no rest for the Germans, and none for us neither. It's funny that when our days are fullest, we can write least about them, because all the events are in the "must keep quiet" class at least for weeks to come. Yesterday I added a few more good stories to tell of my war experiences.

I have something extra to write you for 11/23 but the war will probably hinder sending it to you, as things are moving too fast & furious for carefully written letters. Besides, I can't mail anything out either for the same reason.

Lenny

11/22

Darling,

Today is 7 years that we met. I don't think any special comment is

344   ᐳ   <i>We Are Going to Be Lucky</i>

necessary — just I love you! The mailman had to tie your letters in a package this morning.

Lenny — I have just read the 4 summary letters with your experiences very carefully. A lot that you wrote I was able to guess — for instance that you were in Wales — and when you got to France. I'm glad to know about all the places you have been and where you fought. Now of course, since I know what division etc., you are with, I know much more from newspaper reports. Right now I just feel gripping fear as I read and such happiness that you are all right to write me about it. You asked how I feel about days without mail. They are like months and even worse as you know.

Diana

Nov 23, V, Thanksgiving Day

Dearest Lenny,

Today is also our 55th anniversary.[17] Happy anniversary, darling — Perhaps in the not too distant future we will be celebrating together again.

I don't think I wrote you that I bought a book on child care about a week ago. I wanted it ever since Betty Lou was born but it costs $4.00. It is called "Child Care & Development" by Gesell & Ilg. They are two psychologists who have an experiential clinic in Yale. It discusses how to handle almost every problem that arises and it deals with children up to the age of five years.

Diana

Nov 23, V

Dear Diana,

We're over here where things are sort of hot and not sure if today is Thanksgiving or not.

Uncle Sam has given us all nice warm wool sweaters, with long sleeves so I won't need the one Mrs. Zimmerman made this winter, so do with it whatever you feel.

It's been impossible to write to my folks for some days now and will continue so (in fact, impossible to mail any letter for 4 or 5 days already) — so please let them see whatever mail comes through, when you can.

Lenny

---

17. Lenny and Diana continued to count months, as well as years.

11/24, V

Dear Lenny,

How are you, darling? I follow your exploits as carefully as I can through the newspapers and I wonder how much mail I shall be able to have for a while, considering how busy you are.

Diana

Nov 24, V, not photographed

Dearest,

My calendar says the 30th but "Stars & Stripes" says the 23rd but in either case we got no turkey — but the "C"-ration meat & beans are filling anyway. Days and nights continue to be all too dramatic.

Eagerly awaiting the next set of Betty photos and hoping you are in them too: only I'm so drowsy as I write now, it's doubly hard — besides the usual long hours of night guard, we had a little surprise, something of an emergency, in which a German "language" speaking GI was needed & that cost some more sleeping time. But all goes well — the promise of no winter lull suits me fine, & the progress is all that can be hoped for.

Lenny

11/25

Dear Lenny,

The baby was feeling much better today — I think the worst of the vaccination is over. I was able to take her out. Since it became quite cold, I felt it was time for her to wear her snowsuit so she did. She looked so grown up in it — like a little "mensch."

Diana

Nov 25, V, Germany

Dearest,

Yesterday wasn't Thanksgiving but it was Turkey day for us anyhow, & all you could eat.

Yesterday I sent you by slow mail some of your letters (only 4 — such a long time 'til they came) and also another kind of armband, different from the 3 previously sent, this is a Hitler Jugend armband.[18] I've seen Nazi party bands but couldn't get any for myself so far. They seem

---

18. Youth paramilitary organization of the Nazi party.

to have been mostly destroyed or carried off — part of their plans to go underground, no doubt.

Lenny

Nov 26, V

Dear Diana,

Surprise gift packages — from Welfare Center 73 and a wonderful one from my cousins Bea & Leon! Delicious the stuff is — but, as ever, each package in itself was more than I can carry — and so many packages are coming that we all have too much — I passed out cookies, plus big hunks of fruitcake, & gobs of candy & I still have stuff left galore.

My darling, there was blue sky this afternoon and so rare in Germany I got a chance to sit in the sun and read.

Lenny

11/26

Darling,

Today is the day — 9 V-mails from you from 10/4–10/12 — swell. So you are in Germany dearest — I kinda thought so. I'm glad to know where you are and what you are doing — Betty Lou and I are mighty proud, and also concerned. I know this may sound a little silly but take care of your self and be OK, my Lenny.

Gosh, darling — I would love to have a picture of you. I'm still hoping to get the one that was taken of you in Belgium. If any opportunity arises, take advantage of it — I know you will. I love you so.

Diana

Nov 26

Dearest Diana,

By dim candle in a leaky, wet barn & by grey dawn light this morning finally I've finished Asch's "Apostle."

'Tis a quiet (relatively) day, a Sunday that for once is a Sunday. Last night for a change I allowed myself to think back on our former apartment, in describing some principles of decoration to my friend. (Evoked by the ruins of the town we are in) & it's close to mind & eye & heart today.

I still have no answer to any letters of mine after Oct 21, & your most recent one is about 3 weeks old.

Burned a batch of other letters today because my pocket was too bulky — that always hurts — there are so many nice letters that come that are so pleasant to read & reread.[19]

Lenny

Nov 27 & 11/28, V

Dearest,

Much war again today, no sleep last night — but we are driving the Nazis back town by town. Had a little business with a prisoner who's from Alsace Lorraine, and claimed to be French but spoke far better German, & betrayed his quisling soul by letting himself get tripped up linguistically. I alternated between French & German, & caught him tangled up in the French repeatedly.

Lenny

Six Months Apart

Nov 29, V

Dear Diana,

Glory, we did get a long ride back, past many towns and scenes familiar from recent action there, now quiet once more, and took a hot shower in a mine now under our administration.

I continue concerned as to the affect of Betty's pressure on your family — is it hard on your parents, on Lucy? Write me just how it is, please. It is something I don't dwell on, beloved, as you know — still, today is the full six months since we parted last — it is the longest we've ever been separated and the end is still far off: but happily this experience is also — for us — part of our loving, and a part we shall never regret. As often you have said too — we'll not regret the price we've had to pay — all my love, "Dulcissima."

Lenny

Nov 29, V

Dear,

You are not the only one who writes their husband that they follow the newspapers! By the way, you were right about the First Army — but

19. Presumably, these weren't letters from Diana. Lenny burned her letters and photos only when he was in imminent danger of being captured.

now I am in the Ninth Army. While we are still limited by place & time restrictions, we hear that there was a radio broadcast about the whole record of the 30th Division, back home, and that the current achievements are reported within 10 days. The division is really an outstanding one of the war — you know, we were the first Allied troops in Belgium & in Holland. We hung up some real records in France — and set the pace in Germany.

Lenny

11/29

Dear Lenny,

   Betty Lou had the first letter from her daddy today. I read it to her twice. It's one of the best poems of all those you have written in the last year — maybe I like it so well because it expresses so much how we feel. *To Betty Lou, Age 3 Months*

> Betty Lou, do I owe you
> A word of explanation
>
> Betty, my kid, my Betty Lou
> (Sweet loved child that yet I've never seen)
> To every evening star one prayer up high I send:
> Fortune grant you'll never know
> That father's gone, way across the seas,
> Fortune grant we be united
> Long ere you wonder where I am.

   Someday when Betty Lou will be a big girl and she'll ask us about the war, we'll show it to her. I want to know if you are satisfied with my letters to you since the baby has been born. I think I write you almost everything about her. Are there other things about her I leave out?

   I thought a little about the type of home I would like us to have when you come home. I want plenty of room when we have a new home — mostly I'd like us to have lots of drawers and closets and bookshelves. And we'll have to allow room for expansion — so let's be very careful when we choose our new home.

Diana

11/30, V

Dearest Diana,

   Relaxed by the shower, and a bit of afternoon sunshine, sitting in the place we laughingly call our dayroom — and then suddenly the day is made memorable in a way we'd far rather not have. Blind chance, plain luck, is for individuals the greatest single factor in war.

Lenny

Dec 1, Service Club paper

Dear Diana,

Another month begins; When comes the finish? I do not share the very common idea that the war necessarily ends when we have crossed the Rhine or Ruhr. It will help enormously, of course, but so long as the main body of German troops remain on the Russian front it is there they must be annihilated.

You write of oiling Betty. What the? Why does she need lubrication? I never heard of such a thing. Please explain! Also, what grade oil — do you have to change it "for winter"?[20]

Lenny

Dec 1, V, Germany

Dear Darling,

It was, it seems, only yesterday when we took this town — it's vivid in my mind the way it looked that sunny morning — how surprised we were that it was so quiet, after a couple of days of heavy shelling in the town before it. How we examined the ruins — and yelled at civilians to get back to the cellars and evacuated prisoners.

Tonight we are back here for a breather — and the ruins are a bit more bedraggled, but with no business at all, GI's roam the blackout streets going to a big movie being shone to a jammed house in some building that escaped the general ruin.

Lenny

December 1

Dear Diana,

Some little items of big significance:

a) German houses are plastered with mottoes & slogans; & so are their army mail forms. Here are two of the latter —

"Deutsch sein heist: character haben"[21] — a gross falsehood and

---

20. Sometimes Lenny asked the same questions again, because Diana's mail, with the answers, was delayed.

21. "To be German means to have character."

"Untrrhaltungen ohne waffen sind wie noten ohne instrunente."[22]

b) We found a big book full of horrible pictures of dead folk of all ages, entitled "The Polish Cruelties against German People Resident in Poland" — (here is only the title page as I'd rather use my mailing rights to send pleasanter things) dated 1940 — in other words, the Nazis photographed their own bestial atrocities in Poland in 1939–40, & use it for propaganda.

c) Mimeographed description of the bravery of the 30th Division written by a captain.

Lenny

12/2

Dearest,

Betty Lou knocks herself out these days when she plays. She kicks so hard and is so happy and enthusiastic she screams with pleasure. It's really funny — sometimes she screams so loud that no sound comes out of her at all — just a lot of wind.

Diana

SOMEWHERE IN HOLLAND: WELL-EARNED R AND R

Dec 2, Somewhere in Holland — Red Cross paper

Dearest,

R & R in schoolroom — far from action — sleeping on the floor — Of course one is here very much "out of range" — not even a distant rumble of artillery reaches here — only by airplane can Jerry come this far.

Things are pretty much at ease at the moment. The Germans remind us there's war every few hours, but mostly time's a wasting. My friend calculates at the present rate we may expect to get to Paris next October. Best thing would be to finish the war and all come home.

Lenny

12/2

Dear Diana,

Some interesting copies of "Stars & Stripes" — especially the articles on my division — The headline reads, "1st and 9th Armies Hurl Nazis to Banks of Roer River." The article reads, "Two American armies pushed the

---

22. "Negotiations without weapons are music notes without instruments."—Frederick the Great.

Wehrmacht back against the German River Roer, last major water barrier to the Cologne plain and lower Rhine. U.S. First Army forces pushed on in cold rain and heavy mud to within three miles of the river." An additional clipping reads, "With the 30th Inf. Division laden with combat packs, their feet heavy with mud-coated four-buckle overshoes, men of the 30th (Old Hickory) Inf. Div. double timed over the rain-soaked terrain to surprise and overcome garrisons defending two German towns when the Allies launched their attack along the Western Front, Nov. 16th. Advancing while artillery was pounding German positions, 30th infantrymen were atop the Jerries when they emerged from shelters to see what the shooting was about."

Lenny

12/3

Dear Lenny,

I got some of the election figures you wanted.

National Vote
Roosevelt   24,900,000, 36 states
Dewey   21,500,000, 12 states

Diana

Dec 3, Red Cross paper

Sweetheart,

A quiet Sunday here at the Recreation area in Holland — slept well through the night and feel quite refreshed. One ambles about — kids with the guys — goes to lunch — then to the theater here — a USO show, better than the average.

Dear, as to the 4 long review letters — truly: you want to know that, don't you? Or would you rather just have me write "I am well & love you always?" Personally, I believe it would be better if lots of folks at home know more realistically what goes on — and so you can show those letters to "All the world."

By the way, when I come to write of our experiences in Germany, the story will be much more terrific than anything that happened in France or Belgium.[23]

But — I am lucky — and hope to continue lucky 'til the job is done.

Lenny

---

23. When things were quiet, Lenny wrote long review letters of his experiences. Educated as a historian, he was recording what happened, with the goal of writing a book after he came home.

12/4, V

Dearest,

This morning I had a very nice surprise. I had a letter from you from 11/24 which is only 10 days old.

Diana

Dec 4, V, not photographed

Dear Diana,

In this soupy miserable German mud, we've got a secure cellar with lots of hay to sleep on tonight.

I wonder if I've unnecessarily given you cause for worry — please believe me, 1) Fear on your part is 99% emotion — remember I am a well-trained soldier, 2) I've had all kinds of experience during 5 months, which makes all the difference in the world, 3) The law of averages is in favor of the majority of soldiers, 4) For the first period in my life, I've actually been lucky, consistently lucky — although 75% of "luck" is really profiting from past experience, 5) And there are much fewer days of danger to relative safety.

Lenny

Dec 5, V

Dearest,

The ten snapshots came last night grand as they are by candlelight, I still could hardly wait for daylight to see them clear. Now one can see that we have a young lady in the family!

Lenny

12/5

Dearest Lenny,

I took Betty Lou to the Dr. today for her monthly check up. He was very pleased with her. She weighs 16 lbs. She is fine in every respect. She can now have all kinds of fruits and vegetables. She is also to have an egg for breakfast. I have to start with 1 drop of the yolk tomorrow. She will be on formula until 6 months. Then she'll have regular milk.

Darling, I'm glad I can write you such glowing reports about Betty Lou. I hope you don't think I am exaggerating. She's really a healthy little girl and we're lucky to have her, and she's good as can be.

Diana

BETTY IS FOUR MONTHS OLD

Dec 6, V

My dear girls,

Wherever we move in, we clean up a mess left by Germans (civilians or soldiers), fix up heat, doors. We ventured into an unholy mess in the cellar and transformed it into a cozy haven.

Lenny

Dec 7 & 8, V

Dearest,

Pearl Harbor Day of gloomy memory. For once our situation is rather comfortable here (as such things go) and things go pretty easy for a couple of days.

Lenny

Dec 9, V, Germany

Dear Diana,

A rainy snowy muddy day of sloshing around in muck and mire — with a day of review training — Miracle of miracles, a pass has struck my way — tomorrow I go to spend a "day" (maybe 9 hours) in a provincial Dutch town — don't know what it offers & Sunday in Holland tends to be a blue law day — but a pass is a pass! (Even, if it isn't Paris?)

Lenny

Dec 10, Red Cross stationery, Holland

Dear Diana,

I am sitting in a quite elegant café in this provincial Dutch capital — sipping cider. It's been a pretty pleasant day here on pass. Best plan would have been to get in with a family for the day but the families we know are rather a ways off — so we just ambled around town. On an outside chance, I asked after the synagogue, & finally tracked it down — but was informed that the Germans closed it down.

Still seeking to get a photo for you we searched the town but all places were closed or out of supplies. Finally by a tip from a Dutch miss we hiked out to a suburban cottage where the youngish head of the house invited us in but apologized, sorry, Sunday, day of rest, no can do & so on. It became a job of explaining tactfully we couldn't exactly make an appointment, & come back at leisure — & that while we hated to disturb his Sunday, well, some of our Sundays have been disturbed too. Presently his missus spoke up. It turns out she's a photo expert of a century-old family of photographers. We made arrangements for later pick up of the pictures (ready next week) by (we hope) other buddies who will be in on pass. And then we gave the family cigarettes & a box of chocolates — so it was all very graceful.

The missus photographer contributed a dramatic moment. She said we had no call to be giving the cigarettes & chocolate — and we said they had given up part of their Sunday. "But you," she came back very quickly, "You have liberated Holland!" Naturally we came back with the rejoinder — it was both, Netherlands & Americans etc. But it was a good moment.

Lenny

Dec 10, V, Holland

Dear Diana,

With a day pass, in a very good-looking town here, had my photo taken by a professional photographer today. I hope and pray some buddy will be on pass, here later on & pick them up. That makes the 6th effort I've made to get you a picture.

Lenny

Dec 11, V

Dear Lenny,

I have much fun with Betty Lou these days. She responds to play so well now — better each day. She loves to be bounced around and when you hold her up and sing. She waves her hands and feet to the music.

Diana

12/11, V

Darling,

Things are pretty much at ease at the moment. The Germans remind us there's a war every few hours, but mostly time's a wasting. My friend calculates, at the present rate, we may expect to get to Paris next October.

Lenny

Dec 12, V, Germany

Dearest,

It is again nearly 3 weeks sans mail — not to speak of overdue prior letters. Oh, well!

Lenny

Lenny in Germany, December, 10, 1944

12/12,V

Dearest Lenny,

    I just came home from an interesting discussion on Greece. You probably are aware of what is going on there but I'll discuss it in a letter as soon as I have an opportunity. There is a good deal of anti-Churchill sentiment developing because of the stand he has taken and because of all the criminal bloodshed he has caused for the Greek people. This, of course, is very serious because Churchill is still the person who will lead Great Britain to victory against Hitler.

Diana

Dec 13, V, Germany

Dearest,

I am glad you liked the letter to Betty. I took a long time to get up the courage to write how one must feel under the circumstances but it had to be said once.

Lots of guys are asking "How much longer now?" It's hard to keep them satisfied.

Lenny

Dec 13, V

Dear Lenny

I am planning to go shopping for a pair of shoes for myself. I hope I can get them because most of the stores have very inferior shoes and those not in all sizes. I need sturdy everyday shoes. Since I've gotten Betty Lou's ration book, I have her shoe stamps until she will need shoes of her own, which will only be a matter of months now, I guess.

As I've written you, she is all over the vaccination but the scab is still on. She took it like a soldier's daughter.

Lenny, Betty Lou is a joy in our house and my folks are really and truly not inconvenienced by her. Whatever space problem was created, and there is no doubt that we have one — well, the fun they have with her more then compensates. Lucy is slightly crazy about her also. Please, darling, don't let that concern you. They wouldn't think of letting Betty Lou and me move until you come and take us away.

Diana

Dec 15, V, Germany

Dear Diana,

I got to sleep last night about 3 and slept 'til 9 this morning, which was the first sleep since 12/13 — lots of work and especially night work. In particular 3 times in the last two nights, I thank my lucky stars for the days and nights spent in Mississippi swamps. Hitherto, we've been mainly in settled areas in Germany, reaching like mad across open areas. Now we have to face open country — and it is good to be able to strike out boldly across country, with no fear of being lost, unlike some of the city-bred fellows who were along, who have no confidence in being able to keep oriented and find one's way. There are no streets to go by. It was rugged especially night before last, thigh-deep mud morasses & shell holes big enough to swim in.

A buddy picked up the photos and I sent two off by airmail.

When the Germans surrendered the big city,[24] they didn't surrender on the side we were, outside of the pincer, & we had some of the "ruggedest" weeks ever. We still have a gag among the guys — "Well, I was at ..." and that settles any debate or comparison between situations the men of our battalion have been in. So we were given a real break then.

Lenny

Dec 16

Darling,

This is Saturday night darling and I spend it with you. By now I'm sure you must be very busy again. That is one bad feature of mail taking 10–14 days. I never know where you are when you are there — only two weeks later.

Diana

Dec 16, V, Germany

Dear,

As I've always said, if tears help ease things, why, let them come, beloved, only I hope it isn't anything in my recent letters which induced them.

If you feel like it, by all means type up a couple of my lyrics and send them to any publication you want, only sign them " Leonard M. Loewenthal"[25] and you can start a file of rejection slips.

Lenny

12/17

Dearest Lenny,

In a very short time I'll be able to cut out the 11 P.M. bottle so I'll be able to get to bed earlier and then when Betty Lou will be six months old, I'll be able to cut out the 6 A.M. bottle and I'll stop making the formula. That will be very good because I'd begin to get up later in the morning. Of course, it will depend on how well Betty Lou will cooperate with

24. Aachen.

25. Loewenthal was Lenny's mother's maiden name, which he used as a pen name.

these new plans, but I think with some patience she'll fit into the new program.

Diana

Dec 17, V, Germany

Dear Diana,

We came back to the company this morning and found our combat infantrymen badges waiting for us.

One questions, what the devil has been going on in Greece and in Belgium? Stars & Stripes seems to be toeing a very narrow mark in reporting what's going on and it's not clear.

Lenny

12/18

Dear Lenny,

Regarding the Nazi flags — I think I wrote you what people said. They were very enthusiastic and said they could be used in bond rallies.

Your enthusiasm over the 10 pictures you received of Betty Lou at 3 months makes me very happy. I'm so glad that you like her because she is likeable.

My darling — how are you? All is well with Betty Lou and me. Just as long as we keep getting mail from you as we have been — I'm so grateful for it.

Diana

12/19

Dearest,

My folks were surprised when I told them you had written "the baby must make it difficult for them." They were surprised that you should even think such a thought and they told me to reassure you on that score.

I'm so glad you think I'm doing a good job. You know that I'm trying hard. Of course now, I have much more faith in myself. At the beginning I was really scared, as you probably saw from my letters.

Diana

7

The Battle of the Bulge

The Battle of the Bulge was the last major German offensive campaign of World War II. The goal was to surprise the Allies by cutting
through the dense forests of the Ardennes and splitting the Allied
forces and then forcing a negotiated peace on the Western Front.

As the fighting in southern Holland and Germany dragged on,
Lenny and his squad were constantly out on patrol between two op-
posing battle lines. The Allies were anticipating an offensive attack.

On December 16, the attack came through the Ardennes, the
same route the Germans had taken to successfully cut off the Allies
at the start of the war in 1940. Divisions like the 29th and 30th
were rushed back into Belgium. It took a day to get there. The
Battle of the Bulge had begun. Lenny's 120th Infantry Regiment,
30th Infantry Division, was rushed to Malmédy, Belgium, on the
hills on the northeast side of the Bulge, where they took over from
the 117th and a number of other units who had prevented the
German advance into the town the day before, and now moved on
to the important junction and fuel depot at Stavelot.

The 30th Division held the Germans there as the 29th Division
flanked the enemy advance on the north to keep the Germans
from breaking out into open country. Three days later, as German
tanks tried to enter Malmédy, Lenny's squad was assigned to stop
them from crossing a critical stone bridge. They were to blow up
the bridge if orders came. When the rest of his unit pulled back
under heavy fire, Lenny stuck by his wounded buddy in a paper
mill opposite the bridge, for hours, until help arrived. For this action, Lenny was eventually awarded the Silver Star Medal.

Bridge with mill behind it

Dec 19, V, Belgium

Dearest Darling,

During the last two days the war, for us, has lived up to the reputation of being wholly unpredictable. Anything can happen and usually will. And as always it is the unknown, the unforeseen, the not knowing what to expect, which is much more difficult to bear than situations we've been in, which were actually more serious to us directly.

In any case, it was impossible to write you yesterday. In fact, there was no sleeping night before last, and going without sleep is relatively the little thing. And as usual, the days that are most interesting one can write the least — besides which the Germans put on a couple of all-night shows that really held everyone's attention. Only the last night tended to become monstrous as it appeared they were not performing specially for our benefit but that we were only accidental spectators. In many ways things are as they were back in France, only then there was no snow on the heights, which makes a lot of difference.[1]

Lenny

Dec 20, V, Belgium

Dear Diana,

Received your letters of 12/8, 9, & 10 today & was very happy to be-cause I'm blue today. I had to part with some of my treasures today, which hitherto I kept in a corner of the jeep, but I was evicted from it yesterday for no particular good reason. So rather than throw them away (& they don't let me send 'em home, legitimately acquired though they were) I donated them to the Cathedral library here, a beautiful book of 350 repro-ductions of Durer's work, a Virgil, a Homer, a volume of Goethe. It hurt bitterly but it couldn't be helped.

Lenny

12/20

Dear Lenny,

We have our first snow of the winter. Yesterday Betty Lou and I were con-fined to the house because of it, but today we went out. I wrapped her up so that only her nose was showing and we went for a walk. It was 15 degrees.

Darling — you didn't give me any unnecessary worry in the 4 long letters. You know, I have a pretty fair idea of what an infantry soldier does, and so I've said many times, I want to know as much about you as I can. If I sounded a little scared, well darling, I am, and I think I have cause to be, even though I agree with all the reasons that you listed for me not to worry. You know what I mean, don't you? I'm proud and happy in what you are doing — I'm also worried, and waiting so impatiently for a better future. Those are the contradictions, darling. I guess you face them also. I think you're doing a fine job, just keep it up and I'll be OK.

Diana

---

1. Lenny is writing from Malmédy, Belgium, which the Americans had been holding since their arrival in Belgium on December 18. U.S. troops had confined the northern Nazi stab to the area of St. Vith, Stavelot, and Malmédy [the Germans subsequently took St. Vith]. The three Belgian towns were held by Americans up to noon Wednesday, the latest period covered by official reports. "American Infantry, who from four A.M. until this afternoon were fighting tanks, heard on the radio that the First Army had retaken Malmédy. They think that's a hell of a note because they've never lost it, so how could they have to retake it?" (*Stars and Stripes*, December 23)

Dec 20, 2nd V, Belgium

Dear Dena,

By the way, I hunger deeply for the magazine articles I requested. During the strain of our coming here, everyone being tense & very quiet, except when things happened or appeared about to happen. I was singing our favorite songs to myself & it was a great help.

Lenny

Dec 21

Dear Lenny,

As I sit here writing to you, Betty Lou is lying in her play yard next to me and she's very busy. She is carefully examining her feet. By the way, she only discovered them a day or two ago and now she can play with them for hours. Mostly she tries to see if they'll come off and she pulls so hard. I imagine she is hurting herself but she doesn't seem to mind so I guess it's OK.

The newspapers are full of the counter-offensive that the Nazis have launched against the First Army. The newspapers, of course, always scream when we mark one mile forward or if we have to retreat. Some of the more sober commentators, however, know that this is an inevitable attempt by the Nazis and that it bears the possibility for us to turn it into a real defeat for them. We'll have to see what develops.

It's time for our Betty Lou's supper, so darling all our love.

Diana

12/22, V

Dearest,

Each month rolls around and I think "when"? But there's very much to be done before it will be over

Diana

Dec 22

Darling Diana,

Success! After much checking up and asking, we got photos. These 2 photos are for you, of course. If the folks want any, well, here are the negatives. The background is a barn somewhere in Germany — and someday I'll tell you a couple of things that happened there.[2]

Lenny

---

2. The barn was in Langendorf, Germany (November 8 letter), in the town north of Aachen, which they kept "revisiting" during the battle and afterward. Somehow, in between the heat of battle, the two photos of the squad were taken there.

Dec 22

Dearest,

Yesterday I did not write you a letter. In fact yesterday I burned 3 of your letters, together with a batch of other personal papers of interest and value: it hurt but the circumstances did not admit hesitation or doubt. All in all it was one of the most serious days some of us have come through — and while I had some 3 or 4 plans in mind as to what to do, yesterday, while the situation was sort of tight, fortunately luck continued with us & here I am writing you at ease.[3]

After it is over, I find the telling will be more exciting than the experiencing. One can be cool & deliberate in the midst of all kinds of things going on — thanks to the training one has (character building and education, remember). Our Lt. said last night I might get some sort of medal out of yesterday's business, possibly even the Silver Star. Those things have to be approved by all kinds of folks, so there's no saying if it will come or not. The best reward (wonderful beyond all expectations as a decoration might be) was to have one's own feeling of satisfaction from the company commander and the operations officer when we got back.

The letters I had to burn were the pleasant ones about Betty's play yard. Also, my personal memos, which would have served to write up my record of experiences in Holland & Germany, and my copies of the lyrics including some stray beginnings of some.

1944 Merry Christmas from the 120th Infantry somewhere in Germany.

Lenny

---

3. On this December 21, "When it appeared that there was every possibility the Germans would crash into Malmédy itself, Capt. Charles Pritchard, of Nelsonville, Ohio, mustered headquarters clerks, communication men and others and sent them to front positions. Just then, armored infantry arrived" (*Stars and Stripes*, December 23). This letter refers to the events that day. Lenny was there as part of the HQ company that was sent out to the front lines at the bridge at the west entrance to the town. During the Battle of the Bridge that day, Lenny stayed with his wounded buddy at the paper mill on the northeast side on the road opposite the bridge, for which he was eventually awarded the Silver Star. On the other side of the road, Pfc. Francis Currey and supporting Tank Destroyers took out enemy positions and a German tank, for which Currey was awarded the Medal of Honor.

12/22

Dear Diana,

Enclosed is a copy of "Stars & Stripes" to hold for me — of interest to us.[4]

Lenny

12/22,V

Lenny,

You wrote that your stomach acted up. How do you feel now? Asking you that in this letter is a little silly because you won't get it for a few more weeks, but as you can well imagine, I am concerned.

Monday will be Christmas. I'm so glad Betty Lou is very young and doesn't understand much yet.

Your,
Diana

Dec 23,V

Dearest Diana,

Yesterday I just "took it easy." One feels the strain more after the events than during. I was out a couple of hours interpreting. One learns more about dual-loyalty people that one finds in too many places in Europe.

I sent you yesterday, airmail with 2 photos & negatives to make more prints for the boys. The guys mainly want the group pictures, naturally. Please when you send the photos enclose the list with it in case I should be unable to keep my copy. 'Tis a small matter, and yet so pleasant, it bears remark! Such are one's pleasures here. I got into my bed roll yesterday & got a change of underwear out, & washed up head to toe, & new sox on (one can't change nightly so easily here, sometimes it's monthly) — so feel much better. When we finally get home you'll have a real job to civilize me all over again, let alone streets with lights & sleeping on beds.

Lenny

Dec 23

Dear Lenny,

The newspapers and radio are full of conflicting reports about the German counter-offensive in Belgium. In the main the offensive seems to be

---

4. Lenny fought in this area. "Other First Army forces recaptured the Belgian town of Stavelot 10 miles south of Spa, and fought fiercely to re-take Malmédy into which Germans had penetrated." (*Stars and Stripes*)

checked. It's so hard to make sense out of the reports that they are giving, but remembering what the newspapers did in other wars, I don't let the day-to-day reports upset me too much. I'd rather study the overall picture.

Diana

Dec 24

Dear darling,

I just came home and it's very late, but I feel like writing to you, and it's Christmas Eve when loved ones should be together so I want to spend a little time with you before I go to bed.

We did have a small celebration for your folks' 30th anniversary.

Lenny, a funny thing happening this evening, I think it will make you smile. It hasn't happened to me in ages. The conductor on the Brighton Beach train tried to pick me up and wanted me to go out with him, but I didn't give him a chance to. The train was quite empty because it was only 7 P.M. and he came and sat down near me and started a conversation. He told me this was his final trip for the evening and was leading up to my plans for the evening when I let him know very quickly that I have a husband in Germany and a daughter at home.

Diana

Dec 24, V, Belgium

Dearest Love,

My French, which rested a while, is now being exercised again — and even the little Flemish phrases I picked up come in handy.

Lenny

NOEL, NOEL!

"We will never forget this Christmas . . ." Behind these brief couple of lines in the following letters by Lenny to Diana, lies a story.

On Christmas Eve, 1944, Lenny and his buddies were in the center of Malmédy, when the second of three successive waves of Allied bombers, returning from missions, December 23, 24, and 25, mistakenly dropped some of their bombs on Malmédy, with great destruction to the town, and loss of U.S. soldiers' and civilians' lives. The Christmas Eve bombing was the worst. Almost the entire center of the town was reduced to rubble by the bombing and the subsequent resulting raging fires. Miraculously, the beautiful cathedral survived in the destruction of most of the town's central square.

That whole evening was one giant horrific rescue operation as Lenny, those buddies who survived from Companies K and M, arriving MPs, and the Engineers, who dynamited structures to stop the flames—luckily, located in the center of town—frantically dug through the ruins to carry out the few survivors, on stretchers, to the medics, and corralled back those fortunate civilians who began to emerge too early from the few safe havens and buildings that remained.

Lenny's detailed personal written account in "Rifleman's Road" (in the chapter "Noel, Noel!") and in the small notebooks he assembled during his recovery period in England, of what happened in Malmédy center that evening, were filled with the horror, and a touch of the pathos necessary to survive the war, if you were lucky. The two 30th Division websites contain accounts of the bombings, the radio logs of the communications before contact was lost with headquarters, and the list and reports of those soldiers and civilians that were killed or missing. The rest of the story was seared into the memories of Lenny and his buddies as they moved forward in the following weeks, as the 30th and other units began to close the pincers of the Bulge.

"Later through the night we stood guard and watched the city die, while in the sky the serene white moon came out and shone down on the white frosted piney hilltops. It was Christmas." ("Rifleman's Road")

Dec 25, V, Belgium

Dearest,

We will never forget this Christmas. In the bright sunny afternoon yesterday we talked about preparing a little festivity for the evening, but in one short evil moment all was changed — only a minute, then came the new job (so many strange new jobs since we came here) of going out on errands of mercy, for the saving of lives. And when the serene white moon came out shining on the white frosted piney hilltops, and all should have been suited for Christmas Eve, we stood & watched the city of Malmédy suffer, as too many cities have suffered in wars past and present, an awesome thing to see. There were lots of newly made refugees, and I as interpreter, got called on many times, but that was welcome.

Dearly beloved, it is good you & Betty are safe at home — only now I begin to realize the horrors the Nazis brought the world.

Lenny

Dec 26, V, Belgium

Dearest Diana,

A bleak and bitter Christmas Day followed by a lurid Christmas Eve. There are few things worse than having buddies "missing." One can be well adjusted to the normal course of "warfare" but certain unnecessary tragedies set all on edge & wondering what is next.

Lenny

12/27

Darling Lenny,

Let's not talk of furloughs home, darling, as you say there are so many guys who have priority over you. Let's win the war.

Diana

Dec 27, V

Dear Diana,

Under separate cover I'm sending you a little packet of souvenir items, to save: a batch of Nazi insignia — a party member pin, a Hitler Jugend pin (in dismal shape), a Labor Front pin (2 extras you can give away), a combat badge, and a couple of storm trooper decorations, the sword point is up. I'm sorry I lost the Soviet soldier's insignia, & other things like my German compass, that busy day of the 21st, but I'll probably get another of these stars off a Russian soldier when we get to Berlin, & I now have a German compass to use.

It seems we have been honored by the German radio which is complaining of the "fanatically trained Roosevelt SS driving"!!!

Lenny

Dec 28, V

Dear Diana,

Winter is here but definitely. I am mailing you two long (really one long) letters in blue envelopes — it helps "a lot to get things out of our system — please don't let them worry you too much, or at all, if you can help it. Only one is hampered about what to write about, since, as ever the most interesting things are the least write-able about. As the days go on, I marvel more than ever at the way luck favors us — you & me — so it never did in years gone by! But so it is, and all goes well.

Lenny

12/29,V

Dearest,

Hurrah, Hurrah, your picture came today. I was almost beginning to give up hope because each time you wrote that you made an attempt but the picture didn't come. I think you look well — but then I guess I'm prejudiced about you. I received two so I immediately took one over to your mother.

I'm doing very well on the budget — I manage very comfortably on the $95 per month.

Diana

12/29

Lenny,

How are you, darling? Another few days and 1944 will be ended. There's a lot to say for 1944 but I won't take the time to say it now. Let me just say that 1945 has a good precedent. You write that many soldiers are asking "when." It certainly is even truer of civilians, I think. The German counter-offensive the last two weeks has made many people feel discouraged, but now that it is being stopped.

Yours, Diana

Dec 29, Somewhere in Belgium

Dear Darling,

At the moment things are routine & relatively quiet, but one is always set for sudden alarms.

The mailman brought a fruitcake & a can of pecans mailed last October (so I judge from the New York Times book review section used in filling the package).

A lot of the guys are seeing in the German's latest thrust the chance to finish up the war all the sooner. What's civilian opinion like?

Lenny

12/30,V

Dearest,

I am going to a New Year's Eve gathering with friends and Bob promised to take me home. This is one night I'd be afraid to go home alone late, because of all the drunks. Since I won't be able to write you at 12 tonight, here's my New Year's kiss and Betty Lou's and our love goes with them.

And to come back to our budget for a few minutes, I have found that Betty Lou is more expensive than we thought — between $30 and $35 per month.

Diana

Dec 30, Somewhere in Belgium

Dearest Diana,

Still the same wintry cold — It's always pleasant to read the detailed accounts of Betty's progress. I am still looking forward to the elimination of those 6 and 11 o'clock feedings — it still beats me: did, or do, women in a primitive stage of society also feed their kids at so many intervals & such weird hours? Is it necessary?

I look forward to more reading matter from you: while one doesn't need to be always analyzing what it's all about, still it's good to do so.

Lenny

Dec 31, Red Cross stationery

Dearest,

I got hold of some Belgian handkerchiefs, which I am mailing to your sister Lucy. 'Tis little enough, but as you know, it's the only gift I've sent from Europe. It's by way of saying someday we'll really make up to her for moving her out of her room. Also enclosed is a 10 billion mark note from the 1923 inflation wave — it is the largest denomination I have seen. Theoretically its dollar value was $2,500,000,000.

This morning I had "business" contact with a Nazi family: father a blacksmith, mother of about 23, with a beautiful & jolly baby boy of about 1½ and another due in May — simple little cottage and innocent as you please. The only thing that looked bad to me was the husband's want of any expression when we picked the missus up for questioning (at that moment we didn't know their party affiliations). I mention the incident because it illustrates for the nth time how the surface "humanity" appearance of the Germans is used by the Nazis as protective coloration — and the dammed problem of what to do with the Germans after the war still stands.

Lenny

Dec 31, Somewhere in Belgium

Dearest Darling,

New Year's Eve, in a smoky cellar, by kerosene lamp, all is quiet. There's some wine but no more than any other night, and there's no New Year's whoopee, and I hope the people back home have the good sense to stay home & stay sober too. God knows the times demand it!

It seems I can't recall anything from before June 6 — did anything happen from January to May? So much does the invasion campaign overshadow all — the liberation of France & Belgium & the driving of the Germans out of the Balkans & the Baltic. If '45 chalks up as much progress as '44, we shall be well satisfied. I look forward to the coming meeting of the big 3[5] for a deeper development of a United Nations alliance, & maybe a fuller recognition of what the facts of life demand in the de-"Nazified" ex-occupied countries. Tonight, at midnight, when the New Year comes in, I'll be standing guard in the dark night, looking across the dim snow — and my pal, Charlie, alongside, and like soldiers, we won't be thinking about the coming year at all.

Lenny

12-31

Dear Diana,

Enclosed you will find the rough draft of a story — a true story — although the names Tiny & Len are fictitious, and all place names are omitted, and blanks are used for certain names so as to eliminate any possible question about the censorship rules. Enclosed also is the second half of the manuscript story "The Bridge" in rough draft. The blue envelopes I used spare me the embarrassment of comment from the officer who censors my mail, who's rather cynical about such efforts.[6]

Lenny

1945 Begins

Jan 1, 1945

Dearest Lenny,

Best wishes, dearest, for a victorious New Year. Well, your wife is a terrible stay-out. I came home at 4 A.M. and if not for my mother's help I wouldn't be able to walk around at all today. I had a very pleasant time. There were a few couples plus me. They tried hard not to make me feel like an extra person and I didn't. At midnight all the fellows kissed their wives and Bob wanted to kiss me for you. I said no but he looked a little

---

5. US, UK, and USSR refers to the upcoming Yalta Conference in February 1945.

6. Those letters weren't read as carefully as others.

offended so I said he could kiss me a Happy New Year but not for you. He kissed me on the cheek. You don't mind, do you, darling?

Diana

Jan 1, V

Dearest,

The New Year came in with a couple of salvos from the artillery at the usual targets, and a few folks said Happy New Year in a quiet way.

Lenny

Jan 1

Dear Diana,

Every so often your husband gets restless as anything — especially when our job slows down to routine holding. I do my job, & extras too, because of my knowing languages, but it's the honest truth that except for a few days the army has not demanded a fraction of the man-day production power I was giving out in civilian life, and if one seeks to put out more, well, you've got to buck against Army inertia against fellow soldiers who think you're bucking for Section 8 (mental case discharge), that you aren't satisfied to get away with doing as little as possible. So it goes.

Regrettably, my "library" is gone, but even at that, reading only makes me more restless & studying German is dull business without any real incentive at hand — I know enough to handle prisoners & civilians, now.

Lenny

Jan 2, 1945

Dear Lenny,

I don't know whether I wrote you of Betty Lou's latest accomplishment. She can now drink her bottle by herself. When she is finished, she holds the bottle up for me to take away. She gets a lot of pleasure from feeding herself and I like her to be independent. The end of this week, I have to take her to the Dr. She shall get her first anti whooping cough injection. I hope she will be OK. I'm really a little scared, but it must be done.

Diana

Jan 2, V, Belgium

Dearest,

When we first came into Germany, civilians, and particularly women wore very shabby clothes, but 2½ months later passing through a border town, one could observe that apparently they'd changed their minds and were wearing really spiffy outfits, especially the women, who dress to "kill."

Lenny

Jan 3, V

Dear Lenny,

Lucy was accepted in the Washington University (St. Louis) School of Social Work for the Feb. term. She has written them to ask if she can postpone entering until September. She has an idea that Babe may come home in the next few months so she would prefer to wait with school.

Diana

Jan 3, V, Belgium

Dearest,

Business suddenly picked up last night in my line, & another spurt sort of filled up today. As ever, it is not anything to enjoy while the works to be done, but when it's over, it feels better than when there's been only "routine" duty. Immediately it means three battle participation stars whenever they issue our ETO[7] ribbons (Normandy, North France, & Germany each rated one).

Lenny

Jan 4, V, Belgium

Dearest Diana,

If duty doesn't take you out into the snow (which is when you curse it for being wet, blinding, nasty hiding roads & landmarks, blending sky & earth, a bad thing in hill country), it is really a thing of beauty & joy. But these are no days for enjoying snow. Mostly it's a nuisance & a serious hindrance.

Lenny

Jan 5, V, Belgium

Dear Diana,

For some reason a lot of extra things had to happen yesterday — even routine things became special because of special attention devoted to us by "Jerry."

By the way, the latest prisoners are even more scared than usual —

---

7. European Theater of Operations.

perhaps they have even more guilty consciences than usual. Again, no mail — "doggone" P.O.!

Lenny

Jan 5, V, Belgium

Dearest,

Your Xmas eve letter came. Christmas Eve over here was pretty horrendous, never to be forgotten.

Lenny

Betty Is Five Months Old

Jan 6

Dear Lenny,

Our Betty Lou is 5 months old today. Here's a birthday kiss from her and one from her mamma too. We had a fine birthday today — mail from you. I'm glad you have your combat infantrymen's badge — are you getting the extra pay already?

Betty Lou at five months

Lenny, soldiers are much better judges of military affairs than civilians. You ask for civilian opinion of the latest German thrust. Most civilians and newspaper generals were certain that this proved that we should never have opened a second front and that our military leaders had made a mistake. There was terrible pessimism. Of course now that we have taken the offensive and the Germans are stopped, they feel differently again.

Darling, in the 12/29 air mail, you speak of an experience which may win you the Silver Star. Congratulations, darling — even if you do not actually get the decoration, your two gals are mighty proud of you. I'm sorry you cannot write me about it but I understand. I'm sorry you had to destroy some of my letters — were you able to keep the pictures you have? I'm most sorry that you had to destroy the notes with your experiences — when you are permitted to, will you see what you can do from memory?

Diana

Jan 6, V, Belgium

Dearest,

What beats me is that mail is coming thru for others here. I noticed they are again picking up your mail one day in 4. Four similarly were postmarked 12/20 though mailed on different days.

Lenny

Jan 7, Belgium

Dear Diana,

But by luck & nerve, a buddy & I did get in at the last minute, to the showers, so all was swell. And so it became a pass-to-town deal. We shopped us picture postcards, & strolled about the town, which used to be a very fashionable mineral spring resort in peacetime. Riding back we could appreciate the scenery a little better: snow-covered hills, thick evergreens, draped with shaggy limbs, heavy with powdered snow — very beautiful, if only it were peacetime!

Lenny

Jan 7, V, Belgium

Dear Diana,

Stars & Stripes has announced that some Xmas packages were lost because of enemy action, but no letters so here's hoping.

Lenny

Jan 7, V, Belgium

Dearest,

I am sending you some examples of French & German invasion money.

Spent a couple of hours looking thru a big batch of clippings from newspapers. Guess I never realized what a deep gulf exists between the experience & mind of the soldier in action & what passes for life in civilian America, as seen in these papers.

Lenny

Jan 9, V

Dear Diana,

"Stars & Stripes" prints a suggested change in our division patch, in line with the German SS symbol above the XXX and "FDR" below, reflecting their epithet (Roosevelt's SS troops) but I prefer the patch as is. I'd hate to have any Nazi emblem on me.

Meanwhile no mail, of any sort, at all — just a trickle. You'd think we are out at sea somewhere where no mail could reach us. I hope you are still getting mine.

Lenny

Jan 9, V

Dearest,

I spoke awhile with a Belgian girl, who studied at Bonn in Germany, in the philosophy department. She was in Bonn till the end of July, and claims there was much verbal antipathy to the Hitler regime — but no evidence at all of any action, no conciliation or opposition papers, etc. This is in line with what we observed ourselves — verbal claims to be non-Nazi but no sign of action to prove it.

Lenny

Jan 10, V

Dear Lee,

All is well with me — no mail from you. How are you, darling?

Love from your femmes

Jan 10, V

Dear Darling,

So to the newspaper reports of the German counteroffensive — some were really weird, both in misinformation & in mission. Obviously, one can't write details, but one can say that from the limited viewpoint of the soldier in the ranks, the whole episode, including the weeks preceding the breakthrough confirms one's confidence in SHAFE.[8] In the one sphere where weaknesses appeared, it was really heartening to see with what speed supreme headquarters, meaning Eisenhower, reacted to correct the situation.

Lenny

Jan 11, V

Dearest,

A beautiful clear day like January in New York — only in New York I wouldn't be tramping around knee-deep in snow out in the woods. It is a sardonic sight to see so-called Belgian girls with American GI's & showing photo albums which show themselves in the arms of German soldiers — at least some of which come from regiments we have had the satisfaction of wiping out & the particular soldiers are known to be dead.

Lenny

Jan 11

Darling Diana,

It's a long time since I have written you a plain ordinary love letter but right now here goes one to you, beloved. Beloved Diana, I wish every soldier could have a sweetheart like you to carry in his heart always — must kiss you "so long" now, because I'm due on guard in five minutes.

Lenny

THE END OF THE ROAD

From this point on, the Americans and those holding Malmédy on the northeastern flank began moving out in force toward the south. They joined actively in the American counteroffensive that had begun, from positions farther west, to push the Germans out of the Bulge. Lenny's January 15 letter to Diana refers to witnessing, two days after the bodies were found in the snow, of those who had been murdered in the Malmédy Massacre at Baugnez, Five Points, at the beginning of the German incursion. From then on, every day

---

8. Lenny refers to the German incursion into Belgium, which resulted in the Battle of the Bulge. SHAFE means Supreme Headquarters Allied Forces Europe.

was filled with intense artillery barrages, prisoner interrogations, and digging foxholes in frozen ground.

On January 20, Lenny's company was assigned to dig in once again, now on the left flank of the American line four or five miles south of Ligneuville, south of Malmédy, on the map I still have in my possession. There, on the morning of January 21, the Germans penetrated with a 105mm self-propelled gun. Lenny was badly wounded and would have died if it had not been for the warmth of the dead body of a fellow soldier, and the persistence of his friend ET, returning to look for him and the others that day. Several of his comrades had already been killed or badly wounded over the past several days. It was the end of the road for him in the war, and the beginning of a long recovery and return home to Diana and Betty.

Jan 13 & 14, V

Dear Diana,

Did you ever get the newspaper drawing of a soldier writing on his rifle? Once again mine serves as a desk, as we wait further development in one of those much war days. I guess war is just always hell, be it summer heat or winter snows, but just now winter snow is hellish mostly. I am sending you a second sketch of a guy in our outfit. Further installments will have to wait 'til the Germans get beaten some more.

Lenny

Jan 15, V

Dearest,

I had two V-mails from you today from 12/28 and 1/2/45. Yes, luck does favor us at present, beloved.

Diana

Jan 15 V, not photographed, Belgium

Dearest,

Last night was beautiful and starry. Orion, all resplendent, the Milky Way a glimmer, and when about 1 A.M., I got back with Charlie from a "routine" business — delivering a prisoner to the rear. I thawed out my frozen fingers (gosh, the rifle can get cold to hold). 'Tis a rough war — fortunately it is not at its roughest, mostly in my job, although it's plenty rough!!

Today I saw the evidence of one of the crimes that Germany must pay for — you'll see the photos, no doubt in the papers — the bodies of disarmed Americans who were murdered in cold blood by German troops, lying where they were murdered, in the snow.[9]

Lenny

Jan 16, V

Dearest Diana,

Some of my equipment is "missing" — & possibly stolen.[10] The only inexplicable item was my collection of souvenir photos from places in Germany & I'm sorry that I won't be able to send you those — you always said you like to be able to visualize our surroundings. The other stuff is replaceable but it is inconvenient — my shaving kit, my blue envelopes & airmail envelopes & some military equipment that I hope I'll never need but so want to have.

Lenny

Jan 16

Dear Lenny,

You asked me in a letter recently what goes on in Greece & Belgium. Belgium, Greece, all liberated countries — how they should be treated? This is a key problem of the allies today. This problem must be dealt with by Anglo-Soviet-American cooperation. It is necessary to 1) get rid of all the quislings and collaborators, 2) give people arms so that they can defend themselves, 3) set up provisional gov't of political parties that helped to overthrow Nazis, and 4) for the people to have democratic, self-determination to decide for themselves their form of gov't. As far as the gov't in exile, each should be evaluated according to its record. We have the example of Czechoslovakia whose gov't-in-exile is in agreement with all these points. In Greece, Civil War has been waging because Britain has

---

9. Lenny is referring to the Malmédy Massacre, a war crime in which 80 American prisoners of war were murdered by their German captors. The massacre was committed on December 17, 1944, by members of the 1st SS Panzer Division, a German combat unit, during the Battle of the Bulge. The massacre, as well as others committed by the same unit, was the subject of the Malmédy Massacre trial, part of the Dachau Trials of 1946. The Baugnez (Five Points) crossroads was in no-man's-land until the counteroffensive; the frozen, snow-covered bodies weren't discovered until January 14, 1945, when U.S. forces reached the site. Lenny was there within a day of the discovery of the bodies.

10. Lenny had moved ahead with officers and left his possessions with the company.

tried to forcefully stop the Greek people from setting up a provisional gov't that they want and force upon them one not to their liking.

Diana

Jan 17, V

Lenny,

There is a very bad apartment shortage in NY now — so bad it is practically impossible to get an apartment without bribing the landlord or janitor involved. You ask the reasons; well, no new houses have been built for quite a few years. So many people have married and that seems to more than balance the number of homes that have been broken up temporarily because of the war. It is especially hard to get a nice place.

Diana

Jan 17

Dearest,

Our outfit, I see by the papers, has gotten in on the publicity of the current week, believe me, it earned every bit of mention in the hardest way possible.

I am waiting to see what you thought when you first knew I was in Belgium — apparently not before New Year's did you get my letters from here.

Lenny

Jan 18

Dearest,

The papers are just full of the Red Army offensive — 25 miles covered in a day. I also read that the 30th Div. is fighting near St. Vith, the town in the Belgian province of Liège — also part of the Battle of the Bulge. Then I see in another article that the 1st Army is fighting there. Have you guys been shifted again?

Diana

Jan 20

Dear Diana,

A "Stars & Stripes" page to hold for us: "Infantry of the 30th Div., pushing past this crossroads (Five Points) southwest of Malmédy (Belgium) today uncovered the bodies of American artillery observation battalion men murdered by the First SS Panzer Div., Dec 17. The soldiers were lying in groups, some with hands still raised above their heads."

Lenny

Jan 20,V

Dear Lenny,

This is an historic day. Roosevelt was inaugurated for the 4th time. I just heard a rebroadcast of his inauguration speech — very outstanding, only 5 minutes long in all. Now the meeting of the "big three" will probably take place shortly — we are looking forward to it eagerly.

Betty Lou sat up by herself for the first time today. She pulled on her cradle gym so hard that she pulled herself up and she got so excited that she let go and fell back.

Diana

Jan 21,

Darling,

I've just put Betty Lou to sleep and I want to talk to you. Gosh, she is growing up — she has begun to understand so many things. She is a very pleasant child — she only rarely cries unless there is a reason — that is why she always cries with tears, not just yelling like some kids do. She now sleeps from 6 P.M.–6 A.M., which is swell and I think she is a healthy little girl. The doctor says she is and she seems to be normal in all respects.

Diana

Jan 22

Dearest,

No mail from you today. Lenny, I'm also sending you two Valentine cards today from Betty Lou and me — I hope you'll get them in time.

Diana

WOUNDED IN ACTION

Lenny wrote this letter after being wounded, while lying down, with shaky handwriting, in a field hospital in Spa. He hoped the letter would get to Diana before the Army telegram informing her of what had happened.

Jan 22

Dearest,

No letters because 1/20 & 1/21 was a lot of war. 1/21 I was wounded in action, honorably, but seriously. I want this to get to you before the telegram. It took a 105 mm. gun on a German self propelled tank at 10 yards to get your husband. It was because I obeyed orders against my better judgment that my luck ran out.

They are taking good care of me in the hospital. I have compound fracture of leg & ankle, a hole in my left biceps arm & over my right ear & a scratch on my right jaw. They told me that, although I haven't yet got over the shock (so it's a little hard to hear). I've my left leg in a cast. In the group of 6, one was killed outright & 4 are missing. I will surely recover although it is a question of time. Guess I won't see Betty soon, tho. All my love to my girls — Writing on my back so don't worry about the handwriting.

Lenny

P.S. Break the news gently to my folks.

Jan 23[11]

Lenny,

As I wrote you, my sister Lucy has decided to go to social work school in St. Louis. I am going to get her a valise for a going-away present. She can get one at a reduced rate through a friend — $10 for a very nice one. I know that $10 is a lot of money for us to spend now, but I feel like doing something special because of how nice she has been.

You write of too much snow — we've had a lot of it this winter also — it's snowing today as a matter of fact.

Diana

Jan 24

Dearest Lenny,

The radio and newspapers continue full of the Soviet advance — they are on a straight 175 mile road from Berlin. The predictions are coming fast and furious from many sides that we are only a few weeks from victory in Europe. Praise for our fighting allies again.

I want to ask you — you keep writing about the German civilians that you have seen — anti-Nazi in their talk but not in their actions — no real signs of struggle — what can be done with these people? — will they be able to be re-educated? — Perhaps the older ones? When they say they are anti-Nazi, what do they hope for? Do they want to see Hitler and his gang annihilated? Among the civilians you have seen, are there

---

11. Diana has no idea that Lenny has been severely wounded two days before; she doesn't hear that he has been wounded until February 5.

many out-and-out Nazis? As you can see, this is all part of the question —
What's to happen to the Germans? You've asked me for civilian opinion,
now you write me of military opinions.

All my love and a hug from Betty Lou, (She doesn't know how to kiss
yet.)

Diana

Jan 25, V

Dear Lenny,

I'll civilize you as quickly as you wish. There will be many things that
we will have to catch up on — you and I as thousands of others like us.
Such a job I'll take on with pleasure, although I realize it may be somewhat different than I think, but I love you and that is all that matters in
that type of job.

Diana

Part III

Recovery

8

The Long Road Home

JANUARY 25, 1945–MAY 1, 1945

THE HOSPITAL IN PARIS

Jan 25, V

Dearest,

I'm really comfortable in a big modern hospital near Paris. It may take some time but I will be OK. It was not possible to write you while I was being carted here by ambulance & a freight train at a rate rather slower than the pace we hit chasing the Nazis here in July & August. Thanks to plasma (6 pints), penicillin[1] (about a few dozen needles) and sulfa I seem in pretty good shape and much less pain than I would expect — not more than when I had my tonsils out. But I do suffer much discomfort, use of bed pan, left leg & foot in cast, bandage on upper left arm, & head bandage. I didn't realize it but I also got hit enough to call for a couple of stitches back of my ear.

I had one very bad moment psychologically when they carried me in here & laid me on a real bed with sheets, in a warm room, the realization brought back for one moment all the concentrated horrors of the past 5 weeks, & it was hard to bear for a while. Sorry I won't be at the finish line, but I did a good job running intelligence for the guys carrying the ball. And don't worry, I'll be home, & OK too. Please tell the folks not to be too worried, & take care of yourself & Betty Lou. Let our friends know, as I shall not be writing much.

Lenny

---

1. Penicillin was discovered in 1928 and introduced in the 1940s.

Jan 26, V

Darling,

I've been meaning to ask you — what about the Silver Star? Do you just have to wait around and hope it will come thru?[2]

Diana

Jan 26, V

Dear,

Even with all that I'm now going through — all is well. We've done the right thing — no regrets — although it is painful. It's a pity it had to happen just when it did. I was getting a break for the first time, I was acting as battalion S-2 and might have been able to make more out of it & it was good to really get some challenging duties.

Too bad I'm not in a position to really profit from this visit to Paris & France — got an ambulance-eye-view of the Arc de Triumph & Champs Elysees yesterday.[3]

Lenny

Jan 27, V

Dearest,

There's nothing to do but lie abed and wait for time to pass. One talks a bit with the guys but it brings back the front too vividly. What was routine while we were in it is now suddenly beyond endurance. Long days and longer nights — I am bedridden 'til my leg knits up again so I just am taking it easy now that I've done my job.

Lenny

Jan 27, V

Dearest Lenny,

Here I am spending Saturday night with you. The folks are away and I'm home with our sleeping daughter. It's so pleasant the way she sleeps in the evening now. Remember when she was first born? I used to find the evening so difficult — now I look forward to it.

Diana

---

2. Lenny eventually received the Silver Star and other medals as well.

3. The story Lenny told is that he asked the ambulance driver to slow down, so he could see the sights, but the medic said, "Too bad this guy is delirious," and didn't pay attention to what Lenny was saying.

Jan 28, V

Dear Husband,

I'm at a loss about why my mail doesn't reach you. I purposely use both V-mail and air mail in case one service is not working so well. Maybe by now some has caught up. Yes, I've read of the terrific snows you are having — It must be so tough on you.

Diana

Jan 28, V

Dearest Diana,

Mostly I continue at ease: the pain is almost nonexistent, although sleep comes hard & sometimes my head hurts for no apparent reason — still the concussion, I think. But mostly it's just a long patient wait ahead 'til nature takes its course and repairs the damage: fortunately it is mostly repairable. I try to be cheerful, and kid the nurse and ward boy and read what is brought in. The other patients are very helpful — most of them are minor cases & they bring water and reading matter & fill the pen & set up the dinner bed table etc. It's swell of them.

The news of the Red Army's advance arouses the greatest enthusiasm here. I see by Stars & Stripes my own weary outfit is still pushing in those horrible forests & snows. They give me nightmares, peopled with all the weird horrors of such places, the memories of the terrain. Beloved, be well, take care of yourself & Betty Lou & don't worry.

Lenny

Jan 28, V

Dear Lenny,

This morning we went shopping for a high chair. It is maple to match the kitchen furniture. It is a very special design because it can become a small table and chair when the child is older.

Diana

Jan 29, V

Dear Lenny,

The high chair came today. I shall let Betty sit for a few minutes every day and next week I'll start to give her one meal a day in it. She doesn't sit too well yet. She slouches a little but as soon as she learns to sit up a little better, I shall start to toilet train her. That's a long drawn-out process, usually, but well worth the trouble as you can understand. The news from the

Eastern Front continues tremendous — there is also lots of talk of a big offensive on the Western Front very soon.

All my love and a big hug from Betty Lou — She can hug nicely now.

Diana

SHIPPED TO ENGLAND

Through the initial days in England, Lenny's days, in between medical care, were relieved only by the news he received from Diana about Betty Lou's doings and progress, and the reading material made available by the hospital staff.

Lenny, during R&R after Aachen, recollected and summarized for Diana his most vivid experiences, in lengthy letters detailing, day-by-day, his war memories from his earliest days in Europe. Now, while recovering from his wounds, he completed writing down these experiences with the thought of publishing them in magazine articles and, eventually, in a memoir. It is amazing the amount of detail a soldier recalls:

> Once I have written down the story (as much as the censors allow) on paper, the memory fades from my consciousness very quickly. It is not true, by the way, that the soldier doesn't remember vividly and in great detail. That's what I found out not only in my own experience, but speaking with wounded veterans last summer and now. (February 19, 1945, letter to Diana)

Jan 30, V, England

Dearest Diana,

Still waiting at this stopover place, a wretched set-up with wretched service — The nurses & ward boys come in every so often & there is no way to call for them when you need them in between — a heck of a way for a room full of guys with casts on their legs. It beats me: in France they had 2 ward boys on hand all the time for less dependent cases.

My biggest lack is something to occupy my mind, reading matter & such, & with more primary things always in arrears, it's just another headache. No big changes to report in my condition & probably won't be any "big changes," — just long slow ones. Love to my two girls.

We owe an awful lot to a buddy of mine named Elton. He was my closest friend & buddy in the squad & company all along but especially the day I was wounded. I was lying in the dugout where I'd been hit, with one other who was beyond aid, and I was figuring if I was lucky somebody would come by the position looking for us about dark. I'd come to about 10:00 A.M. (must have been hit about 9:30) & figured a wait until 7 or 8 P.M. (not unusual) pretty good.

But about 1 or 2 P.M., Elton & another came by out of their dugout (a way off — good thing for me I had them dig in separately), & I called them. Elton crawled in beside me & sent the other for medics but he never showed up — he deserted his own personal buddy in a similar case in December. Then Elton went himself & brought the medics & although we were in a very exposed forward spot, stayed with me when the aid man left after bandaging me, until the stretcher crew came. Needless to say saving 5–6 hours is a life's difference.[4] By the way, in one way, I got paid back for the time last month when I chose to help save one of our wounded who'd been abandoned by the others. That incident taught a lot of guys a lesson in comradeship.

Lenny

Jan 31

Dear Lenny,

It has been almost 4 weeks that Lucy had mail from Babe and we were concerned especially because she is planning to leave for school next week. She had a letter this morning. He was in the invasion of Luzon and no mail was taken off the ship.

Darling, there is a question I must ask you regarding the account of your first experiences in Germany. I felt this in some of the other experiences that you wrote about, but I attributed it to the fact that you were new. By the time you got to Germany, though you were hardly a rookie, still you write of "not knowing what to do" of confusion and no one knowing what the strategy is. I don't understand it — don't the officers know, even if they don't let the men in on it? If you soldiers don't realize that you are part of the force surrounding Aachen, for instance, who knows it? Am I being naïve, dear?

Diana

---

4. Lenny had lost much blood and needed multiple pints in transfusion.

1/31, England

Dear Diana,

Here is my new address for the time being so now I can expect mail from you again in about a month — naturally I've got none since my injuries. Now I am in a more permanent set up & I hope it will be OK. The last 48 hours in that shotgun place was a nightmare, which I hope is over for good, but I don't expect to see as fine a setup again as was in that French hospital. England is as cold & rainy as I left it. There's no other news — I'm just taking it easy in the new place.

Lenny

Feb 1, V

Dearest,

Today I received the souvenir invasion money you sent. Why is it in so many sizes? It must be hard to carry.

It was so windy today that I was afraid to take Betty Lou out. It was announced on the radio that this Jan. has been the coldest in 5 years and the most snow since 1935.

Diana

2/2

Dear Diana,

Well, Dr. says things are going nicely. He's taken all the bandages off my head. He also thinks he can sew my arm up without having to graft skin, letting the present skin grow together. Right now it does not look pretty, but compared to what I expected at first it is amazing — sulfa & penicillin beat any magic. The leg, of course, is the big thing but the doc seems to take delight in parading the convalescent, not walking cases, with great enthusiasm. Pain is almost nil to my great surprise, but sleep is still not to be had.

Everyone is cheering the Russians — to Berlin.

All my love — Lenny

2/2, V

Dearest,

Life is very dull & doesn't supply much to write about, when bedridden, in a room with one other patient and the window is rough glass, shutting out even the bleak rainy, English out of doors. Doc comes in & looks you over & you joke with him, you eat, you try to sleep & succeed better by day & try to pass the time with whatever reading material the boys bring in. I count the days until a letter from you can reach here. I do hope you do not feel too unhappy about my being hurt. Literally it is a toss-up whether the physical suffering here is worse than the strain we were under going in action, especially in the battle of the German break-through, so if you were reconciled to that, be reconciled to this: & after all I will recover & be up and about in a matter of weeks.[5]

All my love — Lenny

2/3,V

Dearest,

I was moved today to another ward — in preparation for the work on my leg, which is due to begin Monday. Just at the moment I am rather uncomfortable — it hurts to keep my leg up in the air as it has to be now. However, I look forward to having my leg put into usable shape again. Got out into the open air for a few minutes today in being moved and it was swell.

By now, I think you must have got my airmail about my being wounded — dear, now more than ever I say — never regret the price we have to pay.

Lenny

Feb 4,V

Dear Lenny,

I'm tired — there has been so much noise all day — people coming to say goodbye to Lucy. I have finally put Betty Lou on three meals a day — took away her 6 A.M. bottle. The reason I started it today was that she slept until 7 A.M.

Diana

2/4,V, England

Dear Diana,

Civilization comes back slowly after many months of barbarous army: today there was chocolate ice cream at dinner, the first ice cream I've tasted since leaving America — yesterday I had my first Coca Cola: ditto. To the guy who's confined to bed with a plaster cast running from thigh to toe. Tomorrow the cast comes off & they're going to do some work on my leg — don't be concerned in case I can't write for a day or two. Be well, my beloved.

Lenny

---

5. The recovery took almost two years because of the extent of the wounds and the need for experimental skin grafting on his ankle.

News Finally Reaches Brooklyn

Feb 5, V

Dearest Lenny,

I received a V-mail from you this morning dated 1/27/45 in which you say you are in a hospital in France. Dearest, I don't know what to think — my last mail was from 1/16/45. I guess you have been wounded in between. You mention your leg, so you must be hurt there. I'm trying so hard to keep my chin up until I hear from you further. Perhaps you wrote me more before the 27th but I haven't received it yet.

Lenny, dearest, write me all you can about what happened. To write you how I feel — I can't express it well and you must know — I'm proud, I'm worried, I love you so much. I hope you are getting good care, dear. My darling — I'm so grateful that I heard from you before the War Dep't will notify me. A telegram from them is so cold. A letter in your writing — that's quite different.

Diana

2/5, V, England

Dearest,

'Tis this afternoon they will take the cast off & figure out what to do with my leg. The fracture, compound, is in the tibia a little above the ankle, & there's a wound all across the ankle, heel & instep as I recall (I only saw it the day I was hit when the aid men splinted it using 2 entrenching shovel handles).

What is amazing to me is the effect of the plasma — it's like pouring new life into a person, they gave me 6 pint bottles the day I was hit, so I was glad I'd helped get so much donated in the Welfare Dep't victory committee because I sure used up a lot.

Lenny

Feb 5, V

Dear Lenny,

I just came home from your father — I told your father of the letter I had from you from the hospital this morning and I showed it to him. I left it up to him about telling your mother — he said he would wait a few days until I hear from you further.

Lenny — I feel much better now — I've had some time to digest the idea that you are wounded. Darling, is it painful — it makes it more difficult because I don't know what it is, but I hope to know soon. My sweetheart, I hope you'll be alright soon. I love you, Lenny.

Diana

Feb 6, V

Dearest,

As I thought, I had more mail from you today, which explains about your wounds. You were quite banged up — but I'm grateful that you are as you are — so very grateful, dear — we're lucky. I'm taking your word for it. It will take a while but you'll be OK. I'm thankful to you for writing me just where you were hurt, and thankful for the plasma and penicillin you got. Lenny dear, I'm not sorry — I'm proud of you — you are going thru so much now, but we can both feel a real part of the victory which will come (not too far off now). I haven't heard from the War Dept. yet.

Write me all you can about yourself — can you say how it happened?

Diana

Feb 6, V

Dear Lenny,

Today is Betty Lou's 6 month birthday — she's a big girl — I took her to the Dr. for her 2nd whooping cough and diphtheria inoculation and a general check-up. She's fine — 19 lbs, 3 oz. He took her off formula — I have to gradually decrease the water and dextrose-maltose and increase the milk until she is getting whole milk. I can also stop sterilizing — that makes it easier for me — much easier.

Dear, keep getting better.

Diana

2/6, V

To My Girls,

All of 6 months, whee! I can hardly wait for mail & the next pictures.

Nurse gave me a capsule which made me drowsy & presently 2 needles in the right arm. I woke up about 9 P.M. back in my ward, feeling very sleepy. On inspection, I see a new cast on my leg, slightly different in appearance & a new bandage on my arm; but I don't have the slightest notion what was done to me, if anything.

I'm running out of reading material, having exhausted two wards supply of books & magazines & that is giving me a lot of concern, since I can't get out of bed, can't do anything else, & have an awfully long day to fill and so far, no mail to take up any of it. It's a shame to be in England,

doing nothing, within easy reach of all the original Milton manuscripts &
documents & not be able to do anything about them.

Lenny

Feb 7,V

Dearest Lenny,

    I've had no mail from you today. How are you, darling? You write
your leg & foot are in a cast. Can you tell me what is wrong with them?
I've thought much and tried to accept this which I know — that you
are in the hospital. Darling, you have told me all, haven't you? I know
you wouldn't keep anything away from me so I keep my mind focused
on your recovery — and I don't let it imagine things which aren't so. Of
course, dear, it would be foolish to deny how concerned and worried I am
for you. Are you getting good care?

Diana

2/7,V

Dear Diana,

    Well, it seems all they did the other day was look me over & change
the cast in the leg so there's no news to report.

Lenny

2/8

Dearest,

    I think for the first time since you are in the army, I find it difficult to
write you a letter. This is the third time I've started (I destroyed the other
two). It's not that I don't know what to say. It's that I don't know how to
say in words what is in my heart.

    Dearest, how are you? I'm trying very hard to be worthy of you
during this very difficult and painful period you are going thru. You see
Lenny, when I received the letter from you that you were hurt, it took
all my "assuredness" out from under me and I broke down and cried as
I haven't for a long time. I guess all the accumulated months of tension
were all released. Now, of course, since I've had more mail from you and I
know more of the details, I'm back on my feet again and I'm trying to do
you proud.

    I received the telegram from the War Dep't this morning. As I read it, I
was more and more grateful that I had your mail first. This is what it says:
"Regret to inform you that your husband PFC Leo Miller was seriously
wounded in action 21 Jan. in Belgium, mail address follows direct from

hospital with details." At least they're honest, last time they said "slightly wounded."

Diana

2/9

Lenny, dear,

I received two letters from you today — a V-mail from 1/28 and an air mail from 1/22. The air mail is the one you wrote right after you were wounded. I got the V-mail before the air mail. Here you wrote how it happened. It is sure noticeable that you wrote it on your back — it looks like the first letter I sent you from the hospital after Betty Lou was born.

Lenny, you say "break the news gently to your folks" — that has become a very difficult situation for me. As I wrote you, I went to their house as soon as I received the first letter from you on Mon. Your father did not let me tell your mother — as it is now she doesn't know. He finally told your sister Rose who called me yesterday and I told her all I knew. I haven't been to see your mother all week because I can't tell her that I've had mail from you and that you are all right. I don't like to get myself involved in lot of lies so I haven't seen her. I don't want to tell her against your father's and Rose's wishes because it's their responsibility, but you know how I feel about not telling someone the truth. Your father said he is waiting for a letter from you to them and then he'll tell her — so I hope it will come soon.

Diana

2/9, V, England

Dearest,

Today they moved me into a private room, so at last I am out of direct earshot of that blasted radio. Although I'm in solitary, the quiet is worth it. They took some more x-rays of my leg — otherwise no developments. The British leave you to freeze in this cold climate at the mercy of small coal stoves. Sleep is still a treasure to be attained. It will be a long time before the shock & the effects of the concussion wear off. We'll make the best of it, however, and I'll be coming back to you safe & sound again.

Lenny

2/9, V, England

Dearest Diana,

Because of a swell guy, a patient who went over to the Red Cross for me, one of their girls came over and she agreed to inquire through certain

channels about the possibility of contacting a university library, so I can try
to get research facilities, Milton, of course.

Lenny

2/10,V

Dear Diana,

Not much news — Doc showed me some of the X-rays, before and
after the setting. The break across the fibula doesn't look like much but the
tibia (shin) has a big jagged diagonal break, a couple of inches long. The
bones are now joined & held by the cast, and in 5–6 months will have
knit together again. My arm wound is doing nicely, no important muscle
or nerve was damaged, & I can use the arm completely. When some more
skin grows on the edges, they will sew it up — it is still open under the
bandage & kept moistened by a tube running through the bandage. All in
all I am doing well and can only regret that I can now contribute nothing
to the big job going on.

Lenny

Feb 11

Dear Lenny,

I haven't had mail in a few days and I'm so anxious to know how you
are, but I'll have to wait. Maybe tomorrow —

Your sister Rose was over last night to see some of your letters from
the hospital to know the details of your injuries. Your mother still hasn't
been told. I shall leave it up to your father and Rose, since they are so
dead set against telling her. Lenny, I love you — Keep getting better dear.

Diana

2/11,V, England

Dear Diana,

Last night I got into my usual fitful intervals of sleep, but it was without benefit of codeine capsules or pills for the first time, as maybe it will
be better in that respect. They have finally got around to lighting a fire
in the coal stove in my room, which makes it a little more comfortable
in here. Here's something you will like, a request: please send me a little
package — cookies with chocolate (no more unlimited K rations, chocolate, as we had at the front), chewing gum (chocolate or Spearmint, no
cinnamon or "juicy fruit"). Here we are rationed to 3 or 4 candy bars a
week & I get hungry at night.

Lenny

2/12, V, England

Dearest,

Dozed away the morning for which I was grateful — time hangs heavy. For reasons known to the Doc, they've started giving me an enormous quantity of 2 kinds of pills, sulfa, I guess it must be another stage in treatment. Well, here comes another long evening & I wish I had something to do. Imagine me with nothing to do.

Lenny

2/13 V

Dearest,

Well, the evening last night was saved by the Red Cross worker, who came round with wool for mats & rugs but also had a few books. The last 3 nights I've managed to get a little sleep without an opiate as I did with the pills, so I've decided to cut them out. I figure that by today you have my present address, and in 2 weeks I'll see mail from you again (I've had no word of you later than New Year's).

Lenny

Feb 13

Darling Lenny,

How are you, my darling love? I'm so glad that you write you haven't much pain — I hope so much you will be able to relax and sleep after a little time passes. Rose called me before and I gave the address to her. Your mother still hasn't been told, but I guess they'll have to tell her because you write today that you wrote to your folks. I'm so much opposed to keeping it from her — I'm so afraid that she will be hurt terribly when she does find out, but there is no convincing Rose and your father.

You write me to be a good girl. My darling, I'm trying hard to be one. I can't be a bad girl because I'm so very, very grateful that we have been so lucky and that you are the way you are.

Don't be concerned about me — just be calm and do all that is necessary to make yourself well as soon as possible. And keep writing me as much as you can about yourself and how you are progressing. Thank you again, dearest, for all the details. I am so much calmer because I know.

Your mother phoned. She has the letter from you from England. Of course, she was quite upset — I told her all I know and did the best I could to calm her over the phone. She told me the letter said you flew to England from France. Isn't it the first time you ever flew? How was it?

Diana

Feb 13,V (Sent to hospital)

Dearest,

I received your new address today so I'm writing this V-mail. Of course, darling, since I first heard of your injuries last Mon. I've been writing to your old address — maybe these letters will catch up with you in a few weeks. You write in today's mail that you are in England — I expected they would send you there. Lenny, I'm glad they took the bandages off your head and that the Dr. is so encouraging about your arm and leg.

Dearest, I know you will be better, — we must be patient. To say that I am grateful to your buddy Elton is putting it too plainly — he's a fine fellow and worthy of your close friendship as a soldier and I'm eternally grateful to him for what he did for you.

Diana

2/14,V

Dearest Diana,

They keep the lights on so late in this place — 'til 10:30, rather unusual for a hospital, I think and it creates additional problems for me to occupy myself. Of course I can think about my invention, but here what I really need are some tools, some wiring & some batteries & they are not handy. My invention, which I shall patent when I get up & about, is a guaranteed self-warming seat for a bedpan to replace the ice cold ones they are now using. Also I am trying to figure out an apparatus to lift myself onto it without moving a leg which is in a cast. Possibly the solution is a slide in the bed with an "under hung," detachable receptacle on the body. No, dear, I am not delirious — and only had a cup of hot chocolate.

Lenny

2/14,V

Dear Diana,

Today they gave me my Purple Heart.[6] A full colonel came to my room, & saluted — a very handsome gesture — & pinned it on my

---

6. U.S. military decoration awarded to those wounded or killed while serving with U.S. military.

pajama shirt front, shook my hand & saluted again — of course, I saluted
back but it's the first time an officer saluted me first!

Lenny

Feb 14

Lenny,

As far as what to do with your time — It would be fine if you could
work on Milton. Is there anything I can send you — either your manuscript, books or anything that you would need if you decide to do it?
Don't hesitate to ask me for any help at all. You know I would love to do
it. There is so little I can do for you right now.

Diana

Feb 15, V

Dear Lee,

I'm so eager to have mail from you after they take the cast off your leg.
Write me all as you have been doing. I'm proud, dear, that you write me
all the details — because you know that I try to look the truth in the face.

Diana

2/15, V

Dear Diana,

A dreary day — I've just lain here & lain, with nothing to do — a
wretched business. There are 1 or 2 patients who will bring in a new
magazine when they see one but mostly the staff goes by the path of least
effort. Got paid a partial payment today, $16, but I'm holding on to it —
and I doubt if I'll be able to send you money for a while, here one pays
for a lot of things that were free at the front, and I may want to use some
money to provide myself with something to do.

Doc says he may sew up my arm next week — the hole has sort of
filled up to the skin level, & looks like a slice of "wurst" in color — all it
needs is some skin over it. I imagine it will look something like an appendix scar when it's all healed.

Lenny

2/16, V

Dearest,

Last night Chaplain came around at my request! I talked to him
about an activity. I offered to write letters for guys with arm injuries and
I asked about borrowing some commentaries on the gospels or "Paradise
Regained" but I doubt anything will come of it. You can see how it is

with me, from daybreak to 10:30 P.M. I lie, and try to keep from look-ing at the blank walls. I try to sleep away the mornings now & to write a little in the afternoons and try to save a magazine or "Stars & Stripes" for the long evenings. But I still have about 16 hours a day — it is much harder to endure this inactivity than the occasional pain when another nerve in the leg has reestablished contact with the control switchboard.

Lenny

2/17,V

Dearest,

Doc gives me good prospects to look forward to, but time is of course very indefinite.

How are my girls getting along? Drat this wretched mail service. The weeks drag on and on.

Lenny

2/18,V

Dearest Diana,

Another dreary day, dreary with nothingness — just lying here, try-ing to find some interest in some dopey books from the Armed Service editions without success and falling asleep every so often, with the unsat-isfactory knowledge that it gives relief now and will mean more sleepless hours at night.

'Tis a week now it's been impossible to get a sheet of writing paper other than V-mail. One would think we are in the jungle somewhere. Can you read these V-mails without a magnifying glass? I doubt it.

Lenny

Feb 19,V

Dearest,

I know that you are going through a very trying period. Knowing you as I do — I realize that is it most difficult for you to be cooped up in bed. Don't apologize for writing to me how you feel and for not being cheer-ful. If you don't write the truth to me — well, then — and also I know it makes you feel a little better to write about it — but darling, as I started to say — this is part of the test for you and for me too. This period is part of the price we have to pay and considering what others have paid, even some of our personal friends, we've gotten off lucky up until now. I know this doesn't help to solve the immediate problem you have of getting things to read and of some challenging mental work.

Diana

2/19, V

Dearest,

I begin to get a little regular sleep of nights, and to stretch the daily routine out. Not that I want to, but to make this existence endurable, I have to key life down to a dull flat level. So I read tripe.

At last I managed to get about half a ream of writing paper, so I'll keep myself busy scribbling.[7] I've discovered that the communication zone censors fret over things combat zone censors pass without question, so some of my narrative may not reach you by mail. It serves me as catharsis. Once I have written down the story (as much as the censors allow) on paper, the memory fades from my consciousness very quickly. It is not true, by the way, that the soldier doesn't remember vividly and in great detail. That's what I found out not only in my own experience, but speaking with wounded veterans last summer and now.

Lenny

Feb 20, V

Dear Lenny,

I received 4 V-mails from you today. Dear, they made me feel a lot better because you seemed to be feeling better in the mail I received yesterday. Dearest, I'm so glad to read the cheerful report of your physical condition — keep up the good work. I know it will be a long time — but most important is that you will be well.

Diana

2/20, England

Dearest,

In one of the indifferent books here in the hospital there was a witty parody of an old nursery rime — you remember:

> There was an old woman who lived in a shoe
> She had so many children she didn't know what to do.

Well, there's a revised version that runs:

> There is a young woman who lives in a shoe
> She doesn't have so many children; she knows what to do!

It comes to mind because the hospital business has peculiar angles.

---

7. Lenny is writing up his experiences as a novel/memoir.

Take, for example, the institution of the back rub, with which I was totally unacquainted till I came here. There's one nurse, whose hands happen to be warmer than the others', though the bloom of youth has long, long ago faded from her cheeks; and she goes around all day humming happily to herself all the lively tunes that come in over the radio. My ears suddenly stood up like a rabbit's, & I was glad I had my arm across my face shielding my eyes from the light, for she was straightening the sheets and tucking in the blanket to the unmistakable tune which mischievously some GI Joes teach to girls on the continent who don't understand English — it was the high spirited:

> Roll me over, Yankee soldier
> Roll me over, lay me down
> And do it again.

Now you mustn't get the wrong idea. This is a thoroughly respectable and decent hospital, conducted on all the high principles of Florence Nightingale. Smile, beloved, I'm smiling to you.

Lenny

2/20, V

Dear Diana,

Through channels came a book from the Chaplain the first to fulfill the promise. Of course, I finished the book already. They've got my bed in the wrong place — it should be set up in the British Museum reading room. All my love to my girls —

Lenny

Feb 21, V

Dear Lenny,

Well, our little Betty Lou is progressing. She is making a big effort to creep — she makes all the motions but she can't lift herself up, so instead of going forwards or backwards, she goes round and round in a circle.

Diana

2/21, V

Dearest,

Since Doc has postponed my date with the surgical room, so that I could attend, I was duty bound to go — I "vaulted gracefully" into the wheelchair that the ward boy finally brought into the ward where a cinematographic representation was held. The name of the piece was concealed by the initial fluttering of reel, but it was one of those vaude-ville things a mislabeled "musical."

Tomorrow I have my postponed session in the operating room, so maybe the anesthetic will relieve me of any concern as to how to fill the 22nd up. The performance will be primarily to sew up the wound in my left arm and incidentally to extract a stray fragment of shrapnel from be-hind my right ear. I've been wondering why my eyeglass earpiece makes it sting, so Doc looked at it today. It's only a very tiny splinter.

Lenny

2/22, V

Diana,

I am OK — just coming out of the anesthetic — still "woozy" — with my arm all bandaged up, but I didn't want you to miss a day's mail.

Lenny

Feb 23

Darling Husband,

Happy Anniversary — I love you.

Your,
Diana

2/23, V

Dearest Love,

May we have happier anniversaries in the years to come. I came out of the anesthetic for good this morning & found they had put a cast on my left arm now too; which may be a step forward but right now leaves me much more dependent & helpless than before, & the wound may be sewed closed, but it hurts, which it didn't when it was an open hole.

They saved me the piece of shrapnel which Doc excavated from be-hind my ear in a piece of gauze; but not knowing, I used it for a handker-chief & lost it. Anyway the spot feels much better without the fragment of metal in it.

Lenny

Feb 24

Dear Lenny,

This afternoon, your mother and Uncle Morris, your sisters Rose, Harriet and Harriet's friend Dora were all here to see Betty Lou. I like to have people come to see her, but it bothers me when doting relatives come and talk for 2 hours of the baby and make her the center for ev-erything. They refuse to let her be in her own little corner. They insist on making her the center of attraction, and when I'm a lone voice among so many grandparents and aunts, I might as well not be there.

It's not good to have a group of people sit around and discuss her every little move and for her to feel as though she is putting on an act for them. My folks, of course, want to show her off to everyone that comes in and it is beginning to worry me — you know what happens to a child that gets too much attention when they get a little older.

Diana

2/24, V

Dear Diana,

Another invention I shall patent as soon as they take these plaster casts off me is a clinical thermometer in six delicious flavors: mint, anisette, sarsaparilla, ginger, Sherry and Slivovitz. One begins to gag on the tasteless glass which the nurses insist on ramming down my throat, 4 times a day, in spite of the fact that I have repeatedly pointed out that my temperature never varies more a degree either way from 98.6.

Beloved, I am in great anxiety as the month draws to a close — will the mail finally begin to trickle thru? Will it?

Lenny

2/25, V

Beloved:

O happy day! O joy! Exceeding my fondest hopes & expectations, the ward boy just brought in your V-mail of 2/13 & one from my father — the first mail in so long! Though I don't know what your first reactions were, it's plain from this letter than my Diana still carries on like a good soldier, though it must be hard. I do hope my letters got to you before the War Dept's telegram.

Dove, many weeks, if not months, will pass before the letters sent to my old address catch up — so if anything particularly, noteworthy happened between 1/2 and 2/13 it might be worth repeating.

My normal sleep seems to have returned, which means that the shock of the shell burst is beginning to wear off, and also the pain around my head wound has diminished so that if I lie or roll on that side it doesn't awaken me.

Lenny

Feb 26

Lenny,

I received a postcard from the war dep't dated Feb 10 that "You are making normal improvement." The radio reports a big offensive on the Western Front by the 1st, 9th, and 3rd armies and also on the Eastern Front. It looks like the big final push. I know you are sorry not to be in on it, but it's good to know the Nazi beast will soon be eliminated.

Diana

2/26, V

Dearest Diana,

Isn't often that I find a good word to say for something in the way of popular fiction, but I've just finished a little story, called "Prophet by Experience." It would make a good amusing movie too. I could also add a good word for the clever "Murder of Roger Ackroyd" by Agatha Christie.

I have not fully exhausted the available print stuff in the vicinity so I'll probably have to spend some time writing this week. Wish I could write more of my more interesting war experiences, only they give me nightmares to think of them, so better not yet, anyhow.

Lenny

2/26, V

Dear Diana,

Some people are just too wonderful for words. Yesterday afternoon I was trying to kill time with a detective story, when to my delight and surprise in walked my friend from WC 81, S/Sgt. Joan.[8] Think of it — she used up a 48-hour pass, which they don't hand out so often, and traveled an 8-hour trip, and has had to stay out in a nearby town, just so as to be able to come & cheer up a bedridden casualty for a few hours. She was here again this afternoon for a few hours.

It was wonderful to have someone with whom to talk to for a change (the nurses and ward boys are terribly efficient; they can only run in & out again in a second). Also, she sent you a V-mail while she was here, so you can have an impartial testimony on how I am. You can show that to my folks.

Lenny

---

8. A friend from the New York City Welfare Department where Lenny had worked.

Feb 27

Dear Lenny,

Darling, when you say, "Doc gives you good prospects to look forward to," I wish you would be a little more specific.

Diana

2/27, V

Dearest Diana,

Since your V-mail came two mornings ago I've been on pins & needles waiting for more mail again & I can't wait. Needless to say, I've been terribly lonely for you these past weeks lying in bed. When I was in combat, as you know, I wouldn't let myself dwell too long on home, & besides I had my buddies. But since I am temporarily "out" — well, I've lain here for hours talking to you and thinking of you — and even talking to Betty a bit. Here the winds are not racked by rocket bombs, and they are not quite such rugged roads for love's dreams to travel.

Lenny

2/27, V

Dearest,

Finally, as I was all but exploding with impatience, they brought the mail. You're 100% right to oppose keeping the news from my mother but is she sick? Was there some reason in particular?

By the way, I get more raves about Betty from third parties than from her mom.

You ask about my leg cast — I'll be wearing one for many months though it will be changed from time to time. Don't expect me to be walking for 6 to 8 months yet, because it will take that long for the bones to mend.

Lenny

2/28, V

Dear Diana,

This morning I slept away, so now just waiting for mail call — which is 4:30 P.M. — my main activity. It is ten to three and I am most impatient. I wonder where my division is now, now that the front is moving again.

Lenny

2-28-45

Darling,

Enclosed is my copy of the order issuing me the Purple Heart, which is as important as the medal it self. Put it in the case with the medal when it comes, please.

Lenny

3-1-45, V

"Dininka,"

Since so many of your December, Jan & Feb letters are overdue, would you please tell me if you have received a package of coins & Nazi insignias. I guess I missed writing you a couple of days when I was under anesthesia, including the 23rd, I imagine. But did my letter get to you before the War Dep't telegram and what did you think when you got it?[9]

Lenny

3-1-45

Dear darling,

It has been a pleasant day — blue sky for a change; & I have my window open. The grass is already deep green, the same deep green, that surprised me so much last June. It's different from the light spring green in America. And there is a steady stream of all kinds of airplanes flying by, more air traffic than autos on Belmont Avenue![10] While the sound of airplanes still gives me the horrors, a souvenir of some horrible days during the Battle of the Ardennes,[11] they do look graceful and elegant up there amongst the clouds.

About my airplane trip, which you heard from my mother, surely I wrote you about it! I am certain I did but the service was so wretched in the first hospital where I was in England for about 2½ days that maybe the letter didn't get out. Well, after spending a tortured day & night in a huge hangar, a noisy place where I nearly went frantic from the noise, about 10 A.M. I was loaded onto an ambulance & driven out to an

---

9. Lenny was wounded Jan. 21 and here it is March 1 and he still doesn't know if Diana received his letter before the War Department telegram.

10. East New York, Brooklyn.

11. The Ardennes is the area where the Battle of the Bulge (December 16, 1944 through January 25, 1945) took place. It was the last major Nazi offensive against the Allies and the bloodiest battle of the war.

airport somewhere in France. There about 30-odd stretchers with guys like me, loaded onto a cargo plane, & strapped down snug. I was very lucky because my stretcher was at the window level (there were 4 levels) & so I could see all the way. It was cold because the plane is like a barn, & its big double doors were open a long time while ambulances brought the "freight" up. After a while the doors shut, & the motors started, but not very loudly.

Then we began to taxi down the runway & it seemed to go an awful long way, maybe half a mile — and then with no jolt or jar, the ground began to move down away from us, & fences & houses were not beside us anymore but under us, and then we began to see whole villages, & a panorama of snow-white fields & hedgerows. The plane moved like a dream, with not the ghost of a tremor or vibration. Never have I traveled so smoothly, neither on sea or land. If not for the fact that I could see the moving land below, and the somewhat irregular rhythm of the plane's wing rising and dipping, it would have seemed wholly at rest.

What was most surprising was how slowly the landscape moved. I always imagined it would speed by, as it does by a railroad window, but the perspective is different, and so much is seen at a time that the doll houses and villages drift by very lazily. Then all at once the snow-white earth had a foamy fringe to it, and the blue gray surface of the Channel was beneath us. From way up high it seemed very still, except at the beach. And there were no ships in sight, a sharp contrast to that July day I crossed last year, when the two way convoys filled it to overflowing. Then also abruptly we were over land again, & again it was not feasible to determine where. I was tired from craning my head up, so I lay back & rested.

Now — the ironic payoff. The plane came down to ground as gently as a drifting feather, — but riding on the solid ground it bumped & jolted like an auto! I don't know why anyone should ever want to travel on a shaky ship, if a plane can do the distance as reliably.

My mother's letters — 3 this week so far — are tender, & amusing, in a way. She's trying to convince me that I have fulfilled the call of duty, & should concentrate on getting well, & she lectures me on cooperating with the doctor, and that I should try to fortify myself, & not lose courage. She writes beautifully.

As to being cheerful, well, all the patients cooperate to keep up the doctors' & nurses' morale. It is no exaggeration when I tell you that neither doctors nor nurses ever walk out of my room without laughing at some gag I pull, and when a fellow patient comes in — those who walk drop in — it's always for cooperative kibitzing. American soldiers do not complain nor do they whine — not like the Germans, who were a sniveling, whimpering lot.

But dear, you'll forgive me if I am blue for just a minute when I read about our armies crossing the Roer River, & going out on the Cologne Plain, places I scouted & mapped out & expected to go to myself — and when I think of the day my division contacts some Russian outfit — and I would have been called in to interpret! Otherwise I am cheerful! Well, beloved —as you say, there's no regretting the price we have to pay, in fact I'd like to pay some more, only in my own way.

All my love — Lenny

Mar 1, V

Dear Lenny,

Surprise — today I got back the money from last year's income tax — $20.88. I'm going to use the money to buy myself some clothes, dear. I haven't gotten any new dresses since before I became pregnant so I'm going to get some spring clothes and also a pair of shoes. Is it all right? I think I'm going to be able to deduct Betty Lou and myself as dependents on my father's income tax this year. I'm glad to be able to save him that because, as you know, we do cost him quite a bit.

Diana

Mar 1, V

Dearest,

Congrats on the Purple Heart or maybe I shouldn't congratulate you since it is given for wounds received in action.

I can understand the problem of what to do with your time. I wish so much that I could help. One thing I have done is get everyone possible to write to you.

Diana

Mar 2, V

Dear Lenny,

Under separate cover, I'm sending you an airmail letter with Roosevelt's speech on the Yalta Conference. I hope all is well with you, dearest — no mail today. I hope all is well with your arm. I'm so anxious to know what they did to you.

Diana

March 2, 1945

Dearest Diana,

A batch of old mail came today. First off was a letter from a buddy of mine who's also in England, having preceded me by a month, & it was good to hear from him; & another quite independent letter from his wife, thanking me for saving her life (she put it so sweetly, her husband is her life) — he was the guy I hauled out of the river where a tank shell broke his leg.[12]

Then there was a letter, very appropriately on the back of a circular, from the Servicemen's Welfare Committee. It seems that at Welfare Center 11 they spread out the Nazi flag (the one we captured at Fort Eben-Emael) — and the staff proceeded to snow it under by a mere $23,000 in war bonds!!! Now that is using it like I meant! She said there were plans for using it at other offices & places; & she used it to solicit merchandise for the National War Fund. It was thrilling to read; & so I wrote her to promote another campaign — to make up the 6 pints of blood plasma they used on me.

My Purple Heart went to you by mail yesterday. You ask about the Silver Star.[13] I've no idea if it will ever come thru — all I know is they said it was "recommended." If a general wants, he can pin a medal on you on the spot; but if you are passed through channels, it takes a year or more sometimes. In this case, as far as I know, the guy who recommended it, or said he did, is "missing;" one witness is since "killed in action" & the other is in the hospital in England. That's war.

Glad to hear Babe's OK. I hope he got shore leave in the Philippines — it's something to see a newly liberated people.

You ask about my letter on October in Germany. The situation when we were closing that northern pincer was particularly screwed up; but it is a fact that very few soldiers know where they are, or where they are going, at any particular time. Very few ever see a map at all except for the misleading ones in Stars & Stripes.

Lenny

P.S. My brother Eddie's 5th Marine Division is reported today in action on the west coast of Iwo Jima, it says in Stars & Stripes. Wish the kid luck!

---

12. This refers to the buddy Lenny stayed with during the German attack on Malmédy.

13. The Silver Star is the third-highest military decoration awarded for gallantry against an enemy of the U.S.

Mar, 2

Dear Diana,

I'll send you a note to go with some of the clippings enclosed. There are two items about the Roer River crossing. The dams, in the March 1 article, were the biggest topic of conversation from about Nov 15 to Dec 17, when we left the area to meet the German breakthrough into Belgium. I went out to the low-lying flats by the Roer on several occasions, once night patrol, & twice as a guide, & we could see far across the Roer & we knew well what damage the control of those dams could determine. As a matter of fact, the air corps tried for a long time to do a job on the dams & and every day the word came back, disappointment every time.

The other picture of a pontoon bridge across a narrow part of the Roer, being crossed by prisoners, will give you an idea of the procedure I often took part in. The prisoners keep their hands on their heads, because they can keep them up longer that way than if they held them straight up. Since, as you can see by the photo, there are only about 4 or 5 GI's escorting the POW's, the reason for hands up is obvious. You'll also note the Germans do not have helmets — they wear them much less than we do, & helmets are discarded on surrender, but unlike American soldiers, Germans carry their doughboy caps with them & can wear them.

Lenny

Mar 3

Dearest Lenny,

Today is a red-letter day for us. Betty Lou got her first tooth.

The papers are full of news about the offensive on the Western front — the 9th Army seems to be the spearhead of the drive and is getting much publicity.

Diana

3-3-45, V

Hello darling,

Doc just took the cast off my left arm, hurray. He also took out the stitches of which there were 17, leaving a rather jagged and rough-looking seam — they basted it with big stitches, it's not the neat job like our needle trade parents taught us to appreciate. The upper arm where the hole used to be looks a little skimpy, minus the bulge of the biceps, but I do have a functioning arm.

There's a lag of about 10 days between the news of the front, and its effect on this hospital — but I could see today, from what came in that the armies are on the offensive again.

Lenny

Sunday, March 4, 1945

Dearest Diana,

The pleasure is double when it is unexpected. I was sitting abed propped up in the cushions, writing, to keep myself occupied, the continuation of the narrative of my combat experiences — it's still in the form of a letter to you, though I'm not mailing it & it's now up to 12/20 — when in comes mail, which was not scheduled for today. Glory! 17 pieces!

You mention showing "The Bridge," a story I wrote, to my sister Harriet, which indicates you received it. I suppose you guessed it was a true story, in spite of the fictional cast. "Len" must have been obvious. Because of the form, the story, you got, didn't tell all the details of what happened, but it was terrific, both the attack by the First Armored S.S. Division, & the price they paid, & the handful of men (not even 40) who fought on though cut off, & prevented the Germans from pressing on their breakthrough, & saved not only the town they were guarding, but many towns beyond. You know about the Silver Star — but there's one guy up for a Congressional Medal of Honor for that day, and a whole flock of bronze stars. And I still have more nightmares from that day than from the day I was wounded.

As for me, the sewed-up upper arm aches a bit, but it must be mending under the bandage. It doesn't seem to be draining anymore: it did 'til it was sewn & it was very smelly, so they ran a rubber tube into it & squirted some medicine into it then; but that was before it was sewn. They tell me my leg in the cast is powerfully smelly too, but since it's with me all the time, I never, or almost never, smell it. Most folks are thoughtful enough not to say anything. The smell comes from lymph & stuff which drains out of the big open wound I have in my foot — there is no infection, it is clean; but they can't work on the wound until the bones begin to heal, & the draining matter seeps into the gauze of the cast, & smells as it decomposes. That's one reason they change the cast every so often.

The one time I saw the wound was the day it happened, it looked like the one on my arm as far as depth into the flesh but it is much bigger, &

probably will require a skin graft job. Since it is a far future business, I've never asked from what part of me they expect to get the skin, but unless they have skin banks like blood banks I guess it has to come off me somewhere.[14]

Lenny

Mar 5

Dear Lenny,

Last night we received a phone call from my aunt in Boston. She received a cablegram from my uncle in Tashkent that they are all living. Of course he only includes himself and his family — he didn't refer to any of the folks who stayed in Uman,[15] but it's the first word we've had from anyone since June, 1941. The cablegram took 3 weeks to get here and he begs for an answer. It's wonderful that messages can come through now — one of my father's friends also got a cablegram from his family.

Lenny, here it is only 4 days that I've had no mail and I'm so uneasy — and you haven't had any for weeks. I hope some has reached you to the new address.

Diana

3/5

Dear Diana,

About the money order — I'm sending the receipt to you by separate envelope. Please take it to the Post Office; explain that the issuing office is not reachable, being in Germany most likely, & that your husband is a casualty in England, & don't let them argue you into writing to Germany for inquiry. Tell them you need the dough to live on, and there'll be an unholy scandal if the dough isn't forthcoming pronto.

Glad to hear Betty is trying to go places & to climb in the world. A daughter is such a responsibility, such a worry!

Lenny

---

14. Lenny underwent an experimental skin graft procedure to cover the wound, which was not healing, and he was the first for whom the procedure succeeded. It was written up in *Life* magazine in the February 11, 1946, issue.

15. Uman is a large city in Cherkasy Oblast Province in Central Ukraine. Most of Diana's family had been evacuated to Tashkent, Uzbekistan, in Central Asia, during the German invasion of the Ukraine in 1940.

BETTY IS SEVEN MONTHS OLD

Mar 6

Dearest,

Betty's 7 months today. I'd like to see her. Today I did my best to sleep away — nothing to read & until a few minutes ago no writing paper. Once in a while another patient drops in. It gets dreary. Vic writes that my letters (on Mississippi probably) are considered prize items in the collection of servicemen's letters made by the Schomburg Collection (the big Harlem library), according to Dr. Reddick, its head. The letters are being preserved there, but the signatures are all deleted, for regretfully obvious reasons. Life's ironies — a guy works seven years on a book, and a couple of casual letters get filed for "posterity."[16]

Good that the AWOL $20 came & you won't have to wrestle with the Post Office. And I'm glad to have paid for Betty Lou's highchair. At this long distance, reading everybody's raves, one gets to feel as if she's everybody's kid but mine. This highchair reestablishes my position!

The "hamantashen" are a hit — I gave one to a ward boy & a couple of seconds later one of our most graceful brunette nurses appeared & called for one by name, which was amusing.

Lenny

Mar 6

Dearest Lenny,

Happy Birthday to our Betty Lou — 7 months!

Lenny, there is lots that worries me a great deal about you, but I've hesitated to ask you up to now. From some hints that you dropped in the first letters after you were hurt, you seemed to feel that you would not see action in the final push. Do you have any idea what is going to happen to you?

Since you write that it will take 5 or 6 months before you will be better or rather before you can be back to yourself, coming home for your convalescence would be something, no? I cannot say that I don't worry about you — you wouldn't expect me not to worry, but I am hopeful things will be OK for us. Maybe if I could just get a look at you, I would feel much better. It's difficult that I'm so far from the hospital where you are.

Diana

---

16. Lenny refers to the manuscript he is writing about John Milton.

Mar 7

Dear Lenny,

I had a postcard from the War Dep't again saying that you are convalescing. I wonder what they term convalescing since you are still in bed.

Diana

Mar 7

Dearest Sweetheart,

As to sending me books — it isn't practical to return any, so best not send books from our or Lucy's library. As a matter of fact, while I shall be very glad to get those books friends have sent, I'd rather not request. You send me those magazine issues, though! You see, dearest, a book, unless it's something to be studied barely lasts me a couple of hours; and it would take a fortune to amuse me with books, let alone a few ocean liners to carry them. I find myself better satisfied by writing an hour or two than reading half a day.

As to Betty on 2/18/45: this series of photos are the best job I've seen. Now if I have any complaint about how Betty looks in a picture, I can only blame myself for giving her such features. I'm very happy to see my daughter all decked out in a young miss's dress, even though she's still a baldy.

Lenny

Mar 8

Sweetheart,

Lucy is in school in St. Louis and seems to be getting along fine. There has been a wait of 3–4 weeks between Babe's letters recently. Since she hasn't seen him in 16 months plus the delay in mail makes it so difficult for her.

Lenny, darling, I was a little surprised that you wrote that you get more raves about Betty Lou from third parties. You know to me Betty Lou is a real child. I live with her all day long and I love her every minute of everyday — I write you of her as she develops and as I think you want to know of her. Other people — your folks and some of the other people that have seen her — they come in every once in a while for a half hour or so, watch her perform and play a little with her and then they leave. If you only see her once in 2 or 3 weeks, well, tremendous changes have taken place and therefore they rave.

Also, darling, your family talks of Betty Lou as though she were the most perfect, beautiful, remarkable genius that was ever born — and it isn't so. She's very sweet, she has a lovely disposition (which is her best quality, I think) and she is very good — but then there are things in which other children excel and are ahead of her. For instance, the youngster upstairs can get around much better than she can. On the other hand, he is not nice looking at all. I guess that grandparents are that way and also aunts and uncles especially with the first, but you and I have to take a real attitude towards her.

Yours,
Diana

Mar 9, V

Dear Diana,

Got some more V-mail forms, thank goodness — Today they changed the cast on my left leg. The bone apparently has mended enough so they were able to handle my leg freely with no need of anesthetic. There was very little pain, which was compensated by the pleasure of no cast on for a few minutes. The wound on the heel & ankle has also been mending — they can see it only when the cast is off and the Doc's opinion it will soon be ready for the skin grafting job.

Dear, I'm being moved from this hospital, tomorrow, so my mail to you maybe a trifle irregular. I'll send my new address as soon as possible. Tonight I am out in the ward having gladly yielded up my private room for a guy whose condition is very serious.

Mar 9, scribbled note

Dearest,

Hello, Daddy,

How are you?

Betty Lou

Betty Lou just interrupted this letter — I just guided her hand a little but she wrote it. Of course, as soon as she finished — she wanted to eat it up but I convinced her to wait for supper instead. She loves to tear paper — it's the sound, I guess.

Yes, dearest, I received the coins and the Nazi insignia, the narrative called "The Bridge," the Stars and Stripes with the story of how Malmédy was defended, the poem to Betty Lou, and the special love letter in a blue envelope.

Some of my Christmas packages never did get to you, and my letters — I've sent you several packages since you are in England.

Lenny, you ask me how I thought and felt when I got your first letter from France that you were wounded. The first letter I got was dated 1/27 and did not say what happened to you — you had written on the 22nd but I didn't get that till later. I received it 2/5. I was frightfully worried because I didn't know where you were hurt, and I was so happy and lucky that you were alive and able to write to me. The letter brought a flood of tears — I guess it was weeks of pent-up fear and worry that were released by the shock of your having been hurt. Once I cried it out, I was OK and to this very minute, I still am so happy at how lucky we are. I'm OK and I want you to devote all your time to getting better. By the time the War Dept. telegram came, I had had several letters from you and knew in detail what was wrong.

Diana

Mar 10, V

Dearest,

I understand what you mean when you say you think of me much more now. As for me, I have a clearer picture in my mind now for me to send my love to you, and now once in a while I permit myself to think of how it will be to have you home — the three of us living together.

Diana

EVACUATED TO THE U.S.

Mar 11, V

Dear Lenny,

I don't think I've written you that since Betty Lou eats 3 meals a day, she has settled down to 2 naps a day. Now she gets between 12 and 13 hours sleep at night. She is such a good and happy child. She can play by herself for hours if I just change her toys and move her into another room every once in a while. However, even though her schedule is easier than when she was first born, it still takes me most of the day to care for her.

Diana

Mar, 11, Aboard the Queen Elizabeth

Dearest Diana,

This is going to be a very different trip from the voyage coming over to Europe. Confined as I am to bed with my broken leg in a cast, there will be no long days spent up on deck watching the wild expanse of waves, the seabirds dipping in the spray, the Northern Lights and the rainbows; but by some compensation, neither will I have to sleep in the smelly cavern with 600 men jam-packed into a compartment without air or light, nor eat in a subway crowd mob the two starvation "meals" they gave us then — now I have sheets & a mattress in a well-lit cabin, aired by a porthole, since we are on the main deck, & 3 times a day good meals are brought by a waiter.

My 7 fellow patients are pretty jolly company — and we are going home. What a difference that makes!

The sun shone bright as we were loaded onto the ambulance; I craned my neck to see, from the rear window, the winding road & villages and fields, between Burford Hospital in Oxford Shire, & Wheatley Station. There we were loaded onto the hospital train. Unlike the wretched one in which we "traveled" from Verviers to Paris, here we were 3 bunks tiered, not 4, it was light & airy; instead of dry bread & spam, good meals, if scant, instead of being unattended by a Red Cross dame, who could only hand out year-old papers (too dim to read), here we had 3 nurses who really worked heroically and devotedly to make us comfortable. Still one wearies in a cramped litter, in an overnight ride.

Sunday A.M., the 11th we were carried by Negro port men onto a tender at Gourock, Glasgow harbor. A few minutes later the tender pulled along side the Queen Elizabeth & we were aboard the latter with barely a glimpse at the hovering silver gray seagulls.

Remembering the repulsive interior of the Wakefield Ship[17] it was amazing to be carried up the grand stairways & thru the swanky luxurious corridors, and the cabin for 8, only double decked-bunks, well lit, officers in swanky dress uniforms (not seen at the front), and your eyes pop to see the nurses uniforms: the same pin-striped brown & white seersucker that their dresses were in the hospital: but slacks & blouses, what a revelation! What curves & what grace and if any special criterion was used in selecting these nurses, it was looks — what beauties! 'Tis a long wait for us — loading up will last till Tuesday evening. Kibitzing — getting acquainted. Drugged self with the who-done-it, "Farewell My Lovely."

Lenny

---

17. The ship he sailed to Europe on.

Mar 12, V

Dearest,

Swell what Welfare Center 11 did with the flag you captured. As for the blood plasma — several of the welfare people have donated blood in your honor. Lucy is in the Social Work Division. Darling, it's been in the newspapers about the 5th Marines being at Iwo Jima. I haven't mentioned it to your folks because I'm not sure they know. I wrote to your brother Eddie a few days ago.[18]

Diana

3-13 45, V

Dear Diana,

Mail this afternoon brought no letters, but your package addressed here came: the one with the raisins, apricots (a joy!) & candy. Thanks beloved, it is swell, especially the fruit & the chocolate. Although I have been in the hospital much longer, now, than either the time at Shelby or France, it doesn't seem as long as either of those times. Of course, then I was a rookie, in Shelby eager & ambitious, in France impatient to do my job; now I am a wearied veteran who finds altogether too many memories crowding into his thoughts whenever he tries to just lie back & relax. Later I see in tonight's Stars & Stripes that my 30th division is in Germany again — it has some towns of civilians on its hands — as you can understand that my bed has suddenly become very constricting. Oh well, the lameness in my left arm is rapidly disappearing. Maybe, I ought to try out for a local baseball team now that spring is in the air.

Lenny

Mar 15

Darling,

So glad some of my mail is finally reaching you — about time — Darling, Betty Lou is yours — don't have any fears and as soon as you get back to us your position is well established in my heart and will be in hers too. Your asking about price control on diaper service is touching. There is no price control on that and even without price control everything is double and of much inferior quality. They were asking $1.00 per pound for chicken, black market of course, but none is available at .40 which is the ceiling price so we just don't buy any — and it is with an endless number of items.

---

18. Eddie was at Iwo Jima and went on to serve in Japan during the occupation.

Our armies in the West are moving by leaps and it's wonderful to read about it. I only hope that the newspapers are giving us an accurate picture. Churchill said this week that the war will be over in Europe by the end of the summer or sooner.

Diana

Mar 16

Dearest Lenny,

I'm so excited that I can't think straight. I had a postcard from the gov't today dated 3/10 saying that you are "convalescing" and "evacuated to the USA." Darling, is it true? I hope to hear from you shortly in the U.S. and maybe even see you. Of course, I let your Mother know immediately.

Now I fear I must talk to you seriously. Our daughter is not a "brat." If she has difficulty eating when there are too many others around, it's only because they sit around watching her. You would act up also — so I find it is best to feed her alone.

You know, dearest, I write and write and write and every time it comes back to me about the postcard I received. Are you really coming home?

Diana

BACK ON AMERICAN SOIL

March 19, 1945

United States of America
Hooray!
Dearest sweetheart beloved Diana:

Just arrived — and waiting to be carried off. I shall try to phone you tonight when I arrive at the hospital — but just in case not possible — maybe this will reach you by tomorrow morning. I'm very well.[19]

All my love, Lenny

3/23

Dearest,

It's Lowell General Hospital, Fort Devens, Mass. — I'm not there yet — I'm just getting on the Pullman. Before you try coming here, please

---

19. For the first four days back in the U.S., Lenny was at Halloran General Hospital in Staten Island. Diana visited Lenny and he met Betty for the first time. No cars were available for hire in wartime because of the gasoline shortage. Diana's father arranged, through a friend who owned a funeral parlor, for a hearse to take them to the hospital.

check — I'm not sure if the L.G. Hospital is at or near Ft. Devens — but it is LG Hospital — they just told us.[20]

Lenny

P.S. Hell!

3/24

Dear Diana,

Well, it was grand while it lasted — I suppose we should be grateful for the 4 days at Halloran G.H. (in Staten Island) — and that we could be together on our anniversary day — though it was hard saying goodbye again. Honest, I was bluer than any other time since I'm in the army — especially when they told us where we were going. There's a ward full of NY City guys here! That's the army's way, as always.

It's northwest from Boston & northeast from Worcester. There are trains from Boston to Ayer & buses from Ayer to the hospital. Worcester is nearer NY but I don't know how good its bus service & connections are. Visiting hours are 2 to 4 and 6 to 8. Passes are given at the Lowell North and South gates. I'm in the North Hospital. Doc says not to get out of bed yet.

When you come, please bring me my whole Paradise Regained folder, and the Students' Milton, and two packs of notebook paper I used for the mss; & a large red folder to hold the things in. Also, please rush me a complete chart, names & family tree, of your Boston clans.

I'm in a ward of 16 beds. Give my greetings to all. Tell Betty Lou I'll come to see her as soon as I can get a pass. It's so disappointing — all the folks who could have come to Halloran, whom I so much wanted to see. Up here, who can come?[21]

Lenny

Mar 25

Dear Lee,

I had 2 special deliveries today — thanks so much, beloved — one from Staten Island when you found out where you were going and the other when you arrived.

---

20. Lenny had hoped to be in a hospital closer to New York City and his family.

21. On March 25, Lenny was transferred to Lowell General Hospital, North Ward 132, Fort Devens, Massachusetts, where he remained for one year and three months until his discharge.

I called the RR and was told it's about a 5½ hr trip to Ft. Devens. I knew at the dispatcher's office that you were headed for Lowell — I tried to find you to tell you but the ambulance had left. It's about the same distance as Utica — maybe even better because of my Boston relatives. I'm grateful I can make it in a weekend. Dearest, I love you. Betty Lou hugs her papa.

Diana

3-25, Ward 132 North

Dearest,

It's hard not to be lonely up here. You see — they gave weekend passes to everyone who could walk, even with casts, on crutches; & to one, who couldn't walk, whose family brought a car for him; & almost everyone had a crowd of visitors.

Good news: Doc says as soon as I'm in shape — meaning, bone set for sure & skin graft done — all patients are supposed to get a 21-day furlough. GET SET!!! Among other things, dear, find out what coupons a gas rationing board will give for a guy in my condition to 1) travel by car home 2) use a car in N.Y while on furlough.

P.S. Where can you get money to come on your present budget? I can't see it at all.

Lenny

Mar 26

Dearest,

In the last few days, Betty Lou has learned to make pat-a-cake and also peek-a-boo. Her coordination is not so highly developed so she often claps her hands together but they don't meet and it's very funny. She makes peek-a-boo with her dress and picks it up over her eyes.

Diana

March 26

Dear Diana,

Doc says I may walk on crutches even before they fix the leg further — so I've already been up & about a bit — around the ward. It's not easy but it's grand to get out of bed.

Today's paper says the 120th — my regiment — spearheaded the push across the Rhine & is the farthest advanced reported — gee whiz. Dearest — if I can walk enough by Wednesday A.M., they may give me a pass home for Passover, Wednesday to Sunday. Maybe I ought to keep it

secret & surprise you but why shouldn't you be on pins & needles too,
like me now?

Lenny

Mar 27

Dear Lenny,

Regarding your coming home on a weekend, you flabbergast me. You
mean you might get a pass now if we provide the transportation. It would
be terrific if we could work it out. Dearest, did the Dr. give you any idea
when they'll be able to graft the skin? Also what's with the stitches that
opened up on your arm?

Diana

First Trip Home

There is no more information about how Lenny managed to travel home.
There are family stories about Betty's strong negative reaction to Diana's
giving so much attention to him.

4-2-45

Dearest,

Arrived back at the hospital at about 4:30 A.M. — no trouble at all —
but mighty sleepy.

Lenny

Apr 2

Dear Lenny,

I heard the tragic news about Roosevelt's death about two hours ago
and it's hard for me to do anything. What a terrible tragedy for the entire
democratic world and for us in America. The shock is so great for all of us
that it will be a take a little while to gather my thoughts.

Diana

4-2-45

Dearest Diana,

This is "hangover Monday." Everyone is very, very subdued. When Doc
came by this A.M. he asked "How are you?" — I said "OK." He said, "Did
you have a good time?" I said, "Very."

"Dovey," now I miss not only you — but Betty. It was worth all the
effort of coming home just to be with you & Betty.

Lenny

April 2

Dearest Diana,

The radio just announced the death of President Roosevelt. It's a terrible blow. Truman is a second Andrew Jackson — in potentiality. The struggle to keep America on the Teheran-Yalta road will now become very sharp, because the jackals that didn't dare buck Roosevelt will come out howling now. Let's hope the times make the man, & Truman rises above his source. The news came over the radio like the news of Pearl Harbor. Since then — as you likely know — the radio has had nothing else but the tragic news.

Doc advised against a pass this weekend, because my cast is still cut open, & I didn't disagree with him.

The pictures came today. The ones of Betty are grand & you came out swell too; but what happened to my mug? They all look like caricatures — or else I really look bad.

Lenny

Apr 3

Darling,

It was so wonderful to talk to you this morning — I was so happy you called me. I'm so eager to know what the X-rays showed, but I'll have to wait for mail. She's beginning to stand, dearest, just for a minute or two.

Diana

4/3/45

Dear Diana,

It was sweet to hear your voice on the phone this morning & pleasant that Betty looked for me. I look for her too & for you.

Lenny

4-4-45

Dearest Diana,

Just before lunch, the ward boy yelled my name from the corridor — "package for you." Since I can't carry anything while on crutches, as you know, I asked him to bring it in — and a minute later I was flabbergasted to see him come staggering in with a carton big enough for a play yard for Betty Lou — enormous. At first we thought it was a radio — well, it turned out to be a very fancy "ribboned" & decorated Easter basket from Barricini's loaded with boxes of candy (I can see 7) & such from my father's factory shop. It created a sensation, as it's the biggest thing we've ever seen round here.

Spent this afternoon collating Job with the New Testament, in Paradise Regained — and have found several points of value: above all, I've found in Job a clue to the expansion of the New Testament temptation story as Milton gives it.

Lenny

Apr 5

Dearest,

I'm so glad you called this evening. I'm particularly happy because you sounded as though you are OK. You know what I mean, dearest — you sounded quite satisfied with the progress of your leg and with the things you are doing.

Roosevelt was buried this morning at Hyde Park. The first shock is over, and we must turn our eyes on the future. Let's hope Truman will become big with the times we are living in and carry out the Teheran-Yalta talks.

Your,
Diana

4-5-45

Dear Darling,

It's good you're coming as we're not getting passes this weekend. I only hope Betty doesn't take it too hard, but only hugs you all the more Monday morning.

Lenny

April 6, 1945

Dearest,

Tomorrow, if all goes well, I shall see you again. O joy — only I hope Betty Lou doesn't feel troubled about it! "Wrastled" this morning with an essay on the Germans I have known, — only I can't imagine for the life of me what magazine could conceivably want to buy it, and it limps as a result.

All afternoon confined to bed with cast off & leg wrapped in a sterilized towel — waiting for Doc to come & examine it; but he only got halfway thru the ward. The X-ray report (at which I peeked) says the main break shows sign of rejoining in good position, & ankle joint (mortise) is OK; but medial malleolus (is that ankle bone?) is partly lacking & some ankle fragments are necrotic (dead?). I must get a dictionary!

I want my 30th Division patch to sew on my blouse. The radio puts them over the West Yser and still way out ahead. The First Army was the first to cross over the Rhine at Remagen, Germany and is still way out ahead.

Lenny

4/8 V

Dear Diana,

Today I finished my combat narrative "letter," ending it with my arrival at the St. Cloud Hospital, near Paris. I'm glad it's finished — maybe it will help me to forget some things. The stretch of my last week in action is quite "sketchy," as I have found many of the details react immediately, and very badly, on my stomach.

Lenny

April 8, 1945

Dearest,

I need you today. I'm having trouble. No can get started. At hand there is a batch of letters from the Wakefield and from Great Britain. I don't feel up to it. Even conceding they may have been interesting as letters to you. I still can't conceive of any form in which they might be interesting to anyone else. And furthermore, I don't feel as if they're worth the effort.

If library was available I could work on Milton, but it isn't, & being stuck in snag in regard to the sketches, everything is awry. Also I'm lonesome for you & Betty. If I were doing something in action, I wouldn't mind, but doing nothing & still being away from home, just don't make sense.

Lenny

DIANA TRAVELS TO MASSACHUSETTS

Diana visited Lenny in the hospital once a month. She traveled over the weekend when her mom could take care of Betty. She left Friday night after work and returned early Monday morning in time for her mom to go to work in the garment factory. The trains were very crowded with civilians and soldiers, and she often had to stand up for most of the trip.

Apr 9

Darling Lenny,

I got home at 8 A.M. this morning. Please dearest, believe me — I'm OK and the trip was not too strenuous at all.

How are you darling? I hope they've changed the cast: was the walk back to your ward OK last night? I had a lovely weekend with you. I hope you weren't overtired.

Diana

April 9, 1945

Dearest,

A moment's relaxation — how are you beloved? Did you get home OK & how is Betty, after your all-day — 2-day — absence?

Today I put in, so far, a 12-hour day at work; so your visit was a 100% success, see?

Lenny

April 10, 1945

Dear Diana,

Doc looked at my leg again today while Nurse was changing the bandages, so I asked him what's up — he's very non-talkative. He said he thinks it will heal enough by itself not to need skin grafting, so all they will do is put a cast on, & have an open space to be able to clean the wound. After a time they will X-ray again to see progress, & so on 'til it heals.

I worked some more this A.M. on "the Germans." The conclusion is holding me up a bit, but I expect to finish it today. It is 2,800 words or so. Now who wants to pay me $10 for it?

Lenny

April 11

Dear Diana and Betty Lou,

How are you & Betty? In 3 separate envelopes I am sending you the article on the Germans. Give me, please, the benefit of your sharpest criticism. Can you have it typed in double space, one NEAT original, one duplicate on regular paper & one onion-skin paper?[22]

Lenny

---

22. Lenny asks Diana to type his story so he can submit it to magazines. He had no access to a typewriter in the hospital.

April 13, 1945

Dearest,

The death of FDR still is a big thing here, as everywhere, no doubt. Are you saving today's papers for me? We had a minute of silence here, & in its lame way the army cancelled all social functions & stuff, & arranged an open-air prayer meeting. I went to Friday services at the library — a Roosevelt memorial service.

Lenny

Apr 14

Dearest Beloved,

I've just come home from your folks — your mother is planning to leave tomorrow morning to visit you. I hope things won't be too complicated for you and that it works out OK.

Diana

April 14, 1945

Dear Diana,

It's the day of Lincoln's assassination & of Ft. Sumter; & of the Spanish Republic 1931. Radio continues with FDR obsequies & requiem.

How are Betty & her ma? Is she standing? UNRRA[23] is advertising very lucrative jobs for discharges with Welfare experience, but they must go overseas again for a year or more. It's another possibility; but I do want to be with my two girls for a while!!!

I am again filled with trepidation as I approach writing about the sea passage & England letters. The borderline between triviality and transmitting common experience to universals is so close! Look at Tom Sawyer whitewashing a fence. If one is a genius like Mark Twain, you make a story out of it that lives for ages. And if you're a plain-spoken guy like your husband it's so easy to make a dull, boring personal reminiscence out of what, after all, are not such remarkable days.

It hurts — though — sometimes, a wee bit — that it only comes, that damn lyrical imp — when he damn pleases. Don't I feel enough — don't I understand enough to be able to write an "elegy on a soldier fallen in battle" for my friends & our friend Roosevelt? I'll be damned if ever a word will come. A business has got to be in me seething a long time

---

23. United Nations Relief and Rehabilitation Association.

before it erupts — the images in the story "Hospital Ship" were a brewing a long time before they all came out at once.

Lenny

4/15/45

Dearest,

Am waiting for Ma to arrive — she's rather overdue. I've arranged a wheelchair for myself (at last but only for today) so I can get around without taxing myself; & with the aid of the chaplain & USO, I have a kosher family lined up for her to eat and sleep at.

Lenny

Apr 16

Darling Lee,

Lenny, I want to ask you to wait for my criticism on the article on the Germans until I see you. There is quite a bit for us to talk about. The only other magazine I can think of to send "The Bridge" is the Coronet. Have you ever thought you might only have to send it once?

Diana

April 16, 1945

Dear Diana,

Heard Truman's speech today — Let's hope for the best. It was good enough to praise very highly, but an opportunity for another Gettysburg address was there.

Today Mom told me — I don't think you know of it — that some 5 of my Yiddish letters were broadcast by WEVD last autumn — by some dame named Hannah Specter — for the benefit of the war effort, for Caruso's spaghetti and one-a-day vitamins. And a lot of folks heard it, & there was a to-do on Blake Ave & echoes all the way up to the Bronx.

I debate whether to come home & see Betty too — or to take it easy & have you come here. As usual the sensible approach is the unattractive one. If only I didn't have the arm wound, there'd be no doubt.

Lenny

April 19, 1945

Darling Dear,

I get hungrier for you every hour. Some guys left on furlough this morning, others are getting weekend passes. I was almost the only one to be left in the ward this weekend (which I really hoped for!) but two others are being kept in.

Mail: your letter of 4/16 — glad to hear my buddy was able to salvage some of my things — though it seems my notes & papers must have been barred by the censor officer or else didn't seem of value to the casual eye. But if the maps are there, swell! And I'm happy to recover those 3 books; & the photos.

Renting a typewriter is out, dear: I am surprised you considered it. How could we afford it? The "Bridge" is too long for Coronet, & not the kind of thing Coronet features. Coronet is a short story magazine.

Lenny

April 20, 1945

Dear Diana,

So here it's a month since I'm back & I didn't even realize it. In large measure I'm still living mentally over there. Nearly everyone is out on pass or furlough this weekend.

Beloved, you have been here once, & will be again tomorrow. But I become "lonesomer" and "lonesomer" for Betty. How is she?

Lenny

Apr 23

Dearly Beloved,

Happy anniversary, beloved — did you enjoy our anniversary weekend? I'm still tingling all over with joy and delight and ecstasy and I love you so much.

I arrived home this A.M. at 6 because I caught the midnight out of Boston. I was home in time to begin the day with Betty Lou. She was fine, dearest — behaved very well all weekend, my mother said. This morning she didn't cling to me too much, although she was happy to see me.

Diana

April 23, 1945

Dearest,

What a happy anniversary weekend we had! What more could ask — except to have had Betty with us.

Doc worked on me today: on the leg wound he burned off some of the surface tissue with silver nitrate & cut it off — it wasn't painful — & on the arm just scraped the surface with gauze. I guess the idea was to open the wound up. It seems they've got a big shipment of penicillin that they've got no room for or something. So they're pouring it by the gallon on Pete, George & me, & injecting it also. They pour it on both wounds every hour & in the injection every 3 hours.

A nurse I complained about has been acting worse and worse, so I blew my top & gave her a piece of my mind this morning. She declared the ward has been running sloppy, & she would set it to rights. "This is a hospital, not a country club," she keeps announcing while meaning it is to be run like a prison ward. It's a long time since I've had a fight with anybody & there's a lot of surplus fight energy spilling over.

Lenny

April 24, 1945

Dearest,

This morning I have ironed out the "Holland" story by putting it in 3 sections. My long apprenticeship in historical study has me so inured to chronological sequence & accuracy that it is a strain & effort to recast events into a sequence which reads well. Real life is not equally fascinating at all minutes; there are dull times in real life; but in written life that is forbidden.

The penicillin deluge continues. The sprayings of my arm & leg are awkward, but tolerable. But to be waked up all thru the night is another matter. Worse yet is the injected penicillin — every 3 hours — my right arm & leg are aching from punctures. And there's no making up for last night's sleep by day, because every hour it comes again (the spray is once an hour). What is most annoying is the fact that it's all empirical, guesswork. I'm sure the only reason I'm getting this dosage, after not getting anything in the 30 days I've been here, is either a) as a "control" on Pete who needs it because he has gangrene of the bone, or 2) they're experimenting casually to see how much a guy can take without ill effects. The arm wound, however, whether because of Doc's cutting yesterday, or the penicillin application by spray has a much better appearance today, than it has ever had.

How's Betty????? I miss you — and I miss her, too. What is she doing this week? In our anniversary reunion joy we were like young lovers again and all but forgot we were old married folks with a family. From this weekend, short as it was, I guess we must conclude that "we mutually love each other & ain't no use denying it" — "this thing is bigger than us, let's not fight it."

Lenny

April 25, 1945

Dearest,

The penicillin injection torture treatment continues day & night; but from sheer exhaustion I slept in between waking up to be jabbed again, & got some rest.

Lenny

Apr 25

Love,

Your Mon. letter came today. Dearest, are you sure all is well? Why all the penicillin suddenly? I hope there is nothing wrong.

Diana

April 26, 1945

Dear Diana,

Last night I went to sleep all set to tackle the "France" series of letters today — but today I have hardly been able to lift my head, after 3 nights of being waked to be jabbed, plus the effects of the jabbing, swollen right arm & right thigh I'm just about all in. This morning I appealed to Doc, but he says no, it goes on for 8 days which just about confirms my guess that I'm being tormented just as a control on Pete, who's on the same schedule — but needs it — not I.

The arm & leg wounds look better, healing like: though the new surface is warped, it's closed & not horrible like it used to be — even the still-open areas look better.

Does Betty show any effects of handling by other folks over the weekend? Is she worried, insecure? What does she think when a day goes by and she doesn't see you?

Lenny

April 26

Dear Lenny,

Frankly I'm worried — you seem very casual and even a little sarcastic about all the penicillin, but I don't understand why this sudden flooding with penicillin. I hope that everything is OK — please, dearest, write me what you know.

Darling, Betty's fine. She has learned something new. She can creep, but she goes backwards. It's funny — she tried hard to go after something and she keeps going away from it. Also she has begun to do a tremendous amount of jabbering — just as though she were talking but of course only sounds.

Dearest, I came to the same conclusion, "we mutually love each other" — and let's not even try to fight it cause it's so wonderful and beautiful and makes us so happy. It's thrilling to think of our weekend, isn't it?

Diana

4/27/45

Dear Diana,

Got started on "France" this morning & along came the nurse & jabbed me with the hypo & took all the life out of me.

Is Mussolini really captured? And how go the Italian Partisans in the North? What a difference here from Germany!!!

Lenny

April 27

Dearest,

That penicillin has me worried — but in spite of the agony it is causing you, I console myself that perhaps it is helping heal the wounds because you say they look better. I know that being confined to bed and in pain make it close to impossible for you to do much work — I hope you will again soon as this business is over.

Yours,
Diana

April 28, 1945

Dearest Girls,

How are you & Betty this weekend? Today I scribbled some 15 or so pages on my ten days in Belgium in September '44 and I am only indifferently satisfied with it. Doc was mightily pleased with my wounds today. Medical science sees beauty in strange things. But it is a fact that my leg hole, which used to be about 3 inches in diameter is now 1¼ inches in diameter. The penicillin torture is to go on 'til Monday.

The radio is all full of the German surrender report, due, so they say, momentarily. Here's hoping — what a May Day for 1945!

Lenny

April 28

Dear Lenny,

Dearest, you ask about Betty being insecure or strained. You know I've been much worried about it also, but so far she seems to show no ill effects.

She has gotten to love my mother very much also — she seems to accept the times that I leave and return. For the first day or so, she doesn't leave me out of her sight, but then it passes. It's good, I think, that she isn't older.

Diana

April 29, 1945

Dearest,

Put in some more time on "Belgium" story this morning. Perhaps when the penicillin needling ends (tomorrow is the last day) it'll be easier for me to concentrate on work, & maybe they'll let me out of bed. Have been wrastlin' with the "Germans" essay to amend it in line with your criticisms.

The foot hole has gained a clear 1/8 inch — since yesterday — of fresh flesh around the shrinking margin. It doesn't look horrible anymore at all, although hardly pleasant.

The radio reports it's confirmed that Mussolini has been shot by the Partisans. Good! Hitler and Himmler deserve death as criminals on many counts; but Mussolini, before any of his crimes, earned death by his treason to the working class: that is the first count in the indictment against him!

Lenny

April 30, 1945

Dear Diana,

Two years since I am in the army, today. Doc ordered the needle discontinued, thank goodness. My right arm & leg are all but paralyzed from needle stabs & swelling. He says the sequestrectomy can wait indefinitely (that's the operation to remove fragments or scrape ends of bone that are dead); he says if there's no temperature or spread of infection from that point, there's no point in disturbing it. It can always be done when it becomes necessary (What difference to him whether I heal an open wound once or twice?), & some folks have to have it done repeatedly before it's OK. So probably I'm lucky again. The leg hole continues to shrink, but the area will probably always be tender and dull to feeling.

Lenny

April 30

Dearest Lenny,

By today, I'm beginning to count the hours until the weekend. I get so impatient, dearest. I'm planning to come Sat., May 5, as we decided. I'm glad I shall be able to see you. I wish I could bring Betty also, but as we agreed it isn't fair to her. Your sister Harriet spoke to me about taking more pictures but they are running low on film and want to save some for their own offspring.

You raise some questions and by now you must know the answers — you know Mussolini and 18 others were killed by the Partisans — a good example of how to treat dirty fascist dogs.

Diana

May 1, 1945

Dearest,

May 1, 1945 and the Red Flag flies over Belgium, and the greatest alliance of peoples for freedom in all history moves on towards victory. What a May Day! Would we ever have dreamed on our first May Day, together, in 1938?

The surgical major came around & convinced me again that they are only guessing on the penicillin. He asked in such a way that it was obvious he thought 3 applications of penicillin a day was in order — I am getting 15 a day now. He also thinks a sequestrectomy is needed & skin graft. The ward doctor has said not. They discuss us as if we were guinea pigs.

Lights are about to go out so — goodnight, dear. How's Betty's crawling these days?

Lenny

May 1

Dear Lenny,

There is a lot to say this May 1 — this year for the first time in many, a day of rejoicing with much more in the future — let's hope this will be our last May Day at war. I'm glad to write of mail from Babe and Eddie. Babe's is on its way to Lucy. Eddie has left Iwo Jima — but he can't say where he is.

Diana

9

The Final Phase: Recovery

MAY 2, 1945–JUNE 15, 1946

Lenny and Diana continued to write daily letters from May 2, 1945, to mid-June 1946 when he was finally released from the hospital and honorably discharged. Rather than include daily excerpts, only those significant to the story are included.

July 3, 1945

Dearest,

I have sketched out the rest of the Malmédy sections. There is material left over which I don't know whether or how to use: especially "combat" material — the night the colonel was killed, our running the gauntlet of snipers in the Siegfried line — the barn at Langendorf. Where I missed being killed four times (2X by shell, bomb, & ambush) — the launching of the counteroffensive on Jan 3 in the Ardennes. The buzz bombs alone are a story.

Lenny

July 7

Dearest Diana,

One year ago today we walked ashore on the coast of France. The hike inland, unguided, broken by war load, was one of the longest nights I spent in the ETO — and the predawn barrage by the big guns, making the sky white in the middle of darkness, was really our introduction to combat fear. My lungs & heart pounded & panted involuntarily — but it wore off in a week. Faraway memories now —

Lenny

August 7

Dear Lenny,

The "atomic bomb" which has the papers agog is nothing to be very happy about. It's not clear yet whether the bomb is really as Buck Rogerish as the headlines yell. Truman said it equals 20,000 tons of TNT or a load of twenty major air raids, which is big enough, for a single bomb. Necessary as it may be at the moment, it is not an achievement to glory in.

Diana

August 14

Darling Diana,

The war is over! Cheers and laughter resound through the corridors from ward to ward as the Truman announcement makes it official. There are some battles still to be fought — Franco must go — China must be freed from within — but the war for survival has ended with the people surging forward everywhere.

Somebody is banging pots and pans in another ward. It's a great moment. The guns go silent for the first moment since the afternoon of September 18, 1931, when we were kids in school. I remember reading the headlines of the Franco rebellion, when I heard Chamberlain declare he was going to war on Hitler, the invasion of the USSR and Pearl Harbor, the long trail of blood through the years, and at the end of the trail, Mussolini dead, Hitler dead or a fugitive, Hirohito, a prisoner of war. IT IS GOOD TO BE ALIVE THIS DAY!

Lenny

RECOVERY

By mid-June 1945, Lenny could bear weight on his injured leg. However, the flesh wounds on his upper arm and his ankle continued to be a problem. A skin graft for his ankle didn't close the wound. He and a handful of others underwent an experimental procedure called the tube flap, consisting of four surgeries over a four-month period, beginning in October, in which the gaping hole from the wound needs to be filled with living tissue. Human tissue is borrowed from a site where it regenerates, and used as a living bridge of blood and tissue to fill in the hole. The recovery at each phase was painful and incapacitating. The timetable was differ-

Lenny, Diana and Betty Lou in Far Rockaway, New York,
August 13, 1945

ent for each individual, and Lenny knew that the procedure failed for some along the way, while he had to continue, knowing the odds were not promising.

Sept 8

Dearest Diana,

The guy who was in Stage 3 when you were here has come back from post op: his arm is again free, but they left the tube on — the tube "took" to the foot, but not completely — so they left him the tube, pending decision what to do further. We have yet to see a real success. One guy goes into Stage 3 tomorrow, one is in "3"; & 4 of us are waiting for "2."

Lenny

October 4

Dear Sweetheart,

There have been a number of developments — the guy who was in 3rd stage went to 4th today — we are eager to see him back from post-op — to see how it came out. One guy had an infection spoil his tube, & so it was entirely removed today — all waste. Another had to have a skin graft put under the tube where the tube was cut from. There are 3 others in my stage, & one who's a stage ahead.

Lenny

12/14

Dear Diana,

On the tubes: one of the 3 of us in the 3rd stage — is lost. 100% failure in the hand to foot stage — Sam and I continue fingers crossed. Those guys, still in 2nd, of them one is today 48 days in that stage. The "less than 50%" average continues. They cut Rob's rotting tube off his leg today — it couldn't be salvaged; & Pete getting another surface graft. So Doc wasn't in; but with these saline dressings I see the tube every couple of hours — including night sleep? What's that?

Lenny

Date unknown

Dearest,

Today the "tubes" were photographed — not X-rayed, photographed. Why? No doubt so someone can get a promotion or an article published, or an appointment somewhere. Again, we're not asked — just told. "Tis the army & what good is resenting it." To help out, there is a visiting Dr. who is the 3rd to express surprise that a tube is being done when it could be done by one of 3 easier & shorter methods — and Doc agreed with him. So it goes.

Lenny

In the end, Lenny was one of the first for whom the tube graft worked. His story was written up, as a photographic essay, in the February 11, 1946, issue of *Life* magazine. By then, he was able to stand on both feet.

RECOGNITION

While hospitalized, Lenny was awarded the Silver Star, the third highest military decoration in the armed service for gallantry against the enemy on foreign soil, along with the Bronze Star Medal, awarded for heroic deeds during military operations against an armed enemy, the Good Conduct Medal, issued for three consecutive years of "honorable and faithful service," and four miniature, metal, battle star decorations that were added to medals and ribbons to denote additional service.

During the year and a half he was hospitalized, he came home to Brooklyn a number of times, mostly before the experimental surgeries, and Diana visited him as often as she could. He occupied his time, first, by writing a fictionalized memoir of his war experiences and then by writing a book on John Milton that was published years later.

1/12/46

Dearest Diana,

A year ago, we launched the final & bloodiest — & my interior sinks as the details come back — that first morning when we pushed through Geromont, near Liège to Baugnes,[1] the worst for casualties I'd ever seen & the finding of the massacred infantry men at Five Corners — All day long one "bloodied" man after another staggering back — it was rough & ugly.

Lenny

Feb 27, 1946

Dear Darling,

Of all things — my good conduct medal — medal, not ribbon — came through today. It is a good-looking medal; & a fair design in bronze.[2]

Lenny

---

1. The Malmédy Massacre Memorial is located at Baugnez, just outside Malmédy.

2. The Good Conduct Medal is given for active duty enlisted members of the Armed Forces who complete three consecutive years of "honorable and faithful" service. During wartime, it can be given for one year of service.

DISCHARGED AT LAST

June 15, 1946

Dearest Diana,

The paper-work of the transfer was finished hours ago, & since then there's only been drifting round the corridors — a little ping pong — and nothing. The place is deserted. They opened Lowell North with me, & Lowell's closing with me; it was always a gloomy joke & now it's fully true.[3]

"Dininka," I've got a powerful desire to make this the last letter between us for a long, long time. When I phoned you yesterday, I told you not to write here: and if they send me to Halloran, which begins to seem likely (now that it hardly matters!) — I'd rather phone you during the few (very few, let's hope) days I shall be there. And then, from furlough & discharge, to be with you always & no need for letters, especially for such unhappy letters as the past year. All my love to my two girls — perhaps I can phone you from New York tomorrow — I hope so.

Lenny

---

3. Lenny was one of the first patients at Lowell North, and he was one of the last to leave.

Epilogue

Life after the War

1946–1994

In June 1946, after more than a year spent recovering from his wounds, my father left the hospital in Lowell, Massachusetts. He was discharged from the Army and returned home to Brooklyn. I was almost two years old and my father was basically a stranger to me. It took time to adjust and accept his presence. There is a family story that he had worked really hard to carve a wooden toy while in the hospital. He handed it to me and I threw it down, shattering it into multiple pieces.

Due to the severe apartment shortage after the war, he, my mom, and I remained in the two-bedroom apartment with my mother's parents. In the spring of 1947, my parents qualified for an apartment in Stuyvesant Town, a housing development in Manhattan that gave priority to disabled veterans.

The family was extremely lucky. My parents' brother-in-law, Babe, Babe's brother, Paul, and my dad's brother, Eddie, and various cousins all returned home safely.

After recovering from his wounds and adjusting to civilian life, my father returned to the New York City Welfare Department as a social case-worker. In 1952, he left and was hired by a private adult vocational school to oversee the curriculum and to develop new courses. He enjoyed the process of creating and developing original material. The school flourished under the GI Bill. As the GI Bill began to wind down, my father cre-ated additional courses, particularly those for people seeking to advance in the New York City Civil Service arena. He launched his own vocational school venture with a financial partner. For the next twenty years, he was the director of Eastern School, which offered a wide range of adult courses including civil service exam preparation, upholstery, floor covering, hotel and restaurant management and, most noteworthy, a special program accredited by New York State, developed to train developmentally disabled young adults to function independently after leaving public school.

My parents maintained their fierce commitment to fighting for justice after the war was over. From 1948 to 1952, they joined with a dozen other Stuyvesant Town residents and they formed a committee of tenants, whose aim was to integrate the apartment complex. During the long struggle, they were among the families that were targeted for eviction by Metropolitan Life Insurance Company, owner of the complex. Only a small number of the families originally involved chose to remain in their apartments once the eviction proceedings were set to take place. Public pressure and tremendous union support forced Metropolitan Life to stop the eviction proceedings. The struggle inspired the open-housing movement that eventually made housing discrimination illegal nationwide. They continued to live in Stuyvesant Town for the rest of their lives, proudly displaying the eviction notice on the wall.

In 1950, my brother, Frederick Douglass, was born. The name had been chosen in honor of Frederick Douglass, the black abolitionist, orator, and writer in the nineteenth century.

As was typical of the time period following World War II, my mother was a homemaker, devoted to raising my brother and me. She was an active leader in the Parent Teacher Association throughout our school years. Once we were older, she worked alongside my father, as an administrator and registrar, in their adult vocational education school.

RECONNECTING WITH HIS BUDDIES:
RETURN TO EUROPE AND ACROSS THE UNITED STATES

In 1961, my father finally received back pay from the United States Government, owed to him after he was wounded. He considered this a "windfall" and took our family to Europe to retrace his steps in France and to reconnect with his buddy Pierre, from the French underground. I was seventeen, and Pierre welcomed us and kissed my mother's hand in the way only a true Frenchman can. Pierre showed us Paris, and we visited his mother at her chateau outside of Nice. We also toured Normandy including Omaha Beach and St. Lô, where my father fought.

Our family later took a seven-week automobile trip across the country from New York to California in 1963. We visited with three of my father's closest army buddies and their families. One of them was the wounded buddy my dad stayed with in a paper mill, which earned him a Silver Star. It was clearly a special time for my father and gave us a true understanding of the lifelong bonds between soldiers.

In 1978, my parents returned to Europe to visit places in Belgium, Holland, and Germany, where my dad had fought. He found the bridge by the paper mill on the road entering Malmédy. They visited with a Belgian family with whom my dad and his buddies had stayed in 1944. The children were now grown and the older folks were gone. He could never go back to the spot where he was wounded during the Battle of the Bulge because of the still-traumatic memories.

INDEPENDENT SCHOLAR

Throughout his adult life, my father devoted significant time to his scholarly pursuits, especially historical research focused on the seventeenth-century poet John Milton. His interest was sparked after he won an essay contest in graduate school. He worked on this first Milton manuscript while recuperating in the hospital. Since he never completed his PhD, an academic career wasn't open to him. He pursued his passion in his free time, while having another career to support his family. After he retired, he was devoted to his research. My parents loved to travel, and often their travels took them to libraries, such as the Bodleian at Oxford University, with obscure research materials.

My father struggled to achieve recognition as an independent scholar, but eventually published more than thirty articles in scholarly journals, and *Milton Portraits*, a monograph for a special edition of the *Milton Quarterly*. He also published three books, *John Milton Among the Polygamophiles* (1974), *John Milton and the Oldenburg Safeguard* (1985), and *John Milton's Writings in the Anglo-Dutch Negotiations, 1651–1654* (1992). As a result of these works, he was recognized as one of the premiere Milton scholars of his day. His contribution was as a detective, ferreting out details of Milton's life and understanding their significance. In 1990, he was named the Honored Independent Scholar of the Milton Society. In their apartment in New York, he collected a personal library of seventeenth-century books by John Milton and other books related to this time period. He also amassed a large collection of research materials, and his own papers related to his research.

During frequent family visits to Boulder, Colorado, my dad developed a special relationship with the University of Colorado (CU). Nora Quinlan, the university's director of Special Collections, welcomed him and offered him a quiet place to read. The open stacks allowed easy access to research materials, unlike many universities on the East Coast.

My father decided to donate his personal library of seventeenth-century books, his research materials, and his personal papers to CU. After his death, Nora spent a week in my parents' New York apartment. Fifty cartons were packed and shipped to CU for the John Milton Leo Miller Collection. In 1992, in recognition of his contribution both as a scholar and a donor, he was posthumously awarded an honorary doctorate by the University of Colorado.[1]

FAMILY RESEARCHER

Lenny's strong interest in history led him to research both his and Diana's families' genealogies, as best as one could before the internet. He published *Dobromil* (in the original Yiddish and in English), a memoir written by his father in a series of letters to his son Eddie, about growing up in the town he came from in Austria-Hungary. This was followed by a memoir edited by my parents, *Sokolievka/Justingrad*, about the shtetl in the Ukraine my mother's parents came from. It was based on interviews with survivors in Israel, New York City, and Buffalo, New York, where many from the town emigrated. My parents traveled extensively to research the material for this publication.

THEY WERE LUCKY!

During the years following the war, my parents enjoyed successful, fulfilled lives. In their free time, they loved spending time with family, especially their four grandchildren.[2] They also loved to travel to foreign places. In 1966, they traveled to the Soviet Union and visited family members in Rostov, in the Ukraine, who had survived World War II by fleeing to Tashkent.

My father died in 1990, several weeks before their 50th wedding anniversary. My mother died in 1994.

All in all, our family was very lucky.

---

1. This was initiated and arranged by Jim Williams II, dean of libraries, who came to know Lenny through Nora Quinlan, director of Special Collections.
2. A fifth grandchild was born after Lenny's and Diana's deaths.

Lenny and Diana, July 23, 1967

Appendix

Names that Appear in the Letters

Diana's Family

David Feldstein: Diana's father, born in Sokolievka/Justingrad, employed in the New York City garment district in the needle trade.

Adele Logvin: Diana's mother, born in Sokolievka/Justingrad, employed in the New York City garment district in the needle trade.

Lucy: Diana's sister, 4 years younger, graduated from Brooklyn College, moved back into their parents' apartment when her husband, Babe, entered the Navy. She later attended Washington University Graduate School of Social Work in St. Louis.

Babe (John): Lucy's husband, served in the Navy on a destroyer in the Pacific and became an architect after the war.

Sam Zimmerman: Babe's father, offered his tools to Diana to use while she worked in the machine shop.

Celia Zimmerman: Babe's mother, a fabulous knitter, made wool hats for Lenny and other soldiers fighting during the winter in Europe.

Paul Zimmerman: Babe's brother, served in the Navy submarine corps in the Pacific, was one of two on shore leave when his sub sank with all his buddies aboard.

Lenny's Family

Baba Toba: Lenny's grandmother, born in Dobromil, Galicia; when widowed, she immigrated to New York with her five children. Later in life, she lived with Lenny's family. She eloped with the milk deliveryman and moved to Palestine with her new husband when Lenny was in college.

Saul Miller: Lenny's father, born in Dobromil, union organizer and employee in the New York City garment district.

Ida: Lenny's mother, born in Dobromil, homemaker and dry cleaning/alterations business owner for a brief time.

Rose: Lenny's sister, 3 years younger, married Dave Rich after the war, worked as a secretary.

Harriet: Lenny's sister, 6 years younger, married to Mike Weitz, worked as a secretary and travel agent.

Mike Weitz: Harriet's husband, was in the Army, stationed in Texas, until discharged with a medical disability, worked as an insurance salesman.

Eddie: Lenny's brother, 10 years younger, enlisted as a Marine, served in the Far East and saw action at Iwo Jima. Married Mimi after the war, studied under the GI Bill, worked as a waiter, graduated from City College of New York and became an art teacher in New York City.

Aunt Minnie and Aunt Mary: Lenny's mother's sisters, lived in Brooklyn.

Uncle Benny and Uncle Abe: Lenny's mother's brothers.

Leo (and wife Ruth), Bea, and Edith: Lenny's first cousins.

FRIENDS FROM NEW YORK

John: Lenny's buddy from City College of New York.

Edith: John's wife and friend of Diana.

Helen: Diana's best friend, classmate at Thomas Jefferson High School in Brooklyn and lifelong friend.

Irving: Lenny's best friend from City College of New York, lived and worked in Washington, D.C.

Edna: Irving's wife.

Henry: Lenny's buddy from City College.

Pete: friend who introduced Lenny to Diana.

Frank: longtime friend.

Miriam: Diana's friend and wife of Lenny's basic training buddy Hersh.

ARMY BUDDIES

Basic training

Dave, Hersh, and Max: Lenny's three closest buddies from East New York, Brooklyn, who were together at Camp Shelby, Mississippi, in basic training.

Overseas—Lenny's Squad

Charlie Capp, Butler, Indiana: wounded in the same foxhole with Lenny on January 20, 1945, the day before Lenny was wounded.

Elton Thaggard (ET), North Carolina: the buddy who found Lenny after he was wounded, brought the medics, died in 1948.

Biton Constantine (Tiny): helped Lenny with Sulcer at the paper mill, was later wounded and died on way to medics January 20.

Sulcer Harris, Baton Rouge, Louisiana: Lenny stayed with him at the paper mill, which won Lenny the Silver Star.

Overseas—Other Close Friends

Pierre Le Bailly, French Underground: Lenny met him in Belgium and they became lifelong friends. Pierre became a barrister, and the friendship continued after the war with several visits in Paris and New York.

John Conley: Jeep driver who drove Lenny and Captain Pritchard on reconnaissance and scouting missions.

Army Officers (Commissioned and Noncommissioned)

Basic Training

Lieutenant Stevens: sympathetic to Lenny's research.

Sergeant Jameson and Lieutenant Kellogg: recognized Lenny's skill and asked him to teach a class on map reading.

Lieutenant Hamilton: supportive of Lenny during challenging times.

Colonel Lewis: accompanied Lenny on bivouacs.

Corporal Di Matteo: a member of the motor pool, who helped Lenny learn to drive.

Sergeant Major Langley: in the intelligence section, held high expectations for the soldiers under his command, assigned two-hour night patrols following two nights of practically no sleeping on bivouac.

Sergeant Johnson: on maneuvers with Lenny, acknowledged in Lenny's letters as having provided Lenny with the skills to survive the war.

Officers Overseas

Captain Pritchard, Nelsonville, Ohio: Battalion Executive Officer, Lenny served as his interpreter in Holland and Germany, was in charge of operations in Malmédy on the day of the "Battle of the Bridge."

Staff Sergeant Joan: a friend from the New York City Welfare Department, visited Lenny in the hospital in England.

Further Resources

The following resources are helpful to better understand what my parents and their generation experienced during World War II.

BOOKS ABOUT WORLD WAR II

There exists a tremendous number of books about World War II. One that I found most useful for its comprehensive, readable, insightful, and in-depth approach to all key aspects of the war and its significance was *The World at War 1939–45*, by Duncan Anderson (Reader's Digest, *The 20th Eventful Century*, 1999). For example: a comment on the film *Casablanca*: "Bogart and Bergman are in love but the need to fight the Nazis means they must put their own feelings to one side and say goodbye. It was something millions of couples were doing throughout the world."

Among the most widely read recent books written about the war, from the point of view of its participants, are the following:

Ambrose, Stephen E. *Band of Brothers: E Company, 506th Regiment, 101st Airborne: From Normandy to Hitler's Eagle's Nest* (New York: Simon and Schuster, 1992).

Ambrose, Stephen E. *Citizen Soldiers: The U.S. Army from the Normandy Beaches to the Bulge to the Surrender of Germany: June 7, 1944–May 7, 1945* (New York: Simon and Schuster, 1997).

Brokaw, Tom. *The Greatest Generation* (New York: Random House, 1998).

Brokaw, Tom. *The Greatest Generation Speaks: Letters and Reflections* (New York: Random House, 1999).

Edsel, Robert M. *The Monuments Men: Allied Heroes, Nazis, Thieves, and the Greatest Treasure Hunt in History* (New York: Hachette Book Group, 2009).

Hillenbrand, Laura. *Unbroken: A World War II Story of Survival, Resilience and Redemption* (New York: Random House, 2010).

BOOKS OF WAR LETTERS

Two books I found particularly relevant to *We Are Going to Be Lucky* grew out of academic research by two professors, Judy Barrett Litoff and David C. Smith, who sought to bring to life personal stories of men and women in World War II in the context of the times. The first, titled *Miss You: The World War II Letters of Barbara Wooddall Taylor and Charles E. Taylor* (Athens: University of Georgia Press, 1990), paralleled in many ways my parents' journey, encompassing the time from Barbara and Charles's initial courtship through basic training, the home front and overseas experience, and return to civilian life. The context provided by the two professors (Litoff was Barbara Woodall Taylor's niece), working with the Taylors, highlights the importance of letter writing as a lifeline to soldiers and their families during World War II.

Barrett Litoff and Smith's second book on the subject, *Since You Went Away: World War II Letters from American Women on the Home Front* (Lawrence: University Press of Kansas, 1991), is based on hundreds of letters written by women of different backgrounds dealing with topics that range from courtship through marriage and family, work in the war effort, hardship, purpose (why we fought), and loss (the price of victory). The letters were collected as the result of a public appeal to women that garnered 25,000 letters.

The following reflect the points of view of individuals in collections of letters to the home front and back:

Adler, Bill, ed. *WWII letters: A Glimpse into the Heart of the Second World War through the Eyes of Those Who Were Fighting It* (New York: St. Martin's Griffin, 2002). This work is based on letters from a number of soldiers.

Aquila, Richard. *Home Front Soldier: The Story of a GI and his Italian American Family During WWII* (Albany: State University of New York Press, 1999). This is the story of a first-generation Italian American family with four sons in the military.

Ball, Monte. *190 Letters: A Soldier's Story of WWII* (Mustang, OK: Tate, 2013). This book offers a glimpse of war through the eyes of one soldier.

Carroll, Andrew. *War Letters: Extraordinary Correspondence from American Wars* (New York: Scribner's, 2001). The letters in this work are from all American wars and include those of ordinary soldiers as well as legendary figures. This book has been made into a PBS documentary film.

Carroll, Andrew, ed. *Grace under Fire: Letters of Faith in Times of War* (New York: Doubleday and WaterBrook Press, Random House, 2007). This work presents a moving record of the importance of religion and spirituality to soldiers and their families, from the American Revolution to the war in Iraq.

Copeland, Jeffrey. *Inman's War: A Soldier's Life in a Colored Battalion in WWII* (Saint Paul, MN: Paragon House, 2006). This work tells the story of an Iowa-born

African American soldier in World War II, focusing on racism and prejudice. It has been optioned for a film.

Frederick, Clinton. *WWII: A Legacy of Letters* (Scottsdale, AZ: Zonicom Press, 2006). The author presents a collection of letters from those who served in the Pacific Theater.

King, Larry. *Love Stories of WWII* (New York: Crown Publishers, Random House, 2001). This book includes stories of men and women who met during the chaos of World War II and the relationships they formed. Interviewer Larry King captures their heartwrenching accounts through reminiscences, photographs, and the reproductions of letters.

Litoff, Judy Barrett, and David C. Smith, eds. *American Women in a World at War: Contemporary Accounts from World War II* (Wilmington, DE: Scholarly Resources, Inc.1997). This book includes excerpts from books and articles written by women covering broad issues during the war years, on the home front and abroad, and looking forward to the postwar world.

Pinkerton, Elaine, ed. *From Calcutta with Love: The World War II Letters of Richard and Reva Beard* (Lubbock: Texas Tech University Press, 2002). These letters tell the story of an Army psychologist stationed in Calcutta, dealing daily with the emotional traumas of wartime, and of his wife, a schoolteacher at home.

Saywell, Shelley. *Women in War* (Markham, Ont.: Penguin Books of Canada, 1985). This book focuses on women in World War II, on the British home front and as combatants and in resistance movements.

Schaffer, Mollie Weinstein, and Cyndee Schaffer. *Mollie's War: The Letters of a World War II WAC in Europe* (Jefferson, NC: McFarland, 2010). This book shares the experiences of a woman in the Women's Army Corps.

Spero, Estelle, ed. *An Alcove in the Heart: WWII Letters of Sidney Diamond to Estelle Spero* (New Jewel Services, 2011, Author House 2004). The collection comprises letters written by a soldier to his fiancée before he was killed in action.

Stringer, Helen Dann. *Letters of Love and War: A WWII Correspondence* (Syracuse: Syracuse University Press, 1997). This work is based on 575 letters written between a couple during World War II. His wartime experience was as a surgeon, not as a combat soldier.

WORLD WAR II FILMS

The following films are relevant in terms of the experience of ordinary soldiers:

Saving Private Ryan portrays the brutal realities of war as it describes the search behind enemy lines for Private Ryan whose three brothers have been killed in action.

The Longest Day is the story of the Allied invasion and landing on the Normandy beaches.

The Big Red One gives insight into a sergeant's leadership in the U.S. Army's First Infantry Division during World War II.

Flags of Our Fathers recounts the American story of one of the critical battles of World War II on the island of Iwo Jima.

Letters from Iwo Jima shares stories of Japanese troops who fought and died there during World War II, based on long-buried letters.

Band of Brothers is a TV mini-series directed by Steven Spielberg, which presents the story of Easy Company, 506th Regiment of the 101st Airborne Division, U.S. Army.

Monuments Men is a film starring George Clooney based on the book of the same name.

WEBSITES

There are two 30th Infantry Division websites:

The 30th Infantry Division in World War II: www.30thinfantry.org. This newly revised website was organized by Frank W. Towers. It contains a moving history of the 30th Infantry Division, which fought in some of the most significant World War II battles.

The 30th Infantry Division Old Hickory: www.oldhickory30th.com. This is the original 30th Infantry site, with personal stories and additional information on the Malmédy bombings.

Several websites focus on the preservation of wartime letters:

The Center for American War Letters: www.chapman.edu/research/institutes-and-centers/cawl. Andrew Carroll is the founder and director of this project, a national initiative that honors and remembers U.S. troops and veterans by preserving their wartime correspondence. The goal is to collect at least one million letters representing every military conflict in American history.

WWII Netherlands Escape Lines: www.wwii-netherlands-escape-lines.com Founded by Bruce Bolinger in 2010, this website researches assistance given to downed Allied airmen by the Resistance during World War II in the Netherlands, Belgium, and France. Its original purpose was to enable people with shared interests to connect. As the project grew, Bolinger realized that a second purpose was to provide useful tools to researchers.

MUSEUMS IN THE UNITED STATES

World War II U.S. museums that house relevant artifacts and material:

The International Museum of World War II; www.museumofworldwarii.org. Founded by Kenneth W. Rendell in Natick, Massachusetts, it contains the most comprehensive private collection of more than 7,500 items.

The National World War II Museum in New Orleans: www.worldwar2museum. org Founded by Stephen Ambrose, it is affiliated with the Smithsonian Museum.

United States Holocaust Memorial Museum, Washington, D.C, www.ushmm.org.

MUSEUMS AND MEMORIAL SITES IN EUROPE

Anne Frank House and former Jewish Quarter in Amsterdam

Auschwitz Museum

Babi Yar Memorials in Kiev

Churchill War Rooms in London

Imperial War Museum in London

Mémorial des Martyrs de la Déportation in Paris

Museum of the Great Patriotic War in Moscow

Nuremburg Trials Memorial

Omaha Beach in Normandy

Warsaw Ghetto Memorial

World War II cemeteries

Yad Vashem, Jerusalem

About the Editor

Elizabeth L. Fox, the daughter of Lenny and Diana Miller, was born in New York City during her father's military service in World War II. The letters her parents exchanged before and immediately after her birth, which they saved, are the basis for *We Are Going to Be Lucky: A World War II Love Story in Letters.*

Fox has served for more than twenty years in a leadership role on the National Board of Hadassah where her responsibilities include writing, training, and public speaking. She has a BA in history from the City College of New York and an MA in vocational rehabilitation counseling from New York University. She worked for many years as a substitute teacher in middle and high school.

Fox lives in Boulder, Colorado, with her husband. She has three children and six grandchildren.

Index